Understanding Death and Dying

Understanding Death and Dying

AN INTERDISCIPLINARY APPROACH

Third Edition

Sandra Galdieri Wilcox and Marilyn Sutton
California State University, Domiguez Hills

MAYFIELD PUBLISHING COMPANY

Palo Alto and London

Library of Congress Catalog Card Number: 84-061379
International Standard Book Number: 0-87484-718-4

Manufactured in the United States of America

10   9   8   7   6   5   4   3   2   1

Mayfield Publishing Company
285 Hamilton Avenue
Palo Alto, California 94301

Sponsoring editor: Susan Loring
Manuscript editor: Claire Comiskey
Managing editor: Pat Herbst
Art director: Nancy Sears
Designer (interior and cover): Al Burkhardt
Production manager: Cathy Willkie
Compositor: Kachina Typesetting
Printer and binder: George Banta Company

About the cover: *The Sun and Eagle*, a sand painting
by Ernest Hunt: "four winds, four ages, four seasons."
Used by permission of Jane Anderson.

For Stephen, Paul, Matthew, and Meagan

contents

chapter one

Ambrose Bierce

> Whether the attitudes one expresses toward death are indeed the attitudes one will hold at the time of death remains a mystery. Bierce presents the difference between theory and practice by portraying two characters in the dramatic moment of revising their views.

Richard Schulz

> Schulz presents a critical overview of empirical studies that either assess death anxiety independently or relate it to demographic, personality, and environmental variables.

chapter three
Grief, Mourning, and Social Functions   170

chapter four
Death and the Child   252

chapter five

Choices and Decisions in Death

preface

A class in thanatology appeals to diverse audiences. The student of death and dying might be a curious but slightly apprehensive twenty-year-old, a mother of teenage children interested in preparing herself and her family for future crises, a nurse or paramedic wanting to improve patient care, a social worker who regularly sees the impact of violent death on the family, a teacher whose small pupils are in the process of discovering death with their pets, a nursing home staff member who daily works among those at the close of life, a clergyman who is asked to console bereaved families, or a funeral director who wants to improve his or her services to the community. Courses in death and dying are now offered by several disciplines within medicine, the social sciences, and the humanities; and interest in further study is often stimulated by workshops sponsored by university extension divisions, churches, and hospitals. *Understanding Death and Dying* can be adapted to any of these interests and uses.

In the ten years since the first edition of this text appeared, thanatology has drawn from several source disciplines to mature as a distinct field of study. Within the study of death and dying, the focus has moved from the synthesis of early work to the integration of theoretical principles within existing institutions and to the widespread implementation of new programs. The individual who begins the study of thanatology in the mid-1980s is supported by more research data than ever before, but he or she is also faced with increased responsibility over a wider range of decisions.

The third edition of *Understanding Death and Dying*, while blending cognitive structure and experiential applications, retains an interdisciplinary approach. Like the earlier editions, this volume weaves multicultural, humanistic, and life-span perspectives through the chapters. New selections in each chapter reflect advances in theory, research, and application in areas such as the reflection of attitudes in society, individuals' responses to bereavement, children's understanding of both death and the threat of disaster, and the ethical issues embedded in choices at the end of life.

Chapter Organization

Overall, *Understanding Death and Dying* leads the reader from self-study initiated in the Encounter in Chapter One to reappraisal and the formulation of a basis for action in Chapter Five. The readings within chapters proceed through an analogous sequence. Each chapter opens with an integrative essay and personal Encounter, then moves through several readings in a variety of disciplines, and closes with Structured Exercises. Chapter One of the new edition has been reformulated to present the study of attitudes toward death and dying, and their reflection in society. Chapters Two through Four lead the reader through an examination of the experience of dying, a consideration of the dynamics of grief and mourning, and an exploration of the special challenges in the presentation of death and the threat of disaster to children. In Chapter Five readers are presented with an expanded selection of readings that both underscore the ethical implications of available choices and encourage clarification of values for living.

Essays

An introductory essay at the beginning of each chapter provides a thematic framework for the concepts presented within the chapter. By establishing a context for discussion, the essays identify key questions. A chapter overview within each essay integrates the readings in topical subgroupings.

Encounter

Whether it is a set of questions directed to the reader as in Chapter One, short statements written by children as in Chapter Four, or a news account as in Chapter Five, the Encounter confronts the reader with the dominant issues of the chapter. This material roots theoretical study in actual experience, provoking interest that in turn will result in probing questions.

Readings

Though diverse, the readings in each chapter include a significant theoretical statement on the topic of inquiry. That central statement is accompanied by experience-based selections that tie the discussion to life situations, theoretical statements that develop technical skills, literary selections that reflect the understanding of death across time, and analytic pieces that suggest guidelines for intervention. Each reading is introduced by a brief headnote that places the selection in relation to other readings in the chapter. In their diversity, the readings present key concepts in the social sciences (particularly psychology and sociology), in medicine (psychiatry and nursing), in the humanities (philosophy and literature), in gerontology, and in social welfare. They outline germinal concepts in the study of death and dying and embed those concepts in a larger context provided by the history of ideas.

Structured Exercises

Following the readings in each chapter are Structured Exercises, which provide the instructor with a ready means to frame the theoretical examination of death and dying within a personal interaction initiated in the Encounter. By tying together the concepts introduced in the readings, the Structured Exercises encourage students to apply those concepts to their own lives in a structured personal growth experience.

Questions and Projects for Further Study

The Questions and Projects for Further Study at the end of each chapter help students to assimilate information in individual readings and to integrate related information found in several readings. The Questions ask students to synthesize ideas presented *within* the chapter. The Projects lead students *beyond* the readings to further research and independent study. The Projects invite students to apply the tools of research and the accepted patterns of investigation in the social sciences (and humanities). They have been selected to allow for various levels of sophistication: some can be used to introduce students to the ways a professional in the discipline investigates a topic; others can be expanded to provide a serious research problem for more advanced students.

For Further Reading

In a rapidly changing, multidisciplinary field such as the study of death and dying, both instructor and student will be assisted by a selected bibliography. Reading lists at the end of each chapter identify sources for in-depth coverage of topics introduced within the chapter. Taken together, the bibliographies of the five chapters provide an introductory survey of thanatology.

Appendices

The appendices in the third edition have been expanded and updated. Appendix A includes additional materials for use with the Structured Exercises. Appendix B presents statistical information on death and dying. Appendix C is a collection of legal forms and death-related documents that allow students to examine the bureaucracy of death. Appendix D offers a listing of topics for individual class presentations or student projects as well as an updated mediography keyed to the subject of each chapter.

◇ ◇ ◇

We acknowledge with thanks the comments and suggestions made by the following reviewers of a preliminary version of the manuscript for the third edition: Ellen Beck of Sinclair Community College, Allen P. Fertziger of the University of Maryland, and Vincent Rolletta of Erie Community College. Their comments were particularly useful in validating directions we were considering in the new edition.

Sandra Galdieri Wilcox
Marilyn Sutton

NOTE TO THE INSTRUCTOR

the use of structured exercises
in the classroom

The Structured Exercises have been arranged topically at the end of each chapter, but most of them can be adapted to fit topics in other chapters. The kidney machine exercise in Chapter One, for example, could be equally effective as a closing activity for Chapter Five, if the instructor led the class to focus on a different aspect of the exercise or modified the discussion questions. The student could be asked, for instance, to role-play the patients rather than the hospital committee, and the decision under study might be "Who will accept the treatment, and why?" rather than "Who will be given the opportunity for the treatment?"

Some of the exercises are constructed to uncover latent attitudes, and for that reason potentially volatile terms are used. The instructor who has had little experience in handling such material might wish to schedule a separate "experience" group where a staff member of the campus counseling center or an interested and qualified colleague from the psychology department could assist. The "experience" group should be limited to students enrolled in the course. The relationship of the group to the regular class can be determined by the individual instructor. The group could be optional or required, or it could offer additional units of credit. It could meet during regularly scheduled class time or at another time and location.

Some instructors prefer to limit the use of group experiences to an intense daylong or weekend session at the end of the course. An intense encounter of this kind should be conducted only with the participation of a qualified group leader, and participation by students should be contingent upon appropriate screening methods. The American Psychological Association (1973) has provided "Guidelines for Conducting Growth Groups,"* which lists responsibilities of group leaders.

The use of group exercises in any classroom requires responsible planning and constant attention from the instructor. At the beginning of each exercise,

*"APA Guidelines for Psychologists Conducting Growth Groups," *American Psychologist* 38 (1973):933.

students should be reminded that they may choose, without penalty, not to participate and that they may, at any time, withdraw from parts of the exercise that they find uncomfortable or anxiety-evoking. Before an exercise begins, the class as a whole should discuss the obligation to respect each participant's needs. Even an exercise that appears emotionally innocuous may elicit anxiety in a psychologically vulnerable individual. Students often choose their courses for personal as well as for scholarly or professional reasons. In a "death and dying" class these personal reasons may involve unresolved grief, anticipatory grief, or, occasionally, suicidal preoccupations. In addition, adolescents as a group tend to be "mourning at a distance" for developmental losses of their own childhood and for former parental relationships as they struggle toward the independence of adulthood.

From time to time, a difficult moment for one or all students may occur. In such cases the students themselves can usually be trusted to respond supportively and constructively. When tensions in the group seem to be running high, it may be helpful to stop and go around the room, allowing each student in turn to express his or her opinions and feelings. Other students should not interrupt or argue until everyone has had a chance to speak, though the instructor may want to sum up and reflect back to the group the thrust of a series of related comments.

Understanding Death and Dying

CHAPTER | *one*

The Study of Death: Attitudes and Reflections

To the social scientist, attitudinal research is always of interest; but in the study of death and dying, it is of special value. Death, by definition, remains unknowable from personal experience, so any understanding of death depends to some degree on the interpretation a particular culture gives to it.

Ours is a time when the research of the last three decades has given the lie to any earlier charge of denial. Beginning with the early work of Elisabeth Kübler-Ross and moving through two decades of active research, the study of death and dying has now been systematized and conceptualizations consolidated. Research findings have been assimilated into the structures of society as hospice programs have been established within hospitals (the very institutions they were designed to counterpose), right-to-die legislation has become widespread, and individual choices have been clarified in the widespread use of "Living Wills."

The implementation of an enlarged understanding of death and dying intensifies the complexity and responsibility of the individual, for, in practice, it presents a range of choices and decisions earlier not imagined. A first step in responsible implementation of choice lies in the clarification of one's personal attitude. To this end, Chapter One presents an interdisciplinary approach to the examination of attitudes in the social sciences and to their reflection in contemporary media. Indeed, one article goes so far as to argue that the study of death and dying has generated an ideology of its own, one that is not conducive to dispassionate decision making.

In a field as personal as death and dying, however, the sophistication of study does not reduce the essential mystery of death. A single technological development can throw us back to ancient dilemmas; for instance, the social custom of centuries may dictate that disposal of the body follows immediately upon death, but given the medical resources to transplant human organs, the dictates of social custom undergo reassessment. And as they do, we, as a society, are forced to examine our attitudes and to seek out the assumptions that underlie those attitudes: in short, to continually *redefine* the meaning of death.

The scientific tradition has, in certain respects, bequeathed us an adversary relationship with death. Scientific research, often motivated by an effort to conquer death and prolong life, has encouraged us to see the relationship between life and death as one of polar opposition. Although science assumes that we have biological immortality, in the sense that every creature alive today represents an "unbroken line of life that stretches back to the first primitive organism," that immortality is a continuance of the germ plasm rather than of the body. The scientist today is more likely to think of life in the same terms as Xavier Bichat, an eighteenth-century physiologist who described life as the "totality of all those functions that resist death."

Where the scientific heritage weighs death against life, the tradition of mythopoeic thought (including art, literature, philosophy, and folklore) denies the polarity by employing a third category, afterlife, and placing death within the continuum of life–death–afterlife. Death, for the philosopher, has most often suggested a transition to a different state of being: eternal sleep, a world of shades or heavenly reward—in any case, a continuance.

Reformulating the Meaning of Death

The concept of immortality, once accepted quite literally, has come to be interpreted symbolically by many today. Consequently, one may see one's children as biological immortality, one's lifework as social immortality, and one's memorialization in the arts (whether architecture, literature, or painting) as a form of cultural immortality. Unlike the medieval, whose guiding concern was preparation for afterlife, the contemporary has, in the words of Nathan A. Scott, "relocated the ultimate problem of human existence from the dimension of eternity to the dimension of time." The interest in death centers not only on *what follows* but on the more immediate issues of *how* and *when*.

Given the technological ability to alter the time of death, within certain limitations, we are likely to expand that control in the near future. As the power to extend life increases, the question may arise as to whether we should ever accept death. But we must remember that together with the power to extend life, we have the equally potent capacity to dilute the quality of life beyond recognition. Clinical death is no longer synonymous with *death:* it is only the most extreme of many kinds of death, including the social death of the forgotten widower living in isolation and the mental death of the mongoloid child. Now the issue has become, *What constitutes an appropriate death?*

Overview of the Chapter

Chapter One opens with the study of individual attitudes toward death, both as stated and as lived. Then it moves through a historical review of Western cultural attitudes to speculations about an emerging collective consciousness. The Encounter provides the reader with an opportunity to consider his or her own ideas on issues surrounding death and dying. However, the way that one expects to react when faced with death may not predict what actually will happen. In the short story "Parker Adderson, Philosopher," Ambrose Bierce portrays the confrontation between a general and a captured spy who is to be executed. Bierce highlights the two men's shifting personal responses to death as the circumstances change dramatically. In "Thinking About Death: Death Anxiety Research," Richard Schulz, an experimental psychologist, introduces the reader to the empirical study of death-related attitudes, presents an array of data on contemporary attitudes based on controlled studies, and suggests the need for research demonstrating the effects of these attitudes on behavior.

Expanding the discussion from the individual to society, Talcott Parsons and Victor Lidz present a sociological interpretation of death-related behavior in American society. The selection taken from their extended essay "Death in American Society" counters the familiar charge that Americans deny death and traces the emergence of a concept of "appropriate death." Although the term "appropriate death" has been introduced into the study of death quite recently, assumptions about it have long operated in our society, whether it be the biblical "threescore and ten," the expectation of a task completed, or a life expectancy taken from a statistical mortality table.

Similarly, much of what has been "recently discovered" about responses to death is firmly rooted in tradition, as Philippe Ariès, French historian of ideas, shows in "Death Inside Out." He weaves evidence from literature and philosophy together with observations on social customs to construct a historical overview of Western attitudes toward death. As Ariès does so, he traces the changing relationships between ritual observances and personal experience. Next, in "Death in Prime Time: Notes on the Symbolic Functions of Dying in the Mass Media," George Gerbner, a professor of communications, examines how contemporary media both reflect and reinforce attitudes. In his analysis of prime-time television drama, Gerbner demonstrates meanings that television gives to dying.

Finally, sociologist Lyn Lofland uses irreverence to gain analytic distance as she examines the implications of the work of the last two decades in "Emergent Ideology: The Happy Death Movement." Characterizing the recent attention to death and dying as a social movement, Lofland suggests three belief components that are emerging in a new "craft of dying."

Before considering the issues that these writers raise, however, read the questions in Confronting Your Death to encounter your own attitudes and assumptions.

encounter | *Confronting Your Death*

1. Who died in your first personal involvement with death?

   a. Grandparent or great-grandparent
   b. Parent
   c. Brother or sister
   d. Other family member
   e. Friend or acquaintance
   f. Stranger
   g. Public figure
   h. Animal

2. What aspect of your own death is the most distasteful to you?

   a. I could no longer have any experiences
   b. I am afraid of what might happen to my body after death
   c. I am uncertain as to what might happen to me if there is a life after death
   d. I could no longer provide for my dependents
   e. It would cause grief to my relatives and friends
   f. All my plans and projects would come to an end
   g. The process of dying might be painful
   h. Other (Specify) _____

3. What does death mean to you?

   a. The end, the final process of life
   b. The beginning of a life after death; a transition, a new beginning

Source: Copyright © 1970 by Edwin S. Shneidman. Reprinted from *Psychology Today Magazine.*

c. A joining of the spirit with a universal cosmic consciousness
d. A kind of endless sleep; rest and peace
e. Termination of this life but with survival of the spirit
f. Don't know
g. Other (Specify) _____

4. If you had a choice, what kind of death would you prefer?

a. Tragic, violent death
b. Sudden, but not violent death
c. Quiet, dignified death
d. Death in line of duty
e. Death after a great achievement
f. Suicide
g. Homicidal victim
h. There is no "appropriate" kind of death
i. Other (Specify) _____

5. If you could choose, when would you die?

a. In youth
b. In the middle prime of life
c. Just after the prime of life
d. In old age

6. For whom or what might you be willing to sacrifice your life?

a. For a loved one
b. For an idea or a moral principle
c. In combat or a grave emergency where a life could be saved
d. Not for any reason

7. If you were told that you had a terminal disease and a limited time to live, how would you want to spend your time until you died?

a. I would make a marked change in my life style; satisfy hedonistic needs (travel, sex, drugs, other)
b. I would become more withdrawn; reading, contemplating, or praying
c. I would shift from a concern for my own needs to a concern for others (family, friends)
d. I would attempt to complete projects; tie up loose ends
e. I would make little or no change in my life style
f. I would try to do one very important thing
g. I might consider committing suicide
h. I would do none of these

8. If or when you are married, would you prefer to outlive your spouse?

    a. Yes; I would prefer to die second and outlive my spouse
    b. No; I would rather die first and have my spouse outlive me
    c. Undecided or don't know

9. To what extent do you believe in a life after death?

    a. Strongly believe in it
    b. Tend to believe in it
    c. Uncertain
    d. Tend to doubt it
    e. Convinced it does not exist

10. Regardless of your belief about life after death, what is your wish about it?

    a. I strongly wish there were a life after death
    b. I am indifferent as to whether there is a life after death
    c. I definitely prefer that there not be a life after death

11. To what extent do you believe that suicide should be prevented?

    a. In every case
    b. In all but a few cases
    c. In some cases, yes; in others, no
    d. In no case; if a person wants to commit suicide society has no right to stop him or her

12. What efforts do you believe ought to be made to keep a seriously ill person alive?

    a. All possible effort: transplantations, kidney dialysis, etc.
    b. Efforts that are reasonable for that person's age, physical condition, mental condition, and pain
    c. After reasonable care has been given, a person ought to be permitted to die a natural death
    d. A senile person should not be kept alive by elaborate artificial means

AMBROSE BIERCE

Parker Adderson, Philosopher

Responses to the questionnaire in the Encounter having been formulated, questions arise as to how solid those responses are and what changes they might undergo if put to the test. With masterful brevity and irony, Ambrose Bierce presents a confrontation between a general and a captured spy in which cognitive attitudes are put to the test of experience. The death of a captured spy an unquestioned certainty, the interest in the short story shifts to the attitudes both the prisoner and his captor hold toward death. As they wait for the dawn, they respond implicitly to many of the questions you have just considered in the Encounter.

"Prisoner, what is your name?"

"As I am to lose it at daylight to-morrow morning it is hardly worth while concealing it. Parker Adderson."

"Your rank?"

"A somewhat humble one; commissioned officers are too precious to be risked in the perilous business of a spy. I am a sergeant."

"Of what regiment?"

"You must excuse me; my answer might, for anything I know, give you an idea of whose forces are in your front. Such knowledge as that is what I came into your lines to obtain, not to impart."

"You are not without wit."

"If you have the patience to wait you will find me dull enough to-morrow."

"How do you know that you are to die to-morrow morning?"

"Among spies captured by night that is the custom. It is one of the nice observances of the profession."

The general so far laid aside the dignity appropriate to a Confederate officer of high rank and wide renown as to smile. But no one in his power and out of his favor would have drawn any happy augury from that outward and visible sign of approval. It was neither genial nor infectious; it did not communicate itself to the other persons exposed to it—the caught spy who had provoked it and the armed guard who had brought him into the tent and now stood a little apart, watching his prisoner in the yellow candle-light. It was no part of that warrior's duty to smile; he had been detailed for another purpose. The conversation was resumed; it was in character a trial for a capital offense.

Source: Ambrose Bierce, "Parker Adderson," in *The American Short Story*. Edited by Calvin Skaggs. New York: Dell, 1977.

"You admit, then, that you are a spy—that you came into my camp, disguised as you are in the uniform of a Confederate soldier, to obtain information secretly regarding the numbers and disposition of my troops."

"Regarding, particularly, their numbers. Their disposition I already knew. It is morose."

The general brightened again; the guard, with a severer sense of his responsibility, accentuated the austerity of his expression and stood a trifle more erect than before. Twirling his gray slouch hat round and round upon his forefinger, the spy took a leisurely survey of his surroundings. They were simple enough. The tent was a common "wall tent," about eight feet by ten in dimensions, lighted by a single tallow candle stuck into the haft of a bayonet, which was itself stuck into a pine table at which the general sat, now busily writing and apparently forgetful of his unwilling guest. An old rag carpet covered the earthen floor; an older leather trunk, a second chair and a roll of blankets were about all else that the tent contained; in General Clavering's command Confederate simplicity and penury of "pomp and circumstance" had attained their highest development. On a large nail driven into the tent pole at the entrance was suspended a sword-belt supporting a long sabre, a pistol in its holster and, absurdly enough, a bowie-knife. Of that most unmilitary weapon it was the general's habit to explain that it was a souvenir of the peaceful days when he was a civilian.

It was a stormy night. The rain cascaded upon the canvas in torrents, with the dull, drum-like sound familiar to dwellers in tents. As the whooping blasts charged upon it the frail structure shook and swayed and strained at its confining stakes and ropes.

The general finished writing, folded the half-sheet of paper and spoke to the soldier guarding Adderson: "Here, Tassman, take that to the adjutant-general; then return."

"And the prisoner, General?" said the soldier, saluting, with an inquiring glance in the direction of that unfortunate.

"Do as I said," replied the officer, curtly.

The soldier took the note and ducked himself out of the tent. General Clavering turned his handsome face toward the Federal spy, looked him in the eyes, not unkindly, and said: "It is a bad night, my man."

"For me, yes."

"Do you guess what I have written?"

"Something worth reading, I dare say. And—perhaps it is my vanity—I venture to suppose that I am mentioned in it."

"Yes; it is a memorandum for an order to be read to the troops at *reveille* concerning your execution. Also some notes for the guidance of the provost-marshal in arranging the details of that event."

"I hope, General, the spectacle will be intelligently arranged, for I shall attend it myself."

"Have you any arrangements of your own that you wish to make? Do you wish to see a chaplain, for example?"

"I could hardly secure a longer rest for myself by depriving him of some of his."

"Good God, man! do you mean to go to your death with nothing but jokes upon your lips? Do you know that this is a serious matter?"

"How can I know that? I have never been dead in all my life. I have heard that death is a serious matter, but never from any of those who have experienced it."

The general was silent for a moment; the man interested, perhaps amused him—a type not previously encountered.

"Death," he said, "is at least a loss—a loss of such happiness as we have, and of opportunities for more."

"A loss of which we shall never be conscious can be borne with composure and therefore expected without apprehension. You must have observed, General, that of all the dead men with whom it is your soldierly pleasure to strew your path none shows signs of regret."

"If the being dead is not a regrettable condition, yet the becoming so—the act of dying—appears to be distinctly disagreeable to one who has not lost the power to feel."

"Pain is disagreeable, no doubt. I never suffer it without more or less discomfort. But he who lives longest is most exposed to it. What you call dying is simply the last pain—there is really no such thing as dying. Suppose, for illustration, that I attempt to escape. You lift the revolver that you are courteously concealing in your lap, and—"

The general blushed like a girl, then laughed softly, disclosing his brilliant teeth, made a slight inclination of his handsome head and said nothing. The spy continued: "You fire, and I have in my stomach what I did not swallow. I fall, but am not dead. After a half-hour of agony I am dead. But at any given instant of that half-hour I was either alive or dead. There is no transition period.

"When I am hanged to-morrow morning it will be quite the same; while conscious I shall be living; when dead, unconscious. Nature appears to have ordered the matter quite in my interest—the way that I should have ordered it myself. It is so simple," he added with a smile, "that it seems hardly worth while to be hanged at all."

At the finish of his remarks there was a long silence. The general sat impassive, looking into the man's face, but apparently not attentive to what had been said. It was as if his eyes had mounted guard over the prisoner while his mind concerned itself with other matters. Presently he drew a long, deep breath, shuddered, as one awakened from a dreadful dream, and exclaimed almost inaudibly: "Death is horrible!"—this man of death.

"It was horrible to our savage ancestors," said the spy, gravely, "because they had not enough intelligence to dissociate the idea of consciousness from the idea of the physical forms in which it is manifested—as an even lower order of intelligence, that of the monkey, for example, may be unable to imagine a house without inhabitants, and seeing a ruined hut fancies a suffering occupant. To us it is horrible because we have inherited the tendency to think it so, accounting for the notion by wild and fanciful theories of another world—as names of places give rise to legends explaining them and reasonless conduct to philosophies in justification. You can hang me, General, but there your power of evil ends; you cannot condemn me to heaven."

The general appeared not to have heard; the spy's talk had merely turned his thoughts into an unfamiliar channel, but there they pursued their will independently to conclusions of their own. The storm had ceased, and something of the solemn spirit of the night had imparted itself to his reflections, giving them the sombre tinge of a supernatural dread. Perhaps there was an element of prescience in it. "I should not like to die," he said—"not to-night."

He was interrupted—if, indeed, he had intended to speak further—by the entrance of an officer of his staff, Captain Hasterlick, the provost-marshal. This recalled him to himself; the absent look passed away from his face.

"Captain," he said, acknowledging the officer's salute, "this man is a Yankee spy captured inside our lines with incriminating papers on him. He has confessed. How is the weather?"

"The storm is over, sir, and the moon shining."

"Good; take a file of men, conduct him at once to the parade ground, and shoot him."

A sharp cry broke from the spy's lips. He threw himself forward, thrust out his neck, expanded his eyes, clenched his hands.

"Good God!" he cried hoarsely, almost inarticulately; "you do not mean that! You forget—I am not to die until morning."

"I have said nothing of morning," replied the general, coldly; "that was an assumption of your own. You die now."

"But, General, I beg—I implore you to remember; I am to hang! It will take some time to erect the gallows—two hours—an hour. Spies are hanged; I have rights under military law. For Heaven's sake, General, consider how short—"

"Captain, observe my directions."

The officer drew his sword and fixing his eyes upon the prisoner pointed silently to the opening of the tent. The prisoner hesitated; the officer grasped him by the collar and pushed him gently forward. As he approached the tent pole the frantic man sprang to it and with cat-like agility seized the hand of the bowie-knife, plucked the weapon from the scabbard and thrusting the captain aside leaped upon the general with the fury of a madman, hurling him to the ground and falling headlong upon him as he lay. The table was overturned, the candle extinguished and they fought blindly in the darkness. The provost-marshal sprang to the assistance of his superior officer and was himself prostrated upon the struggling forms. Curses and inarticulate cries of rage and pain came from the welter of limbs and bodies; the tent came down upon them and beneath its hampering and enveloping folds the struggle went on. Private

Tassman, returning from his errand and dimly conjecturing the situation, threw down his rifle and laying hold of the flouncing canvas at random vainly tried to drag it off the men under it; and the sentinel who paced up and down in front, not daring to leave his beat though the skies should fall, discharged his rifle. The report alarmed the camp; drums beat the long roll and bugles sounded the assembly, bringing swarms of half-clad men into the moonlight, dressing as they ran, and falling into line at the sharp commands of their officers. This was well; being in line the men were under control; they stood at arms while the general's staff and the men of his escort brought order out of confusion by lifting off the fallen tent and pulling apart the breathless and bleeding actors in that strange contention.

Breathless, indeed, was one: the captain was dead; the handle of the bowie-knife, protruding from his throat, was pressed back beneath his chin until the end had caught in the angle of the jaw and the hand that delivered the blow had been unable to remove the weapon. In the dead man's hand was his sword, clenched with a grip that defied the strength of the living. Its blade was streaked with red to the hilt.

Lifted to his feet, the general sank back to the earth with a moan and fainted. Besides his bruises he had two swordthrusts—one through the thigh, the other through the shoulder.

The spy had suffered the least damage. Apart from a broken right arm, his wounds were such only as might have been incurred in an ordinary combat with nature's weapons. But he was dazed and seemed hardly to know what had occurred. He shrank away from those attending him, cowered upon the ground and uttered unintelligible remonstrances. His face, swollen by blows and stained with gouts of blood, nevertheless showed white beneath his disheveled hair—as white as that of a corpse.

"The man is not insane," said the surgeon, preparing bandages and replying to a question; "he is suffering from fright. Who and what is he?"

Private Tassman began to explain. It was the opportunity of his life; he omitted nothing that could in any way accentuate the importance of his own relation to the night's events. When he had finished his story and was ready to begin it again nobody gave him any attention.

The general had now recovered consciousness. He raised himself upon his elbow, looked about him, and, seeing the spy crouching by a camp-fire, guarded, said simply:

"Take that man to the parade ground and shoot him."

"The general's mind wanders," said an officer standing near.

"His mind does *not* wander," the adjutant-general said. "I have a memorandum from him about this business; he had given that same order to Hasterlick"—with a motion of the hand toward the dead provost-marshal—"and, by God! it shall be executed."

Ten minutes later Sergeant Parker Adderson, of the Federal army, philosopher and wit, kneeling in the moonlight and begging incoherently for his life, was shot to death by twenty men. As the volley rang out upon the keen air of the midnight, General Clavering, lying white and still in the red glow of the camp-fire, opened his big blue eyes, looked pleasantly upon those about him and said: "How silent it all is!"

The surgeon looked at the adjutant-general, gravely and significantly. The patient's eyes slowly closed, and thus he lay for a few moments; then, his face suffused with a smile of ineffable sweetness, he said, faintly: "I suppose this must be death," and so passed away.

RICHARD SCHULZ

Thinking About Death: Death Anxiety Research

Addressing the question "Do people really fear death and, if so, what exactly do they fear about death?" Schulz urges distinctions between death fear and death anxiety. He considers death fears to be grounded in the environment and, therefore, amenable to treatment. Death anxiety, on the other hand, he defines as inherent in the universality of death. After acknowledging the limitations of empirical studies and noting that some conceptualizations respond more effectively to intuitive analysis, Schulz provides a critical summary of attempts both to assess death anxiety and to relate it to demographic, personality, and environmental variables. He concludes by suggesting three directions for the next stages of research.

An Empirical Perspective: Death Anxiety Research

Death anxiety has been measured in a variety of populations and settings with a wide assortment of assessment devices ranging from projective techniques (such as the Rorschach and Thematic Apperception Test) to the measurement of galvanic skin response, a physiological correlate of anxiety. It is the aim of this review to bring order to the existing death anxiety literature and direction to the field by critically evaluating the various methods used to assess death anxiety, deriving conclusions warranted by the available data, and suggesting the direction that future research should follow. Before this literature is examined, one qualifier is in order. The distinction between death fear and death anxiety described earlier has not been made by empirical researchers. As a result, the two terms are used interchangeably in the discussion that follows.

Methodological Issues

Both direct and indirect techniques have been used to assess death anxiety. Direct techniques include questionnaires, checklists, and rating scales, while indirect techniques include projective tests, the measurement of galvanic skin response, and reaction times during death-related word association tasks. Direct techniques are by far the more frequently used, and at present there are six widely used death anxiety questionnaires (Boyar 1964; Collett and Lester 1969; Lester 1967; Sarnoff and Corwin 1959; Templer 1970; and Tolor and Reznikoff 1967). An example of one death anxiety scale is presented in Table 1. After reading each statement, the respondent decides whether a particular

Table 1 | Templer's Death Anxiety Scale

Content
I am very much afraid to die.
The thought of death seldom enters my mind.
It doesn't make me nervous when people talk about death.
I dread to think about having to have an operation.
I am not at all afraid to die.
I am not particularly afraid of getting cancer.
The thought of death never bothers me.
I am often distressed by the way time flies so very rapidly.
I fear dying a painful death.
The subject of life after death troubles me greatly.
I am really scared of having a heart attack.
I often think about how short life really is.
I shudder when I hear people talking about a World War III.
The sight of a dead body is horrifying to me.
I feel that the future holds nothing for me to fear.

Source: From D. Templer, The construction and validation of a death anxiety scale, *Journal of General Psychology* 82 (1970): 167.

statement is true or false for himself. These responses are then coded according to a key, and a death anxiety score is derived.

Only Boyar's (1964) Fear of Death Scale (FODS) and Templer's (1970) Death Anxiety Scale (DAS) have been validated. Validation is a procedure for determining whether a scale measures what it was designed to measure—in this case death anxiety. Exactly how this should be done varies with the type of scale used. Boyar attempted to validate his scale by administering it to subjects before and after viewing a highway accident movie intended to increase their death anxiety. Fear of death scores rose significantly more in the experimental group than in the control group, which saw an innocuous movie. Templer validated his scale both with psychiatric patients in a state mental hospital and with college students. High death anxiety psychiatric patients independently assessed by a clinician were found to have significantly higher DAS scores than control patients. The remaining four scales (Collett and Lester 1969; Lester 1967a; Sarnoff and Corwin 1959; Tolor and Reznikoff 1967) have not been independently validated, although intercorrelations among the scales are high enough to lend each a degree of concurrent validity. Durlak (1972a) found positive intercorrelations ranging from .41 to .65 among five of the scales. He inexplicably omitted Templer's DAS from his study, although Templer (1970) reported a positive .74 correlation between his scale and Boyar's (1964) FODS.

Two remaining scales (Dickstein 1972, 1975; Krieger, Epsting, and Leitner 1974) have neither been validated nor compared to the six scales discussed above. Krieger, Epsting, and Leitner's (1974) "Threat Index" has the interesting feature of being theoretically based but has poor test–retest reliability ($r = .49$ with one of 13 subjects dropped). Test–retest reliability is a measure of the reliability of the scale over time. That is, if an individual completes the same scale at different times, his scores should be very similar even though several months may have passed between the first and second time the scale was administered. This is based on the assumption that the scale measures permanent dispositional characteristics of the individual, which should not vary greatly over time.

Most death anxiety scales treat death anxiety as a unitary concept. This is based on the probably erroneous assumption that death anxiety is a single type of fear or anxiety. The one exception is the Collett and Lester (1969) scale, which is divided into four subscales measuring anxiety over death of self, death of others, dying of self, and dying of others. These subscales are roughly equivalent to the fear of nonbeing and the fear of the process (the pain and suffering) of dying as they apply to oneself and those close to us. Collett and Lester found low intercorrelations among their subscales, especially between the two subscales dealing with self and the two dealing with others, suggesting that death anxiety is a multidimensional concept. An individual may, for example, fear the process of his own dying and not be fearful about the dying process of those close to him. Durlak's (1972a) intercorrelation study showed that other scales correlate best with the death-of-self subscale of Collett and Lester. Many of the inconsistencies in the death anxiety data will probably be clarified once researchers begin paying closer attention to the components of death anxiety instead of treating it as a unitary concept. One such attempt is made below in the section on sex differences, where it is argued that inconsistencies in the literature are resolved when the cognitive and affective components of death anxiety are isolated. The accurate assessment of death anxiety is further complicated by recent findings that the method of administering a death anxiety scale affects reported death anxiety. Schulz, Aderman, and Manko (1976) found significantly lower reported death anxiety among college students on the Templer (1970) and Sarnoff and Corwin (1959) scales when administered individually rather than in group sessions. Death anxiety as measured by a group-administered questionnaire was not significantly different from death anxiety as assessed by the "bogus pipeline method" (Jones and Sigall 1971), in which a fake "emotion monitoring device" is attached to subjects to keep them honest. The rationale underlying the bogus pipeline is that subjects do not want to be second-guessed by a machine, and when asked to predict what the machine says about their attitudes, they respond without many of the social biases that obscure straight paper and pencil measures on sensitive topics. The findings of Schulz, Aderman, and Manko (1976) suggest that there may be a private and public component to death anxiety and that the private attitudes are more likely to be expressed when the respondent is anonymous.

In addition to the problems of the "unitary concept" assumption, death anxiety scales have been criticized by some researchers for their inability to discriminate between private and "unconscious" death anxiety. For example, Fulton (1961) has argued that even with a valid and reliable measuring instrument, a researcher can still only tap the "epiphenomenal" or surface-level attitudes of subjects, while Rheingold (1967) has stated that even the most elegant instrument can measure only public attitudes "passively acquired from culture or religion" (p. 33) and completely miss those attitudes and feelings existing at the unconscious level. In order to delve into the unconscious, according to Rheingold, it is necessary to turn to projective techniques and the intuitive insights of the psychotherapist. It is difficult to argue against such an approach except by pointing out its subjective nature. More objective measurements of unconscious death anxiety are possible by comparing reaction time, recall reaction time, galvanic skin response for death-related and neutral word associations, or through use of the Color-Word Interference Test (Stroop, 1938). Presumably, these indirect techniques assess death anxiety on a level beneath that accessible by questionnaires, although results from such studies must be interpreted with care.

Researchers have assumed that high galvanic skin response or slow reaction time during death-related word association tasks indicate "perceptual defense" and hence death anxiety (Alexander and Adlerstein 1958; Feifel and Branscomb 1973). Using a different indirect technique, Lester and Lester (1970) found that recognition of blurred death-related words was faster than recognition of blurred neutral words. They explained that "perceptual facilitation" makes evolutionary sense since survival requires hasty recognition of threatening stimuli. Since most investigators of unconscious death anxiety use word association rather than recognition tasks, the focus of this research has been on processes of perceptual defense rather than perceptual facilitation.

Another indirect technique is analysis of dream content. Handal and Rychlak (1971) had several judges (inter-rater reliability = .89) classify dreams reported in subjects' morning-after journals as positive, negative, or neutral and as death-related or non-death-related. They considered a high frequency of negative and/or death-related dreams to be evidence of unconscious death anxiety.

Taken together, these studies indicate that the measurement of death anxiety is indeed a more complex task than early researchers had anticipated. At present, it appears that death anxiety is not a unitary concept and may be comprised of four or more subcomponents. To complicate matters even further, it appears that death anxiety can be tapped at any one of three levels: public, private, and unconscious. Table 2 shows the three levels crossed by possible subcomponents. Although it is unlikely that each of fifty-seven possible cells can be clearly differentiated operationally, death anxiety researchers should nevertheless be sensitive to the complexity of their task, if confusion is to be avoided in the future.

Demographic and Personality Correlates of Death Anxiety

Although many variables have been found to relate to death anxiety, few clear and consistent patterns have emerged. The search for such patterns in the data is reviewed below.

Table 2 | Specific death fears by different assessment methods

	Level of Assessment		
Specific Fears Relating to Death of Self*	Public	Private	Unconscious
Pain			
Body misfunction			
Humiliation			
Rejection			
Nonbeing			
Punishment			
Interruption of goals			
Negative impact on survivors			
a psychological suffering of survivors			
b economic hardship			

*All these fears can be experienced vicariously in relation to the death of someone close to us. In addition, the fear of abandonment can be experienced directly.

Sex   Although several early studies yielded no systematic sex-related differences in death anxiety (Christ 1961; Rhudick and Dibner 1961; Swenson 1961; Jeffers, Nichols, and Eisdorfer 1961), it now appears fairly certain that, on the level assessed by questionnaires, females fear death more than males. Templer's (1970) DAS has been administered to samples of apartment residents, hospital aides, psychiatric patients, ninth graders, and high school students and their parents (Templer, Ruff, and Franks 1971; Iammarino 1975), and in all cases females scored higher than males. This finding was replicated by several other researchers.

Only when death anxiety is broken up into its components do researchers find any evidence of a greater fear of death among males. According to Thematic Apperception Test (TAT) responses, males have more fear of the effects of their death on dependents (Diggory and Rothman 1961) and more fear of the violence of death (Lowry 1965). In contrast, women show more fear of the dissolution of the body and the physical pain associated with death (Diggory and Rothman 1961).

Degner (1974) identified two clusters of responses to the concept of death by having subjects fill out 36 semantic differential scales. Among males she found an "evaluative" dimension to be strongest and an "emotional" dimension to be weakest. In an earlier study, Folta (in Degner 1974) found the reverse to be true for women. These studies suggest that there may be a cognitive and emotional component to death anxiety, with women viewing death in more emotional terms and men viewing death in more cognitive terms.

Consistent with these findings is the preliminary work of Krieger, Epsting, and Leitner (1974) with their Threat Index, a scale that measures death anxiety by measuring the "cognitive distance" subjects place between the concepts "death" and "self." Males tend to have higher death anxiety scores than females—a finding directly contrary to that obtained when Lester's Death

Anxiety Scale is used. Since the Threat Index is a cognitive measure and Lester's Death Anxiety Scale is a more affective one, these results, and those of Degner and Folta, can be understood if it is accepted that male death anxiety tends to be cognitive and female death anxiety more emotional. Further support for the existence of these two components of death anxiety is the lack of correlation between Lester's affective Death Anxiety Scale and the more cognitive Threat Index (Krieger, Epsting, and Leitner 1974) and also the lack of correlation between Lester's Death Anxiety Scale and Boyar's FODS, which is also supposedly a more "cognitive" scale (Krieger, Epsting, and Leitner 1974; Berman and Hays 1973). Finally, Krieger et al. reported a very high positive (+.73) correlation ($p<.01$) between the two cognitive scales: the Threat Index and Boyar's FODS. In summary, these findings suggest that researchers who use affectively oriented death anxiety scales will find higher death anxiety among females than males while the reverse is likely to be true when cognitively oriented death anxiety scales are used.

Age Although most of the death anxiety data have been collected from college students and the aged, there are some pertinent data available for every age group, from infants to the very old. Hall and Scott (in Hall 1922) attempted to assess death concern in children by asking adults to recall their earliest experiences with death. Using this retrospective technique, they concluded that the young child's view of death is characterized by specific objects and feelings associated with a specific death. A more informative study on children's views of death was conducted by Nagy (1959), who directly interviewed 378 boys and girls three to ten years old. Nagy's results yielded three relatively discrete developmental phases: for ages three to five, death is seen as a temporary departure or sleep; for ages five to nine, death is seen as final and is personified as either a separate person or the dead person himself; beyond nine years of age, children recognize death as not only final, but also inevitable. Nagy's data suggest that the association between death and anxiety is established as early as three years of age, when death is viewed as separation.

According to Rothstein (in Kastenbaum and Aisenberg 1972), death anxiety is relatively low throughout young adulthood until the middle adult years. Relying on extensive interview data, he found that death anxiety peaks in the middle years. This is especially true for men, perhaps because this is the first time men become aware of their own vulnerability as a result of deaths among friends and acquaintances their age. Contrary to Rothstein's findings, Feifel and Branscomb (1973) found that subjects over the age of fifty tended to answer "no" to the question, "Are you afraid of your own death?" more frequently than younger subjects. On the other hand, a study by Templer, Ruff, and Franks (1971) yielded results contrary to both Rothstein and Feifel and Branscomb. Testing over 2,000 subjects of various ages, they found no significant correlation between age and death anxiety scores.

This discrepancy in findings remains unresolved and is further complicated by a study of death anxiety at the unconscious level. Feifel and Brans-comb (1973) found that the same elderly subjects who reported below-average overt death anxiety exhibited unconscious death anxiety that was just as high as that of younger subjects. Corey (1961) similarly found that older adults tend to show avoidance of death in projective tests. While no explanation can account for all these data, they can perhaps in part be understood if it is assumed that people are more likely to deny their fears as death becomes a more immediate threat. Researchers frequently invoke the concept of denial to explain low death anxiety scores in populations such as the aged, who because of their nearness to death are expected to have high death anxiety. Unless other corroborating data are available, such interpretations of low scores are unjustified. Individuals who score low in death anxiety just may not be very concerned with death, regardless of their temporal nearness to death. The study by Feifel and Branscomb (1973) is one example of a study where a denial interpretation can be entertained. The relative discrepancy between overt death anxiety and unconscious death anxiety in the same population of elderly subjects could be the result of denial influencing the expression of overt death fears.

Physical Health   Evidence on the relationship between health and death anxiety follows a pattern similar to that of death anxiety and age. There is conflicting evidence on overt death anxiety and a possibility of denial among subjects most threatened by impending death. Lucas (1974) studied 60 hemo-dialysis and surgery patients and did not find their DAS scores to be significantly different from the normal mean scores reported by Templer (1970). Templer, however, found a significant negative correlation between scores on the DAS and a measure of physical health, indicating that the higher an individual's death anxiety, the lower his physical health status. Swenson (1961) suggested that people who are unhealthy might look forward to ending it all and so fear death less than the healthy. His finding that individuals in poor health tended to look forward to death more than fear it supports this view, although his sample included only aged individuals. Feifel and his colleagues (Feifel 1974; Feifel, Freilich, and Hermann 1973) found that terminally ill patients reported fearing death no more frequently than other subjects but demonstrated higher death anxiety on an unconscious level. Kübler-Ross (1969) reports some impressionistic data based on interviews with 200 terminal patients. She found that although patients experience a great deal of shock and anxiety when first informed of their terminality, most patients eventually come to accept their impending deaths. In a review of the literature on the feelings and attitudes of dying patients, Schulz and Aderman (1974) concluded that the predominant response of most terminal patients is depression rather than anxiety shortly before death. In sum, there is little evidence that persons closer to death, because of their health status, exhibit greater overt death anxiety than their healthy counterparts, and there is no evidence to suggest that extraordinary denial processes are operating in these populations.

Religiosity While Lester's review (1967a) reported considerable confusion on the relationship between religious beliefs and death anxiety, recent findings have been refreshingly clear. It is possible that the disparate results from earlier studies (e.g., Faunce and Fulton 1958; Kalish 1963) are attributable to different conceptualizations of religiosity. Indicators of extrinsic religiosity (frequency of church attendance) might result in a positive relationship between religiosity and death anxiety, but religiosity measured in terms of fundamental values might produce the reverse relationship. Recent studies show that degree of religiosity (measured by self-report of beliefs and churchgoing) is unrelated to death anxiety for the general population (Feifel 1974; Kalish 1963; Templer 1970) but is negatively related when subjects are religiously involved (Templer 1972a; Shearer 1973). That is, for Templer's sample, which included many ministers, religiosity was correlated with low levels of death anxiety.

Belief in afterlife has been suggested as an intervening variable reducing death anxiety for highly religious people. Jeffers, Nichols, and Eisdorfer (1961) found that individuals with strong religious commitments were more likely to believe in afterlife and also showed less fear of death than less religiously committed persons. Osarchuck and Tatz (1973) found that for subjects scoring high in a Belief in Afterlife Scale, a death-threatening slide show induced still greater belief in an afterlife. In general, the link between belief in afterlife and religiosity has been amply demonstrated. Osarchuck and Tatz (1973) and Kalish (1963) reported that active Protestants and Catholics had higher belief in afterlife when compared to religiously inactive persons of any faith. The other link—the relationship between belief in afterlife and death anxiety, independent of degree of religiosity—is in need of further study.

Emotional Disorders Research on the death anxiety of psychiatric patients is inconsistent. Brodman, Erdman, and Wolff (1956) and Templer (1971a) found psychiatric illness positively associated with high death anxiety. Similarly, Templer and Ruff (1971) reported above average DAS means for samples of psychiatric patients. However, contradictory findings are reported by Feifel and Hermann (1973). Using a wide range of death anxiety measurement devices, they found no differences between the death anxiety of mentally ill and normal subjects. They also found degree of mental illness to be unrelated to death anxiety.

Working with samples of "normals" from the general public, Templer (1970, 1972a) reported small positive correlations between Templer's DAS and the neuroticism scales of the Eysenck Personality Inventory and the Welsh Anxiety Scale, respectively. Other scales of general anxiety correlate similarly with the DAS (Templer 1970; Lucas 1974), as does the Minnesota Multiphasic Personality Inventory (MMPI) depression scale (Templer 1971a). Using projective measures, Rhudick and Dibner (1961) found significant positive correlations between death concern and four MMPI scales of neurotic preoccupation. These findings indicate that death anxiety shares features with more general forms of anxiety, neurosis, and depression. While it is important not to ignore this aspect of death anxiety, it is also important to note that Templer (1970) reports data suggesting that death anxiety is a concept distinct from general anxiety. The intercorrelations among various death anxiety scales are consistently and significantly higher than their correlations with general anxiety.

It might be expected that people who attempt suicide would fear death less than the general population. Lester (1967a) found this to be the case when he administered his and Boyar's (1964) FODS to attempters and threateners of suicide and compared their scores to those of subjects who never considered suicide. Similarly, Tarter, Templer, and Perley (1974) found a significant correlation between the DAS and the judged "potential for rescue" following the act of attempted suicide. One possible interpretation of these data is that those who fear death less are more serious about acting on their suicidal desires. The only evidence contrary to these findings comes from an unpublished study carried out by Lester and reported in his review (1967a). He found that suicide-threateners fear death more than suicide-contemplaters, who in turn fear death more than those who have never considered taking their lives; Lester admits this evidence is weak because of the small sample studied. The best conclusion is that suicidal individuals have lower death anxiety than comparable nonsuicidal populations.

Need for Achievement, Sense of Competence, and Purpose   At least three hypotheses have been generated relating need for achievement, sense of competence, and sense of purpose in life to death anxiety: (1) individuals with high need for achievement (nAch) will fear death more because it ends their chance for further achievement (Diggory and Rothman 1961); (2) individuals with a high sense of competence will fear death less because they are satisfied with their lives (Goodman 1975); and (3) persons with low fear of death will have a greater purpose in life because a crucial step in developing the latter is confronting death without fear (Frankl 1965).

Two studies (Nogas, Schweitzer, and Grumet 1974; Ray and Najman 1974) investigated the first hypothesis and failed to find a relationship between nAch and death anxiety, although Ray and Najman pointed out that the undergraduate samples used were too high in need for achievement to provide a sufficiently wide range of scores. The second hypothesis was partially supported by Nogas, Schweitzer, and Grumet (1974), who found a significant negative correlation between death anxiety and sense of competence. The data may indicate, however, that sense of competence includes competence in confronting death. The third hypothesis is supported by convincingly high negative correlations (ranging from -.54 to -.82) between overt death anxiety and Crumbaugh and Maholick's (1964) Purpose in Life Test (Blazer 1973; Durlak 1972b, 1973). Ignoring the fact that correlations say little about causality or about direction of causality, Blazer and Durlak suggest that children taught to accept death will become adults with more meaning in their lives.

Cognitive Style   A provocative study by Mishara, Baker, and Kostin (1972) indicated that college students differing in cognitive style hold different attitudes toward death. Cognitive style was determined by the Kinesthetic Figural After-effects task, which classifies subjects as "augmenters" if they overestimate the width of a wooden block held between their fingers after holding a wider "intervening stimulus" block. Subjects who underestimate the block's width after the intervening stimulus are classified as "reducers." Augmenters tend to magnify stimulus intensity; they tend to be more comfortable with stimulus deprivation and less comfortable with aversive stimuli. When asked to imagine the final year of their lives, augmenters avoided mentioning death (presumably an aversive stimulus) significantly more than reducers. While no death anxiety scale was administered in this study, these data suggest that augmenters have higher death anxiety than reducers.

This attempt to link death anxiety to cognitive functioning is a refreshing change from the usual pattern of relating death anxiety to other questionnaire measures.

Other Variables   A host of other variables have been researched as possible correlates of death anxiety. No significant correlations were found for the following variables: projective measures of fear of failure (Cohen and Parker 1974); a dependency scale (Selvey 1973); guilt about hostility (Selvey 1973); race (Pandey 1974; Pandey and Templer 1972); and Eysenck's Extraversion Scale (Templer 1972b). Three of four studies relating death anxiety to Rotter's I-E locus of control scale reported no relationship (Selvey 1973; Dickstein 1972; Berman 1973); only Tolor and Reznikoff (1967) found a significant relationship between Rotter's I-E scale and death anxiety. Externally oriented subjects had significantly greater death anxiety than subjects with internal orientations.

Denial of Death Anxiety   The idea that death anxiety can exist at both the conscious and unconscious level has been a theme throughout this chapter. While researchers have occasionally found consistencies between self-reported and unconscious death anxiety, more often than not the two are discrepant. When such discrepancies occur, researchers typically invoke the concept of repression, or denial, of death anxiety to explain these findings.

Handal and Rychlak (1971) found a much higher proportion of negative and death-related dreams among subjects scoring high or low on self-report death anxiety scales than among those with moderate scores. They concluded that many of those with low conscious death anxiety were denying their deeper fears. Feifel and his colleagues (Feifel and Branscomb 1973; Feifel and Hermann 1973) concluded that death anxiety is greater at unconscious than at conscious levels, especially for aged and unhealthy subjects. For this reason, the concept of denial has been invoked to explain the lack of increased death anxiety scores among dying subjects. Similarily, the failure to find a relationship between death anxiety and contact with death may be attributed to the exclusive use of conscious death anxiety measures in these studies.

Other evidence of denial of death anxiety makes use of Byrne's (1964) Repression-Sensitization scale. Subjects who tend to repress threats (according to the Repression-Sensitization scale) also tend to be low in conscious death anxiety as measured by the DAS (Templer 1971b). Templer found no evidence for the relationship between Repression-Sensitization score and unconscious death anxiety. Apparently repressors, while low in conscious death anxiety, are not high in unconscious death anxiety either.

Templer (1971b) also found a .30 correlation between DAS and unconscious death anxiety as measured by a galvanic skin response to death-related stimulus material. This moderately positive correlation suggests that the two levels of death anxiety are not totally independent.

Donaldson (1972) argues that operational and theoretical definitions of denial must be determined before conclusions are drawn about its existence. The discrepancies between conscious and unconscious death anxiety found in the research reviewed above represent a step in this direction. Research employing discrepancy between conscious and unconscious death anxiety as a variable and searching for its correlates appears promising. The internal dynamics resulting from disharmony between different levels of a person's attitudes toward death may prove to be more important than death anxiety itself.

Environmental Influences on Death Anxiety

Three classes of environmental variables are found in the literature. Researchers have examined the effects of educational intervention, contact with death, and the impact of the family on death anxiety. Lucas (1974) and Templer, Ruff, and Franks (1971) reported high correlations ($r = .59$) between spouses' DAS scores; child–parent correlations were less ($r = .40$) but tended to be somewhat higher when the two are of the same sex. Although these data say nothing about the relative importance of environment and genetics as determinants of death anxiety, they do support the notion that the environment, through parents' influence, affects death anxiety (Templer, Ruff, and Franks 1971).

Lester and Templer (1972) found a striking developmental trend in child–parent correlations. During adolescence, daughter–parent DAS correlations decreased steadily and were statistically insignificant by age eighteen or nineteen. No explanation is offered for the apparent tendency for adolescent boys to continue to be influenced by their parents while their sisters are cutting the death anxiety apron strings. Another finding of family influence was reported by Iammarino (1975). Ninth-graders living with only one parent feared death more than their two-parent peers. This could be interpreted as evidence that separation anxiety can be an antecedent of death anxiety. More generally, this serves to demonstrate the effect of family environment on death anxiety.

Since death anxiety has been shown to be a socially influenced phenomenon, one might expect it to respond to direct intervention. However, attempts to verify the success of intervention, in the form of nursing curricula and college courses, have met with mixed success. Nurses nearing graduation accept death more than students earlier in their training (Yeaworth, Kapp, and Winget 1974). Their death anxiety is lower (Lester, Getty, and Kneisl 1974), and thoughts of death are less frequent (Snyder, Gertler, and Ferneau 1973). With the exception of Lester and his colleagues, most researchers attribute the changes in death anxiety to the nursing curriculum, ignoring alternative explanations such as contact with patients. All that can be concluded with certainty is that something in a nursing student's experience reduces death anxiety.

Several specific "death education" programs have been evaluated, but only one caused a significant reduction in death anxiety. Murray (1974) found nurses' DAS scores significantly reduced after a six-week course. It is possible that the practical work of the students interacted with the program to lessen death anxiety since courses for college students have not been found to change death anxiety significantly (Bell 1975; Leviton 1973; Wittmaier 1975).

While death education courses will certainly continue in colleges and nursing schools, an indirect approach to lessening death anxiety was shown to be effective by Templer, Ruff, and Simpson (1974). They evaluated the death anxiety of subjects before and after therapy dealing exclusively with reduction of depression. DAS scores declined significantly along with depression, demonstrating that depression and death anxiety covary to some extent.

In spite of many attempts, no study has shown that contact with death or with high-risk situations influences death anxiety. Self-report of previous death-threatening experiences is unrelated to death anxiety (Durlak 1973; Berman 1974). Nurses' death anxiety is not related to the patient death rate on their unit (Shusterman and Sechrest 1973) or within their area of specialization (Lester, Getty, and Kneisl 1974). Parachute jumpers (Alexander and Lester 1972) and widows (Kalish and Reynolds 1974; Rhudick and Dibner 1961) score no higher than controls on death scales, although Swenson (1961) found that widows tend to deny their death anxiety when direct methods are used. The mixed pattern of results obtained on environmental determinants of death anxiety is most likely attributable to the lack of conceptual and methodological rigor in designing and executing research in this area. Researchers should know at what level death anxiety is being assessed and should be sensitive to possible confounding variables when carrying out their research.

Future Research

This review of the death anxiety literature suggests that future research should move in three directions. First, researchers should be sensitive to the multidimensionality of death anxiety. Much of the confusion of past research may be avoided by recognizing that death anxiety is comprised of several independent components, each of which can be tapped at a public, private, and unconscious level. An immediate goal should be the investigation of the various subcomponents of death anxiety. Some components—such as anxiety over nonexistence and the anxiety over the process of dying (that is, the humiliation, pain, and suffering) in relation to self and others—have been identified. Other components might include anxiety about the impact of one's death on survivors and about having one's plans interrupted.

A second endeavor should be the untangling of discrepancies between conscious and unconscious death anxiety. The consequences of this discrepancy may eventually prove more interesting and important than simple death anxiety per se. One perspective on this problem is presented in a recent excellent review of the psychological death literature by Kastenbaum and Costa (1977). These authors suggest that fear of death and death anxiety are two different and independent phenomena. Thus, an individual may be high on specific fears associated with death and yet exhibit little death anxiety. Viewed from this perspective, there is no reason to expect a consistent relationship between conscious and unconscious death anxiety. At any rate, further attempts at enlarging the list of paper-and-pencil correlates of death anxiety appear to be of little use in understanding or demonstrating its relevance to human behavior.

Third, an effort should be made to demonstrate the functional or behavioral consequences of death anxiety. One such example is Templer's (1972b) study of death anxiety in smokers. Templer found that while nonsmokers and smokers did not differ in death anxiety, smokers with high death anxiety tended to smoke less. Another example is Kastenbaum and Briscoe's (1975) study of street-crossing behavior. The authors demonstrated the feasibility of relating naturalistically observed behavior to unobserved psychosocial variables: they found strong relationships between risk-taking in street-crossing and suicidal tendencies, marital status, and desired and expected life span.

Conclusion

Thinking about death has been one of man's major preoccupations. Many early speculations were based on intuition and individual case studies and yielded a rich and complex perspective on what it is that man fears about death and how these fears affect his functioning. Some researchers (Becker 1973; Meyer 1975; Zilboorg 1943) have used this perspective to argue that death anxiety has been the inspiration for many great individual achievements. Turning to the empirical studies of the relationship between death anxiety and a multitude of other variables, we found the existing empirical approach to be somewhat simplistic. Death anxiety does not appear to be a unidimensional concept. Instead, it appears to have many components, each of which can be assessed at different levels. However, recent research shows signs of tapping into the richness of this topic.

References

Alexander, I. E., and Adlerstein, A. M. 1958. Affective responses to the concept of death in a population of children and early adolescents. *Journal of Genetic Psychology* 93:167–77.

Alexander, M., and Lester, D. 1972. Fear of death in parachute jumpers. *Perceptual and Motor Skills* 34:338.

Becker, E. 1973. *The denial of death*. New York: Free Press.

Bell, W. 1975. The experimental manipulation of death attitudes: A preliminary investigation. *Omega: Journal of Death and Dying* 6:199–205.

Berman, A. 1974. Belief in afterlife, religion, religiosity, and life-threatening experiences. *Omega: Journal of Death and Dying* 5:127.

———. 1973. Smoking behavior: How is it related to locus of control, death anxiety, and belief in afterlife. *Omega: Journal of Death and Dying* 4:149–55.

Berman, A., and Hays, J. E. 1973. Relationship between death anxiety, belief in afterlife and locus of control. *Journal of Consulting and Clinical Psychology* 41:318.

Blazer, J. 1973. The relationship between meaning in life and fear of death. *Psychology* 10:33–4.

Boyar, J. I. 1964. "The construction and partial validation of a scale for the measurement of fear of death." Unpublished doctoral dissertation, University of Rochester, Rochester, New York.

Brodman, K., Erdman, A., and Wolff, H. 1956. *Manual for the Cornell Medical Index*. Ithaca, New York: Cornell University Medical College.

Byrne, D. 1964. Repression-sensitization as a dimension of personality. In B. A. Maher (ed.), *Progress in Experimental Personality Research,* vol. 1. New York: Academic Press.

Christ, P. E. I. 1961. Attitudes toward death among a group of acute geriatric psychiatric patients. *Journal of Gerontology* 16:56–59.

Cohen, R., and Parker, O. 1974. Fear of failure and death. *Psychological Reports* 34:54.

Collett, L., and Lester, D. 1969. Fear of death and fear of dying. *Journal of Psychology* 72:179–81.

Corey, L. G. 1961. An analogue of resistance to death awareness. *Journal of Gerontology* 16:59–60.

Crumbaugh, J. C., and Maholick, L. T. 1964. An experimental study in existentialism: The psychometric approach to Frankl's concept of noogenic neurosis. *Journal of Clinical Psychology* 20:200–207.

Degner, L. 1974. The relationship between some beliefs held by physicians and their life-prolonging decisions. *Omega: Journal of Death and Dying* 5:223.

Dickstein, L. 1972. Death concern: Measurement and correlates. *Psychological Reports* 30:563–71.

———. 1975. Self-report and fantasy correlates of death concern. *Psychological Reports* 32:147–58.

Diggory, J. C., and Rothman, D. Z. 1961. Values destroyed by death. *Journal of Abnormal and Social Psychology* 63:205–10.

Donaldson, P. J. 1972. Denying death: A note regarding some ambiguities in the current discussion. *Omega: Journal of Death and Dying* 3:285–90.

Durlak, J. 1972a. Measurement of the fear of death: An examination of some existing scales. *Journal of Clinical Psychology* 28:545–47.

———. 1972b. Relationship between individual attitudes toward life and death. *Journal of Consulting and Clinical Psychology* 38:463.

———. 1973. Relationship between various measures of death concern and fear of death. *Journal of Consulting and Clinical Psychology* 41:162.

Faunce, W. A., and Fulton, R. L. 1958. The sociology of death: A neglected area of research. *Social Forces* 36:205–9.

Feifel, H. 1974. Religious conviction and fear of death among the healthy and the terminally ill. *Journal for the Scientific Study of Religion* 13:353–60.

Feifel, H., and Branscomb, A. 1973. Who's afraid of death? *Journal of Abnormal Psychology* 81:282–88.

Feifel, H., and Hermann, L. 1973. Fear of death in the mentally ill. *Psychological Reports* 33:931–38.

Feifel, H., Freilich, J., and Hermann, L. 1973. Death fear in dying heart and cancer patients. *Journal of Psychosomatic Research* 17:161–66.

Frankl, V. E. 1965. *The Doctor and the Soul.* New York: Knopf.

Fulton, R. 1961. Discussion of a symposium on attitudes toward death in older persons. *Journal of Gerontology* 16:44–66.

Goodman, L. 1975. Winning the race with death, fear of death and creativity. Symposium, American Psychological Association Convention, Chicago, Illinois.

Hall, G. S. 1922. *Senescence.* New York: Appleton.

Handal, P. J., and Rychlak, J. F. 1971. Curvilinearity between dream content and death anxiety and the relationship of death anxiety to repression-sensitization. *Journal of Abnormal Psychology* 77:11–16.

Iammarino, N. K. 1975. Relationship between death anxiety and demographic variables. *Psychological Reports* 17:262.

Jeffers, F. C., Nichols, C. R., and Eisdorfer, C. 1961. Attitudes of older persons to death. *Journal of Gerontology* 16:53–56.

Jones, E. E., and Sigall, H. 1971. The bogus pipeline: A new paradigm for measuring affect and attitude. *Psychological Bulletin* 76:349–64.

Kalish, R. A. 1963. Some variables in death attitudes. *Journal of Social Psychology* 59:137–45.

Kalish, R., and Reynolds, D. 1974. Widows view death. *Omega: Journal of Death and Dying* 5:187.

Kastenbaum, R., and Aisenberg, R. 1972. *The Psychology of Death.* New York: Springer.

Kastenbaum, R., and Briscoe, L. 1975. The street corner: A laboratory for the study of life-threatening behavior. *Omega: Journal of Death and Dying* 6:33.

Kastenbaum, R., and Costa, P. T. 1977. Psychological perspectives on death. In M. R. Rosenzweig and Porter, L. W. (eds.) *Annual Review of Psychology* 8:225–49.

Krieger, S., Epsting, F., and Leitner, L. M. 1974. Personal constructs, threat, and attitudes toward death. *Omega: Journal of Death and Dying* 5:299.

Kübler-Ross, E. 1969. *On Death and Dying.* New York: Macmillan.

Lester, D. 1967. Experimental and correlational studies of the fear of death. *Psychological Bulletin* 67:27–36.

Lester, D., Getty, C., and Kneisl, C. 1974. Attitudes of nursing students and nursing faculty toward death. *Nursing Research* 23:50–53.

Lester, D., and Lester, G. 1970. Fear of death, fear of dying, and threshold differences for death words and neutral words. *Omega: Journal of Death and Dying* 1:175–79.

Lester, D., and Templer, D. 1972. Resemblance of parent–child death anxiety as a function of age and sex of child. *Psychological Reports* 31:750.

Leviton, D. 1973. Death education and change in students' attitudes. *Final Research Report,* National Institute of Mental Health Research Grant MH 21974-01. Washington, D.C.

Lowry, R. 1965. Male–female differences in attitudes toward death. Doctoral dissertation, Brandeis University.

Lucas, R. 1974. A comparative study of measures of general anxiety and death anxiety among three medical groups including patient and wife. *Omega: Journal of Death and Dying* 5:233.

Meyer, J. E. 1975. *Death and Neurosis.* New York: International Universities Press.

Mishara, B., Baker, H., and Kostin, I. 1972. Do people who seek less environmental stimulation avoid thinking about the future and their death? Proceedings of the Annual Convention of the American Psychological Association 7:667–68.

Murray, P. 1974. Death education and its effect on the death anxiety level of nurses. *Psychological Reports* 35:1250.

Nagy, M. 1959. The child's view of death. In H. Feifel (ed.), *The Meaning of Death.* New York: McGraw-Hill.

Nogas, C., Schweitzer, K., and Grumet, J. 1974. An investigation of death anxiety, sense of competence, and need for achievement. *Omega: Journal of Death and Dying* 5:245.

Osarchuck, M., and Tatz, S. 1973. Effect of induced fear of death on belief in afterlife. *Journal of Personality and Social Psychology* 27:256–60.

Pandey, R. E. 1974–75. Factor analytic study of attitudes toward death among college students. *International Journal of Social Psychiatry* 21:7–11.

Pandey, R. E., and Templer, D. 1972. Use of the death anxiety scale in an inter-racial setting. *Omega: Journal of Death and Dying* 3:127–30.

Ray, J. J., and Najman, J. 1974. Death anxiety and death acceptance: A preliminary approach. *Omega: Journal of Death and Dying* 5:311.

Rheingold, J. C. 1967. *The Mother, Anxiety, and Death.* Boston: Little, Brown.

Rhudick, P. J., and Dibner, A. S. 1961. Age, personality and health correlates of death concern in normal aged individuals. *Journal of Gerontology* 16:44–49.

Sarnoff, I., and Corwin, S. M. 1959. Castration anxiety and the fear of death. *Journal of Personality* 27:374–85.

Schulz, R., and Aderman, D. 1974. Clinical research and the stages of dying. *Omega: Journal of Death and Dying* 5:137–43.

———. 1977. Physician's death anxiety and survival of patients. Unpublished manuscript.

Schulz, R., Aderman, D., and Manko, G. 1976. Attitudes toward death: The effects of different methods of questionnaire administration. Paper presented at the meeting of the Eastern Psychological Association, New York, April.

Selvey, C. 1973. Concerns about death in relation to sex, dependency, guilt about hostility, and feelings of powerlessness. *Omega: Journal of Death and Dying* 4:209–19.

Shearer, R. E. 1973. Religious belief and attitudes toward death. *Dissertation Abstracts International* 33:3292–93.

Shusterman, L., and Sechrest, L. 1973. Attitudes of RNs toward death in a general hospital. *Psychiatry in Medicine* 4:411–26.

Snyder, M., Gertler, R., and Ferneau, E. 1973. Changes in nursing students' attitudes toward death and dying: A measurement of curriculum integration effectiveness. *International Journal of Social Psychiatry* 19:294–98.

Stroop, J. R. 1938. Factors affecting speed in serial verbal reactions. *Psychological Monographs* 50:38–48.

Swenson, W. M. 1961. Attitudes toward death in an aged population. *Journal of Gerontology* 16:49–52.

Tarter, R., Templer, D., and Perley, R. 1974. Death anxiety in suicide attempters. *Psychological Reports* 34:895–97.

Templer, D. 1970. The construction and validation of a death anxiety scale. *Journal of General Psychology* 82:165–77.

———. 1971a. The relationship between verbalized and nonverbalized death anxiety. *Journal of Genetic Psychology* 119:211–14.

———. 1971b. Death anxiety as related to depression and health of retired persons. *Journal of Gerontology* 26:521–23.

———. 1972a. Death anxiety in religiously very involved persons. *Psychological Reports* 31:361–62.

———. 1972b. Death anxiety: Extraversion, neuroticism, and cigarette smoking. *Omega: Journal of Death and Dying* 3:53–56.

Templer, D., and Ruff, C. 1971. Death anxiety scale means, standard deviations, and embedding. *Psychological Reports* 29:173–74.

Templer, D., Ruff, C., and Franks, C. 1971. Death anxiety: Age, sex and parental resemblance in diverse populations. *Developmental Psychology* 4:108.

Templer, D., Ruff, C., and Simpson, K. 1974. Alleviation of high death anxiety with symptomatic treatment of depression. *Psychological Reports* 35:216.

Tolor, A., and Reznikoff, M. 1967. Relationship between insight, repression-sensitization, internal-external control, and death anxiety. *Journal of Abnormal Psychology* 72:426–30.

Wittmaier, B. 1975. The impact of a death course. Unpublished manuscript, Kirkland College, New York.

Yeaworth, R., Kapp, F. and Winget, C. 1974. Attitudes of nursing students toward the dying patient. *Nursing Research* 23:30–34.

Zilboorg, G. 1943. Fear of death. *Psychoanalytic Quarterly* 12:465–75.

TALCOTT PARSONS & VICTOR LIDZ

selection from
Death in American Society

While the preceding selection reviewed empirical research methods on individual attitudes, the next essay turns to an analysis of the cultural context in which those attitudes are embedded. Using a sociological model, Parsons and Lidz demonstrate that the interpretation of death in America has concentrated on two factors: the completion of a normal life cycle and the technological control of random causes. They counter the often-heard generalization that ours is a death-denying society by asserting that American society demonstrates an attitude of acceptance, qualified by a concept of appropriate timing.

The present paper will examine the basic patterns of orientation toward death in American society, their cultural roots, and their relations to the social structure. We hope also to suggest problems for further research, as social science clearly lacks crucial knowledge about the subject, as well as to shed light upon some related aspects of American society and, e.g., attitudes toward life purposes or strivings and toward aging, problems occasioned by the increasing proportion of older people in our population and by the high incidence of suicide, and the nature of current funeral practices.

We shall begin with a foil—the widespread view that the realities of death are characteristically met with "denial" in contemporary American society,[1] an opinion that seems dubious to us. Usually cited as evidence of this opinion are practices such as embalming, the elaborate dressing of corpses, and the use of cosmetics upon them, as well as more extreme ones such as concern with coffins' impermeability to decay and the seeming apathy of many terminal patients about their diseases.

Such practices are commonly interpreted as indications that Americans are "going soft," becoming progressively less capable of facing the harsh reality of the actual world. In such interpretations, reality and harshness are often equated, whereas the pleasant things of life are considered not very "real." Americans are said, then, to live in a world of illusion, constructing elaborate defenses against intrusions of reality. Our handling of death is considered only one striking manifestation of a general deplorable tendency.[2]

This paper will present an alternative view, namely that American society has institutionalized a broadly stable, though flexible and changing, orientation to death that is fundamentally not a "denial" but a mode of acceptance

Source: Talcott Parsons and Victor Lidz, "Death in American Society," *Essays in Self-Destruction.* Edited by Edwin S. Shneidman. New York: Science House, Inc., 1967, 133–140. Copyright © by Jason Aronson, Inc., New York, New York. Reprinted by permission.

appropriate to our primary cultural patterns of activism. We cannot develop our argument until we have reviewed some of the salient characteristics of American society and have discussed some aspects of death and dying. However, it seems appropriate to register immediately a basic difficulty of the denial hypothesis: it would be very anomalous for a society that has no thoroughly institutionalized scientific values to adopt an attitude so drastically discrepant with the realism of science in an area so close to biology and medicine.

Death is a "natural" phenomenon rooted in the conditions of the biological existence of man and all the higher organisms. Moreover, modern biological science has established that death is not only inevitable among higher organisms but is also a positive factor in species' adaptations within the broader physical and organic system.

The differentiation between germ plasm and somatoplasm, which is the crux of the mortality of the higher organisms, enhances both stability and variability of genetic materials in adaptational terms. Bisexual reproduction favors controlled genetic variation by combining two independent genetic lines to produce a new, unique genetic constitution in practically every individual of the offspring generation. However, if the resulting adaptive changes are to accumulate with much efficiency, the parental generation must die off so that its genetic materials can be replaced by those of the offspring. Hence death is positively functional for biological adaptation.[3]

The death of the individual human personality seems to be similarly functional for the sociocultural system to which it belongs. Human kinship systems tend to ascribe reproduction and its correlate in the sociocultural system, the socialization process, to each other, though there is certainly some independent "play" between the two. Through its structuring of marital selection and family maintenance, a kinship system determines both what organic-social components in the society are combined for perpetuation and how the resultant offspring are submitted to the primary learning processes that introduce them to members within the continuing society. In maturing through the life cycle, a new generation comes to internalize the cultural patterns of the society as communicated by the parental generation.[4] It then becomes important that the older generation be "on the way out" so that its offspring can "take over" the controlling positions of the society, perhaps especially those of reproduction and socialization, and can be free to innovate, both socially and culturally.[5] Like genetic patterns, the cultural patterns communicated to specific offspring seem to vary with both generation and the particular "lines" in the kinship system which the parents represent. Clearly, death plays an important part in the genesis and utilization of new variations in the cultural patterns that will have adaptive significance for the society.

Thus death must be regarded as a fundamental aspect of the human condition, not only by us in our roles as social scientists but by all men as members of their various social groups. All who attain even a moderate longevity must undergo the strains of losing at least some persons to whom they have been closely attached. And, by virtue of being human and being oriented in action by long-accumulating, complex symbol systems, all will have anticipatory knowledge of, and must contemplate, their own deaths. Furthermore, it seems that mortality must always be a particularly important example and trenchant symbol of the finitude of the concrete human being. It is the barrier to omnipotence and the limit to capacities that simply cannot be overcome but must be adjusted to and accepted.

Because death inherently has such critical meaning for humans, it must be given an important position in the "constitutive symbolism" of all viable religious systems. In terms of its own fundamental patterns of orientation, each culture must attribute some "ultimate" meaning or reference to death. If a religion is to remain a workable, institutionalized complex, it can *never* simply deny the ultimate relevance of such a basic condition, although it can (and must) select among the many possibilities which are viable within the human condition, including some rather extreme ones.[6] It must provide a framework for interpreting death that is meaningful and appropriate, in relation to other elements of the culture, for defining attitudes regarding both the deaths of others and the prospect of one's own death. Closely associated with such a framework, of course, are the conventions for occasions of death, particularly the complex of funeral practices.[7]

Some massive facts indicate that modern Western society stands very far along in a major evolutionary development in the biological–demographic sphere. It is well known that "nature" is generally prodigal with the potentials of reproduction at the lower levels of evolution. Among the lower species, the ratio of ova produced to ova fertilized is exceedingly high, as is the ratio of fertilized ova to those which develop into mature organisms. The general evolutionary trend is toward reducing these ratios and increasing the species' "investment" in the probability that particular organisms will perpetuate its patterns.[8] For example, the long periods of gestation and postnatal care that characterize mammals are evidence of this trend. Man has a particularly prolonged gestation period and a relatively extreme postnatal dependency, but he also has a generally high rate of successful maturation (and reproduction). Modern societies seem to accentuate this development within the broad range of possibilities that comprises the biologic basis of the human condition.

Most striking is the recent prolongation of the individual life and concomitant reduction in the ratio of, first, conceptions and, then, live births to completions of a relatively maximum life cycle. The dramatic demographic fact is that in modern societies life expectancy at birth has approximately doubled in the last century, from in the thirties to about seventy years. However, this has occurred without a marked change in the typical maximum life span—the proportion of centenarians has increased little, if at all. The essential fact, then, is that a substantially larger proportion of a birth cohort, or cohort of young adults, lives to approximate completion of the life cycle. Premature death, relative to a normality of attaining "old age," has been enormously reduced.

This broad development comprises a gain in control over the effects of death in that we need not fear its caprices so acutely now that we have fair (statistical) assurance of living out our most active days. Nevertheless, in some other senses the problem of death has concomitantly come to be posed even more massively and trenchantly.

Modern societies contain a rapidly increasing class of persons who have attained old age. Over 9 percent of the American population is now over 65 years of age, as opposed to only 4 percent only 60 years ago.[9] A very large proportion of these people have completed their more obvious and important life tasks, as valued by the ordinary criteria of our society. In general, they have retired from their occupational jobs, and their children have matured and become independent and have families of their own. By the nature of their social positions, they are "on the way out" and are living "in the shadow of death," having entered what is—by most *institutional* criteria—a terminal period of their lives. Thus, there is a relatively large group institutionally placed so that, in some sense, it must rather directly confront the problem of inevitable death. Moreover, this situation affects a much wider group, as those associated with the aging, particularly their children, must prepare to lose them in the relatively near future.

Both for the individual as he faces death and for the social groups intimately attached to him, the problem of the *meaning* of death is coming in a new sense to be concentrated about death occurring as the completion of a normal life cycle. This central, irreducible problem is becoming disentangled from the problem of adjusting to deaths that occur earlier in the life cycle, particularly in infancy and early childhood, which was much more general in the premodern period.

This development may be regarded as differentiating two aspects of the historic problem of death: that stemming from the inevitability of death and that pertaining to deaths which are potentially subject to some kind of human control. We generally value very highly efforts to minimize deaths of the latter type and are particularly upset by such deaths when they do occur. This seems to be the underlying reason why we feel deaths in automobile accidents to be so shocking and their rates to warrant so much public concern. Similarly, lapses in control over avoidable deaths that we now take for granted are experienced as especially disturbing—e.g., the great international concern over the Zermatt typhoid epidemic. Similarly, a major rise in deaths due to smallpox or plague would be highly traumatic, very largely because it is now so completely unexpected and considered to be unnecessary.

This basic differentiation within the complex of orientations toward death has some important correlates. We have come to expect that death will occur primarily among the old and only rarely in other groups. Parents no longer frequently experience the deaths of young children, nor do they ordinarily expect that they will. Similarly, the death of young adults, once so closely associated with tuberculosis, is now relatively uncommon—Violetta and Mimi, though characters still as tragic as when *La Traviata* and *La Bohème* were composed, no longer represent a common fate. The fact that people killed in automobile accidents are often the young probably contributes greatly to our concern over such deaths.

With the prevention of premature death being so heavily and broadly emphasized, difficult problems of meaning are raised by instances in which death either is deliberately imposed or could be avoided through greater care. Significantly, the imposition of capital punishment has been declining, even in proportion to convictions for capital crimes, and is being opposed by widespread movements to abolish the death penalty altogether. Similarly, the contemporary world has newly developed general and intense convictions about the ethical unacceptability and irrationality of war.

Death also has a very broad, if complex, association with suffering and violence. On the one hand, it is an ultimate severity on the scales of punishment, violence, and suffering. On the other hand, it is just as ultimate a release from them. Our modern concerns with control clearly bear upon these scales, and the minimization of suffering in general has certainly become highly valued. The deliberate imposition of physical suffering through torture has generated very great humanitarian opposition, so much so that torture is now almost considered basically unacceptable in the main Western tradition, no matter how "good" its cause may be. Throughout our era, torture has been a major focus of the moral objection to totalitarian regimes. Increasingly, the aggressive employment of violence for overt political ends seems to be attracting opposition of a similar moral generality, except in the cases of certain extreme situations. The most massive developments in the control of suffering, however, have been those in modern medicine. These are salient, not only in the prevention and cure of disabling diseases but also in the reduction of the physical suffering that is involved in illness, including mortal illness. Anesthetics and narcotics have been the most important means for this accomplishment (note that even those who are alarmed by contemporary American attitudes toward death object very little to such "denial" of pain) and have enabled modern man almost to exclude physical suffering from the problems which death inevitably presents.

Thus, modern institutions differentiate three components of the more diffuse problem of death from the core phenomenon of "inevitable death": "premature" death that can be avoided by human measures; deliberately imposed death; and the physical suffering that dying may entail. The modern tendency has been to mobilize control measures to minimize the undesirable impact of each of these three components. In a sense, all three comprise the "uncertainty" of death, as distinguished from its inevitability, and it is this adventitious uncertainty that we strive to control. Although it is unlikely that any of three components will ever be completely eliminated, all have already been sufficiently reduced to be distinguished clearly from the category of the inevitable "natural" death of all individuals. They need be involved in only a small and varying minority of deaths—they are no longer constitutive components of "man's fate." Moreover, when they occur, they may be seen as "irrational" relative to the "normal," natural aspects of death.

Here we may note how radically these ideas contrast with most pre-modern orientations toward death. Many primitive societies evidently regard *all* deaths as a result of the adventitious play of human or magical factors and lack a clear conception of "natural death." Deaths can then be warded off or adapted to on some combination of political and religio–magical grounds, but they cannot be the foci of distinct cultural complexes that discriminate between their "ultimately" and scientifically meaningful aspects. Most of the classical civilizations adopted a rather fatalistic attitude toward death and illness, when early in life as well as in old age.[10] They regarded the loss of a large proportion of a population cohort before maturity as quite normal. Furthermore, they would have considered any very elaborate efforts to save the dying and to mitigate suffering as interference with Divine provision. Thus, the modern development of both a pattern for valuing the prolongation of life and a highly rationalized schema for identifying the controllable components of the death complex must not be taken for granted.

The comparative evidence suggests that the concomitant emergence in modern societies of the two general developments we have noted, the prolongation of actual life expectancy and the orientation toward controlling the "adventitious" components of the death complex, can hardly be fortuitous. It suggests that we should view the modern, differentiated orientation toward death as a component of a much broader orientation system which emphasizes dedication to activity that can be expected on rational grounds to maximize human control over the *conditional* elements of the life situation. A major tradition of sociological research, stemming largely from Max Weber's comparative studies in religion, has shown that such a general orientational system, which may be conveniently called instrumental activism, characterizes modern Western civilization, particularly American society,[11] and underlies much of the modern day's rather spectacular reconstruction of the human condition.[12] A major theme in our analysis as it develops will be that American attitudes and practices regarding death can be interpreted very generally as elements of that reconstruction.

This bears directly on our rejection of the view we have set as a foil, that American attitudes tend to "deny" death. Instrumental activism is a rational orientation in that, when specified to a particular sphere of action, it can develop the type of control that it values only by accurately recognizing the facts and conditions of the relevant situation. Here, the development of science that it has fostered is evidently prototypical—surely science is not grounded primarily in fantasies that deny basic realities of the empirical world, no matter how problematic is any sense in which it simply reflects these realities. It would seem that the modern orientation toward controlling the adventitious aspects of death must involve a very similar realism, both because of its interpenetration with science (e.g., medicine) and because of its need for highly rationalized means for meeting human strains. However, it is evident that the orientation of control cannot apply to the "inevitable" aspect of death, which is its core phenomenon, in quite the same sense. Rather, the differentiation between the adventitious and inevitable aspects of death has rendered the latter still more irreducible—something that must be faced still more squarely than ever before. The sense in which such facing of death has been incorporated in the value pattern of instrumental activism is extremely complex; it can be treated only after we have considered the "ultimate" meaning that Western tradition has given to the fact of death.

Notes

1. Herman Feifel states that "denial and avoidance of the countenance of death characterize much of the American outlook," by way of summarizing a predominating theme in the book he edited, *The Meaning of Death* (New York: McGraw-Hill, 1959), which contains contributions by many distinguished people in a variety of disciplines. Quotation is from p. xvii.

2. Perhaps the most sociological discussion of funeral practices and such a hypothetical general trend is Peter Berger and Richard Lieban, "Kulturelle Wertstruktur und Bestattungspraktiken in den Vereinigten Staaten," *Kolner Zeitschrift für Soziologie und Sozial Psychologie*, No. 2, 1960.

3. George Gaylord Simpson, *The Meaning of Evolution* (New Haven, Conn.: Yale University Press, 1949).

4. Talcott Parsons, *Social Structure and Personality* (New York: The Free Press, 1964), especially chap. 4.

5. S. N. Eisenstadt has probably made the most important contribution to the understanding of problems in this field. See his *From Generation to Generation* (New York: The Free Press, 1956).

6. Max Weber's *Sociology of Religion*, English ed. (Boston: Beacon Press, 1963) is probably still the best single statement of the broad analytical position we are taking toward religion.

7. These last paragraphs are intended to give death its due in terms of its general implications for action systems. We wish to note, however, that our account is quite distinct from that of much current existentialism, which seems to claim that, very generally, life purposes and a great many life activities gain their meaning *only* from being contrasted with and opposed to death. Analytically, this seems extreme and perhaps hinges upon a rather pejorative use of the term "meaning."

8. See Simpson, *Meaning of Evolution*.

9. M. Gendell and H. L. Zetterberg, *A Sociological Almanac for the United States*, 2nd ed. (New York: Scribner's, 1961), p. 42.

10. Buddha, we may recall, viewed sickness, old age, and death, with their attendant suffering, as the aspects of this world that led him to recognize the need for adopting a radical other-wordly orientation.

11. The best statement on the characteristics of the pattern of instrumental activism that is yet in print is given in Talcott Parsons and Winston White, "The Link Between Character and Society," chap. 8 in *Social Structure and Personality*. It should be clear that we are referring to a general orientational pattern that can be specified, in principle, to all contexts of social action. We are not simply talking about the "scientific" orientation.

12. Talcott Parsons, *The System of Modern Society* (Englewood Cliffs, N.J.: Prentice-Hall, 1971).

PHILIPPE ARIÈS

Death Inside Out

Philippe Ariès, noted French historian of ideas, enters the discussion of attitudes about death from a European vantage point. Rather than focus on distinctions in contemporary society, he provides a historical context as a perspective for understanding modern attitudes. The following selection traces a pattern of reversal in sentiment toward the dying person, the mourning process, and funeral rituals. This reversal, Ariès suggests, provides a direct link between two modern crises: the crisis of death and the crisis of individuality.

The attitudes commonly held about death by modern man—whether sociologists, psychologists or doctors—are so novel and bewildering that scholars have not yet been able to detach them from their modernity and situate them within a broader historical perspective. This is what I shall attempt to do in the following chapter, with respect to three themes: the dispossession of the dying person, the denial of mourning, and the new funeral rites in America.

I. How the Dying Person Is Deprived of His Death

For thousands of years man has been the sovereign master of his death and the circumstances attending it. Today he no longer is and these are the reasons why.

First of all, it was always taken for granted that man knew he was going to die—whether he came by this knowledge on his own or was told by somebody else. The story-tellers of former times assumed as a matter of course that man is aware of his forthcoming death. La Fontaine is an example. In those days, death was rarely sudden, even in cases of accident or war. Sudden death was very much feared not only because it did not allow time to repent but more importantly because it deprived man of his death. Most people were forewarned of their death, especially since most diseases were fatal. One would have had to be a fool not to perceive the signs of death; moralists and satirists took it upon themselves to ridicule those who refused to admit the obvious. Roland was aware that death was about to carry him off; Tristan felt his life ebbing away and knew that he was going to die; Tolstoi's peasant, responding to an inquiry about his health, says: "Death is at hand." For Tolstoi as for La Fontaine, men adopted a familiar and resigned attitude before death. This does not mean that thinking about death remained the same over this long period of history. Nonetheless, some basic similarities survived in certain classes from one age to another despite the emergence of other attitudes.

Source: Philippe Ariès, "Death Inside Out," translated by Bernard Murchland, reprinted from Peter Steinfels and Robert M. Veatch, eds., *Death Inside Out: The Hastings Center Report* ® 1975, Institute of Society, Ethics and the Life Sciences. Harper & Row. Reprinted by permission.

When the dying person failed to perceive his lot, it fell to others to tell him. A pontifical document of the Middle Ages made this a responsibility of physicians, and for centuries they executed it faithfully. We find one at Don Quixote's bedside: "A physician was sent for, who, after feeling his pulse, took a rather gloomy view of the case, and told him that he should provide for his soul's health, as that of his body was in a dangerous condition." The *Artes Moriendi* of the fifteenth century stipulated a "spiritual" friend for this task (as opposed to a "carnal" friend) who was called the *nuntius mortis,* a title and a role that is more than a little shocking to our modern sensibility.

As we advance through history ascending the social ladder in an urban environment, we find that man adverts less and less to his impending death. He must be prepared for it by others upon whom he consequently becomes more and more dependent. Probably sometime in the eighteenth century, the physician renounced a role that had long been his. By the nineteenth century, the doctor spoke only when questioned and then with certain reservations. Friends no longer intervened as they did in the time of Gerson or even as late as Cervantes. From the seventeenth century onward, the family assumed this responsibility, which may be taken as a sign of the evolution in family sentiment. For example: The year is 1848 and we are with a family called La Ferronnays. Madame La Ferronnays falls sick. A doctor diagnoses her case as serious and shortly afterwards calls it hopeless. The woman's daughter writes: "When she finished her bath and as I was about to tell her what the doctor had said, she suddenly said to me: 'I can no longer see anything and fear I am going to die.' She then recited a short prayer. How consoling those calm words were to me in that terrible moment!" The daughter was relieved because she was spared the painful task of telling her mother that she was going to die. Such relief is a modern trait but the obligation to inform another of imminent death is very ancient.

The dying were not to be deprived of their death. Indeed, they had to preside over it. As one was born in public so too one died in public. This was true not only of kings (as is well known from Saint-Simon's celebrated account of the death of Louis XIV) but of everyone. Countless tapestries and paintings have depicted the scene for us! As soon as someone fell ill, the room filled with people—parents, children, friends, neighbors, fellow workers. All windows and doors were closed. The candles were lit. When people in the street saw the priest carrying the viaticum, custom as well as devotion dictated that they follow him to the dying person's bedside, even if the person were a stranger. As death approached, the sick-room became a public place. In this context we understand the force of Pascal's words: "We die alone." They have lost much of their meaning for modern man because we literally do die alone. What Pascal means was that, despite the crowd gathered about, the dying person was, in the end, alone. Progressive doctors in the late eighteenth century were firm believers in the curative powers of fresh air and complained bitterly about this public invasion of the rooms of the dying. To their minds, it would have been far healthier to open the windows, put out the candles, and send everyone home.

The public presence at the last moments was not a pious practice imposed by the Church, as we might think. The clergy, or at least the more enlightened of them, had tried long before the doctors to restrain this mob in order to better prepare the sick person for an edifying end. Beginning with the fifteenth century, the *Artes Moriendi* recommended that the dying person be left alone with God so as not to be distracted from the care of his soul. As late as the nineteenth century, very pious individuals, having submitted to all these customary practices, might request that the many onlookers leave the room so that nothing would disturb their final conversations with God. But these were cases of rare and exemplary devotion. Long-standing custom dictated that death be the occasion of a ritual ceremony in which the priest had his place, but so did numbers of other people. The primary role in this ritual was played by the dying person himself. He presided with controlled dignity; having been a participant himself in many such occasions, he knew how to conduct himself. He spoke in turn to his relatives, his friends, his servants, including "the least of them," as Saint-Simon put it in describing the death of Madame de Montespan. He bade them adieu, asked their forgiveness, and gave them his blessing. Invested with a sovereign authority by approaching death (this was especially true in the eighteenth and nineteenth centuries), he gave his orders and made his recommendations. This was the case when the dying person was a very young girl, virtually a child.

Today, nothing remains of this attitude toward death. We do not believe that the sick person has a right to know he is dying; nor do we believe in the public and solemn character accorded the moment of death. What ought to be known in ignored; what ought to be a sacred moment is conjured away.

A Reversal in Sentiment

We take it for granted that the first duty of the family and the physician is to keep the dying person uninformed about his condition. He must not (exceptional cases apart) know that his end is near; he dies ignorant of his death. This is not merely an accidental feature of our contemporary mores; on the contrary, it has taken on the force of a moral rule. Vladimir Jankélévitch made a clear statement in proof of this at a recent medical conference on the theme: Should We Lie to the Sick?[1] "In my mind," he declared, "the liar is the one who tells the truth. I am against the truth, passionately against the truth. For me there is one law that takes precedence over all others and that is the law of love and charity." Since traditional morality made it mandatory to inform the dying of their state, Jankélévitch's law presumably has been universally violated until recent times. Such an attitude is the measure of an extraordinary reversal in sentiment and thought. What has happened? How has this change come about? We might suppose that modern societies are so fixed upon the goals of affluence and material well-being that there is no place in them for suffering, sorrow, or death. But this would be to mistake the effect for the cause.

This change in attitude toward the dying is linked to the changing role of the family in modern society and its quasi-monopoly over our emotional lives. We must seek the cause of modern attitudes toward death in the relationship between the sick person and his family. The latter does not consider it dignified or a mark of self-esteem to speak frankly about the imminence of death. How often have we heard it said of a loved one: "I at least have the satisfaction of knowing that he died without being aware of it." The "without being aware of it" has replaced the "being aware of one's approaching death" of other times, when every effort was made to make the dying aware of what was happening.

In fact, it may be that the dying frequently know perfectly well what is happening, but remain silent to spare the feelings of those close to them. (Of course, the dead do not share these secrets.) In any case, the modern family has abdicated the role played by the *nuntius mortis,* who from the Middle Ages until the dawn of modern times was not a member of the immediate family. As a result, the dying have also abdicated their role. Why? Because they fear death? Hardly. Fear of death has always existed, and was always countered, often with humor. Despite a natural fear of death, society obligated the dying to play out the final scene of farewell and departure. The fear of death, it is said, is ancestral, but so are the ways of overcoming it. No, the fear of death does not account for the modern practice of denying one's own death. Again, we must turn to the history of the family for an explanation.

In the late Middle Ages (the age of Roland which lives on in the peasants of Tolstoi) and the Renaissance, a man insisted upon participating in his own death because he saw in it an exceptional moment—a moment which gave his individuality its definitive form. He was only the master of his life to the extent that he was the master of his death. His death belonged to him, and to him alone. From the seventeenth century onward, one began to abdicate sole sovereignty over life, as well as over death. These matters came to be shared with the family which had previously been excluded from the serious decisions; all decisions had been made by the dying person, alone and with full knowledge of his impending death.

Last wills and testaments provide evidence of this. From the fourteenth to the beginning of the eighteenth century, they were a spontaneous and individual means of expression, as well as a sign of distrust—or, at least, the absence of trust—toward the family. Today the last will and testament has lost its character of moral necessity; nor is it any longer a means of warm and personal expression. Since the eighteenth century, family affections have triumphed over the testator's traditional distrust of his heirs. This distrust has been replaced by a trust so absolute that written wills are no longer necessary. Oral wills have recently become binding for the survivors and are now scrupulously respected. For their part, the dying confidently rely on the family's word. This trusting attitude, which emerged in the seventeenth and eighteenth centuries, and developed in the nineteenth, has become, in the twentieth, a prime source of alienation. No sooner does a member of the family fall mortally ill than the rest conspire to conceal his condition from him, depriving him of information, as well as his freedom. The dying person becomes, in effect, a minor like a child or mental defective. His relatives take complete charge of him and shield him from the world. They supposedly know better than he what he must do, and how much he should know. He is deprived of his rights, particularly the formerly sacred right of knowing about his death, of preparing for it, and organizing it. Now he allows this to be done for him because he is convinced that it is for his own good. He gives himself over to the affection of his family. And if, despite all, he divines his condition, he pretends not to know. In former times, death was a tragedy—often lightened by a comical element—in which one played the role of the dying person. Today, death is a comedy—although not without its tragic elements—in which one plays the role of the "one who does not know" he is going to die.

Of itself, the pressure of family sentiment probably would not have changed the meaning of death so drastically, had it not been for the progress of medical science. It is not so much that medicine has conquered disease, however real its achievements in this realm, but that it has succeeded in substituting sickness for death in the consciousness of the afflicted man. This substitution began to take place in the second half of the nineteenth century. When a sick peasant in Tolstoi's *Three Deaths* (1859) is asked how he is, he answers, "death is at hand." On the contrary, in *The Death of Ivan Ilych* (1886), after overhearing a conversation that leaves no doubt in Ivan's mind about his condition, he obstinately believes that his floating kidney and infected appendix will be cured by drugs or surgery. His illness becomes an occasion for self-delusion. His wife supports this illusion, blaming his illness on his refusal to obey the doctor's orders to take his medicine regularly.

Of course, it is true, with advances in medical science, serious illness terminates less frequently in death. And chances of recovery are greatly improved. Even when recovery is partial, one can still count on many years of life. Thus, in our society (where we so often act as though medicine had all the answers, or look upon death as something that happens to others, but never to oneself) incurable disease, and especially cancer, has taken on, in the popular imagination, all the frightening and hideous traits depicted in ancient representations of death. Even more than the skeletons or macabre mummies of the fourteenth and fifteenth centuries, cancer is today the very image of death. Disease must be incurable, and regarded as such, before we can admit the reality of death and give it its true name. But the anguish caused by this kind of honesty is so great that it constrains society to hastily multiply those many inducements to silence that reduce a moment of high drama to the banality of a Sunday afternoon picnic.

As a consequence we die in virtual secrecy, far more alone than Pascal could have imagined. This secretiveness comes from a refusal to openly admit the death of those we love and a proclivity to soften its reality by calling it a disease that may be cured. There is another aspect to this problem that

American sociologists have noted. In what one might be tempted to regard as nothing more than illusory conduct, they have shown the de facto presence of a new style of death, in which discretion is the modern form of dignity. With less poetry, this is the kind of death approved of by Jankélévitch in which the hard reality is coated over with soothing words of deception.

A New Model of Death

In their *Awareness of Dying* Glaser and Strauss report on their study of six hospitals in the San Francisco Bay area.[2] They recorded the reactions to death of an interrelated group that included the patient, his family, and the medical personnel (doctors and nurses). What happens when it becomes clear that the patient is near death? Should the family be told? The patient? And when? How long should a life be artificially maintained? At what moment should the patient be allowed to die? How should doctors and nurses act in the presence of a patient who does not know, or at least appears not to know, that he is dying? Or one that does know? Every modern family is certainly confronted by such questions, but in a hospital context an important new factor is present: the power of modern medicine. Today, few people die at home. The hospital has become the place where modern man dies, and this fact lends added importance to the Glaser and Strauss study. But the interest of their book goes beyond its empirical analysis. The authors have in fact uncovered an ideal of death that has replaced its traditional public character, as manifested for example in the theatrical pomp of the Romantic era. We now have a new "style of dying" or rather "an acceptable style of living while dying," "an acceptable style of facing death." The emphasis is on *acceptable*. What is important is that one die in a manner that can be accepted and tolerated by the survivors.

Doctors and nurses (although the latter less so) wait as long as possible before telling the family, and scarcely ever tell the patient himself, because they fear becoming involved in a chain of emotional reactions that would make them lose self-control. To talk about death, and thus admit it as a normal dimension of social intercourse, is no longer socially acceptable; on the contrary, it is now something exceptional, excessive, and always dramatic. Death was once a familiar figure and the moralists had to make it hideous in order to inspire fear. Today, mere mention of the word provokes an emotional tension that jars the routine of daily life. An "acceptable style of dying" is, therefore, a style which avoids "status forcing scenes," scenes which tear one from one's social role and offend our sensibility. Such scenes are the crises of despair the sick go through, their tears, their cries and, in general, any exceptional emotive or noisy outburst that would interfere with hospital routine and trouble others. This is an example of what Glaser and Strauss call, "embarrassingly graceless dying," the very opposite of an "acceptable style of dying." Such a death would embarrass the survivors. This is what must be avoided at all costs and this is the reason why the patient is kept uninformed. What basically matters is not whether the patient knows or does not know; rather, if he does know he must have the consideration and courage to be discreet. He must conduct himself in such a way that the hospital staff is not reminded that he knows and can communicate with him as though death were not in their midst. For communication is necessary. It is not enough for the dying to be discreet; they must also be open and receptive to messages. Their indifference in this matter should be as embarrassing to the medical personnel as an excessive display of emotion. Thus, there are two ways of dying badly: one can be either too emotional or too indifferent.

The authors cite the case of an old woman who was at first well behaved, in accord with acceptable conventions; she cooperated with the doctors and nurses and bore her illness courageously. One day she decided that she had struggled enough, that the time had come to give up. Whereupon she closed her eyes, never to open them again, signifying in this way that she had withdrawn from the world and wished to await her end alone. In former times, this withdrawal would have been respected and accepted as normal. But in a California hospital it disconcerted the medical staff so much that they flew in one of her sons from another city to persuade her to open her eyes on the grounds that she was "hurting everybody." Sometimes patients turn to the wall and refuse to move. We recognize in such acts one of the oldest gestures of man in the face of death. In this way did the Jews of the Old Testament die. So did Tristan who turned toward the wall and exclaimed that he could no longer keep a hold on life. But in such ancestral reactions the California doctors and nurses saw only an antisocial refusal to communicate, a culpable renunciation of the will to live.

Let us note that patients are not blamed in such cases merely because they have demoralized the medical staff, or because of failure to perform their duty, but more seriously because they are considered to have lessened the capacity to resist the sickness itself—an eventuality that becomes as fearsome as a "status forcing scene." That is why American and English doctors are today less inclined to keep patients in the dark about their condition. But we must not exaggerate the significance of such signs. They may indicate no more than the pragmatic hope that the patient will respond better to treatment if he knows his condition and will, in the end, die as discreetly and with as much dignity as if he knew nothing. In *Reflections on America*, Jacques Maritain describes the good American's death: The medical staff induces in him a kind of dream-like state in which he thinks that to die amidst these smiling faces and these uniforms, white and immaculate like the wings of angels, is a genuine pleasure, or at least a moment of no consequence—"Relax, take it easy, it's nothing."[3] Take away the professional smile and add a little music, and you have the contemporary philosopher's ideal of the dignified, humanistic death: "To disappear *pianissimo* and, so to speak, on tip toe" (Jankélévitch).

II. The Denial of Mourning

We now see how modern society deprives man of his death. Whatever dignity remains must be purchased at the price of not troubling the living.

Reciprocally, modern society forbids the living from showing too much emotion over the death of a loved one; they are permitted neither to weep for the departed nor to appear to mourn their passing.

In times past mourning was the ultimate expression of sorrow. It was both legitimate and necessary. Grief over the death of a close one was considered the strongest and most spontaneous expression of emotion. During the Middle Ages, the most hardened warriors and the most renowned kings broke into tears over the bodies of friends and relatives. They wept, as we would say today, like hysterical women. King Arthur is a good example. He often fainted, struck his breast, and tore at his skin until the blood flowed. On the battlefield, he fell to the ground in a swoon before his nephew's body and then set out in tears to find the bodies of his friends. Upon discovering one of them, he clasped his hands and cried out that he had lived long enough. He removed the helmet from the dead man's body and, after gazing upon him for a long time, kissed his eyes and mouth. We find many instances, in those times, of the most extraordinary and uninhibited emotional outbursts. But, with the exception of those few whose sorrow was so great that they had to retire to a monastery, the survivors soon resumed normal life.

From the thirteenth century on, we notice that expressions of mourning begin to lose their spontaneity and become more and more ritualized. The grand gesticulations of the early Middle Ages are now simulated by professional mourners (who can be found in some parts of Europe even today). The Spanish hero, El Cid, requested in his will that there be no flowers or mourners at his funeral, as had been the custom. The iconography of fourteenth- and fifteenth-century tombs depict mourners around the body of the deceased, clothed in black robes with their heads buried in penitent-like cowls. We learn from sixteenth- and seventeenth-century documents that funeral processions were composed largely of substitute mourners: mendicant monks, the poor, and orphans, all clothed for the occasion in black robes furnished by the deceased. After the ceremony, each received a portion of bread and a little money.

Apparently close relatives did not attend the funeral services. Friends were offered a banquet—banquets so excessively festive that the Church tried to suppress the practice. Last wills refer to such festivities less and less, or mention them only in censorious language. We notice that the dying frequently requested and sometimes insisted upon the presence of a brother or a son in the funeral procession. Often this was a child, who was offered a special legacy for his much desired presence. Would this have been the case had the family attended funerals as a matter of course? Under the old regime we know that women did not attend funerals. It is probable that from the end of the Middle Ages with the increasing ritualization of mourning rites, society imposed a period of seclusion upon the immediate members of the family, a seclusion which would have excluded them from the obsequies. They were represented by priests and professional mourners, religious members of pious organizations, or simply those who were attracted by the alms distributed on such occasions.

The period of seclusion had two purposes. First of all, it gave the bereaved some privacy in which to mourn their loved ones. Protected from the gaze of the world, they waited for their sorrow to pass as a sick person waits for his illness to abate. One, Henri de Campion, makes mention of this in his *Mémoires*. In June, 1659, his wife died in childbirth and the child, a daughter, died shortly afterwards. He wrote:

> I was heartbroken and fell into a pitiful state. My brother and my sister took me to Conches where I remained seventeen days and then returned to Baxferei to put my affairs in order. Not being able to inhabit my house because it reminded me too much of my beloved wife, I bought a property in Conches and lived there until June, 1660 (which is to say until the first anniversary of my wife's death) at which time I perceived that my sorrow had followed me. So I returned to my former home in Baxferei with my children, where I am presently living in great sadness.

Second, the period of seclusion prevented the survivors from forgetting the deceased too soon. It was in fact a time of penance during which they were not permitted the activities and pleasures of normal life. This precaution was not unhelpful in preventing a hasty replacement of the dead person. Nicolas Versoris, a Parisian merchant, lost his wife to the plague on September 3, 1522, one hour after midnight. On December 30 of that same year, he was engaged to a doctor's widow, whom he married as soon as he could, which is to say on January 13, 1523, "the first festive day after Christmas."

This custom continued through the nineteenth century. When someone died the immediate family, servants, and often the domestic animals as well, were separated from the rest of society by drawn curtains and black mourning crepe. By this time, however, the period of seclusion was more voluntary than obligatory: it no longer prohibited close relatives from participating in the funeral service, pilgrimages to the graveside, or the elaborate memorial cults that characterized the Romantic Age. Nor were women any longer excluded from the obsequies. In this regard, the bourgeoisie were the first to break with tradition, followed some time later by the nobility, among whom it had been considered good taste for a widow not to attend her husband's funeral. At first the nobility ceded to the new practices discreetly, usually hidden in some dark corner of the church with ecclesiastical approval. Little by little the traditional custom of seclusion gave way to the new practice of honoring the dead and venerating their tombs. Women's presence at funerals, however, did nothing to radically change the private character of mourning: entirely clothed in black, the *mater dolorosa*, she is hidden from the world's sight except as symbol of sorrow and desolation. Nonetheless, mourning was now more moral than physical in nature. It was less a protection of the dead from oblivion than an affirmation that the living must remember them; that they could not go on living as before. The dead no longer needed society to protect them from the indifference of their close relatives; nor did the dying any longer need written testaments to make their last will known to their heirs.

The new family sentiment of the late eighteenth and early nineteenth centuries thus combined with the ancient tradition of seclusion to transform the mourning period from an imposed quarantine into a right to express, with all due propriety, deeply felt sorrow. This marked a return to the spontaneity of the high Middle Ages while conserving the formal rituals that had been introduced around the twelfth century. If we were to trace the historical curve of mourning it would look like this: until the thirteenth century, a time of uninhibited and even violent spontaneity, followed through the seventeenth century by a long period of ritualization, which gave way in the nineteenth to an age when sorrow was given full and dramatic expression. It is likely that the paroxysm of mourning in the nineteenth century stands in some direct relationship to its attenuation in the twentieth century in somewhat the same way as the "dirty death" of Remarque, Sartre, and Genet in the post-war period emerged as the other side of the "noble death" celebrated by Romanticism. Thus, the significance of Sartre's gesture, more laughable than scandalous, of urinating on Chateaubriand's tomb. It took a Chateaubriand to produce such a Sartre. It is a relationship of the sort that links contemporary eroticism to Victorian sexual taboos.

Mourning Becomes Forbidden

Some form of mourning, whether spontaneous or obligatory, has always been mandatory in human society. Only in the twentieth century has it been forbidden. The situation was reversed in a single generation: what was always commanded by individual conscience, or the general will, is now rejected. And what was, in former times, rejected is now recommended. It is no longer fitting to manifest one's sorrow or even give evidence of experiencing any.

Credit for uncovering this unwritten law of our civilization goes to the British sociologist, Geoffrey Gorer. He was the first to understand that certain facts, neglected or poorly understood by the humanistic moralists, did, indeed, constitute a characteristic attitude toward death in industrial societies. In an autobiographical introduction to his *Death, Grief and Mourning,* Gorer recounts some personal experiences which led him to the discovery that death is the principal taboo of our time.[4] The sociological inquiry he undertook in 1963 on attitudes toward death and mourning in England merely confirmed, detailed, and enriched ideas he had already published in his "The Pornography of Death," a remarkable article based upon his personal experiences and reflection.[5]

Gorer was born in 1910. He recalls that the whole family mourned the death of Edward VII. He learned, as do French children, to take off his hat when a funeral procession passed in the street and to treat those in mourning with special respect—practices which seem strange to the British today. In 1915, his father was lost in the sinking of the *Lusitania,* and Gorer was, in his turn, given special attention. "I was treated with great kindness, like an invalid; no demands were made on me, I was indulged, conversation was hushed in my presence." One day during a walk, he attempted to convey his desolation by telling his Nanny that he would never be able "to enjoy flowers again," whereupon she reprimanded him and told him not to be morbid.

Because of the war his mother was allowed to take a job where she found diversion from her sorrow. She would not have had such a recourse at any earlier date; but at a later date she would not have had the support of the mourning ritual. Thus Gorer experienced in his childhood the traditional manifestations of mourning and they must have made a strong impression on him for they remained vivid in his memory many years later. During his youth in the postwar period, he had no further experience of death. Once he saw a cadaver in a Russian hospital he visited in 1931; unaccustomed to the sight of death, this chance viewing seems to have captured his imagination. Gorer's case was not unusual. Unfamiliarity with death is common today—the long, unnoticed consequence of greater longevity. J. Fourcassié has shown how it is possible for today's children to grow to adulthood without ever seeing anyone die. Gorer was, however, surprised when his inquiry revealed that more people had witnessed death than he would have suspected. But he also observed that they quite spontaneously adopted the same behavior patterns as those who had never seen a death, and forgot it with all possible haste.

Gorer was later surprised when his brother, a well-known physician, fell into a state of depression after his wife's death. Intellectuals in England had already begun to abandon the traditional funeral rites and external manifestations of sorrow as so many primitive and superstitious practices. But Gorer did not at the time see any connection between his brother's pathological despair and the absence of mourning rituals. The situation was different in 1948 when he lost a close friend who left a wife and three children. Gorer wrote:

> When I went to see her some two months after John's death, she told me, with tears of gratitude, that I was the first man to stay in the house since she had become a widow. She was being given some good professional help from lawyers and the like who were also friends; but socially she had been almost completely abandoned to loneliness, although the town was full of acquaintances who considered themselves friends.

Gorer then strongly suspected that the changes that had taken place in mourning customs were neither anecdotal or insignificant. He was discovering the importance and serious consequences of these changes, and a few years later, in 1955, he published his famous article.

Decisive proof came in 1961 when his brother, who had remarried, was diagnosed as suffering from incurable cancer. His brother's doctor, a friend since they were in medical school together, "asked me to decide whether his wife, Elizabeth, should be informed; he had already decided to hide the truth from Peter; and he and his colleagues engaged in the most elaborate and successful medical mystification to hide from Peter's expert knowledge the facts of their diagnosis." He consulted an old and respected friend about his dilemma and was advised that Elizabeth should be told. "One of the arguments he advanced was that, if she were ignorant, she might show impatience or lack of understanding with his probably increasing weakness, for which she would reproach herself later; she could use the final months of their marriage better if she knew them for what they were." The prognosis was for a lingering illness but much to everyone's surprise Peter died suddenly in his sleep. Everyone concerned congratulated themselves that he had died without knowing it, an eventuality widely regarded as a desirable one in our culture. In this family of intellectuals, there would be no funeral vigil and no exposure of the body. Since his death took place at home, the body would have to be prepared. Gorer evokes what took place in colorful language:

> It was arranged for a pair of ex-nurses to come to lay out the body. They imparted a somewhat Dickensian tone; they were fat and jolly and asked in a respectful but cheerful tone, "Where is the patient?" Some half hour later their work was done, and they came out saying, "The patient looks lovely now. Come and have a look!" I did not wish to, at which they expressed surprise. I gave them a pound for their pains; the leader, pure Sarah Gamp, said, "That for us, duck? Cheers!" and went through the motions of raising a bottle and emptying it into her mouth.

No mention was made through all of this of either death or the corpse. Peter was still regarded as a "patient" despite the biological transformation that had taken place. Preparing the body for burial is an ancient rite. But its meaning has changed. It formerly had as its object to make the body reflect the ideal image of death prevalent in society; the intention was to create a sense of dependency, to present the body in a helpless state, with crossed hands, awaiting the life to come. The Romantic Age discovered the original beauty that death imparts to the human face and these last ablutions were designed to rescue this beauty from the pain that had generated it. In both cases, the intention was to create an image of death: to present a beautiful corpse but a corpse nonetheless. Today we no longer have a corpse but something almost alive. "The patient looks lovely now." Our fairy's touch has given it the appearance of life. All signs of pain have been erased, not in order to capture the hieratic beauty of the dead or the majesty of those in repose, but to present a cadaver that retains the charms of something living, something "lovely" and not at all repulsive. The preparation of the body is today intended to mask the reality of death and give the pleasing illusion of life. We must remember that in Gorer's England this practice was just emerging, which is why the family could not share the old nurses' enthusiasm for their handiwork. In the United States, on the other hand, embalming is a fine art and corpses are exhibited in funeral homes with great pride.

The Meaning of Cremation

Gorer's family was deluded by neither the beliefs of another age nor the flashy talents of American morticians. Peter's body was to be cremated, and cremation in England (and no doubt in Northern Europe generally) has a special meaning which Gorer's study clearly brought out. Cremation is no longer chosen, as was long the case, in defiance of the Church and traditional Christian customs. Nor is it chosen solely for reasons of convenience or economy, reasons which the Church would be disposed to respect in memory of a time when ashes, like those of Antigone's brother, were as venerable as a body that was buried. The significance of cremation in modern England cuts deeper; it reflects the rational spirit of modern times and is nothing less than a denial of life after death, although this was not immediately apparent from the results of Gorer's inquiry. Of sixty-four persons interviewed, forty favored cremation over burial and they offered two basic reasons for this preference. It was first of all considered the most efficient means of disposing of the body. Thus one of the respondents in the study had her mother cremated because it was "healthier" but stated, "I think for my husband, who was buried, cremation would have been too final."

The second reason is connected to the first: cremation makes cemetery rituals and periodic visitation to the graveside unnecessary. But it should be noted that such practices are not necessarily eliminated by cremation. On the contrary the administrators of crematoriums do everything in their power to enable families to venerate their dead just as they do in the traditional cemeteries. In the memorial rooms of crematoriums one can have a plaque installed which performs a function analogous to that of the tombstone. But of the forty persons interviewed by Gorer, only one had opted for such a plaque and only fourteen wrote their names in the memorial book which is opened each day to commemorate the day of the death. This may be seen as a kind of intermediary solution between complete oblivion and the permanency of the engraved plaque. If families choose not to adopt commemorative practices available to them it is because they see in cremation a sure means of avoiding any form of cultic homage to the dead.

It would be a serious mistake to see in this refusal to commemorate the dead a sign of indifference or insensitivity. The results of Gorer's study and his autobiographical testimony are evidence to the contrary that the survivors are and remain deeply affected by a death in the family. For further proof of this let us turn to Gorer's account of his brother's cremation. Elizabeth, the widow,

> decided not to come to the cremation herself—she could not bear the thought that she might lose control and other people observe her grief; and she wished to spare the children the distressing experience. As a consequence, their father's death was quite unmarked for them by ritual of any kind, and was nearly even treated as a secret, for it was several months before Elizabeth could bear to mention him or have him mentioned in her presence.

Notice that her absence was not due to any of the traditional reasons or to indifference but to a fear of "losing control." This has become a new form of modesty, a convention which requires us to hide what we were formerly obliged to manifest, even if it had to be simulated: one's sorrow.

Notice, too, that children are also affected by this modern mandate. Even in France, where traditional practices are more in evidence, middle-class children rarely attend the funerals of their grandparents. Old people who are several times grandparents are buried by adults who are more rushed and embarrassed than grieved, with no grandchildren present. I was especially struck by this when in the course of my research I came across a number of documents dating from the seventeenth century in which the testator insisted that at least one of his grandchildren be in his funeral procession, although he may have been indifferent to the presence of other relatives. At that time, we might recall, mourners were often recruited among orphans. In numerous representations of the dying, the painter or engraver always included a child among those gathered about the deathbed.

So Elizabeth and her children stayed in their country home on the day of her husband's cremation. Geoffrey joined them that evening, overcome with grief and fatigue. His sister-in-law welcomed him in her usual self-assured manner. She told him that she had passed a pleasant day with the children. "They had taken a picnic to the fields where the grass was being cut for silage." Elizabeth, who was born in New England, quite naturally adopted the conduct she had been taught in America and which the English expected of her: she acted as if nothing had happened and so made it easier for others to do the same and thus permit social life to continue without even momentary interruption by death. Had she risked a public demonstration of her sorrow, society would have censored her like a fallen woman. She was, moreover, avoided by her and Peter's friends. They treated her, she said, "like a leper." Only if she acted as though nothing of consequence had happened was she again socially acceptable. Gorer observes that "at the period when she most needed help and comfort from society she was left alone." It was in the months following Peter's death that he decided to undertake a study of the modern refusal to mourn and its traumatizing effects.

From the Cabbage Patch to the Flower Garden

Gorer argues that this state of affairs began with the decline of social support for funeral rituals and the special status of the mourning period. He perhaps accords too much importance to the two World Wars as catalysts in this evolution. New conventions made their appearance gradually, almost imperceptibly in such a way that their originality went unnoticed. Even today they are not formalized in the manner of traditional customs. Yet they are just as powerful an influence on behavior. Death has become a taboo, an unmentionable subject (as Jankélévitch says over and over again in his book on death), something excluded from polite conversation. Gorer mounts impressive evidence to show that in the twentieth century death has taken the place of sex as the principal taboo. He writes that in our time,

> there has been an unremarked shift in prudery; whereas copulation has become more and more "mentionable" . . . death has become more and more "unmentionable" as a natural process. . . . The natural processes of corruption and decay

have become disgusting, as disgusting as the natural processes of birth and copulation were a century ago; preoccupation about such processes is (or was) morbid and unhealthy, to be discouraged in all and punished in the young. Our great-grandparents were told that babies were found under gooseberry bushes or cabbages; our children are likely to be told that those who have passed on (fie! on the gross Anglo-Saxon monosyllable) are changed into flowers, or lie at rest in lovely gardens. The ugly facts are relentlessly hidden; the art of the embalmers is an art of complete denial.

Children used to be told that a stork brought them but they could be present at deathbeds and attend funerals! Sometime after the middle of the nineteenth century, their presence caused a kind of malaise and there was a tendency to at least limit their participation when in fact it was not prohibited altogether. Children were present at the deaths of Emma Bovary and Ivan Ilych but they were permitted only a brief visit and then escorted from the room on the pretext that the agonies of the dying would be too much for them to bear. Although their presence at the deathbed was gradually prohibited, they were allowed their traditional place at the obsequies, clothed from head to foot in black.

Today children are initiated at an early age into the physiology of love and birth, but when they express curiosity about why they no longer see their grandparents they are told (at least in France) that they have gone on a long trip or (in England) that they are resting among the flowers. It is no longer a case of babies being found under the cabbages but of grandparents who disappear among the flowers! Relatives of the deceased are thus forced to feign indifference. Society demands of them a form of self-control similar to that demanded of the dying themselves. For the one as for the other, what is important is to show no sign of emotion. Society as a whole behaves like a hospital staff. Just as the dying must control their feelings and cooperate with the doctors and nurses, so must the bereaved hide their sorrow, reject the traditional period of seclusion (because this would betray their feelings), and carry on their normal activities without so much as missing a step. Otherwise, they would be ostracized by society, a form of seclusion that would have consequences quite different from the traditional mourning period. The latter was accepted by all as a necessary transition period and carried with it forms of behavior that were equally ritualistic such as obligatory visits of condolence, letters of sympathy, and the succors of religion. Today the bereaved are treated like sexual deviants, those afflicted with contagious diseases, or other asocial types. Whoever wishes to spare himself this stigma must hide his true feelings in public and reveal them only to his closest friends. As Gorer puts it, one weeps in private just as we undress and go to sleep in private, "as if it were an analogue of masturbation."

Society today refuses to recognize that the bereaved are sick people who need help. It refuses to associate mourning with illness. The traditional custom was in this respect more comprehensive, perhaps more "modern," more sensitive to the pathological effects of repressed moral suffering. Gorer considers it a mark of cruelty to deprive anyone of the beneficence guaranteed by the ancient custom. In their mourning, Gorer notes, those stricken by the death of a loved one need society's help more than at any other time, but it is precisely then that society withdraws its assistance and refuses to help. The price of this failure is very great in misery, loneliness, despair, and morbidity. This prohibition of a decent period of mourning forces the bereaved to bury himself in work; or to push himself to the very limits of sanity by pretending that the deceased in still living, that he never went away; or, what is worse, to imagine that he himself is the dead person, imitating his gestures, his voice, his idiosyncrasies, and sometimes simulating the symptoms of the sickness that carried him off. This is clearly neurotic behavior. We see in such behavior instances of those strange manifestations of exaggerated grief which seem new and modern to Gorer but are nonetheless familiar to the historian of customs. They once found an outlet in rituals which were acknowledged, recommended, and, indeed, even simulated during the prescribed period of mourning in traditional societies. But it must be admitted that only the appearances are the same. In former times such rituals had the purpose of liberating. Even when, as often happened in the Romantic Age, they exceeded the limits of custom and became pathological, they were not repressed as something monstrous but were patiently tolerated. This tolerance appears in a striking manner in a novel by Mark Twain in which a woman refuses to accept the death of her husband and each year lives out his impossible return. Her friends conspire to support this illusion. Today we can't imagine anyone participating in such a dark comedy. Twain's characters acted out of kindness and generosity but their action would be viewed by today's society as something embarrassing and shamefully morbid, indeed, a sign of mental illness. We thus ask ourselves, with Gorer, whether or not a large part of contemporary social pathology does not originate in our refusal to confront the reality of death—in society's denial of mourning and the right to weep for the dead.

III. New Funeral Rites in the United States

Based on the foregoing analysis, we might be tempted to conclude that our suppression of the reality of death is part of the very structure of contemporary civilization. The elimination of death from conversation and from the communications media goes hand-in-hand with the priority of material well-being as the principal trait of industrial societies. This is especially the case in Northern Europe and America, the main geographical areas of modernity, although there are exceptions where older thought-patterns still prevail. I am thinking of some sectors of Catholic France and Italy, of Presbyterian Scotland, and of the lower classes even in countries that are industrially advanced. Modernity depends on social conditions as much as geography and even in the most progressive countries is limited to the educated classes, whether believers or sceptics. Where modernity has not penetrated we find that eighteenth- and nineteenth-century Romantic attitudes toward death still prevail, such as the cult of the dead and veneration in cemeteries. We should not be misled by the survival of such attitudes, however; while they characterize large numbers of people, they are seriously threatened today. They are doomed to inevitable decline, along with the earlier, less developed mentalities with which they are linked. They are also jeopardized by a model of future society which would continue the process of emptying death of all existential meaning, a model that already dominates middle-class families, whether liberal or conservative. We need not be entirely pessimistic about this evolution because it is probable that the denial of death is so bound up with industrial civilization that the one will disappear with the other. Nor is the denial of death universally the case, as we pointed out, because it is not found in many sectors of society. I am not thinking now of backward parts of Old Europe but of the stronghold of modernity, the United States. America has been the first among modern societies to attenuate the tragic sense of death. There we can observe firsthand the new attitudes toward death. Some of these were satirized in *The Loved One,* Waugh's novel, written in 1948.[6] In 1951, Roger Caillois saw in them an example of hedonistic sleight of hand:

> Death can be faced without fear, not because of some moral ability to transcend the fear it provokes, but because it is inevitable and because in fact there is no reason to dread it. *What we must do is simply not think or talk about it.*[7]

Everything we have said about death in the preceding pages—the alienation of the dying person, the denial of mourning, etc.—holds true for America with the one exception of burial practices. The Americans have not simplified funeral rites as much as the English. To understand this singularity we must continue our earlier account of how modern man dies, with the emphasis now on the time between death and burial. The time before death and after burial, together with the peculiar mourning rites modern man affects, is no different in American than in any other modern society. The difference comes in the intermediary period. We recall how the two nurses charged with preparing the body of Gorer's brother admired their own work. But in England this kind of enthusiasm is not shared by society at large. What matters to the English is to get rid of the body as decently and quickly as possible. That is why they favor cremation.

In America, on the other hand, the art of laying out the body forms part of a series of new rites that are both complicated and sumptuous. These include: the embalming of the body, its exhibition in a funeral parlor, visitation by friends and relatives, flowers and music, solemn obsequies, and finally, interment in a cemetery that looks like a park. The latter is embellished with monuments and is intended for the moral edification of visitors who are more like tourists than pilgrims. There is no point in describing these rites further. They are well known to a wide public as a result of Waugh's book, which has been made into a film, and Jessica Mitford's *The American Way of Death.*[8] Such books are misleading, however, insofar as they suggest that these rituals are no more than a form of commercial exploitation or a perversion of the cult of happiness held dear by Americans. More deeply, they testify to a refusal to have death emptied of all meaning, a refusal to let death pass without solemnizing the occasion ritualistically. This is one reason why cremation is less widespread in the United States.

American society is very attached to these rituals, although they seem somewhat ridiculous to Europeans and American intellectuals (whose attitudes are reflected in Mitford's book). So much so that for a time death is something familiar, something one can talk about. Ads of this sort are common in America: "The dignity and integrity of So-and-So Funeral Home costs no more. Easy access. Private parking for over one hundred cars." Of course, there is no doubt that death is a consumer product. But what is noteworthy is that it has become so, together with all the publicity attendant upon its commercial status, despite the banishment of death elsewhere in society. American attitudes toward the immediately deceased constitute an exception to modern attitudes toward death in general. In this case, they break the normal pattern of modernity and grant the deceased the social space traditional societies had always reserved for them, space that has been practically eliminated in industrial societies. In their way, Americans are carrying on the tradition of bidding a solemn farewell to the dead, and this in spite of the iron-clad rule of expediency that governs conduct in technological and consumer societies. In France many of the hospitals date from the seventeenth century (when the sick were subjected to humiliating and coarse treatment at the hands of vagabonds and delinquents) and the bodies of the dead are still kept in cold rooms like so much meat. The French are, consequently, in a good position to appreciate the need for a time of recollection and solemnity that strikes a balance between the anonymity of a collective morgue and the finality of burial.

In another age such a time could have been observed in the home. But modern attitudes are set against having the corpse too close to the living. In Europe the intelligentsia rarely keep the body in the house, even if the death occurs there. This is partly for hygienic reasons, but more because of a nervous fear of losing control. The American solution is to deposit the body in a neutral place, halfway between the anonymity of the hospital and the privacy of the home. This place is called a funeral home, a special building that is in the charge of a kind of innkeeper who specializes in welcoming the dead. The time spent here is a compromise between the decent but hasty and deritualized services of Northern Europe and the more archaic ceremonies of traditional mourning. The new funeral rites created by the Americans are also a compromise between their desire to observe a period of solemnity after death and their general acceptance of society's taboos. That is why these rituals are so different from those we are used to and why, consequently, they strike us as somewhat comical, even though they retain some traditional elements. The half-closed coffin exposing the upper half of the body is not an invention of American morticians. It is a practice dating from the Middle Ages and can still be found in

Mediterranean areas like Marseilles and parts of Italy. A fifteenth-century fresco in the church of St. Petronius in Bologna depicts the remains of Saint Mark reposing in a coffin of this type.

The Mortician's Art

Still, it must be borne in mind that these funeral home rituals have quite radically changed the meaning of death. In fact, it is not death that is celebrated in these rituals; it is rather death transformed into the appearance of life by the mortician's art. Formerly embalming was intended primarily to impart something of the incorruptibility of the saints to the dead, especially those who had been celebrated and venerated in life. One of the miracles required for sainthood is an uncorrupted body. By helping to make the body more incorruptible, embalming was looked upon as a way of cooperating in the work of sanctification.

In modern America chemical techniques for preserving the body make us forget death by creating an illusion of life. What friends and relatives pay respect to amidst the banks of flowers and the soothing music is the lifelike appearance of the deceased. The idea of death is banished from this ritual as is all deep sorrow. Roger Caillois grasped this point so well when he noted that those fully clothed corpses give the impression that they are merely taking a nap. While it is a fact that this illusion is dispensed with in those sectors of English society described by Gorer and in the American intelligentsia, it is also a fact that the general public goes along with it and this is no doubt evidence of a profound trait in the American character.

The idea of making a dead person appear alive as a way of paying one's last respects may well strike us as puerile and preposterous. As is often the case in America, this practice is part and parcel of a syndrome that includes commercial interests and the language of advertising. But it also testifies to a rapid and unerring adaptation to complex and contradictory conditions of sensibility. This is the first time in history that a whole society has honored the dead by pretending that they were alive.

Something like this happened once before in history, but involved one person only. I refer to Louis XIV, King of France. When he died he was embalmed, clothed in the purple robes of his consecration, laid out on a bed that looked something like a judge's bench—all as though he would wake up at any moment. Banquet tables were set up, no doubt reminiscent of the ancient funeral festivities but more a symbol of the rejection of mourning. The king did not die in the minds of his subjects. Dressed in festive garments, like a rich Californian in a funeral parlor, he received his court for a last time. The idea of the continuity of the Crown dictated a funeral rite that was, in effect, much like those of contemporary America despite a time difference of several centuries, and like them it may be regarded as a compromise between the desire to honor the dead and the desire to put them out of mind as something unmentionable.

The Americans, who believe in their way of death (including the practices of their funeral directors) as they do in their way of life, give these rituals a further justification that is very interesting because it bears out in an unexpected way Gorer's theory about the traumatizing effects of the denial of mourning. Jessica Mitford reports this case: "Recently a funeral director told me of a woman who needed psychiatric treatment because her husband's funeral was with a closed casket, no visitation, and burial in another state with her not present." (In effect, this represents the practice of the progressive Englishman.) "The psychiatrist called him (the funeral director) to learn about the funeral or lack of one. The patient was treated and has recovered and has vowed never to be part of another memorial-type service," that is to say a simplified commemoration of the dead.[9]

Funeral directors, whose interests are threatened by a trend toward simplicity, draw upon expert psychological opinion to defend their business. They argue that by replacing sorrow with sweet serenity they are providing an important public service. Because it tempers the anguish of the bereaved and designs cemeteries for the happiness of the living, the funeral industry sees itself as having a beneficient moral and social function. In America today cemeteries play a role that was intended for future necropolises by French urban-planners at the end of the eighteenth century when a royal edict prohibited burial within the city walls. As a result, provisions for new cemeteries had to be made, and a vast literature described what they should be like and what in particular Père Lachaise of Paris (which became the model of all modern cemeteries in both Europe and America) should be like. One is struck by the resemblance between these eighteenth-century texts and the prose of modern American Funeral directors and the moralists who support them. Mitford's book offers abundant evidence of this similarity. America is rediscovering the tone and style of the Age of Enlightenment. Rediscovering? Perhaps we should say that they have never lost them. Some historians of American society think that the Puritanism of the eighteenth century impeded the development of a hedonistic attitude toward death and that contemporary optimism does not predate the twentieth century. Whether the influence is direct, then, or a repetition, after a century's interlude, in either case the similarity is striking.

Had it not been for the influence of Romanticism, Père Lachaise would have become another Forest Lawn, the famous cemetery in Los Angeles caricatured by Waugh. Romanticism thwarted a development in this direction and its influence still persists in the popular representations of death and in graveside cults. On the other hand, we get the impression that in America the Romantic influence was short-lived and that the spirit of the Enlightenment, although diminished by Puritanism, was more influential. If this is the case, Puritanism would have had the same braking effect in America as Romanticism did in Europe, but would have died out earlier, thus fostering a mentality much like that of the Enlightenment, the seedbed of so many modern attitudes. We cannot help thinking that in this matter as in so many others (in constitutional law, for example) America is closer to the eighteenth century than Europe is.

The Crisis of Death and the Crisis of Individuality

We conclude that in the last third of the twentieth century something of monumental significance is taking place of which we are just becoming aware: death, that familiar companion of yore, has disappeared from our language. His name is anathema. A kind of vague and anonymous anxiety has taken the place of the words and symbols elaborated by our ancestors. A few writers like Malraux and Ionesco make some attempt to restore death's ancient name which has been obliterated from our language and social conventions. But in normal existence it no longer has any positive meaning at all. It is merely the negative side of what we really see, what we really know, and what we really feel.

This represents a profound change in attitude. In truth, death did not occupy a large place in the minds of men during the high Middle Ages or for some time afterwards. It was not outlawed by edict as it is today; rather its power was weakened by reason of its extreme familiarity. But from the twelfth century onwards, people became more and more preoccupied with death, at least this was the case among the clergy and the educated classes. This concern emerged gradually in connection with two distinct themes: in the twelfth and thirteenth centuries in connection with the theme of the Last Judgment and in the fourteenth and fifteenth centuries in connection with the theme of the art of dying. The *Artes Moriendi* depicted the whole universe in the death-room: the living of the earth, the blessed of heaven, and the damned of hell, all in the presence of Christ and his heavenly court. The life of the dying person was thus summed up for all time and, whoever he might be, he was in this restricted space and for this brief moment the very center of the natural and supernatural worlds. Death was the occasion for individual self-awareness.

We know from several sources that the late Middle Ages was a time of emerging individuality, when men began to define themselves as entities distinct from the collective representations of the human race. It was a time of rampant individualism in religion, in economics (the beginnings of capitalism), and in culture at large. The most conclusive evidence of this individualism is, in my opinion, to be found in the wills and last testaments of the time. These became a literary form in their own right and a means of individual self-expression. When a will is reduced to a mere means of disposing of the deceased's wealth as it is today, it is a sign of a decline or at the very least of a change in our conception of individuality. The progress of science, the affirmation of the rights of man, and the rise of the middle class in the eighteenth century testify that that age was also a heyday of individualism. But it was an individualism already in eclipse, for in the unnoticed intimacy of daily life, individual freedom was already threatened, on the one hand, by family constraints and, on the other, by the demands of professional life. The clear correspondence between the triumph over death and the triumph of individuality during the late Middle Ages invites us to ask whether a similar but inverse relationship might not exist today between the "crisis of death" and the crisis of individuality.

Notes

1. Vladimir Jankélévitch, *Médecine de France* [177] (1966) 3–16; reprinted in *La mort* (Paris: Flammarion, 1966).

2. B. G. Glaser and A. L. Strauss, *Awareness of Dying* (Chicago: Aldine, 1965).

3. Jacques Maritain, *Reflections on America* (New York: Scribner's, 1958).

4. Geoffrey Gorer, *Death, Grief and Mourning* (New York: Doubleday, 1965).

5. Ibid., pp. 192–99. See Gorer, for this article and subsequent quotes.

6. Evelyn Waugh, *The Loved One* (London: Chapman and Hall, 1950).

7. Roger Caillois, *Quatre essais de sociologie contemporaine* (Paris: Perrin, 1951).

8. Jessica Mitford, *The American Way of Death* (New York: Simon & Schuster, 1963).

9. Ibid., p. 93.

GEORGE GERBNER

Death in Prime Time: Notes on the Symbolic Functions of Dying in the Mass Media

George Gerbner, a professor of communications, attempts to decipher the meaning given to death by prime-time television. The context with which the media surround death and dying, he argues, is an invented world of symbols. When the symbolic environment of death on television is examined, Gerbner finds that dying is most often presented as violent retribution for some weakness. He elaborates the implications of this connection in the following selection.

Death in Prime Time

Dying in the mass media—both news and entertainment (a distinction increasingly hard to make)—has a symbolic function different from death in real life but investing it—and life itself—with particular meanings. We can begin to consider what these might be by reflecting on the nature of representation.

A symbol system is an artifact par excellence. It is totally invented to serve human purposes. It can serve these purposes only if those interpreting it know the code and can fit it into a symbolic context of their own. They must share the rules of the invention and the interpretative strategies by which it should be understood.

Symbolic narrative, a story, has two basic elements of invention: fictive and selective. Selective invention is factual narrative such as news. Presumably true events (facts) are selected from an endless stream of events. A narrative is invented to convey some meaning about the selected facts as interpreted in a previously learned framework of knowledge.

Fictive invention is fiction and drama; the "facts" are invented as well as the narrative. (Selection is of course involved in both.) The function of fictive invention is to illuminate (literally to embody and dramatize) the invisible structure and dynamics of the significant connections of human life. It is to show how things *work*. Invention that can only select events but not create them must be more opaque; it can only show what things *are* but rarely why or how they work. The full development of the connections between events and

Source: George Gerbner. "Death in Prime Time: Notes on the Symbolic Functions of Dying in the Mass Media." *Annals of the American Academy of Political and Social Science,* Vol. 447, 1980.

human motivations and powers requires the freedom and legitimacy to invent the "facts" in a way that illuminates the otherwise hidden dynamics of existence.

In this totally invented world of symbols—selective and fictive—nothing happens without some purpose and function (which need not be the same). Let us use as an example the world of television which we have studied for some years.[1] This discussion also applies to other media and cultural forms, with the difference that television is the generally non-selectively used universal storyteller of modern society. It is, therefore, more a symbolic *environment* than a traditional medium.

People are not born into the world of television. They are selected or created for a purpose. The purpose is usefulness to the symbolic world (called news values or story values) that the producing institutions and their patrons find useful for *their* purposes. More numerous in both news and drama are those for whom that world has more uses—jobs, power, adventure, sex, youth, and all other opportunities in life. These values are distributed in the symbol system as most resources are distributed in the society whose dominant institutions produce most of the symbols: according to status and power. Dominant social groups tend to be overrepresented and overendowed not only absolutely but also in relation to their numbers in the real population. (For example, men outnumber women at least three to one in television and most media content.)

Minorities are defined by having less than their proportionate share of values and resources. In the world of television news and drama, this underrepresentation means lower numbers, less usefulness, fewer opportunities, more victimization (or "criminalization"), more restricted scope of action, more stereotyped roles, diminished life chances, and general undervaluation ranging from relative neglect to symbolic annihilation.

Death in News and Drama

Death in such a context is just another invented characterization, a negative resource, a sign of fatal flaw or ineptitude, a punishment for sins or mark of tragedy. It is always a reminder of the risks of life, cultivating most anxiety and dependence for those who are depicted as most at risk. In other words, death is one feature of the more general functions of social typing and control.

Obituaries are the Social Register of the middle class. Even a "nobody" of modest status and power (i.e., a person of no symbolic existence in the common culture) becomes a "somebody" if the flicker of his or her (and it's mostly his) life can leave its final symbolic mark of existence in the obituary column.

Death in the news is a tightly scripted scenario of violence and terror. Murders, accidents, "body counts" and catastrophes scatter a surfeit of impersonal corpses in ghoulish symbolic overkill across the pages of our family newspapers and television screens. By the time we grow up, we are so addicted to this necromania of our culture (and we are not alone), that its constant daily cultivation seems to add to a morbid sense of normalcy.

Yet it is all well (if unwittingly) calculated to cultivate a sense of insecurity, anxiety, fear of the "mean world" out there, and dependence on some strong protector. It is the modern equivalent of the bloody circuses in the Roman empire's "bread and circuses" that were supposed to keep the populace quiescent.

At the center of the symbolic structure of death is the world of stories invented to show how things work—fiction and drama. The most massive and universal flow of stories in modern society (and history) is of course television drama, most of it produced according to the industrial formulas developed to assemble large audiences and sell them to advertisers at the least cost.

That is a world in which practically no one ever dies a natural death. Assembly-line drama generally denies the inevitable reality of death and affirms its stigmatic character. Violent death, on the other hand, befalls 5 percent of all prime-time dramatic characters every week, with about twice as many killers (many of whom also get killed) stalking the world of prime time. The symbolic function of death in the world of television is thus embedded in its structure of violence, which is essentially a show of force, the ritualistic demonstration of power.

The Structure of Violence—and Power

Dominated as it is by males and masculine values, much of the world of prime time revolves around questions of power. Who can get away with what against whom? How secure are different social types when confronted with conflict and danger? What hierarchies of risk and vulnerability define social relations? In other words, how power works in society.

The simplest and cheapest dramatic demonstration of power is an overt expression of physical force compelling action against one's will on pain of being hurt or killed, or actually hurting or killing. That is the definition of violence used in our studies of television drama. Violence rules the symbolic world of television. It occurs at an average 10-year rate of 5 violent incidents per hour in prime time and 18 per hour in weekend daytime children's programming—a triple dose.

Violence as a demonstration of power can be measured by relating the percent of violents to the percent of victims within each social group. That ratio shows the chances of men and women, blacks and whites, young and old, to come out on top instead of on the bottom. Conversely, it shows the risks of each group to end up as victims instead of victors.

Table 1 is a summary of these "risk ratios" based on annual samples of prime time and weekend daytime (children's) programs major dramatic characters, a total of 3,949, from 1969 through 1978. It shows for each of several demographic and dramatic groups the ratio of violents over victims (including killing) and of only killers over killed (or the other way around) within each

Table 1 | Risk Ratios[1]: Major Characters in All Programs (1969–1978)

	All Characters				Male Characters				Female Characters			
	N	Involved in Violence	Violent-Victim Ratio	Killer-Killed Ratio	N	Involved in Violence	Violent-Victim Ratio	Killer-Killed Ratio	N	Involved in Violence	Violent-Victim Ratio	Killer-Killed Ratio
All Characters	3949	63.3	−1.20	+1.90	2938	68.4	−1.18	+2.02	956	46.1	−1.34	+1.20
Social Age												
Children-Adolescents	415	60.5	−1.60	+3.00	297	65.0	−1.69	+3.00	116	49.1	−1.33	0.00
Young Adults	813	64.5	−1.36	+2.00	539	69.6	−1.23	+2.17	270	53.7	−1.82	+1.33
Settled Adults	2212	59.8	−1.12	+2.07	1698	65.7	−1.12	+2.13	513	40.0	−1.12	+1.60
Elderly	106	47.2	−1.15	−1.75	80	50.0	+1.07	1.00	26	38.5	−3.33	−0.00
Marital Status												
Not Married	1873	65.6	−1.23	+1.90	1374	69.7	−1.18	+2.02	491	53.8	−1.44	+1.30
Married	987	45.5	−1.27	+1.67	626	52.9	−1.27	+1.82	361	32.7	−1.25	+1.11
Class												
Clearly Upper	269	59.5	−1.38	+1.50	182	67.6	−1.26	+1.57	87	42.5	−2.00	+1.25
Mixed	3549	63.4	−1.19	+2.07	2650	68.3	−1.17	+2.20	844	46.3	−1.29	+1.20
Clearly Lower	131	69.5	−1.25	−1.11	106	73.6	−1.20	−1.13	25	52.0	−1.71	1.00
Race												
White	3087	60.1	−1.19	+1.97	2235	65.1	−1.16	+2.11	852	46.9	−1.31	+1.26
Other	360	55.0	−1.33	+1.69	280	61.1	−1.27	+1.69	77	31.2	−1.83	0.00
Character Type												
"Good"	2304	58.4	−1.29	+2.93	1659	63.7	−1.24	+3.85	622	43.2	−1.51	−1.60
Mixed	1093	61.4	−1.22	+1.33	807	65.8	−1.21	+1.27	262	44.7	−1.31	+1.50
"Bad"	550	88.0	1.00	+1.84	471	89.4	−1.01	+1.86	71	77.5	+1.15	+1.67
Nationality												
U.S.	3100	58.1	−1.20	+2.06	2263	63.2	−1.16	+2.23	827	43.9	−1.38	+1.18
Other	264	73.5	−1.31	+1.31	203	80.8	−1.29	+1.27	61	49.2	−1.47	+2.00

[1]Risk ratios are obtained by dividing the more numerous of these two roles by the less numerous within each group. A plus sign indicates that there are more violents or killers than victims or killed and a minus sign indicates that there are more victims or killed than violents or killers. A ratio of 0.00 means that there were no victims or killers or violents or killed. A +0.00 ratio means that there were some violents or killers but no victims or killed; a −0.00 ratio means that there were victims or killed but no violents or killers.

group. It also shows the percent of characters in each group involved in any violence as either violents or victims (or both). For example, of the 415 children and adolescent characters studied, 60.5 percent (65.0 percent males and 49.1 percent females) were involved in violence. Of the males, victims outnumbered violents by 1.69 but killers outnumbered killed by 3.00. In other words, for every 10 child and adolescent violents there were about 17 victims, but for every 10 killed there were 30 killers in that group of characters.

Overall, 63 percent of all characters were involved in some violence. For every 10 violents there were 12 victims, but for every 10 killed there were 19 killers. However, as we have just seen, involvement in violence and its outcome—as with values and resources—is not randomly distributed.

Some features of the distribution of violence as a demonstration of power can be illustrated by selecting a few risk ratios from Table 1, showing how these victimization rates define a hierarchy of risks within which the depiction of dying (and killing) is embedded.

A Hierarchy of Risks

Combining prime-time and daytime characters, we find that victimization rates define a social hierarchy of risks and vulnerabilities. For every 10 characters who commit violence within each of the following groups the average number of victims for

white men is	12
nonwhite men is	13
lower class women is	17
young women is	18
nonwhite women is	18
old women is	33

If and when involved in violence, women and minorities, and especially young and old as well as minority women characters, are the most vulnerable.

Now let us look at dying (and its dramatic counterpart, killing) in that context. We can compute a lethal pecking order by relating the number of killers to the number of killed within each group. Unlike violence in general, killing eliminates a character and must be used more sparingly, either as curtain-raiser or as the "final solution." Therefore, in most role categories, there are more killers than killed. "Good" men, the male heroes of prime-time drama, are at the top of the killing order. For every 10 "good" men killed, there are 38 "good" men killers. Next are young men and American men; for every 10 young males killed, there are 22 young male and American male killers. The killed–killer ratio of all white males is only slightly lower: 21 killers for every 10 white males killed. In other words, if and when involved in some fatal violence on prime time television, "good," young, American, and white males are the most likely to be the killers instead of the killed. They kill in a good cause to begin with or are the most powerful, or both.

Women do not fare so well. Their most favorable ratio is 20 killers for every 10 killed, and that goes to foreign women. The second highest female kill ratio goes to "bad" women: they kill 17 characters for every 10 "bad" women killed. Next are middle-aged women who kill 16 for every 10 killed. Thus women who tend to kill, kill much less than men, have relatively more lethal power when they are foreign, evil, or past the romantic-lead age, than when they are "good," American, young, and white, as is the case with men. Their killing is more likely to be shown as unjust, irrational, and "alien" than is killing by men.

At the very bottom of the lethal pecking order are old women who get involved in violence only to get killed and "good" women who get killed 16 times for every 10 killers. Old and "good" women get into violence mostly as sympathetic (or only pathetic) victims, rousing male heroes to righteous (if lethal) indignation. Next in line are lower class men, lower class women, and old men. For every ten killers in each group there are, respectively, 11, 10, and 10 killed. Unlike those of greater ability to survive conflict or catastrophe, older and lower class characters pay with their lives for every life they take.

Provocation and Retribution

In general, then, as can be seen on Table 1, the pecking order of both mayhem and killing is dominated by men—American, white, middle class, and in the prime of life. At the top of the general order of victimizers are "bad" women, old men, and "bad" men, in that order. The presence of evil at the top of the power hierarchy suggests the dramatic role of villains provoking heroes to violent action. Heading the ranking of killers over killed are "good" and other majority-type males. We can begin to discern not only the provocative role of the "bad" but also the retributive function of the "good" and the strong.

Lowest on the dramatic scale are women, lower class, and old people. Of the 20 most victimized groups (both total violence and killing), all but three are women.

Old women are at the bottom of the heap of both the battered and the killed. "Good" women are among the characters most likely to be both general and fatal victims of violence rather than the perpetrators. "Good" men have power as indicated by their heading up the killer–killed list; "good" women, on the other hand, end up near the bottom of the power hierarchy. When it comes to violence, "good" are the strong men and the weak women of the world of television.

Dying on television is a violent retribution for weakness, sin, or other flaw in character or status. It is part of the social typing and control functions of centralized cultural production. Our research has found that heavy viewers (compared to light viewers in the same social groups) derive from their television experience a heightened sense of danger, insecurity, and mistrust, or what we call the "mean world" syndrome. It can be conjectured that the symbolic functions of dying are part of that syndrome, contributing not only to a structure of power but also to the irrational dread of dying and thus to diminished vitality and self-direction in life.

Note

1. The long-range project was first described in my article on "Cultural Indicators: The Case of Violence in Television Drama" in the *Annals*, Vol. 388, March 1970. The most recent report, including a description of methodology, appears in George Gerbner, Larry Gross, Nancy Signorielli, Michael Morgan, and Marilyn Jackson-Beeck, "The Demonstration of Power: Violence Profile No. 10," *Journal of Communication*, Vol. 29 (Summer 1979).

LYN LOFLAND

Emergent Ideology:
The Happy Death
Movement

Lofland puts forth the thesis that so much attention has been paid to death and dying that a general social movement has resulted. In order to gain analytic distance from a current phenomenon, she terms the social movement "the happy death movement." The movement, Lofland suggests, has created an ideology evoking an enemy and constructing a "craft of dying," promoting the notion that in our efforts to avoid denial of death, we have constructed a new form of denial.

Social movements are not merely the creators of activities or new organizational forms. They do not merely attempt to rearrange social furniture. They are also, importantly, creators of ideology, constructors of conceptions. The women's movement, for example, is not merely a mover behind divorce reform or the ERA attempt or the creation of child care facilities. It is also the creator or the synthesizer or the carrier of ideas about the proper relation between the sexes, about the appropriate meanings of male and female. The ecology movement is not merely a force which battles to enlarge parks or pass legislation involving the necessity for environmental impact reports. It is also the constructor of conceptions about the appropriate relationships between human beings and the planet earth, conceptions about the priority of certain long-term values over other shorter-term concerns. So, too, the happy death movement is not just concerned with hospices and euthanasia legislation and new therapeutic opportunities. It is profoundly involved as well with conceptions of the appropriate character and meaning of death and dying.

I want here to consider two fundamental aspects of the movement's complex and emergent ideology: the evocation of an enemy and the developing articulation of some important belief components of a "dying craft." Before turning to these matters, however, some qualifications are necessary.

First, I am attempting to capture in print something which is in the process of creation. As such, there is necessarily the possibility, however unintended, of distortion. Second, in speaking of "ideology" as a unitary thing capable of being dissected, I do not mean to suggest that there is any coordinated effort at

Source: Lyn Lofland, pp. 87–104 in *The Craft of Dying: The Modern Face of Death*. Copyright © 1978 by Sage Publications, Inc. Reprinted by permission of Sage Publications, Inc.

its creation. As with reform activities, the movement's emergent ideology is the product of diverse voices expressing similar but not identical points of view. Finally, the relationship between movement ideologues and structural reformers is not one of total harmony. As with many social movements (the women's movement, for example), the ideological creators of the happy death movement are considerably more "radical" and more "extreme" in their thinking than are the majority of movement participants and sympathizers.

The Evocation of Enemy

Enemies—real or created—are indigenous to social movements. As Turner and Killian have pointed out, a "movement is inconceivable apart from a vital sense that some established practice or mode of thought is *wrong* and ought to be replaced" (1972, 259). That sense of something wrong is sustained by a sense of "righteous indignation," a sense of injustice. "A sense of injustice that is vital enough to have consequences seems to require not only a situation that appears unfavorable by comparison with some reference group, but also an oppressor, so that the situation can be seen as a product of human will." In short, Turner and Killian argue (1972, 268), social movements need *enemies* (see also Gerlach and Hine 1970, xvii).

Some movements—the nineteenth-century women's suffrage movement, for example—are "fortunate" in facing an opposition that is organized and articulate. The members of such organizations can be identified and personified. The oppressor is concrete; is real. But not all movements have "enemies" that are so clearly identifiable. It may be that the thing which is wrong, the practice which is abhorred, is merely a de facto creation—simply the consequence of "the way things are done," with no one especially defending that way nor especially opposed to change but not especially anxious to undergo all the effort change entails, either. De facto enemies are not very useful in creating righteous indignation. They do not articulate any opposition. They do not seem in fact to be enemies at all. If they are to be useful to a movement, if they are to provide the emotional springboard for a sustained sense of injustice, they must be *evoked* by the movement itself. If they will not speak for themselves, they must be "articulated" by the movement.

There are undoubtably many means for evoking an enemy, for articulating de facto opposition. The means utilized by the happy death movement is one of the simplest, and probably one of the most common. It involves doing only two things: set up an "ideal" and then point to the imperfect presumed real. Let us look at how this is done, first by critics of the modern family and then by happy death movement apologists.

The sociologist William Goode has described with insight the manner in which critics of contemporary family arrangements and practices evoke an ideal—what he calls the "classical family of Western nostalgia."

It is a pretty picture of life down on grandma's farm. There are lots of happy children and many kinfolk live together in a large rambling house. Everyone works hard. Most of the food to be eaten during the winter is grown, preserved and stored on the farm. The family members repair their own equipment, and in general the household is economically self-sufficient. The family has many functions; it is the source of economic stability and religious, educational and vocational training. Father is stern and reserved and has the final decision in all important matters. Life is difficult, but harmonious because everyone knows his task and carries it out. All boys and girls marry, and marry young. Young people, especially the girls, are likely to be virginal at marriage and faithful afterward. Though the parents do not arrange their children's marriages, the elders do have the right to reject a suitor and have a strong hand in the final decision. After marriage, the couple lives harmoniously, either near the boy's parents or with them, for the couple is slated to inherit the farm. No one divorces. (Goode 1970, 6)

Similarly, ideological creators of the happy death movement evoke "the classical death of Western (or other) nostalgia." There are many versions, but Elisabeth Kübler-Ross provides a classic example of the genre:

I remember as a child [in Switzerland] the death of a farmer. He fell from a tree and was not expected to live. He asked simply to die at home, a wish that was granted without questioning. He called his daughters into the bedroom and spoke with each one of them alone for a few minutes. He arranged his affairs quietly, though he was in great pain, and distributed his belongings and his land, none of which was to be split until his wife should follow him in death. He also asked each of his children to share in the work, duties, and tasks that he had carried on until the time of the accident. He asked his friends to visit him once more, to bid good-bye to them. Although I was a small child at the time, he did not exclude me or my siblings. We were allowed to share in the preparations of the family just as we were permitted to grieve with them until he died. When he did die, he was left at home, in his own beloved home which he had built, and among his friends and neighbors who went to take a last look at him where he lay in the midst of flowers in the place he had lived in and loved so much. (Kübler-Ross 1969, 5–6)

Having created an image of an ideal and allegedly "preferable" state of affairs, the ideological crafts-person then has only to describe the way in which the "presumed" real world fails to measure up. In so doing, the opposition is "articulated"; a social problem is *created* (Blumer 1971).

For the happy death movement, the "presumed real" against which the ideal is measured involves a set of assertions about death and dying in contemporary America which I shall label, "the conventional view of death." It has been variously formulated, but essentially the view holds that America is a death-denying society, that death is a taboo topic, that death makes Americans uncomfortable so they run from it, that death is hidden in America because Americans deny it, and so forth. The consequences of all this denial and repression are asserted to be quite terrible: exorbitant funeral costs and barbaric funeral practices, inhumane handling of dying in hospitals, ostracism of the dying from the living, inauthentic communication with the fatally ill, an unrealistic, mechanical, non-organic view of life, and so forth. Philippe Ariès, widely cited in movement literature, provides an articulate example of the view:

> For thousands of years man was lord and master of his death, and the circumstances surrounding it. Today this has ceased to be so. . . . Today nothing remains either of the sense that everyone has or should have of his impending death, or of the public solemnity surrounding the moment of death. What used to be appreciated is now hidden; what used to be solemn is now avoided. . . . We have seen how modern society deprives man of his death, and how it allows him this privilege only if he does not use it to upset the living. In a reciprocal way, society forbids the living to appear moved by the death of others; it does not allow them either to weep for the deceased or to seem to miss them. (Ariès 1974, 136, 138, 143)

So does a recent (1977) advertising circular for a new "death book": "The editors describe death as the contemporary taboo that holds enormous terror for many persons." And a brochure from the University of Minnesota's Center for Death Education and Research:

> Every society *must* find the means to deal with this recurring crisis. "Death," as such, however, has been a "taboo" topic and hence has evoked little public discussion. People today are characteristically unwilling even to discuss the process of dying itself; they are even prone to avoid telling a dying person that he is, in fact, dying. This is partly a moral attitude: life is preferable to whatever may follow it, and one should not look forward to death unless he is in great pain.
>
> This moral attitude is shared by many professional people who work with or near the patients who die in our medical institutions. Most of the training that physicians and nurses receive in schools of medicine or nursing equips them principally for the technical aspects of dealing with patients. Little, if any instruction is offered on how to deal with the issue of death.

As many scholars have pointed out, the empirical evidence for all these assertions is something less than overwhelming. (See, for example, Dumont and Foss 1972; Donaldson 1972.) And one might consider it somewhat odd that the statement that death is a taboo topic in America should continue to be asserted in the face of nearly a decade of non-stop talking on the subject. But if one appreciates the *functions* these statements serve in enemy evocation, one can also appreciate that their questionable empirical basis is hardly a serious obstacle to endless repetition. The importance of the "conventional view of death"—of the conventional wisdom about death—as propounded over and over again by movement intellectuals, is not its "truth" but its utility.

Finally, it is important to appreciate the degree to which the happy death movement's "critique" of contemporary death attitudes and practices "meshes" with a broader intellectual tradition in the modern United States. I refer to the "humanistic-counterculture" denouncement of modern society in general, which denouncement emphasizes the Western world's dehumanizing, unemotional, technologically dominated, inauthentic, and constricted character. It may be that the movement's "conventional wisdom" draws much of its "believability" from what it shares with this broader tradition.[1]

The Components of a Craft of Dying

In a secular age, large numbers of humans confront the modern face of death unarmed with any certainties about what it might mean. A part of the ideological work of the happy death movement is, therefore, the construction of some larger meaning system into which the experiences modern humans are having with death may be placed. While the ideological edifice is at present incomplete, it is still possible, tentatively, to identify three components which may eventually be central to the finished structure. These are *immortality*, *positivity*, and *expressivity*.

Immortality

The fact of an afterlife has, in the late seventies, emerged as an increasingly central tenet of the happy death movement's ideology. What began in the early seventies as allusion has become assertion. What was born as vague suggestion is becoming creed. What could first be heard at conferences and workshops and symposia clothed in subtlety—as in the following:

> I said, "Russell, let go now; let go, easy, easy, this is it; let go and move on out now, please let go . . . now!" And so he did. There was a sudden release of tension, the breathing stopped, his head dropped forward, and he was very still. The color paled, the expression left his face, and, after eight months, he had "broken free. . . ." We all stayed up until dawn. *Soon after he died, the lightning flashed and by daylight it had begun to rain on the Mesa area of Santa Barbara, on a cliff overlooking the ocean on the south.* I sat by the window, deep in hazy thought, yet still and contemplative. *Was it really over?* What was "it," this awesome, marvelous thing we had been carried along by? *This was a cosmic experience,* I thought, and it doesn't matter if I ever do anything worthwhile again—ever. (Kerr 1974, 29, emphasis added)

unfolds into stark forthrightness:

> Dr. Elisabeth Kübler-Ross who has counseled thousands of terminally ill patients is convinced that "people don't really die."
>
> The 49 year old Swiss-born psychiatrist, author of *On Death and Dying* and two other books on death, says she knows "beyond the shadow of a doubt" there is life after death.
>
> "This is not just the spooky stories of someone who has worked with too many dying patients," she said. "It is a good feeling to be able to say after many years that people don't really die." ("Specialist on Dying Says People Don't," *Sacramento Bee,* October 16, 1975)[2]

Befitting a movement largely composed of presumably secular upper-middle-class professionals, the immortality claim rests not on revelation but on "research." That is, Kübler-Ross and others *know* there is an afterlife not as a consequence of any direct communication with a deity but because of "evidence," such as the following accounts, provided by the recovered "clinically dead."[3]

> One patient, a 32-year-old female kidney dialysis patient, described her experience when she suffered liver and kidney failure, lapsed into a coma and had been given up for dead by doctors at Shands Teaching Hospital.
>
> The woman found herself in a beautiful, serene environment where, across a border, she saw "people I knew who had died."
>
> Without any fear or apprehension, the woman found herself approaching the border, she said, adding, "I would get almost across and they would seem to push me back. 'It's not time,' they said." (Life After Death Experiences Cited," *Sacramento Union,* August 2, 1977)

> Barbara Feldman's experience is typical. "I was in the Intensive Care Unit following lung surgery. Suddenly I felt a sharp pain in my chest," she remembers. "I knew it was my heart. . . . Then I heard one of the doctors say, 'We've lost her.'
>
> "I noticed that a blue mist surrounded my body and was drifting up off the operating table. It was beautiful. I kept saying to myself: How can I be dead? I'm still conscious! . . .
>
> "After a while I gave up trying to tell them I was alive. Then I realized that I was travelling through a long tunnel. There was a humming sound in my ears; not music, but it was pleasant. Up ahead was a brilliant light and I knew that I wanted to get to it. I had the most irresistible urge to become one with the light. I was travelling fast.
>
> "Then an image of my three children appeared. I felt a tremendous tugging on my soul and I stopped travelling. I knew at that moment that I could either go on toward the light or return to my body. It was the hardest decision I ever had to make. I decided to return. . . . I started descending toward my body and felt very sad. Then a voice, unlike anything I had ever heard, spoke. It said, 'You will be very happy for many years. And then you will return." (Panati 1976, 78)

For some movement ideologues, then, the question of an afterlife is resolved; its exact character, however, remains undetermined. Despite the certainty of the three panelists at a late seventies seminar on "An Excursion into the Undiscovered Country,"[4] who undertook to chart "the different stages of consciousness experienced in the afterlife," most writers leave the issue open—perhaps reincarnation, perhaps a "spirit world," perhaps some ecstatic absorption into cosmic energy, perhaps something else altogether. On one aspect, however, there is consensus. Whatever the character of human immortality, it is *pleasant.* As such, the idea of immortality "fits" with a second component of movement ideology: positivity.

Positivity

One could argue that in its developing commitment to immortality as a component of its "craft of dying," the happy death movement is breaking away from the long trend of Western secularism and materialism.[5] Certainly, to the degree that the movement links with one or another version of mysticism, it would appear to move outside the stream of scientific rationalism which is the familiar milieu of most of its participants. In its commitment to the positive view, however—what I am calling "positivity"—the movement is firmly planted in the rich soil of tradition. If it is at all meaningful to speak of an "American culture"—or at least to speak of the culture of America's long-dominating Anglo group—then it is certainly plausible to argue that a recurring and important theme of that culture is positivity: a belief in progress, personal or societal; a belief in the possibility of solutions for all problems; a belief that life is potentially just and that one can get what one deserves.[6]

As a component of the ideology of the movement, positivity involves three interrelated assertions: (1) that the dying process may be the occasion for self-improvement and personality "growth" for the dying person; (2) that the dying process and subsequent grieving may be the occasion for self-improvement and personality "growth" for the family and friends of the dying/dead person; and (3) that death itself (the moment of death and what follows) may be blissful, serene, pleasurable, intensely contenting—perhaps even orgastic.

(1) An important message of movement rhetoric is that dying, for the dying, need not be dismal. If one is prepared to take advantage of the opportunities, dying and death may be—as Kübler-Ross subtitled her 1975 edited book—"the final stage of growth." For example, on the dust jacket of Stanley Keleman's widely and positively reviewed book, *Living Your Dying* (1974), we are asked: "Is there a person alive who isn't really curious about what dying is for them? Is there a person alive who wouldn't like to go to their dying full of excitement, without fear and without morbidity? This book tells you how." Similarly, in the introduction to her book, Marjorie McCoy promises to teach us how *To Die with Style:*

> My intention [in writing the book] has emerged from this new interest in death but at the same time I have sought a different, more radically positive way to view dying. I propose we look at death not primarily as a thing to be suffered but rather as an action to be anticipated and prepared for. Dying need not be equated with a watch running down or a flower withering away, a stream drying up or a rock falling at last into a dark abyss. Why not, with Carl Jung, speak of "the *achievement* of death" and view dying as the final creative task of our lives? (1974, 16)

The quintessential version of this view is perhaps that of Mwalimu Imara:

> We abhor and reject the moment when we will confront the nearness of our death. But the dying stage of our life can be experienced as *the most profound growth event of our total life's experience*. The shock, the pain and the anxiety are great, but if we are fortunate enough to have time to live and experience our own process, our arrival at a plateau of creative acceptance will be worth it. (1975, 149, emphasis added)

(2) One does not have to be dying oneself, however, to reap benefits. An ad for Peter Koestenbaum's *Is There an Answer to Death?* (1976) informs us

that "a positive confrontation with death can be a personally liberating experience . . . it can help us develop our individual identity and give us the security we need to live our lives courageously." That is, the dying and death of another is also an occasion for self-improvement and growth. Reflecting on the death of his son, Keith Kerr, a California marriage and family counsellor writes:

> In retrospect, even after some four years have elapsed, not all of the benefits, insights and awarenesses have become clear to us. It may seem strange to speak of "benefits" as coming from the death of anyone, not to mention a son or someone so close emotionally. The following have emerged to date: (1) A release from virtually all feelings of guilt. Whatever omissions in our rearing or relationship with Russell, they were compensated for and there are few regrets; (2) I, personally, began to shed—through our experience in his death—a lifelong compulsion to overwork and to "push" myself; (3) we felt we had "proven" ourselves in an act of fullest love and affection, and there was a consequent building of our self-esteem in a basic way; (4) personally, again, my own death became an absolute and eventual certainty to me through Russell's death. So not only did that reality emerge to me; I had looked death full in the face and it held no sense of foreboding or terror as I had in advance fantasized it would; (5) the tremendous energy depletion lasted for months. During that time, and up to the present, I was and am now totally unable to force my body or mind beyond their natural endurance limits. I withdraw and rest sooner, before being depleted of energy and I "listen" to my body more attentively. (Kerr 1974, 29–30)

The same argument, more generally stated, is made by Roy Nichols and Jane Nichols in an article on funerals:

> The ultimate goal of the grief work is to be able to remember without emotional pain and to be able to reinvest emotional surpluses. *While the experience of the grief work is difficult and slow and wearing, it is also enriching and fulfilling.* The most beautiful people we have known are those who have known defeat, known suffering, known struggle, known loss, and have found their way out of the depths. These persons have an appreciation, a sensitivity, and an understanding of life that fills them with compassion, gentleness, and a deep loving concern. Beautiful people do not just happen. (1975, 96, emphasis added)

(3) Finally, the positivity component offers the possibility that death itself and what ensues will be pleasurable. Again the experiences of the recovered "clinically dead" are brought forth as evidence (see above), but so are the perceptions of death witnesses.

> Throughout human history, recorders of death-bed scenes tell of a frequent and strange phenomenon. They note that the visage of the newly deceased is quite often wreathed in a gentle smile or in a look of uncommon peace. Interpreters offer many explanations, all of them guesses. . . . My guess is that the smile or look of peace reflects a satisfaction limited to men of any creed who died in peace. They expired without earthly strings of any kind choking their hearts and they realized that they had bequeathed no strings to choke the hearts of those they left behind. (Kavanaugh 1972, 79)

In the above extract, Robert Kavanaugh, a former priest and current counselling psychologist offers only the hope for death as serene. Other writers have suggested a more tantalizing possibility. One example can stand for many:

> Death is the ultimate unification experience. As part of his eternal cycle and ceaseless becoming, man in death merges with himself, others, and all. . . . There is an analogy here to the search for the perfect orgasm. Since time immemorial, or for as long as the recorded history of sexuality, man has attempted to perfect, prolong, and/or multiply the orgasm for himself and his partner. . . . Death does not represent destruction, evil, meaningless oblivion, or the dark forces of man. It is the quintessence of what man has always desired most and what has been the chief motivational factor in his life, the search for, and repetition of, the spontaneous unification experiences he has encountered sporadically and at random during the course of his life and existence. It is the final, ultimate, and eternal experience of unity. (Gordon 1970, 106, 108, 109)

As can be seen from these extracts, the positive character of dying and death is not simply given in the nature of things. Quite the contrary: the growth and self-improvement that may emerge out of the dying process—one's own or others—and the ecstasy of death itself are largely to be *achieved*. Understandably enough, writers vary in their prescriptions for salvation. But at least one element in those prescriptions is widely shared: one of the coins with which a "happy death" is purchased is *expressivity*.

Expressivity

The expressivity component of the happy death movement's emergent craft of dying specifies that whatever the emotions engendered by dying and death, they *should be expressed*. To supress expression is to sacrifice the opportunities for "growth" which death provides.

> Most people live their dying as they have lived their lives. People who rarely express themselves emotionally, or those whose lives are lived as misery and defeat, tend to die that way. People whose lives are rich in self-expression tend to die self-expressively. (Keleman, 1974, 4)

> If survivors are made to feel ashamed of their spontaneous reactions to loss and the memory of the deceased, they suffer more distress than if they could acknowledge these in relation to others. In time, the failure to find opportunities for these grief efforts impairs the survivors' ability to cope with the recent as well as future bereavement. Every survivor needs opportunities to deal with his personal reactions to any death. The closer the relation, the greater the needs, and the greater the necessity of providing opportunities to talk about death, before, during, and long after termination. (Cutter 1974, 128)

The emphasis on expressivity meshes nicely with the movement's utilization of "talk" (see above) as reform activity. It is important to stress, however, that expressivity calls not simply for talk but for *talk about one's varying emotional states, which talk "authentically" expresses those states*. Talk which is "mere" intellectualizing is proscribed. Expressivity demands, rather, a good deal of emotional temperature-taking and considerable concern for the genuineness of one's emotion. It is acceptable to feel very little, for example, only if this isn't "masking" some other denied feeling state. In sum, for the constructors of happy death movement ideology, the scenes of death and dying are more appropriately written by Eugene O'Neill than by Noël Coward.

Notes

1. See, for example, Back (1972); Fair (1974).

2. The extract from Kerr is from the written version (available for purchase from him) of the account of his son's death which he presented *orally* at a number of death and dying conferences and symposia.

See also on newspaper accounts of Kübler-Ross' "testimony": "Understanding death: the final stage of human growth," *Sacramento Union* (May 27, 1975); "Psychiatrist sees afterlife," *Sacramento Bee* (September 20, 1975); "Expert on death, the dying, is not turned off on life," *Sacramento Bee* (November 4, 1975). For additional accounts, see Gildea (1977); Balfour (1976); Woodward (1976); Hoover (1977a, 1977b); Panati (1976); Moody (1975); Kron (1976/1977); "Life after death experiences cited," *Sacramento Union* (August 2, 1977).

Unquestionably, from the late sixties to the late seventies, Kübler-Ross served as a patron saint for important segments of the movement. She was "canonized" repeatedly at death and dying conferences—her name spoken in "hushed" and respectful tones. Some flavor of this sacred esteem is found in the following extract from a discussion of Kübler-Ross published in the *San Diego Reader* in 1978.

> Behind all the sociological terminology, behind the systematization of the stages of dying, behind the anecdotes and the moral advice [in her written work] there are the same age-old truths that in an earlier age were expressed by Saint Benedict or Guantama Buddha and by the institutions they helped to found.
>
> Dr. Kübler-Ross fits this role perfectly. Her modest demeanor, her quiet humor, her staunchness, her cheerfulness, her mixture of compassion and certainty, of gentleness and toughness, of delicate little body and tremendous moral strength: these are the characteristics of the nuns who work in hospitals, or among the extreme poor, or with the incurably ill. They are the recognizable characteristics of a certain kind of saint—in this case a thoroughly secular saint, let it be said. Dr. Kübler-Ross brings us the inescapable religious message, shorn of religion; and if *The Shadow Box* [a play about dying] does no more than make us turn to her writings and to her millennial wisdom, it will have served an invaluable function, whatever its artistic merits may be. (Saville 1978)

3. I do not mean to suggest that this emerging ideological component has gone unchallenged. More traditional thanatology scholars have reacted with something less than enthusiasm. As Joan Kron, a senior editor for *New York* and a seasoned observer of the movement has written:

> Members of the thanatology community (who study death), however, had fits. After working for years to convince skeptics that the psychology of death and dying was a worthy subject for scientific study, one of their own members, Kübler-Ross (who was already getting flak from her colleagues for her stages-of-dying theory), was now steering thanatology into spiritualist waters. "I admire Elisabeth tremendously," said one colleague, "but I don't believe in mixing one's religious beliefs with science." "I have left instructions," said another, "not to let that woman within a mile of my deathbed."
>
> But most of the critical blasts are aimed at the 32-year-old Moody, a psychiatry resident, now on leave from the University of Virginia to write a sequel to his best-seller (*Life After Life,* 1975). "As anecdotes, I'd give the book B-minus," says University of California professor of thanatology and suicide expert, Dr. Edwin Shneidman, "and as research, I'd give it D-minus." (Kron 1976/1977, 71)

It is interesting to note also that Kübler-Ross has moved increasingly in the direction of mysticism. She does not report receiving messages from the deity, but she is hearing from spirits. (See, for example, Hoover 1977a). In the late seventies it remains unclear whether her exalted standing among movement participants will be sufficient for her to carry significant numbers of them with her into mysticism.

4. The seminar was sponsored by Reminding ("an organization which designs and coordinates seminars, workshops and conferences led by distinguished individuals in the humanities and sciences"), in cooperation with Dominican College, San Rafael, California and was held on the Dominican College campus, March 12–13, 1977, as part of the 1977 Dominican Series of Seminars. Dominican College was also the locale of a lecture by Dr. Cicely Saunders, on "The Philosophy of Hospice Care," sponsored by Hospice of Marin, August 26, 1977; and of a conference on "The How To of Hospice Care" in May of that year.

5. One could also, of course, argue the obverse. The justification for my suggestion is primarily rhetorical rather than empirical.

6. The literature which might be viewed as supporting this assertion is considerable. See, for example, Hofstadter (1955); Rieff (1966); Halmos (1966); Schneider and Dornbusch (1958); Fair (1974); Meyer (1965); Back (1972); Sennott and Travisano (1976); Wolfe (1976); Noyes (1876); Treffert (1974).

References

Ariès, Philippe. 1974. The reversal of death: Changes in attitudes toward death in Western societies. In *Death in America*, ed. David E. Stannard. Philadelphia: University of Pennsylvania Press, 134–158.

Back, Kurt W. 1972. *Beyond words: The story of sensitivity training and the encounter movement.* New York: Russell Sage Foundation.

Balfour, Malcolm. 1976. Trappist monk describes his ecstatic experience of life after death. *National Enquirer,* 19 November.

Blumer, Herbert. 1971. Social problems as collective behavior. *Social Problems,* Winter, 298–306.

Cutter, Fred. 1974. *Coming to terms with death.* Chicago: Nelson-Hall.

Donaldson, Peter J. 1972. Denying death: A note regarding some ambiguities in the current discussion. *Omega,* November, 285–290.

Dumont, Richard G., and Dennis C. Foss. 1972. *The American view of death: Acceptance or denial?* Cambridge, Mass.: Schenkman.

Fair, Charles. 1974. *The new nonsense.* New York: Simon & Schuster.

Gerlach, Luther P., and Virginia H. Hine. 1970. *People, power and change: Movements of social transformation.* Indianapolis: Bobbs-Merrill.

Gildea, William. 1977. Life . . . after death. *Sacramento Bee,* 27 June.

Goode, William J. 1970. *World revolution and family patterns.* New York: Free Press.

Gordon, David Cole. 1970. *Overcoming the fear of death.* New York: Macmillan.

Halmos, Paul. 1966. *The faith of the counsellors.* New York: Schocken.

Hofstadter, Richard. 1955. *The age of reform.* New York: Vintage Books.

Hoover, Eleanor Links. 1977a. Mystical portents. *Human Behavior,* March, 14.

———. 1977b. Charting life after death. *Human Behavior* April, 9.

Imara, Mwalimu. 1975. Dying as the last stage of growth. In *Death: The final stage of growth,* ed. Elisabeth Kübler-Ross. Englewood Cliffs, N.J.: Prentice-Hall.

Kavanaugh, Robert E. 1972. *Facing death.* New York: Penguin.

Keleman, Stanley. 1974. *Living your dying.* New York: Random House.

Kerr, Keith W. 1974. Death and grief counseling. Paper presented in part at "Alternative Death Systems in America" Conference, University of California, Berkeley, 21–23 February 1975. Earlier version published in *The Marriage and Family Counselors Quarterly,* Winter 1972.

Koestenbaum, Peter. 1976. *Is there no answer to death?* Englewood Cliffs, N.J.: Prentice-Hall.

Kron, Joan. 1976/77. The out-of-body trip: What a way to go! *New York*, 27 December/3 January, 66–72.

———. 1976. Designing a better place to die. *New York*, 1 March, 43–49.

———. 1975. The good news about the bad news. *New York*, 21 July, 38–40.

Kübler-Ross, Elisabeth, ed. 1975. *Death: The final stage of growth*. Englewood Cliffs, N.J.: Prentice-Hall.

———. 1969. *On death and dying*. New York: Macmillan.

McCoy, Marjorie C. 1974. *To die with style!* Nashville, Tenn.: Abingdon Press.

Meyer, Donald. 1965. *The positive thinkers*. New York: Doubleday.

Moody, Raymond A. 1975. *Life after life*. Simons Island, Ga.: Mockingbird Books.

Nichols, Roy, and Jane Nichols. 1975. Funerals: A time for grief and growth. In *Death: The final stage of growth*, ed. Elisabeth Kübler-Ross. Englewood Cliffs, N.J.: Prentice-Hall, 87–96.

Noyes, John Humphrey. 1876. *Mutual criticism*. Oneida, N.Y.: Office of the American Socialist in Oneida.

Panati, Charles. 1976. Is there life after death? *Family Circle*, November, 78, 84, and 90.

Rieff, Philip. 1966. *The triumph of the therapeutic*. New York: Harper & Row.

Saville, Jonathan. 1978. Death mask. *San Diego Reader*, 13–19 April.

Schneider, L., and S. Dornbusch. 1958. *Popular religion: Inspirational books in America*. Chicago: University of Chicago Press.

Sennott, Roger S., and Richard V. Travisano. 1976. Puritanism and rationality: The socially impossible consciousness. Paper presented at the meetings of the Society for the Study of Symbolic Interaction, New York, 31 August.

Treffert, Darold A. 1974. Why Amy didn't live happily ever after. *Prism*, November.

Turner, Ralph H., and Lewis M. Killian. 1972. *Collective behavior*. Englewood Cliffs, N.J.: Prentice-Hall.

Wolfe, Tom. 1976. The me decade and the third great awakening. *New West*, 30 August, 27–48.

Woodward, Kenneth L. 1976. Life after death. *Newsweek*, 12 July, 41.

structured exercises

Before beginning these exercises, please read "Note to the Instructor" on page xxi.

1. *Coat of Arms*. The discussion of death is closely tied to values in life. This exercise is meant to help students examine what values they hold in life. Have each student draw the outline of a large shield or "coat of arms" on a sheet of paper and divide it into six fields. In each field, have students draw a picture to represent the answer to each of the following questions:

   a. If you were to die right now, what do you think your friends would miss most about you? Draw a picture to show what they might miss.
   b. Think of something about which you feel very strongly, something for which you would be willing to give your life. Draw it.
   c. What was the closest you ever came to losing your life? Draw a picture to represent that event.
   d. Think of someone who was close to you who died. Draw a picture to show what you miss most about that person.
   e. What are you doing to help yourself live a long, healthy life? Illustrate this on your coat of arms.
   f. Imagine that you have one year left to live. Draw something to represent what you would do in that year, what kind of activity you would pursue.

   After completing their drawings, have students discuss their choices with each other in pairs. Then have the pairs return to the large group for a summary of similarities and differences. Finally, have the group as a whole consider the implications of the range of values represented.

2. *Kidney Machine Decision*. Although the competition for dialysis units that originally prompted the following exercise no longer exists, the dilemma forced by competing priorities continues in other instances, as for example the competition for organ transplants. To help the class experience how their own attitudes, values, and past experiences with death would influence their decision making, the class can be divided into groups of five to seven. Copies of the *Kidney Machine Description Sheet* and the *Kidney*

Machine Biographical Sheet can be distributed to each group. Additional information, the *Kidney Machine Psychological Reports Sheet,* is included in Appendix A-1. Its use is optional. If it is to be used in this exercise, the student should not turn to the additional material until the middle of the decision-making process. The groups will need time to read through the materials and about 30 minutes to arrive at a solution. Each group can list the criteria the participants used in decision making. At the end of the allotted time, the groups can evaluate their work in terms of the following:

a. Whom did you choose? Why?
b. Did you feel you had enough information about each candidate to make a decision?
c. What effect did the psychological data have on your decision?
d. To what extent were you motivated to *avoid* making a decision, (e.g., leaving the decision to chance in some way)?
e. Were any novel or unusual solutions proposed?
f. To what extent did your group try to "objectify" the decision, i.e., by rating candidates or devising a formula? Were such efforts helpful?

The decisions of all the groups can then be shared for a discussion of criteria. If time allows, the class can then discuss what factors in subjects' profiles would change their decisions.

Kidney Machine Description Sheet*

Located at Swedish Hospital in Seattle, Washington, is the famous kidney machine. A marvel of technological ingenuity, it is the only hope of life for people with a rare kidney disease.

In actuality, the machine functions as a kidney for people who have lost the use of their own. By connecting themselves to the machine for twenty-four hours each week, people with renal failure can remain alive indefinitely—or until they are killed by some other ailment not connected with their kidneys.

There are several problems associated with using this machine, for there are many more people who need it than there is time available on the machine. In fact, only about five people can be placed on it at any one time. Doctors examine all potential patients and determine those who could profit most from connection to the machine. They screen out those with other diseases, for whom the machine would be only a temporary expedient, and they turn their list of recommended patients over to the hospital administration. At present, the doctors have submitted the names of five persons for *one* place on the machine.

The committee assembled to make the decision has been given a brief biography of each person appearing on the list. It is assumed that each person has an equal chance of remaining alive if allowed to use the machine. Thus, the committee is asked to decide which *one* of these may have access to the machine.

Source: © Gerald M. Phillips. "Kidney Machine." 1974 *Annual Handbook for Group Facilitators.* Edited by J. William Pfeiffer and John E. Jones. La Jolla, California. University Associates Publishers, Inc., 1974, 78–83. Used by permission of Gerald M. Phillips.

You are asked to act as if you were a member of this committee. Remember, there is only one vacancy, and you must fill it with one of these five people. You must agree, *unanimously*, on the single person who is permitted to remain alive, and you must decide your own criteria for making this choice.

The only medical information you have is that people over forty seem to do more poorly on the machine than those under forty (although they do not necessarily find it useless). It is up to you.

Kidney Machine Biographical Sheet

Alfred: White, male, American, age 42. Married for 21 years. Two children (boy 18, girl 15), both high school students. Research physicist at University medical school, working on cancer immunization project. Current publications indicate that he is on the verge of a significant medical discovery.

On the health service staff of local university, member of county medical society, member of Rotary International, and Boy Scout leader for 10 years.

Bill: Black, male, American, age 27. Married for five years. One child (girl 3), wife six months pregnant. Currently employed as an auto mechanic in local car dealership.

Attending night school and taking courses in automatic-transmission rebuilding. No community service activities listed. Plans to open auto-transmission repair shop upon completion of trade school course.

Cora: White, female, American, age 30. Married for eleven years. Five children (boy 10, boy 8, girl 7, girl 5, girl 4 months). Husband self-employed (owns and operates tavern and short-order restaurant). High school graduate. Never employed.

Couple has just purchased home in local suburbs, and Cora is planning the interior to determine whether she has the talent to return to school for courses in interior decoration. Member of several religious organizations.

David: White, male, American, age 19. Single, but recently announced engagement and plans to marry this summer. Presently a sophomore at large eastern university, majoring in philosophy and literature. Eventually hopes to earn Ph.D. and become a college professor.

Member of several campus political organizations, an outspoken critic of the college "administration," was once suspended briefly for "agitation." Has had poetry published in various literary magazines around the New York area. Father is self-employed (owns men's haberdashery store), mother is deceased. Has two younger sisters (15, 11).

Edna: White, female, American, age 34. Single, presently employed as an executive secretary in large manufacturing company, where she has worked since graduation from business college. Member of local choral society; was alto soloist in Christmas production of Handel's *Messiah*. Has been very active in several church and charitable groups.

questions

1. Define the following terms and give examples of each where appropriate. Terms marked with an asterisk are psychological, sociological, or medical terms that the authors of the selections expect readers to know. If you are not familiar with the meanings of those terms, consult the appropriate dictionary.

Schulz

*test validation
death anxiety
denial
*operational definition
*correlation
*projective test
*demographic variable

Parsons and Lidz

germ plasm
somatoplasm
constitutive symbolism
premature death
adventitious aspects of death
natural death
instrumental activism

Ariès

Artes Moriendi
nuntius mortis
acceptable style of dying

Ariès (continued)

*iconography
ritualization of mourning
Romanticism
Age of Enlightenment
necropolis

Gerbner

selective invention
fictive invention
symbolic structure of death
social typing
social control
risk ratio

Lofland

ideology
social movement
craft of dying
enemy evocation
Happy Death Movement
immortality
positivity
expressivity

83

2. Schulz supports the widely held belief that death anxiety is, on occasion, constructive in that it may serve as inspiration for great individual achievements. Drawing from literature, philosophy, music, art, and film, suggest works that might be offered as evidence of this theory.

3. What are the functional applications of the ability to measure death anxiety? In what groups might it be particularly interesting to study levels of death anxiety? In what situations would you expect differences in levels of death anxiety to influence behavior?

4. The ability to "make sense of" death depends in large measure on the degree to which we find it appropriate. (Parsons and Lidz suggest death at the end of a complete life cycle as one way.) The following statements suggest different ways of justifying death. What factors make death acceptable to the speakers? Compare each attitude to your own idea of appropriate death.

    a. Mother, 42, speaking of her son who died suddenly at age 19 as a result of a previously undetected congenital heart defect:
       "He died at the right time. He had decided on his major, made the track team, and had just fallen in love. Life had never been better for him. He seemed to have found himself. In another year, things might have fallen apart."
    b. Woman, 55, at a study group discussion of funeral practices:
       "My family will not have to fight about my funeral. I have worked hard and I have got it all paid for. I have always made do with second best, but this I am going to do right."
    c. Male student, 28, in a seminar on death and dying:
       "What's all this talk about appropriate death? If I have lived my life well, why should the circumstances of my death matter to me?"

5. In his reference to wills, Ariès uses changes in social customs as an indicator of attitudinal shifts. What other long-established social customs might be studied as indicators of such change?

6. Ariès describes the moral obligations of the *nuntius mortis* and notes that the role of the dying person has undergone a reversal with respect to the management of death. Yet many contemporary writers would claim a subsequent shift. Would you want to be informed of your own death? Why or why not? If so, by whom?

7. Gerbner asserts that the portrayal of violent death in television drama contributes to the "irrational dread of dying." What meanings of death do television newscasts construct? What effect might this have?

8. a. Ariès develops a specialized notion of "acceptable death." What are its characteristics, and how does it differ from the concept of "appropriate death" that Parsons and Lidz propose?
    b. What examples of Lofland's three components of the "craft of dying" can you find in the papers by Ariès and by Parsons and Lidz?

9. a. Both Ariès and Lofland present exaggerated views of "acceptable ways" in which a dying person is expected to behave. Describe positive models of the dying person in your own experience. What qualities, reactions, or behaviors were responsible for your choice?

   b. How does the death of Parker Adderson differ from his model of an appropriate death? Outline the disparity between the expectation and the outcome for General Clavering.

projects for further study

1. Violent death and terminal illness have become popular subjects for movies and television. Watch three different medical series on television during a one-week period and observe the portrayal of death and its effects on the participants: patient, family, nurse, and doctor. Profile the dying patient in terms of age, sex, occupation, personal and social attractiveness, and social status. What is the cause of death? Where does the patient die? Note the attitudes of each person toward death. Based upon your analysis, what do you feel television presents as appropriate death? As inappropriate death?

2. Cultural attitudes determine what one does to "put his (or her) house in order" before death. Our society has very different expectations, for instance, from a community in medieval times or more recent Eskimo culture. Research the types of arrangements that are expected and available in our society. Include psychological, financial, legal, and religious factors in your research.

3. Debate the following proposition: The more acceptable that death is in itself, the less worth will be ascribed to the dying life.

4. Coining the phrase "happy death movement," Lofland uses humorous exaggeration to provide analytic distance from a difficult subject. Collect similar instances of humor in jokes and cartoons. What themes are represented in your collection? What functions does humor serve in expressing these themes?

5. Read *The Loved One* by Evelyn Waugh and develop a summary of the ways in which the society presented there "attenuates the tragic sense of death." Based on your own experiences of the handling of death, identify points of similarity and dissimilarity with the world of *The Loved One*.

for further reading

Ariès, P. 1981. *At the hour of our death*. New York: Alfred A. Knopf.

Becker, E. 1973. *The denial of death*. New York: Free Press.

Charmaz, K. 1980. *The social reality of death*. Reading, Mass: Addison-Wesley.

Choron, J. 1963. *Death and Western thought*. New York: Collier Books.

Feifel, H., ed. 1977. *New meanings of death*. New York: McGraw-Hill.

Fulton, R., ed. 1976. *Death and identity*. Rev. ed. Bowie, Md.: Charles Press.

Kalish, R. A., and D. K. Reynolds. 1976. *Death and ethnicity: A psychocultural study*. Los Angeles: University of Southern California Press.

Kastenbaum, R. 1977. *Death, society, and human experience*. St. Louis: C. V. Mosby

Kastenbaum, R., and P. T. Costa, Jr. 1978. Psychological perspectives on death. *Annual Review of Psychology,* 28:225–249.

Shneidman, E. S. 1973. *Deaths of man*. New York: Quadrangle.

Stannard, D. S., ed. 1975. *Death in America*. Philadelphia: University of Pennsylvania Press

Toynbee, A., ed. 1969. *Man's concern with death*. New York: McGraw-Hill.

Vernon, G. N. 1970. *Sociology of death: An analysis of death-related behavior*. New York: Ronald Press.

Whaley, J., ed. 1982. *Mirrors of mortality: Studies in the social history of death*. New York: St. Martin's Press.

CHAPTER | *two*

*The Experience
of Dying*

The person who is dying passes through a social transition from being alive to being dead. Yet all too often, upon entering that transition, the dying person is treated as if he or she were already dead: left alone and forced to conspire in the fiction that "nothing is wrong." More and more, we are coming to recognize that the interval of dying can be a time for the resolution of conflicts, achievement of personal closure, and even a time for continued psychological growth. But if a person is to make his or her dying a time for growth, he or she must be informed and allowed to assume a more active role than has been customary in recent times.

Early Voices

When social scientists began the study of death, they did so "at a distance," focusing more on organizational structures in the hospital than on the individual dying patient. Humanists like physician Sir William Osler, at the beginning of this century, and, more recently, psychotherapists like Kurt Eissler and Lawrence and Eda LeShan recognized the needs of the dying and urged their peers in medicine, psychiatry, and psychology to remain with dying patients even when nothing more than palliative care was possible. But the advice of those perceptive individuals was directed to a professional audience that was limited and often skeptical about the patient's willingness or ability to confront death.

Dialogue with the Terminally Ill

When Elisabeth Kübler-Ross first attempted to involve terminally ill patients in a seminar for hospital staff in 1965, she repeatedly heard, "We have no dying patients." Yet, once encouraged to discuss their feelings about impending death, many patients were grateful for the opportunity, speaking honestly and freely. Faced with the openness of the patients, the hospital staff realized that they would have to confront their own feelings about death and dying before they could face death directly with their patients. The resulting demand for seminars, classes, and special training has moved thanatology, the study of death, into the health curriculum. Significant changes in health care have taken place both within hospitals and in alternative social structures like hospice programs.

Popular Response

The public interest in studies of the terminally ill has been so great that shortly after the publication of *On Death and Dying* (1969), Kübler-Ross came to be regarded as a spokesperson for the "death and dying movement." Her work created a widened audience for the earlier research that had seldom been noticed beyond professional circles. The one-time public silence on the subject of death has been shattered. Now the media frequently treat such themes as the unique and complex character of the dying person, the value of the terminal patient's discussing death with his or her family, and the rewards (as well as the costs) of sharing another person's dying.

Dying: Transition vs. Institution

Indeed, the current interest in death and dying is so great as to threaten saturation. Given the machinery to prolong dying and the steadily increasing study of the dying patient, there is a danger that the experience of dying will not only be recognized but also be institutionalized, in much the same way as society has institutionalized death. Dying, like mourning, could become a scripted performance with expected roles. Montaigne warned against such an imbalance: "If we have not known how to live, it is wrong to teach us how to die, and to give the end a different shape from the whole."

Overview of the Chapter

To encounter the personal experience of dying is to give substance to theoretical understanding that would otherwise remain abstract. The Encounter in Chapter Two is a first-person account of a heart attack by a patient confronting complex reactions to impending death. The first reading examines, from the vantage point of clinical experience, the process of facing death through terminal illness. In "The Sequence of Dying," E. Mansell Pattison, a psychiatrist, sets the knowledge of death as a crisis that begins a three-phase "living–dying interval." Sorting out a range of fears evoked by the expectation of death, he frames specific problems that the dying face and identifies ways for the helper to aid in their resolution. As Pattison notes, generalizations can only guide the helper, and so, for contrast, individual statements are presented in the form of two modern poems. In the first poem, "Do Not Go Gentle into That Good Night" by Dylan Thomas, the persona rages against easy acceptance of death. In "I Heard a Fly Buzz When I Died," Emily Dickinson moves to the perspective of the dying person, drawing the reader to the point of death itself. Returning to the vantage point of clinical experience, psychiatrist Elisabeth Kübler-Ross describes her early and influential work on the stage theory of dying. In "What Is It Like to Be Dying?" she sets out to answer the question from the patient's point of view in order to provide better information on which helpers can base their efforts.

Clinical experience, however, is only one ground for understanding, as psychologist Robert Kastenbaum shows in his objective assessment of Kübler-Ross's theory. In "Do We Die in Stages?" he urges expanded research both to validate the stage theory and to identify its limitations. Kastenbaum urges examination of the total context of the dying person's experience. The next two selections draw back to view the interaction between the dying individual and the organizational structure within which the dying occurs. In "Reaction to Extreme Stress: Impending Death by Execution," psychiatrists Harvey Bluestone and Carl McGahee present brief case studies of prisoners condemned to execution. The reactions displayed by individual inmates demonstrate a wide variety of approaches to death. In "Awareness of Dying," sociologists Anselm Strauss and Barney Glaser analyze organizational strategies that hospital personnel use to manage the patient's knowledge of impending death. Strauss and Glaser offer advantages and disadvantages to both patient and staff for each of the awareness contexts they present, and they conclude by urging the benefits of open awareness of death in the hospital structure.

The chapter closes with two pieces that raise the issue of one's knowledge of the temporal approach of death in old age. William Carlos Williams's poem "To Waken an Old Lady" uses delicate but compelling images from nature to move the discussion to a consideration of aging and a consciousness of mortality. In "Age and Awareness of Finitude in Developmental Gerontology," gerontologist Victor Marshall disputes the validity of correlating age with awareness of finitude. Noting that awareness of finitude is held to initiate processes of disengagement, self-focusing, and life review, he links the social reminiscence of aging to social comparison as the aged attempt to uncover and resolve past conflicts.

This essay began by focusing on *dying* as the social transition that takes one from being alive to being dead. However, the readings in the chapter indicate that the living–dying interval is not as clear-cut as it might seem. The limits of the definition are pressed in the following Encounter, in which it becomes clear that a heart attack may result in a rebirth, or the death of a life-style, or physical death, or simply a suspended sentence.

encounter | *Autobiography of a Heart Attack*

The first sign was vomiting and diarrhea, but I didn't know I had a heart attack because the flu was going around. It was about eight on a Saturday morning, and I'd gone downstairs to get myself a cup of coffee. Fran, my wife, was still asleep and when I went back up, I just kept on going and vomiting, but I still didn't think I was having a heart attack. I figured I had just come down with the bug.

But when I got back in bed, I just couldn't get comfortable. I didn't have any pain, but I just felt poor even in bed. Fran said I felt cold and clammy, and I figured I ought to call the paramedics.

They were there in minutes, and after giving me an IV and checking me all over they told me I was in trouble. I knew that already, but they wouldn't tell me what was wrong. They've got to be careful that way. I still didn't think I had a heart attack, but I knew my body was getting ready for some big battle, what with it being cleaned out at both ends.

A lot of people, including me, at least before my heart attack, think that the only signs of a heart attack are chest pains and pains shooting down your arm, but that isn't always true. It depends on what part of your heart is affected. Mine was the left ventricle. Also, a lot of people have "silent attacks." They never feel any symptoms, and after a time they keel over because the heart never had a chance to repair itself.

I was so sedated in the CCU (Coronary Care Unit) that I wasn't apprehensive at all. I remember a few friends and relatives coming by, but I didn't feel I was deathly ill. You know, I was sedated 20 out of the 24.

Source: As told to Dana Prom Smith. Reprinted by permission of Dana Prom Smith, Senior Associate, St. Paul's Foundation.

93   *encounter*
Autobiography
of a Heart Attack

I didn't get anxious until I was out of CCU and in a regular ward with a monitor. The man in the room with me, we got to know each other pretty well, was in bad shape and was being transferred to St. Vincent's for open heart surgery. At that time St. Vincent's was taking all the high risk cases. I called his home the next day, and they told me he died on the table. That kind of got me. I hadn't really thought about dying.

There are three critical stages. If you make it the first twenty-four hours, you're over the first hurdle because you aren't dead. Then you've got to get through the next four or five days. You've got to get enough scarring to stop a blowout because if you blow, you're gone. And then you've got to keep the stress down to let the heart keep on scarring. During this time you begin to walk, but they keep you on Valium. I don't like that stuff because I don't trust drugs.

About this time things start getting grim because you become aware you'll never be the same again.

Some people begin to treat you like an invalid, and then you hear that some of the men at work are saying that "old Charlie isn't ever going to come back." They figure that if you're out for a month, you're out forever. I didn't like that at all. When I got home even some of the women tried to help me down the stairs as if I were a cripple. I didn't like that either.

I never thought I wouldn't make it, though. I don't know why, but I guess it's because I've had a couple of close calls before and squeaked by. You know, when you're in a crisis, that's not the time to give up, it's the time to hold on and keep your head.

A heart attack is hard on your sex life. You just can't get worked up too much if you're worried about your pulse rate and blood pressure, and then the medication depresses your ability and desire. It took a little time to work around that one. I like sex as much as the next man, but I sure didn't want to die for it.

The thing that bothered me the most was the way I had to change my life. Some things turned out for the better, because with better diet and exercise I've had fewer colds and casual illnesses, but the truth is that you never fully recover because you're about ninety percent of what you used to be. Mostly that doesn't bother me because most of us function way below our capacities.

But I can never be more than an hour away from a hospital or doctor. I can't chance accidents like capsizing in a boat because the cold water might be too big a shock for my heart. I can't go hiking in the mountains. You live on the margin.

I guess you're apprehensive as long as you live. I knew I could go back to work, and when I finally put in a full eight-hour day, I felt a lot better. I came home dog-tired, but I knew I'd made it, but still nothing was going to be the same anymore. That damned clot had changed everything.

1. How did the heart attack change life for this speaker? Consider three or four ways in which your own life would change were you to experience a similar attack.

2. Apply the concept of appropriate death to the speaker. Would his death have been appropriate? Inappropriate?

3. Acceptance of death often depends on a person's readiness to begin the grief work before the death occurs, whether it is his own death or that of another person. Based on the account above, what indications of readiness were present before the heart attack? After the heart attack?

E. MANSELL PATTISON

The Sequence of Dying

Even a brush with death, such as the heart attack described in the Encounter, sets up a psychological trajectory for the rest of one's life. In the following article, Pattison separates the process of dying from the fact of death. He identifies the living–dying interval as a psychological crisis period in which unresolved conflicts from one's earlier life are reactivated. He then identifies a "sequence of dying" beginning with an acute crisis phase, moving through a chronic living–dying phase, then ending with a terminal phase. This sequence, Pattison suggests, provides a framework for understanding the specific experience of dying for each individual and suggests new roles for the helper when the goal is no longer to cure.

Death itself is not a problem of life, for death is not amenable to treatment or intervention. We may consider death only as an issue between man and God. But the process of dying is very much a part of a person's life. Advances in medical technology now make it possible to prolong the period of dying, so that dying may stretch over days, weeks, months, and even many years. For perhaps the first time in history, we have many people who experience a new phase of life—*the living–dying interval.*

The human dilemma of this living–dying process was first illuminated for me personally by a letter from a lady unknown to me:

Dear Mr. Pattison: Quite by accident I read your treatise on dying. Because I am so grateful for your guidance I am writing not only to thank you but to suggest that the article be made available to relatives who care for patients . . . My husband has been treated for chronic glomeruli nephritis for nine years. For the past five years, he has had biweekly dialysis, which equates to a living–dying stage of long duration. In these times, when there is no doctor–patient relationship in this type of indirect care, the entire burden of sharing the responsibility of death falls to the member of the family. . . . Your listing of the fears was so apparent when I read your paper, yet when my husband experienced them I was unprepared to see them or even acknowledge them. When a patient is accepted on a kidney program, he knows he is dying. Would it not be a kindness to the person caring for him to know his fears and how to help?

As said so clearly by this wife, the period of living–dying is most important to the patient, family, friends, relatives, and professional staff.

Source: From the book *The Experience of Dying* by E. Mansell Pattison. © 1977 by Prentice-Hall, Inc., Englewood Cliffs, N.J.

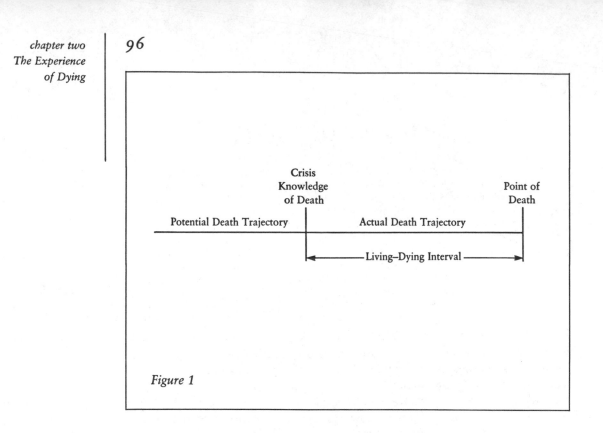

Figure 1

The Living–Dying Interval

All of us live with the potential for death at any moment. All of us project ahead a *trajectory* of our life. That is, we anticipate a certain life span within which we arrange our activities and plan our lives. And then abruptly we may be confronted with a crisis—*the crisis of knowledge of death*. Whether by illness or accident, our potential trajectory is suddenly changed. We find that we shall die in days, weeks, months, or several years. Our life has been foreshortened. Our activities must be rearranged. We cannot plan for the potential, we must deal with the actual. It is then the period between the "crisis knowledge of death" and the "point of death" that is the living–dying interval (see Figure 1).

The period of living–dying can be divided into three clinical phases: (1) the acute crisis phase, (2) the chronic living–dying phase, and (3) the terminal phase. We cannot intervene with the ultimate problem of death. However, we can respond to the acute crisis, so that it does not result in a chaotic disintegration of the person's life during the process of dying. Thus, our first task is to deal appropriately with the crisis of knowledge of death, so that the dying person can move into an appropriate trajectory that integrates his or her dying into his or her life-style and life circumstances. The second task is to respond to

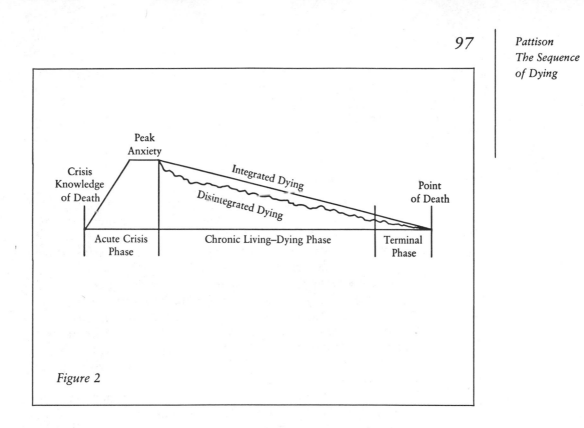

Figure 2

the adaptive issues of the chronic phase. And, finally, the third task is to assist the patient to move ineluctably into the terminal phase when it becomes appropriate. (See Figure 2.)

Dying Trajectories

The phases of dying are related to several different types of trajectories or "death expectations" that are set up by the crisis of knowledge of death. Glaser and Strauss (1965, 1968) suggest four different trajectories: (1) *Certain death at a known time.* In this trajectory it is possible to move rapidly from the acute phase to the chronic phase, because the time frame for resolving dying issues is quite clear. In very rapid trajectories, such as in acute leukemias or accidents, the dying process may remain only within the acute phase. (2) *Certain death at an unknown time.* This is the typical trajectory of chronic fatal illness. Here the problems tend to center on the maintenance of effective living in an ambiguous and uncertain time frame. (3) *Uncertain death but a known time when the question will be resolved.* One example here is the radical surgery, where a successful outcome will be known. Thus, the patient and family must live through a continuing period of acute crisis. On the other hand, there are long-term problems, such as possible arrest of cancer, where ambiguity may remain for years. (4) *Uncertain death and an unknown time when the question will be resolved.* Examples are multiple sclerosis and genetic diseases, which leave the person beset with a life of ambiguity.

The effect of these different trajectories upon the living–dying process will be examined.

Denial and Openness

Before we examine the phases of living–dying, we must clarify our approach to the dying patient. About 10 years ago a common question was: Should we tell the patient or keep it a secret? The question is false. The care of the dying does not revolve around telling or not telling but rather the whole panorama of human interactions that surround the dying person.

Further, there are many levels of communication between people, and many degrees of awareness. For example, the acutely ill patient who is barely conscious should not be subjected to long discussions about the severity of his or her illness. He or she knows that he or she is ill and may well die. Care and comfort are foremost. On the other hand, a patient who is experiencing progressive physical deterioration and is told there is nothing to worry about may say nothing but wonder much.

It is difficult to keep secrets. The problem is when our actions say one thing and our words another. This is what is termed "closed awareness" of dying. You know and I know, but we both know we cannot let each other know. This blockage of communication does nothing but set up trouble for all involved.

The questions a patient has are many. "Am I going to die?" is only the first of many questions that the patient may need to pose and receive specific answers to, not only from the physician but from many people around him or her. To avoid questions about death means that one also must avoid all other questions about his or her life that the patient has. Kalish (1970) has listed a variety of information inputs that come to the patient:

1. Direct statements from the physician.
2. Overheard comments of the physician to others.
3. Direct statements from other personnel, including aides, nurses, technologists.
4. Overheard comments by staff to each other.
5. Direct statements from family, friends, clergy, lawyer.
6. Changes in the behavior of others toward the patient.
7. Changes in the medical care routines, procedures, medications.
8. Changes in physical location.
9. Self-diagnosis, including reading of medical books, records, and charts.
10. Signals from the body and changes in physical status.
11. Altered responses by others toward the future.

It is evident that the dying person is engaged in multiple communications with many people. If the messages are congruent, the dying person can make sense out of the experience. But if the messages are confused, ambiguous, contradictory, the result is needless apprehension, anxiety, and the blockage of appropriate actions on the part of both the dying person and those around him or her.

On some fronts we have seen a frontal attack on denial, as if it were a terrible pathology. As a result we sometimes see brutal, blunt, and tactless confrontations in the name of openness.

What do we mean by denial? I suggest four levels of denial. The first is *existential denial,* the fundamental approach to mortality and place of death in one's life. We engage in degrees of existential denial as a necessary mechanism for existence. Second is *psychological denial,* an unconscious defense mechanism by which we repress that which is known. Both hospital staff and patients use denial mechanisms rather frequently. It is doubtful that we could eradicate denial mechanisms, and they often fulfill useful purposes. It is only when denial is pervasive, and the sole or predominant defense, that it becomes a major problem. Third is *nonattention denial.* We engage our attention elsewhere, and for the moment we are unaware of the undesirable.

We should not expect that at all times we always look at ourselves in the stark cold light of reality. There is an interplay of levels of denial and levels of awareness. Human communication is full of nuances. Thus, it seems absurd to expect that suddenly when it comes to discussions with the dying, all of our patterns of human communication should change. If we are able to talk with people about their lives in many ways that are comfortable and acceptable to both of us, then we should be able to talk about dying in many ways that are acceptable and comfortable. Thus, I am not concerned with the issue of how much denial or openness there is. But I am concerned that there be *opportunity, availability,* and *possibility* for open communication with the dying.

The Acute Phase

The crisis of knowledge of death can be seen as a crisis in the life of the person. During the period of acute crisis, there is an increasing anxiety that will reach a peak of tolerance. No one can continue to function long at peak anxiety, and, therefore, the patient will call upon whatever psychological mechanisms are available to reduce the anxiety. If ineffective mechanisms are used, a disintegrative dying style will follow.

The knowledge of death as a crisis event can be analyzed in terms of five aspects of crisis (Parad 1965):

1. This stressful event poses a problem that by definition is insolvable in the immediate future. In this sense, dying is the most stressful crisis because it is a crisis to which we bow but do not solve.

2. The problem taxes one's psychological resources since it is beyond one's traditional problem-solving methods. One is faced with a new experience with no prior experience to fall back on, for although one has lived amidst death, that is far different from one's own death.

3. The situation is perceived as a threat or danger to the life goals of the person. Dying interrupts a person in the midst of life, and even in old age it abruptly confronts one with the goals one set in life.

4. The crisis period is characterized by a tension that mounts to a peak, then falls. As one faces the crisis of death knowledge, there is mobilization of either integrative or disintegrative mechanisms. The peak of anxiety usually occurs considerably before death.

5. The crisis situation awakens unresolved key problems from both the near and distant past. Problems of dependency, passivity, narcissism, identity, and more may be activated during the dying process. Hence, one is faced not only with the immediate dying process but also the unresolved feelings from one's own lifetime and its inevitable conflicts.

The first response to this state may be one of immobilization. It is as if life is standing still. One's life flashes before one. There may be no panic, no anxiety, no trace of despair, no pain, but rather an altered state of consciousness. Noyes and Kletti (1976) term this a "depersonalization" phenomenon—"This is not really happening to me, I'm just watching."

Then may come an overwhelming, insuperable feeling of inadequacy—a potential dissolution of the self. There is bewilderment, confusion, indefinable anxiety, and unspecified fear (Montefiore 1973). There is seemingly no answer, and the anxiety makes it difficult to look at what needs to be done.

As part of this process in the acute phase, we may see many pathologically appearing defenses, such as Kübler-Ross (1970) describes as the stages of denial, anger, and bargaining. Yet Kübler-Ross described patients mostly seen in the hospital in the acute phase, where we might expect to see initial mobilization of pathological defenses.

We should not be surprised to see many pathological defenses in this acute stage, nor perhaps react too vigorously to them. For if we focus on the reduction of anxiety through a focus on reality issues and appropriate emotional support, it is likely that the dying person will move on toward appropriate emotional responses to his or her living–dying.

The Chronic Living–Dying Phase

During the chronic phase the dying patient faces a number of fears. It is important at this time to specify the precise issues the dying person faces so that he or she can resolve each specific issue in an appropriate manner. One cannot deal with all issues of dying simultaneously. Rather, our task is to separate each issue, take one at a time as it occurs. Then the dying person can resolve the issues of dying in a rewarding fashion that enhances self-esteem, dignity, and integrity. The dying person can take pride then in having faced his or her crisis of dying with hope and courage, and come away having dealt successfully with his or her dying. One might call this "healthy dying."

Now let us consider the specific fears of the living–dying interval.

Fear of the Unknown

The initial phase of crisis may involve a bewildering array of concerns. However, as the dying person looks forward on his or her dying trajectory, he or she may fear the fact that he or she does not know what lies ahead. It is important to separate those things that can be known from those for which there is no answer. Diggory and Rothman (1961) suggest the following fears of the unknown:

1. What life experiences will I not be able to have?
2. What is my fate in the hereafter?
3. What will happen to my body after death?
4. What will happen to my survivors?
5. How will my family and friends respond to my dying?
6. What will happen to my life plans and projects?
7. What changes will occur in my body?
8. What will be my emotional reactions?

It is evident that some of the above questions can be answered rather well immediately, some answers will be found in the process of time, and some cannot be answered. The issue is summed up rather well in the ancient prayer of serenity: "Grant me the courage to accept the things I cannot change, the strength to change the things I can, and the wisdom to know the difference."

Fear of Loneliness

When one is sick, there is a sense of isolation from oneself and from others. This is reinforced by the fact that others tend naturally to avoid a sick person and leave him or her alone.

This mutual process of withdrawal is even more evident when a person is dying. The isolation attendant to dying is not only a psychological phenomenon but is also a reflection of our social management of dying. No longer does our culture afford us the luxury of dying amidst our family, friends, and belongings, for over 60 percent of deaths now occur in impersonal, isolated hospital rooms. We have given medicine and hospitals the social responsibility of caring for the dying, yet the hospital is not geared to care for the dying (Krant 1974).

There have been many critiques of the depersonalized and mechanized care of the dying in general hospitals. Yet our criticism of hospitals and their staff may be misplaced. Most hospitals are socially constructed to provide acute remedial care. To then ask the same social institution to provide chronic supportive care is to place the hospital staff in a double bind. Which priorities do they respond to? In fact, recent studies show that hospital staff do not necessarily ignore dying patients, but that they give priority to patients for whom they can provide life-saving measures. This is not unreasonable.

The dilemma is that acute care hospitals are not well equipped to care for the dying. As a result, the dying are isolated, ignored, and left with little human contact, although perhaps given good technical care. The solution, to my mind, does not lie in depreciation of acute care hospital staff, but rather in the provision of chronic care facilities that are devoted to the appropriate care of the dying. An example is St. Christopher's Hospice in London, directed by Cicely Saunders, which is a hospital for the dying.

The acute care hospital is necessarily geared toward *curative* functions; the dying require *caring* functions. Oliver Wendell Holmes stated the difference well: "Our task is to cure rarely, relieve sometimes, and comfort always."

The fear of loneliness is perhaps sensed by the dying from the beginning. The necessary withdrawal from work or recreational activities may begin to accentuate the loss of everyday contacts. It may become difficult to maintain social relations. The dying person may not know what to say to others, and others don't know what to say in return. This social awkwardness is revealed in the autobiography of a dying woman (Kelly 1970). An insurance salesman came to the door. When asked if she was interested in life insurance, she replied: "Yes, I'm dying and need the insurance right away!"

Increasing physical debilitation and confinement to bed further may limit social contacts with family and friends. Hospitalization may do so even more. In the hospital the dying person may be placed in a private room, which isolates him or her to a greater degree. Where only supportive technical care is provided, the dying person may be left essentially alone most of the time.

The impact of this social isolation is a sense of human deprivation. As shown in many experiments of sensory deprivation, the human deprived of contact with other humans quickly disintegrates and loses a sense of ego integrity. For the human who is dying, human isolation and deprivation sets the stage for what may be termed "anaclitic depression." This depression is not due to loss but to *separation*—the sense of being away from those we love and depend upon (Schoenberg et al. 1970).

Without human interaction the dying person is vulnerable to the confusional syndrome of human deprivation that we call *loneliness*. It is one thing to choose to be alone at times—as we all desire—it is another to be left alone. It seems that the fear of loneliness is paramount when the person first faces the prospect of death and fears that he or she will be deserted in dying.

Fear of Sorrow

We do not like to face situations of grief and sorrow; if possible we would like to avoid them. Yet the dying person is faced with many losses, which he or she may fear to face. "Can I stand thinking about what I am losing?" There is the fear that one cannot tolerate the painful experience of sorrow. There is the loss of job, of future plans, of strength and ability, of the ongoing pleasure of relationships and activities (Fulton and Fulton 1971).

The task that faces the dying person may seem formidable. Yet not all of these losses are likely to occur simultaneously; some joys and pleasures may be taken from some aspects of life during the living–dying interval. This requires that we help the dying person to avoid *premature* sorrow that cuts the person off from available satisfactions (Aldrich 1963).

On the other hand, it is also necessary to help the dying person engage in *anticipatory grief.* That is, to handle each episode of grief as it occurs, so that one can work through the grief and set it aside. Thus, one is not beset by constant grief and sorrow but may have interludes of satisfaction and accomplishment. One may grieve over that given up, but then proceed to engage in what is present in life now (Schoenberg et al. 1970, 1974).

Fear of Loss of Family and Friends

The process of dying confronts the person with the reality of losing one's family and friends through one's death, just as much as if they were dying. This is a real loss to be mourned and worked through (Glaser and Strauss 1965). Rather than denying this real separation and preventing the grief work, it is possible for both the person and his or her family to engage in anticipatory grief work. The completion of such grief work may allow the person and the family to work through the emotions of separation and part in peace (Gordon and Kutner 1965; Vollman et al. 1971).

The grief of separation before death is akin to the Eskimo custom of having a ritual feast of separation before the old person steps onto an ice floe, waves goodbye, and drifts off into the sea. Similarly, in the Auca tribe of South America, after a farewell ceremony, the old person leaves the village and climbs into a hammock to lie alone until death.

Failure to recognize this real loss ahead of time may block the normal and healthy process of grief. This makes it difficult for the dying person to distinguish between his or her own problem of death and the problem of grief and separation from those he or she is leaving. Thus, the grief of separation should be accomplished *before* death.

Fear of Loss of Body

Our bodies are not just appendages but a vital part of our self-concept. When illness distorts our bodies, there is not only physical loss but a loss of self-image and self-integrity (Szasz 1957). This narcissistic blow to the integrity of self may result in shame, feelings of disgrace and inadequacy, and loss of self-esteem. As before, we may help the dying person to grieve these losses of body without incurring a loss of integrity or esteem.

Since we humans do not tolerate ambiguity well, it is more difficult to tolerate ambiguous distortions of the body. External disfiguring disease may be more acceptable because one can see what is wrong, whereas an internal silent process, such as a failing heart or brain, may be more dismaying.

On the other hand, external disfigurement may provoke a sense of being ugly and unacceptable. The dying person may despise his or her distorted body image and may feel like rejecting his or her ugly body. Then the dying person may try to hide his or her unlovely self from loved ones, for fear that the family will also despise the ugly body, reject him or her, and leave him or her alone.

Fear of Loss of Self-Control

As debilitating disease progresses, one is less capable of self-control. There is less energy, less vitality, less strength, less responsiveness. These all are part of one organism. We think less quickly, less accurately, and we may fear this loss of body and mind.

This problem is particularly acute in our society, which has placed strong emphasis on self-control, self-determination, and rationality. As a result, most people in our culture become anxious and feel threatened by experiential states that pose loss of control or obtundation (dulling) of consciousness. This is reflected in our cultural ambivalence over the use of psychedelic drugs and alcohol, which produce diminished states of self-control and altered states of consciousness. In contrast to Eastern mystical experiential states that many participate in, it is unusual in Western culture to experience any acceptable loss of self-control. Even alcoholic "highs" are viewed with ambivalence. Thus, we come ill-prepared to times of life when we must give up some degrees of control over ourselves (Tart 1969).

When we come to the experience of dying, the loss of control over body and mind, with a diminished sense of consciousness, may then create anxiety and fear about the integrity of ourselves. One is placed in a position of dependency and inadequacy so that in a sense the ego is no longer master of its fate nor captain of the self.

Therefore, it is important to encourage and allow the dying person to retain whatever authority he or she can, to sustain him or her in retaining control of daily tasks and decisions, avoiding shaming for failure of control, and help the person to find rewarding experience in the self-determination yet available.

Fear of Suffering and Pain

Our social and cultural experiences precondition us in our response to pain. Some ethnic groups are pain accentuators; others are pain minimizers (Petrie 1967). But, more importantly, we learn the *meaning* to give to pain. Thus, pain is not the issue per se but our response to pain makes it either *sufferable* or *suffering*.

A certain level of awareness of one's body and one's consciousness is necessary to engage in the experience of suffering. Suffering does not occur when we are unaware. This self-awareness may either diminish or exacerbate pain and transform it into suffering (Shontz and Fink 1959).

We may deal with the problem of pain by using medical means of pain relief and thus diminish suffering. This is all to the good, and those who say that pain is not a problem have likely not felt much pain nor had to live with it.

But the mere diminution of pain does not eradicate suffering, nor is oblivion the answer.

Another alternative is to diminish suffering through awareness and understanding. David Bakan (1968) suggests that a humanistic approach to pain and suffering lies in our understanding of and awareness of pain. The patient who fears pain is more likely expressing a fear of suffering. And what is suffering? It is pain that has no meaning, no location, no explanation. Clinically, studies of pain in the dying bear this out: pain relief is not closely related to the dosage of pain-killing drugs, but rather relief is closely tied to the person's attitude toward pain.

The fear is not just a physical fear, but a fear of the unknown and unmanageable. Senseless pain is perhaps intolerable. On the other hand, pain may be accepted and dealt with if that pain does not mean punishment, or being ignored, or not being cared for. People will not suffer long, but they will endure pain.

Fear of Loss of Identity

The loss of human contact, the loss of family and friends, the loss of body structure and function, the loss of self-control and total consciousness all threaten the sense of one's identity. Human contacts affirm who we are, family contacts affirm who we have been, and contact with our own body and mind affirms our own being–self.

We can see that the dying process faces the person with many threats to self-identity. How does one maintain identity and integrity in the face of these forces of dissolution? Bowers (1964) concluded: "When life cannot be restored, then one can accept the fact with a meaning that gives dignity to his life, and purpose even to the process that is encroaching on his own vitality."

Willie Loman, the salesman in *Death of a Salesman*, says of his own death: "A man must not be allowed to fall into his grave as an old dog."

It is not *that* we die but *how* we die. The tasks are to retain self-esteem and respect for the self until death, to retain the dignity and integrity of the self throughout the process of living we call dying. There are three major mechanisms for this:

The first mechanism is most important. We maintain our identity through contact with those who have been and are part of our life. We do not become a number, a case, an object, if others continue to see us, react to us, talk to us, relate to us, *as the unique person I am.* Here again is the familiar theme of dying; maintaining contact with the familiar that keeps on reaffirming to the dying person that he or she is the person he or she has been always.

A second mechanism is reinforcement of identity through the continuity of one's life in family and friends. One sees one's self in one's children, life work, and in the bequeathing of one's possessions to others. One can not only leave a will but can leave parts of one's body in bone banks and eye banks. This personal sense of continuity was illustrated by a middle-aged man who was dying of lung cancer. I had spent much time talking with him about his life as he lay dying on my ward. He was transferred to another ward where the surgeons wanted to perform a biopsy. He refused until he could talk to me. I explained to him that the biopsy would not change his disease, but it would help my understanding of it. Then he was pleased to comply, for he felt he was giving me something, his diseased tissue, that in a sense I would carry with me in my professional life. He had given me a part of himself to be with me after his death.

A third mechanism maintains identity through a desire for reunion with loved ones who have died before or who will die and join one. These reunion fantasies include the sense of return to the primordial mother figure as well as reunion with specific loved ones (Brodsky 1959; Greenberg 1954). There will be reunion with one's parentage and one's progeny. Hence, one can place oneself at one point in the continuum of ongoing human relationships, of which my death is merely one point in the more universal span of existence.

Fear of Regression

Finally, there is fear of those internal instincts that pull one into retreat from the outer world of reality, into a primordial sense of being where there is no sense of time or space, no boundaries of self and others. We have all had this sense of pull toward regression into self when we awaken in the morning. As the alarm rings, we drowsily douse the noise, turn over, feel the immense weight of our sleep pulling us back into slumber. We luxuriate in the indefinite sense of our boundaries, the relaxation of our awareness, the freedom from the demands and constrictions of the real world that await our awakening. With exquisite pleasure we allow ourselves to float back off into a timeless, space-less, self-less state of nonbeing (Needleman 1966). Certain religious mystical experiences, psychedelic experiences, and body awareness exercises produce similar altered states of consciousness.

In most of life the ego fights against this instinctual regression into self-lessness. In our culture we have difficulty regarding such states as acceptable. We fear such states.

For the dying person, especially as he or she approaches and enters the terminal phase of living–dying, the fear of regression begins to loom. With the diminution of physical capacity and the clouding of consciousness, the sense of regression may be frightening. The dying person may fight against the regression, trying to hold onto concrete, hard, reality bound, consciousness of him or herself (Montefiore 1973). This may produce the so-called death agonies, the struggle against regression of the self.

It is here that we must help the person shift away from reality and turn inward toward the self, to allow regression and withdrawal to occur. With such support the dying person may then accept the surrender to the internal self, allow oneself to turn away from life, seek reunion with the world out of which he or she has sprung. Then psychic death is acceptable, desirable, and at hand.

The Terminal Phase

The onset of the terminal phase of living–dying is not precise. However, we can roughly state that it begins when the dying person begins to withdraw into him or herself in response to internal body signals that say he or she must now conserve energies unto him- or herself (Rioch 1961; Shontz and Fink 1959). Perhaps it is like the experience we may have with a bad case of the flu. We feel terribly sick, lose interest in food, activities, and friends. All we want to do is curl up in a warm bed and be left alone in quietness. The onset of this withdrawal is the onset of the terminal phase.

Lieberman (1965), has found that the terminal phase is marked by both physical withdrawal and subtle signs of emotional disorganization. Hinton (1963) has observed that there is a decrease in anxiety and an increase in depressive involution. Davies et al. (1973) have found that this psychological withdrawal is a type of "apathetic giving up," which accompanies a deterioration of the physical state of the person.

This turning from the outside world to the internal self is clearly described in this case report by Janice Norton (1963):

> She told me her only remaining fear was that dying was strange and unknown to her, that she had never done it before. Like birth, it was something that only happened once to any individual, and similarly one might not remember what it was really . . . She no longer worried about what was to happen to her after death . . . she felt that she might be unnecessarily concerned with the actual process of death itself.

Changes of Hope

At the outset of the living–dying interval, the dying patient has an *expectational hope*. That is, a set of expectations that have some possibility for fulfillment. There may be remissions, arrests, sometimes possible cures. There may be weeks, months, years of some rewarding life yet to be fulfilled. And it well may be that the dying person will cling to this expectational hope in a useful sense throughout the living–dying interval.

However, as a person enters the terminal phase, it may be signaled by a change in hope. Stotland (1969) has clarified the point that expectational hope now changes to *desirable hope*. That is, I may still hope that I might not die, that is a desirable thought but no longer expectable as a hope. This transformation from expectancy to desire may herald the psychological process of "giving up." It is for this reason, as Cappon (1959) notes, that hope should not cease until shortly before psychic death. However, we should also attend to the fact that we may aid the dying person in making the necessary transition from expectancy hope to desirability hope as he or she enters the terminal phase.

Types of Death

When we consider the terminal phase, we must take into account the four definitions of death: (1) *Sociological death,* the withdrawal and separation from the patient by others. This may occur days or weeks before terminus if the patient is left alone to die. The person is treated as if dead. Some families desert the aged in nursing homes, where they may live as if dead for several years. (2) *Psychic death*, the person accepts death and regresses into him- or herself. Such psychic death may accompany the appropriate diminution of the physical body status. But anomalies can occur; psychic death can precede terminus as in voodoo death (Cannon 1942) or in patients who predict their own deaths and refuse to continue living (Barber 1961; Vollman et al. 1971; Weisman and Hackett 1961). (3) *Biological death*, organism as a human entity no longer exists. There is no consciousness nor awareness, such as in irreversible coma. The heart and lungs may function with artificial support, but the biological organism as a self-sustaining mind–body is dead. (4) *Physiological death*, where vital organs such as lungs, heart, and brain no longer function.

The importance of these four types of death is that they can occur out of phase with each other. And that becomes a major source of ethical and personal confusion. As shown in Figure 3, as the person enters the terminal phase, this can be considered as the onset of giving up and withdrawal. Social death would be allowing the dying person to withdraw, leading to psychic death, which is usually shortly followed by biological and then physiological death.

However, there are distortions of this process also shown in Figure 3. Where there is social rejection of the patient, he or she may become socially dead long before the other aspects of death occur. On the other hand, where there is social and personal rejection of the dying process, we have the problem of precipitous death that is not anticipated nor dealt with. This also can occur when a patient suddenly deteriorates and dies contrary to expectation. It may precipitate a shocked reaction in all involved, because the anticipated trajectory has been upset. Another pattern is where the patient rejects life. This is usually met with social disapproval. For example, old people are not supposed to say they are ready to die, nor is the acutely ill person. We want people to want to live. In so doing, we may interfere with their own dying trajectories. And, finally, there is the case of death of mind and body—the artificial preservation of life—in which there is social denial of the fact that both psychic death and biological death have occurred. This is currently a source of much medical–ethical controversy in our culture.

In summary, our task is to synchronize each type of death dimension so that optimally they will converge together in an appropriate fashion, rather than being disjointed and out of phase with each other.

The Sequence of Dying

I have sketched a rough outline of the sequence of dying. However, I must caution that this is not a format but rather a framework that may guide our clinical thinking. Always we must keep in mind that human life is unique for each person. Our generalizations are just that. Therefore, we must beware of

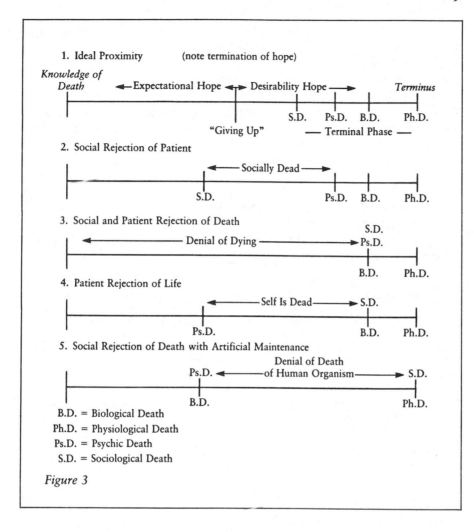

1. Ideal Proximity   (note termination of hope)

Knowledge of Death   ←—Expectational Hope ←—→ Desirability Hope —→   *Terminus*

S.D.   Ps.D.   B.D.   Ph.D.

"Giving Up"   —— Terminal Phase ——

2. Social Rejection of Patient

←——— Socially Dead ———→

S.D.   Ps.D.   B.D.   Ph.D.

3. Social and Patient Rejection of Death

S.D.
←——————— Denial of Dying ——————→ Ps.D.

B.D.   Ph.D.

4. Patient Rejection of Life

←——— Self Is Dead ———→ S.D.

Ps.D.   B.D.   Ph.D.

5. Social Rejection of Death with Artificial Maintenance

Denial of Death
Ps.D. ←——— of Human Organism ———→ S.D.

B.D.   Ph.D.

B.D. = Biological Death
Ph.D. = Physiological Death
Ps.D. = Psychic Death
S.D. = Sociological Death

Figure 3

fitting a dying person into a procrustean bed (a doctrine of conformity) of "scientific facts." Human life does not fit into neat categories and sequences. Thus, our charge is to understand the specific experience of dying for each person.

To recapitulate; at first the person is faced with the seeming impossible crisis of knowledge of death, which threatens to overwhelm the self. Human beings seem always to have recognized that no one has the capability to face this crisis alone, for we develop cultural customs whereby we actually and literally help people to die. Given our interest, support, and guidance, the dying person can face death as an unknown with the realization that he or she cannot know, and instead he or she can turn to deal with living–dying.

In the chronic living–dying phase, if not deprived of human contact, the person can learn to endure the inevitable degrees of separation without loneliness. He or she can face the loss of relatives, friends, and activities if he or she can actively mourn their loss where grief is defined and accepted. He or she can tolerate loss of body and structure if others accept that loss too. He or she can tolerate the loss of self-control if it is not perceived by him or herself and others as a shameful experience and if he or she can exercise control where feasible. The dying person can tolerate pain if he or she can see the source of pain and its meaning so that it is not transformed into suffering. He or she can retain dignity and self-respect in the face of the termination of the life cycle if he or she can place his or her life in perspective within his or her own personal history, family, and human tradition.

It is then possible to enter the terminal phase, in which expectational hope is transformed into desirability hope, where it is possible to give up one's grappling with life, and an acceptable regression occurs where the self gradually returns to the state of nonself.

References

Aldrich, C. K. The dying patient's grief. *Journal of the American Medical Association* 184:329–331, 1963.

Bakan, D. *Disease, Pain, and Sacrifice: Toward a Psychology of Suffering.* Chicago: University of Chicago Press, 1968.

Barber, T. X. Death by suggestion: a critical note. *Psychosomatic Medicine* 23:153–155, 1961.

Bowers, M., ed. *Counseling the Dying.* New York: Nelson, 1964.

Brodsky, B., Liebestod fantasies in a patient faced with a fatal illness. *International Journal of Psychoanalysis* 40:13–16, 1959.

Cannon, W. Voodoo death. *American Anthropologist* 44:169–181, 1942.

Cappon, D. The dying. *Psychiatric Quarterly* 33:466–489, 1959.

Davies, R. K., D. M. Quinland, F. P. McKegney, and C. P. Kimball. Organic factors and psychological adjustment in advanced cancer patients. *Psychosomatic Medicine* 35:464–471, 1973.

Diggory, J. C., and D. Z. Rothman. Values destroyed by death. *Journal of Abnormal and Social Psychology* 63:205–210, 1961.

Fulton, R., and J. Fulton. A psychosocial aspect of terminal care: anticipatory grief. *Omega* 2:91–100, 1971.

Glaser, B. G., and A. L. Strauss. *Awareness of Dying.* Chicago: Aldine, 1965.
———. *Time for Dying.* Chicago: Aldine, 1968.

Gordon, N. B., and B. Kutner. Long term and fatal illness and the family. *Journal of Health and Human Behavior* 6:190–196, 1965.

Greenberg, I. M. An exploratory study of reunion fantasies. *Journal of the Hillside Hospital* 13:49–59, 1954.

Hinton, J. The physiological and mental distress of dying. *Quarterly Journal of Medicine* 32:1–21, 1963.

Kalish, R. A. The onset of the dying process. *Omega* 1:57–69, 1970.

Kelly, J. *Free Fall.* Valley Forge, Pa.: Judson Press, 1975.

Krant, M. J. *Dying and Dignity: The Meaning and Control of a Personal Death.* Springfield, Ill.: C. C. Thomas, 1974.

Kübler-Ross, E. *On Death and Dying.* New York: Macmillan, 1970.

Lieberman, M. A. Psychological correlates of impending death. *Journal of Gerontology* 20:181–190, 1965.

Montefiore, H. W., ed. *Death Anxiety*. New York: MSS Information Corporation, 1973.

Needleman, J. Imagining absence, nonexistence, and death: a sketch. *Review of Existential Psychology and Psychiatry* 6:230–236, 1966.

Norton, J. Treatment of a dying patient. *Psychoanalytic Study of the Child* 18:541–560, 1963.

Noyes, R., Jr., and R. Kletti. Depersonalization in the face of life-threatening danger: a description. *Psychiatry* 39:19–27, 1976.

Parad, H. J., ed. *Crisis Intervention: Selected Readings*. New York: Family Service Association of America, 1965.

Petrie, A. *Individuality in Pain and Suffering*. Chicago: University of Chicago Press, 1967.

Rioch, D. The psychopathology of death. In *The Physiology of Emotions*, ed. A. Simon. Springfield, Ill.: C. C. Thomas, 1961.

Schoenberg, B., et al., eds. *Anticipatory Grief*. New York: Columbia University Press, 1974.

———. *Loss and Grief: Psychological Management in Medical Practice*. New York: Columbia University Press, 1970.

Shontz, F. C., and S. L. Fink. A psychobiological analysis of discomfort, pain, and death. *Journal of General Psychology* 60:275–287, 1959.

Stotland, E. *The Psychology of Hope*. San Francisco: Jossey-Bass, 1969.

Szasz, T. *Pain and Pleasure: A Study of Bodily Feelings*. London: Tavistock, 1957.

Tart, C. T., ed. *Altered States of Consciousness*. New York: Wiley, 1969.

Vollman, R. R., A. Ganzert, L. Picher, and W. V. Williams. The reactions of family systems to sudden and unexpected death. *Omega* 2:101–106, 1971.

Weisman, A. D., and T. Hackett. Predilection for death: death and dying as a psychiatric problem. *Psychosomatic Medicine* 23:232–256, 1961.

DYLAN THOMAS

Do Not Go Gentle into That Good Night

The foregoing selections have necessarily generalized patterns in the dying process, but as the following poem makes clear, the style of dying is a highly individual choice. Writing about the death of his father, Dylan Thomas calls for a powerful resistance to death as a way of affirming all that has been valuable in life.

Do not go gentle into that good night.
Old age should burn and rave at close of day;
Rage, rage against the dying of the light.

Though wise men at their end know dark is right,
Because their words have forked no lightning they
Do not go gentle into that good night.

Good men, the last wave by, crying how bright
Their frail deeds might have danced in a green bay,
Rage, rage against the dying of the light.

Wild men who caught and sang the sun in flight,
And learn, too late, they grieved it on its way,
Do not go gentle into that good night.

Grave men, near death, who see with blinding sight
Blind eyes could blaze like meteors and be gay,
Rage, rage against the dying of the light.

And you, my father, there on the sad height,
Curse, bless, me now with your fierce tears, I pray.
Do not go gentle into that good night.
Rage, rage against the dying of the light.

Source: The Poems of Dylan Thomas. Copyright © 1952 by Dylan Thomas. Reprinted by permission of New Directions Publishing Corporation.

EMILY DICKINSON

I Heard a Fly Buzz When I Died

In the following poem, Emily Dickinson "ties on" the persona of an individual at the moment of death. In doing so, she hypothesizes what it is like to be dying, a question that Elisabeth Kübler-Ross will undertake.

I heard a Fly buzz – when I died –
The Stillness in the Room
Was like the Stillness in the Air –
Between the Heaves of Storm –

The Eyes around – had wrung them dry –
And Breaths were gathering firm
For that last Onset – when the King
Be witnessed – in the Room –

I willed my Keepsakes – Signed away
What portion of me be
Assignable – and then it was
There interposed a Fly –

With Blue – uncertain, stumbling Buzz –
Between the light – and me –
And then the Windows failed – and then
I could not see to see –

Source: Reprinted by permission of the publishers and the Trustees of Amherst College from *The Poems of Emily Dickinson,* edited by Thomas H. Johnson. Cambridge, Mass.: The Belknap Press of Harvard University Press. Copyright 1951, © 1955, 1979, 1983 by the President and Fellows of Harvard College.

ELISABETH KÜBLER-ROSS

What Is It Like to Be Dying?

Philosophy has always concerned itself with death, and great literature speaks of the enduring conflicts common to all ages. Only recently, as death has been pushed farther and farther away from everyday life, has it become a subject of study for the social sciences. Sociologists have compiled bodies of data on the organization of death and dying, and Elisabeth Kübler-Ross has done much to establish dying as a discipline of its own within psychiatry and psychology. In the following selection, she summarizes her best-known work with the dying. Although she readily admits that all patients do not follow "a classical pattern" and that a patient may well remain in one "stage" or another, by outlining a psychological process of dying, she provides a structure for understanding the reactions and needs of the dying person. Kübler-Ross emphasizes, as Pattison did, how those close to the dying patient must work to understand their own attitudes toward death in order to be able to help the patient.

What is it like to be dying? Not from the nurse's point of view, nor from the doctor's, nor the family's, but from the patient's point of view: what is it like? Because, if we have some idea of what the answer might be, then we're going to be in a better position to help.

At the University of Chicago Billings Hospital, some of us have made it our business to find out a little more about what it is like to be dying. Before sharing this information with you, though, let me first raise another question: why—at this time, in this society—must we have so many books on death and dying, so many lectures and seminars on the subject? After all, we should be experts on dying. It is the one thing that has been with mankind as long as man himself. So why has it suddenly become such a big issue?

Death has always been a fearful thing to men. We have a hard time conceiving of our own death. We believe with the psalmist who says, "A thousand shall fall at thy side, and ten thousand at thy right hand: *but* it shall not come nigh thee." Deep down, we believe, or would like to believe, that we are immortal. We cannot conceive of dying a natural death at the end of our lives, just falling asleep one night and not waking up. Instead, when we have to conceive death, we see it as something malignant and catastrophic: a destructive intervention from the outside that hits us suddenly and finds us unprepared.

Death in the old days came in the form of epidemics: produced by nature, not by man. Man tried to master epidemics, he mastered illness, he developed antibiotics and vaccinations, he learned to prolong life, he was able to master

Source: Copyright © January, 1971. The American Journal of Nursing Company. Reproduced, with permission, from *American Journal of Nursing,* January, Vol. 71, No. 1.

many, many causes of death. But in his fear of death and his need to master things, he has also developed weapons. If he has the choice to kill or be killed, he chooses to kill.

In the old days, an enemy in the battlefield could be seen. You had a chance to defend your family, your tribe, or your honor; you could choose a good weapon or a good hill. You had a chance to survive.

But today, out of man's need to be stronger, to defy death, he has developed bigger and more horrible weapons. One reason for our present death-denying society, I believe, is that man has now created weapons of mass destruction—man-made, mind you, not like nature's epidemics. He has developed weapons which, in a very concrete way, represent our fear of death, the catastrophic death that hits us from the outside when we are not prepared. You can't see, you can't smell, and you can't hear this enemy, whether it be chemical or bacteriological warfare, atom bombs, or even pollution.

What do we do when we have created such weapons of mass destruction? We cannot defend ourselves physically against them, we have to defend ourselves psychologically. We can pretend that nobody will push the wrong button. We can build ourselves bomb shelters in the garden, or we can build anti-missiles and have the illusion that we are safe.

But none of these defenses really works. What works partially is that we can deny that we are finite. That it shall happen to thee and thee but not come nigh to me. We can pretend that we are not finite by developing "deep freeze societies," where we freeze those who die and put them into some sort of mausoleum and promise the next of kin to defrost them in 50 or 100 years from now. These societies really exist; they serve the need to deny that people actually die.

We see this same need and tendency in the hospital. When we are assigned to dying patients, we feel very, very uncomfortable. In fact, even when we know that a patient is dying, we have a hard time facing that fact and acknowledging it—not in the head but in the gut. And our patients very often die with more difficulty than they used to.

In the old days, people were more likely to die at home rather than in the hospital. When a person is at home, he's in his own familiar environment, with his family and his children around him. Dying, under these circumstances, is not only easier and more comfortable for the patient, but it also does something for his family—especially the children, who can share in the preparatory grief for a person who is dying in the house. Such a child will grow up and know that death is part of life.

But if the sick person is shipped off to the hospital, with visits limited to perhaps five minutes every hour in the intensive treatment unit, it is not the same experience. And children are not allowed to see those patients, those parents. In Europe, even now, there is no embalming, no make-believe sleep, no slumber rooms, no euphemisms. All this, I think, helps us to face death as part of life. But today, in the United States, we have a long way to go before we can accept death as part of life. Dying, as many patients have expressed to us, has become not only more lonely and more isolated, but very often more impersonalized, dehumanized, and mechanized.

Some five years ago, four theology students asked me if I couldn't help them in a project. They had to write a paper on crisis in human life, and they had chosen dying. That's the biggest crisis people have to face, they said, and they asked, "How do you go about it? How do you do research on dying? You can't experience it. You can't experiment with it, you can't verify it, you can't do all the things that one ought to do with a good research project."

So I suggested to them that it would be very simple to ask dying patients, "What is it like? How does it feel? What fears, needs, fantasies do you have? What kind of things are we doing that are helpful? What kind of things do we do that are detrimental?" The students agreed, and I volunteered to work with them and to find a seriously ill patient for our first interview.

How naive I was: I discovered that there was not a single dying patient in a 600-bed hospital! I went from ward to ward and told the nurses and doctors that I would like to talk to a terminally ill patient.

"What about?"

"About dying."

"Oh, we have nobody dying."

If I pushed, they said, "He's too weak" or "too sick" or "too tired" or "he doesn't feel like talking." A lot of not only denial and rationalization but also hostility and some very aggressive behavior emerged. One nurse asked me, "Do you enjoy playing God?" and another: "Do you get a kick out of telling a 20-year-old that he has one week to live?" And, of course, there was much well-meant protectiveness for the patients.

I had had the same experience a few years earlier in another hospital. There, the only way I was able to find a dying patient was to go through the wards and look at the patients and guess that somebody was very sick. That way I saw an old man who looked very sick and who was reading a paper with a headline, "Old Soldiers Never Die." I asked him if he wasn't afraid to read that, and he said, "Are you one of those doctors who can't talk about it when you can't help us no more?" So I gave him a pat on the back and said, "You're the right kind of man and I want to talk with you."

Eventually, though, we started to receive an ever-increasing number of referrals. Our first patient was perhaps the most troubling one—to me, anyway. I went to see this old man the day before I was to see him with the students. He put his arms out and with pleading eyes said, "Please sit down *now*." With the emphasis on *now*. But I did what we always do. I could only hear my own needs, I was frustrated and tired of running around, and tomorrow was the day I was supposed to see him with the students. So I told him, "No, I can't stay now, I'll be back tomorrow," and I left.

When I came back with the students the next day, it was too late. He was in oxygen, he could hardly breathe, and the only thing he was able to say was, "Thank you for trying, anyway." And he died a short time later. He helped us a lot, however, although not in any verbal way. What he told us was that when a terminally ill patient says, "Sit down *now*," you have to sit down *now*. Because somehow these patients sense that *now* is the time that they can talk about it. There may not be such a time again, so even if you can sit down only two or three minutes, you will feel better, and so will the patient.

The students and I had so many feelings when we left that man's room that we did something that we have continued to do for almost five years now: we went to my office and shared our gut reactions. Not nice things. Not the kinds of things that one ought to say and feel: those come from your head. But how does it feel in the gut? That's what we talk about. We try to get to know each other's feelings—to understand them, not to judge them. We try to help each other express them so that we can learn to listen to our gut reaction and to differentiate between the patient's needs and our own.

So far, we have interviewed over 400 terminally ill patients. By "terminally ill," I mean patients with a serious illness which may end fatally. They don't necessarily die the next day or the next week. Many of them have gone home or have had a remission. Some have lived only 12 hours, and others have lived for a year or two.

What have we learned from them? We have learned that our patients all know when they are dying, and I think that's consoling for us to know. Half of them have never been told that they have a serious illness. We are often asked what or whether a patient should be told. Actually, I don't think any patient should be told that he is dying. He will tell *you* that when you dare to listen, when you are able to hear it.

But patients should, I think, with very few exceptions, be told when they have a serious illness. Our patients say that they would like to be told this under two conditions: one is that the person telling them allows for some hope, and the second is that "you are going to stick it out with me—not desert me—not leave me alone." If we can, indeed, "stick it out" with them, then I think that we can help them the most.

We have learned, too, that dying patients generally go through a series of stages. The stages don't always follow one another; they overlap sometimes and sometimes they go back and forth.

Most patients, when told they have a serious illness, react with shock and denial. "No, it can't be me. It's not possible." Only three of our 400, however, maintained this denial to the very end, although many have maintained denial in the presence of other people—usually family or staff members—who need denial themselves. If a family needs denial, the patient will not talk to them about the seriousness of his illness or how he feels. But if they, or we, can tell him that we are ready to talk about it, that we are willing to listen, he will drop the denial quite quickly and will talk about his situation.

Our patients usually drop part of their denial when they have to take care of unfinished business or financial matters, especially when they begin to worry about their children. But they also drop their denial if they know that the person with them will help them to express the multitude of feelings that emerge when they face the given reality.

Perhaps the second most important and common response is anger. When a person can no longer say, "No, not me," the next question is usually "Why me?" The patient should be allowed to express this, and you don't have to have an answer because none of us will ever have an answer to that question. Just listen.

At this stage these patients will be very difficult; not only with the family (they visit too early or too late or with too many people or not enough people), but also with the nurses. You come in and shake a pillow and the patient complains, "Why are you bothering me now? I just want to take a nap." When you leave him alone, he protests that you don't straighten out his bed. The physician doesn't have the right prescriptions or the right diet or the right tests. In short, these are extremely "difficult and ungrateful" patients.

What do you do when you have a patient like that? What is your gut reaction? Remember, the harder you try, the harder the time he gives you. What do you do? You withdraw, you get angry at him, maybe you wait twice as long until you answer his light.

In one study, they measured the time it took nurses to answer the patients' lights. And they discovered that patients who were beyond medical help—terminally ill patients—had to wait twice as long as the others.

That, too, you have to try to understand and not judge. It is very hard to be around patients like this for very long, especially if you try to do your best and all you get is criticism and abuse. What we have found to be most helpful to the patients and ourselves is not to get angry back at them or take their abuse personally (which we normally do) but to try to find out what they are so angry about.

We asked our patients about this. What came out was that the peppier, the more energetic, the more functioning you are when you come into that room, the more anger you often provoke. And the patient says angrily to you, "*You* can walk out of here again, you know. *You* can go home again at five and see your kids. *You* can go to work." They're not angry at you as a person, but at what you represent—life, functioning, pep, energy, all the things they are in the process of losing or have already partially lost.

We tried to see if it would help if we poured fuel on the fire, if we let them ventilate, let them express their anger. If we can say to them, "You know, I would be angry, too. Get it off your chest. Scream if you feel like screaming," then they will express their rage and anger, but it never comes out as loud and frightening as you might think.

The best example is the mother of a small child who died. She looked very numb, so I said to her, "You look as though you need to scream." And she said, "Do you have a screaming room at the hospital?" She was serious. I said, "No, but we have a chapel," which was a silly answer because she immediately replied, "I need just the opposite. I need to scream and rage and curse. I've just been sitting in the parking lot and cursing and screaming at God. 'God, why do you let this happen to my child? Why do you let this happen to me?' " And I said, "Do it here. It's better to do it *with* somebody than out in a parking lot all alone."

And that's what I mean by the stage of anger, of rage, of a sense of impotence, of helplessness. You can help not only the patient to express this rage and anger, but the family, too, because they go through the same stages. And, from a practical point of view, the nursing staff will be saved many, many steps. The nurse will be called less, the patient will be more comfortable.

Sometimes the patient gets to this point—loses his anger—without any external help, and you wonder what happened. Very often it is because he has entered the state of bargaining. Most bargaining is done with God. "If you give me one more year to live, I will be a good Christian or I will donate my kidney or this or that." Most of the time it is a promise, in exchange for some prolongation of life.

We had one patient who depended on injections around the clock to control her terrible pain. She was one of our most difficult patients, and it became very hard to keep on visiting her. Then one day she was very friendly and she said, "You know, if you help me get out of this hospital for one single day, I will be a good patient." She wanted that one day to get up and get dressed and attend her son's wedding. This was finally possible, and she left, looking like a million dollars.

And we began to wonder, "What is it like? How must it feel to ask only for one single day? It must be terribly difficult to come back to the hospital."

When she returned, she wasn't happy to see me. Before I could ask a single question she said, "Dr. Ross, don't forget I have another son." That's the briefest, quickest example of the bargaining stage I know.

In the denial stage it's "No, not me!" In the anger, "Why me?" In the bargaining, "Yes, me, but. . . ." When the patient finally drops the "but," then it's "Yes, me." And "Yes, me" means that he has the courage to acknowledge that it has indeed "come nigh" to him, and he is naturally very depressed.

After a while, these patients become silent. It's a kind of grief which is difficult for us to accept—where they don't talk much any more, where they don't want any more visitors. How do we react to them when we come into their rooms and find them crying or silently mourning? What do we do? Can we tolerate this?

This is sometimes even more difficult to bear than the angry patients. As long as they complain about all the things they have lost, it's something we can grasp. But when they become quiet and the tears are running down—and especially if it's a man—then it's very hard. We have a tendency to say, "What a beautiful day outside. Look at those lovely flowers. Cheer up. It's not so bad."

It *is* bad. If I were to lose one beloved person, everybody would allow—even expect—me to grieve. It would be perfectly normal because I would have lost one person I loved. But the dying patient is about to lose not just one beloved person but everyone he has ever loved and everything that has been meaningful to him. That is a thousand times sadder. If the patient has the courage to face this, then he should be allowed to grieve; he has a right to it.

We call this the preparatory grief. If he can prepare himself slowly, if he is allowed to grieve and, if necessary, to cry, then he becomes able to decathect, to separate himself. He will have the courage to ask for no more relatives to come after a while, no more children. And at the very end he will want perhaps only one loved person—someone who can sit silently and comfortably by his side, without words, but just touching his hand or perhaps stroking his hair or just being there.

That's when a patient has reached the stage of acceptance. And acceptance is not resignation! Resignation is a bitter kind of giving up ("What's the use?"), almost a defeat. But acceptance is a good feeling. "I have now finished all of my unfinished business. I have said all of the words that have to be said. I am ready to go."

These patients are not happy, but they are not terribly sad. They usually have very little physical pain and discomfort, and they slip into a stage which very often reminds us of the beginning of life: when a person has physical needs and needs only one person to give him some tender, loving care and compassion—who can be with him but doesn't have to talk all the time. It's the comfort of being together that counts.

"Do you have to be a psychiatrist to work with these people?" I am often asked. No. Many of our patients are angry when a psychiatric consultation is called because they have dared to become depressed. What I have talked about so far is the normal behavior of a dying patient, and it doesn't take a psychiatrist to help him. It doesn't take much time, either—only a very few minutes.

Last fall, we saw a young man who was the father of three small children. He had never been sick, never been in the hospital before, and now he was admitted with acute leukemia. Every day when I saw him, he was on the verge of talking. He wanted to talk but he couldn't. So he would say, "Come back tomorrow." And I would come back the next day, but he would say again, "Come back tomorrow."

Finally, I said to him, "If you don't want to talk about it, that's alright." He quickly responded: "No, if I don't do it now, I'll never be able to do it. Why don't you come back tomorrow morning very early, before rounds, before anybody else comes? I have to get it out." (We never talked, by the way, about what "it" meant, but both of us knew.)

The next day I came very early and the nurses told me that this patient had been dying during the night, that he had put up a physical fight for about three and a half hours, that he was really not in a condition to talk. But when I promise a patient I will see him, I keep that promise even if he is comatose or not in a position to communicate. So I went to his room and, to my surprise, he almost sat up in his bed. "Come on in," he said; "close the door and sit down." And he talked as he had never talked before.

He said, "I have to tell you what happened last night, you will never believe it." (I'm using his own words because I want to show you what we mean about talking about dying. Patients do not always use the word "dying" but you can talk about dying in many languages.)

"Last night," he continued, "I put up a fight for several hours. There was a big train going rapidly down the hill towards the end, and I had a big fight with the train master. I argued and fought with him. And I ordered him to stop this train one tenth of an inch short."

Then he paused and asked me, "Do you know what I am talking about?" I said, "I guess the train that goes rapidly down toward the end is your life. And you had a big fight with the train master—for just a little bit more time." Then I smiled and added, "You made it." (That's bargaining. He bargained for one tenth of an inch.)

At that moment his mother came in and I said, "How can I help you with the tenth of an inch?" using his language since I didn't know on what level this mother and son communicated. And he said, "Try to help me convince my mother that she should go home now and bake a loaf of bread and make my favorite vegetable soup; I want to eat that once more." And the mother did go home and he did get his bread and soup—his last solid food. He died about three days later.

I think this man went through all the stages of dying in this overnight struggle. He tried to maintain his denial as long as possible—and then he dropped it in that one night. The anger, the bargaining and the depression, preceded the final stage of acceptance.

My last example is a woman whose story illustrates what hope means and how the nature of hope changes from the healthy to the sick to the dying. If we can elicit the patient's hope and support *his* hope, then we can help him the most.

This woman came to our hospital feeling very sick and weak, and her doctor said that she should go to a specialist in another hospital. So she hoped at that time that it was nothing serious, that it could be treated, that she would get well. After a while she was told that she had a serious kidney disease; then she hoped for treatment that would cure it. Next, she was told her life could be prolonged if she were accepted on a dialysis program for indigent people. This, too, was something for her to hope for—but she was rejected.

The social worker and the nurses, who were really fond of this woman, could not accept this. It was hard for them to visit her after dialysis had been denied, so they asked us to see her in our death and dying seminar.

The patient was very relieved when we were frank and told her why we wanted to see her. Many little but unfortunate things had happened to her at the hospital to which she was sent—hurriedly and unprepared—to be considered for dialysis. Confusion and misunderstanding grew until finally, when all the doctors stopped at her bedside on rounds, she realized that this was the moment of truth.

"A big cloud came over me," she said, "and I had the idea that I had a kidney operation and didn't need those doctors. When I woke up they were gone." In other words, she had a fantasy that she didn't need the doctors to save her life. Considered to be psychotic and hallucinating, she was rejected for dialysis.

We explored a lot of feelings about that, and then we discussed with her what kinds of things we could do now to make whatever time she had left more meaningful or more bearable.

She said, "Don't be so upset. When I die, it will be just like going from this garden to God's garden." But something was really bothering her, she added. She didn't know quite what it was and it was hard to talk about it.

Two days later, I said to her, "You know, there was something that bothered you, and that's what we call unfinished business. What is it?" And she kept saying, "I'm bad, I'm bad, I'm bad." Because what she was really saying was that she had to confess something that she felt guilty about, but she didn't know the origin of this guilt. And we searched like two children who are looking in the dark for something they have lost.

Finally, I gave up and I said, "God only knows why you should be bad," which was a genuine gut reaction on my part. And she looked up and said, "That's it: God. I called on God for help for the last few days. 'God help me. God help me.' And I heard Him say in the back of my mind, 'Why are you calling me now, why didn't you call me when things were all right?' What do you say to that, Dr. Ross?" And my gut reaction was to take off. Why couldn't a priest be here? Or a minister? Or somebody? But not me.

But you can't give a patient like this a phony answer. You have to be you and you have to be honest. So I struggled, and finally I said, "Just imagine that the children are playing outside and the mother is in the house and the little boy falls and hurts his knee. What happens?" And she said, "The mother goes out and helps him back on his feet and consoles him." I said, "OK, and he is all right now. What happens next?" And she said, "The boy goes back to his play and the mother goes back in the house." "He has no use for her now?" I asked, and she said "No," and I said, "Does the mother resent this terribly?" She looked at me almost angrily and said, "A mother? A mother wouldn't resent that." And I said, "If a mother wouldn't resent that, do you think that our Father would?"

Then the happiest, most beautiful smile came over her face, and she asked me something I'll never forget: "What is your concept of death?" (I felt like saying, "How dare you ask me!" It shall not "come nigh" to me, even after seeing so many dying patients.) So I said something about liking her idea about the garden, but she just shook her head and asked again, "What is your concept of death?" Then I looked at her face and said, "Peace." That was a genuine answer. And she said, "I'm going very peacefully, now, from this garden into the next one."

This patient taught us how hope can change: from hoping it's nothing serious, then hoping for treatment, then hoping for a prolongation of life. And finally hoping that "If I'm not accepted in this garden, I hope I'll be accepted in the next garden."

It is the patient's hope that we should support. I had known this woman less than an hour, yet I learned from her. And I think I helped her.

It didn't take much time. But what it did take, and will always take, is a sense of comfort in the face of death. What all of us have to learn is to accept death as part of life. When we have learned this, then maybe we can help our patients learn it, too.

ROBERT KASTENBAUM

Do We Die in Stages?

In developing the stage progression approach to the dying experience, Kübler-Ross provided an effective vocabulary for discussions of dying. Evaluating her work and noting the limitations of any stage theory, Kastenbaum raises the issue of standards of evidence for clinical research. He calls for empirical research to validate the stage theory of dying and to identify significant variables in its application.

Do We Die in Stages?

The concept of stages is abundantly familiar in developmental theory and research. Freud, Erikson, and Piaget are perhaps the most influential of the theorists who have offered stage-progression approaches, but there are many others also available to choose from. Stage theories are characterized by emphasis upon qualitative differences that are thought to appear in a relatively fixed sequence. Change along a simple quantitative dimension is usually not regarded as the stuff of stage theory. The 12-year-old is taller than the 6-year-old, but it is the contention that he *thinks differently* that constitutes the grounds for locating him in a different stage.

Popular as a technique for observations and for teaching, stage theory might also be expected to surface in the area of dying and death, which until recent years has attracted few researchers, theoreticians, and clinical specialists. With the publication in 1969 of Elisabeth Kübler-Ross's *On Death and Dying,* such a theory did become available and widely disseminated. It is this approach that will be described and examined in the next section.

A. A Stage Theory of the Dying Process

1. *The Five Stages*   Kübler-Ross proposes that the dying person passes through five stages. These begin with the impact of mortal tidings, and terminate as life itself terminates. Individuals may differ in the rapidity through which they move from stage to stage. Further, some people do not reach the final stage at all. One can be caught or arrested at a particular stage of dying, as in any stage in life-span development. The stages are normal modes of responding to the harsh reality of death. Further, there can be some slipping back and forth between stages, and the coexistence of two stages.

Denial is the first stage. The person is, in effect, saying "No!" to death. This stage takes place whether terminal status is communicated by medical authorities or surmised by the individual himself. Denial can be displayed in

Source: Excerpt from Robert Kastenbaum, "Is Death a Life Crisis?" in Nancy Datan and Leon H. Ginsberg, eds., *Life-Span Developmental Psychology: Normative Life Crises,* © 1975, Academic Press. Reprinted by permission.

straightforward fashion or obliquely. By words and actions the person resists acknowledging the reality of impending death.

Anger comes next. The lid blows off. Angry feelings may be vented upon family, medical staff, the environment. Even God is not exempt. It is as though somebody must be blamed for the overwhelming disaster, which is no longer denied. The typical question the person is struggling with at this time is "Why me?" Frustration builds and anger overflows as the question resists satisfactory answer.

Bargaining is the middle stage. The person attempts to make a deal with fate. He changes his strategy and asks for a favor. Kübler-Ross compares this maneuver with the child whose request for an overnight visit with a friend has been turned down. After stamping his foot, "No!" and expressing anger, the child eventually comes around to ask, "If I am very good all week and wash the dishes every evening, then will you let me go?" (Kübler-Ross 1969, p. 72). The terminally ill patient attempts to bargain for an extension of life, a postponement of the death event. Much of the bargaining is likely to proceed covertly between the dying person and God, but the process sometimes can be seen as well in interactions with others.

Depression sets in "when the terminally ill patient can no longer deny his illness, when he is forced to undergo more surgery or hospitalization, when he begins to have more symptoms or becomes weaker and thinner, he cannot smile it off anymore. His numbness or stoicism, his anger and rage will soon be replaced with a sense of great loss" (Kübler-Ross 1969, p. 75). The depressive state may involve feelings of guilt and unworthiness, fear of dying, and attenuation of communication with family and others.

Acceptance is the final stage. The struggle is over. Tired and weak physically, the patient nevertheless is no longer sunk in the anguish of depression. "Acceptance should not be mistaken for a happy stage. It is almost void of feelings. It is as if the pain had gone, the struggle is over, and there comes a time for 'the final rest before the long journey' as one patient phrased it" (Kübler-Ross 1969, p. 100).

2. *Context of the Stage Theory*   Kübler-Ross illuminates her presentation of each stage with brief synopses of terminally ill people she has interviewed, and transcribed dialogue between the patient and herself. This sharing of clinical material helps the reader to grasp the essence of the various stages. Moreover, it provides a person with "something to go on" or "something to look for" when entering into a relationship with a dying person oneself. She also comments upon some of the ways in which family or staff might respond helpfully to the dying person in each stage. The difficult problem of relating to the dying person when anger is the dominant affect, for example, receives her attention. A separate chapter is devoted to examples from her therapeutic efforts with the dying.

Interwoven through all five stages is the phenomenon of *hope,* which also is discussed in a separate chapter. Perhaps her key point here is that

In listening to our terminally ill patients we were always impressed that even the most accepting, the most realistic patients left the possibility open for some cure, for the discovery of a new drug, of the last minute success in a research project.... It is this glimpse of hope which maintains them through days, weeks, or months of suffering. It is the feeling that all this must have some meaning, will pay off eventually if they can only endure it for a little while longer. It is the hope that occasionally sneaks in, that all this is just like a nightmare and not true. (Kübler-Ross 1969, p. 123)

B. Stage Theory of Dying as a General Contribution

The stage theory of dying has made a number of contributions to our culture's general orientation toward dying and death. Not the least of these is the awakening or legitimation of interest in a topic that has been taboo to many Americans, whether laymen or professionals (Feifel 1959). Kübler-Ross has reached the feelings of people who previously did not know where to begin in relating themselves toward their terminally ill friends, family or patients. *On Death and Dying* became for many their first exposure to systematic description of the dying process, and their first guide for their own explorations. Although books on death have been published before and after, it is this contribution by Kübler-Ross that established the topic as one of general concern.

Thoughts and feeling stirred by this book have added to the impetus of a nationwide death education movement. The existence of stage theory also has provided a coin of communication: The social worker from Utah meeting the nurse from New York can both talk about Stage 3, and the student of death education has his or her five stages to copy down and memorize.

The book, then, has opened the subject of death and dying to many people and provided a basis for communication. This stepping-over-the-threshold is significant action, when we reflect that even experienced health professionals often place physical and emotional distance between themselves and the palpabilities of dying and death. The humanism and the case material account for part of this effect. What about the stage theory itself? It is my impression that the stage theory gained rapid acceptance because it is a clear, understandable schema that provides structure and reduces anxiety for the reader. Death becomes subsumed under dying, and dying transformed from a vague, overpowering, and terrifying mass to a delimited, coherent, orderly sequence. There are rules now to govern this part of the universe that has for so long been considered out of bounds. The reader, researcher, or health professional thus can approach the topic with less anxiety and foreboding.

It is not surprising that many people have felt remarkably better after becoming acquainted with the stage theory of dying. Anxiety and lack of cognitive structure are replaced by the security of knowledge. The reader now knows what happens during the process of dying, has greater feeling for the patient's situation, and has some idea about what might be done to be of value to the patient or his family. There is no doubt that stage theory has increased the dialogue, both oral and written, about care of the dying person. And there is little doubt that more people have taken heart to draw closer to the dying person. Not all the consequences have been favorable, however, and some of the problems involved will be examined in what follows.

C. Stage Theory of Dying as a Contribution to Knowledge

We raise now a sampling of those questions that come to mind in evaluating any model of human behavior. Particular attention will be given to issues that link the stage theory of dying with other developmental approaches.

1. *Overview*   The stage theory of dying draws primarily upon the clinical experiences of psychiatrist author Elizabeth Kübler-Ross. In her words, this theory is intended "to summarize what we have learned from our dying patients in terms of coping mechanisms at the time of a terminal illness" (Kübler-Ross 1969, p. 33). The theory is intended to encompass feelings and behaviors of the dying person from awareness of terminality to the death event itself. In company with other stage theories, the stage theory of dying specifies a strongly directional set of transitions with each way station characterized by fairly distinct phenomena. The source, intention, and general nature of Kübler-Ross's theory do not present any difficulties. Personal experience with dying patients is obviously a sensible basis for deriving the principles of a theory or general formulation. The stage theory of dying comes into being as a means of summarizing and sharing those experiences. And the idea that the process of dying can be usefully viewed in terms of some orderly progression of adaptive states does not tax credibility. In broad outline, then, the theory deserves consideration as a plausible approach toward understanding the dying process. Does it also deserve acceptance as the "true account" or the "most useful" theory? This is quite another question.

2. *The Data Base*   Experiences with approximately 200 terminally ill people provided the basis for the stage theory of dying; since that time Kübler-Ross has interviewed approximately another 200 terminally ill in her own setting, and has seen many others as consultant–lecturer. It is clear that her theory is grounded in relevant information.

However, virtually every operation that might be performed on clinical information for conversion into research data has been neglected. The sample itself has not been described. Terms have not been defined. Transcripts have not been subjected to analysis and no interrater reliability procedures that might demonstrate the existence of the five stages have been performed. The interaction between the method of data gathering and the results has not been discussed. The most basic types of statistical information have not been provided. (How many patients, for example, were seen for what periods of time? How many, in fact, did die while the interview series was in process? How many were interviewed only on a single occasion? etc.).

There are sensitive issues here that could easily be distorted. Systematic research and finesse may be unreasonable to expect when a person is helping to pioneer an emotion-laden growing edge of knowledge and concern. One-to-one with a dying person, a psychiatrist or other interested person has more pressing concerns than the abstract demands of science. Kübler-Ross had to discover her own pathway to understanding the terminally ill, and then had the generosity of spirit to share it with others.

But all of this does not permit us to relax standards of evidence. Perhaps a theory has emerged whose ties with its original data base are personal and difficult to share or open for objective evaluation. This circumstance in itself neither supports nor undercuts the specifics of Kübler-Ross's theory. However, the rapid acceptance of the stage theory of dying has quite outdistanced any attempt to examine the theory empirically or logically. It is taken typically as proven fact. But the fact is that the theory was not offered with a close and coherently developed data base at the start, and no effort has been made to test out the theory as it continues to become more widely disseminated and applied. Few who center their approach to dying and death around the stage theory of dying see it as in need of analysis, examination, evaluation. It is useful in some way, therefore it is self-perpetuating. Moreover, as will be seen later, those who find this theory less than useful tend to drop it without necessarily subjecting either the theory or their own uses of it to searching analysis. In short, there is conviction that the stage theory of dying is an empirically valid formulation of human experience during the dying process, when little effort has been expended to study the relationship between theory and fact. The present criticism is not directed at the paucity of information brought forth to support or test the stage theory of dying, but the attitude that research is superfluous.

As a person who has some experience with the terminally ill, I appreciate the fact that companionship, caring, and intervention cannot wait until scientific formulations have been purified and validated. Sounding the caution about a particular theory is not equivalent to discouraging people from bringing their best selves to interactions with the dying, or to using whatever insights the theory provides. But I must reject the contention that the stage theory of dying is so important and useful that research can wait. It is precisely because the experiences of the dying person and all those around him are so important that we ought not to base our work indefinitely upon an untested theory. If the theory is substantially correct, then we should use it for all that it is worth; if it has decided limitations or inaccuracies, then we should move without delay to find alternatives.

3. Factors Insufficiently Considered by the Stage Theory of Dying   It is here suggested that Kübler-Ross's theory suffers from what could be described either as overreliance upon one component of the total situation or underappreciation of the total context. In this regard, the theory perhaps is suffering a flaw common to most stage theories. Mentioned in the following paragraphs are several other sources of variance that are neglected by the emphasis upon the five hypothesized stages of individual adaptation to terminal illness.

Nature of the disease   There have always been physicians who maintain that a person "dies the death of his disease." In other words, the patterning of the pathology dominates all else. This contention, like those of the stage theory of dying, has yet to be tested critically. But it is evident that the nature-of-the-disease process can greatly affect pain, mobility, trajectory of dying, and the social stimulus value of the dying person, to mention just some of the dimensions involved. Within the realm of cancer alone, for example, the person with head or neck cancer looks and feels different from the person with leukemia. The person with emphysema, subject to terrifying attacks in which each breath of air requires a struggle, experiences his situation differently from the person with advanced renal failure, or with a cardiovascular trajectory. Although Kübler-Ross's theory directs welcome attention to the universal psychosocial aspects of terminal illness, we also lose much sensitivity if the disease process itself is not fully respected.

Sex differences   Do men and women experience terminal illness identically, even if both are afflicted by the same condition? Clinical experience suggests that the sexes differ with respect to the type of discomfort, impairment, and limitations of function that are of greatest concern. Some of our research in progress further suggests that pain, dependency, and loss of occupational role rank very high for men, while women are more distressed by the impact of their illness and death upon others. It is possible, then, that sex-role attitudes may be a significant source of variance in adaptation to terminal illness.

Ethnicity   Is it legitimate to die in a hospital or other public institution? How is pain to be experienced and expressed? Is it most important to keep up the strong front or the family name? Does the death event signify triumph and release or dismal failure? For some people, the answers to these questions may be found most clearly in their ethnic identity. The total interpersonal situation that surrounds a terminally ill person as well as his own responses can differ radically depending upon the ethnic patterns involved—as thousands of nurses can testify.

Personality or cognitive style   Whatever makes a person the particular person he is has much to do with the nature of his terminal phase of life. No single personality or cognitive style is invariably adaptive; in fact, any of a number of cognitive style variables might be equally adequate. The point is that we approach our death to some extent as the type of person we have always been—reflective or impulsive, warm or aloof, whatever. A view of the dying process that excludes personality as such must also exclude much of reality.

Developmental level   The meaning of dying and death differs for the infant who has known little of life and for the aged man or woman who has known much. Additionally, whatever merit there is in classifying people according to developmental level applies as well to appreciating their experiences in the terminal phase of life. People come to death as more or less mature organisms, and with very different positions along with their own potential life cycles. In other words, the person's general developmental situation must be taken into account as well as any modes of development that are specific to the dying process itself.

Sociophysical milieu   What is the nature of the environment in which the person is dying? Is it an efficient, professionalized world of strangers? A slow-paced nursing home? A room in the house where the person was born many years before? Is the environment over- or underprotective? Does it value expression or suppression of feelings? Is this an environment in which there are clear, conflicting, or no expectations of the dying person himself? However we may choose to analyze the sociophysical milieu, it is obviously a major source of variance in influencing what the dying person says and does, and perhaps also what he feels.

Formulations of the dying process could be derived from each of the areas sketched earlier. Some appear as promising or more promising than a stage theory, some less promising. Useful theories of dying could be grounded, for example, in the sociophysical milieu. The work of Glaser and Strauss (1965) moves in this direction. The milieu also has the advantage of being somewhat amenable to change. A formulation that incorporates two or more sources of variation could be even more powerful (e.g., the developmental and the sociophysical). There is no compelling reason to limit our thinking to any single realm.

Even if Kübler-Ross's theory could be supported as an accurate representation of adaptive strategies on the part of the dying person, it would still tell us little that we need to know about the interaction with disease process, ethnicity, personality style, and so on. Were less claimed for her theory, more could be granted to it. Hastily accepted as *the* account of the dying process, Kübler-Ross's theory emphasizes one possible set of dynamics to the virtual exclusion of all others.

One of the consequences is establishment of the image of *the* dying person moving through the universal five stages. Yet it is always a specific person dying in a specific environment that has its own social and physical dynamics, and the person approaches death through one or more specific disease modalities, responding in terms of the idiosyncratic integration of personality, ethnic, sex-role, and developmental resources. Viewed in this light, each death is individual. The five stages, if they do exist, are found within the context of the situation but do not necessarily dominate it.

4. Other Problems with the Stage Theory of Dying   In keeping with most developmental theories, the stage theory of dying assumes a single primary path of movement. We grow up one way. We die one way. Variations are acknowledged, but are seen as deviations from a central mode of progression. This approach is objectionable in the stage theory of dying as well as other forms of developmental theory—objectionable because the uncritical perpetuation of the one-path conception (a) impedes the appreciation and discovery of alternate approaches and (b) has the effect of stereotyping uncommon or idiosyncratic patterns as deviant.

Both the stage theory of dying and developmental theories in general sometimes fail to distinguish adequately between what usually happens and what *should* happen. The problem may, however, be more severe in the present use of the stage theory of dying, where conception and application are closely linked, and both under intense emotional pressure. Kübler-Ross herself has cautioned that people should not be rushed through the stages. Yet the theory implies that there is a valued destination to be reached, and that one should keep moving toward acceptance, if at his or her own pace. Less a problem of the theory itself than of some of its applications, there is nevertheless a disturbing tendency for description to be converted imperceptibly into prescription. In general, the relationships between fact and surmise, surmise and theory, and theory and value orientation remain obscure and vulnerable in the stage theory of dying.

Clinical research concerning the dying process by other investigators does not clearly support the existence of the five stages or of any universal form of staging. A recent review of the literature, scant as it is, finds no evidence for five predictable stages of psychological adaptation. Other investigators' data "show the process of dying to be less rigid and even stageless. There is some consensus among all researchers that terminal patients are depressed shortly before they die, but there is not consistent evidence that other affect dimensions characterize the dying patient" (Schulz and Alderman 1974). We must add that this negative conclusion is based upon studies conducted by various clinical investigators with equally various populations, techniques, and objectives, none of which were to make critical tests of stage theory. Nevertheless, the fact that available data do not make a strong case for the stage theory of dying obviously must be kept in mind.

D. Concluding Note on the Stage Theory of Dying

Although this has been perhaps the most systematic exploration yet made of the stage theory of dying, much remains to be learned and discussed. It is possible that the theory, either in its present or a revised form, might eventually become established as a faithful representation of central facts in the dying process and a dependable guide to education and action. For the moment, however, what we have is the early social history of a simple formulation about some vital aspects of human existence. This theory fills various individual and social needs; it is illuminated by the experience and insight of its author; and it can be appealing to those who are avid collectors of stage theories. We hope to have suggested that the application of stage theory to significant—literally life-and-death—experience should be accompanied by the critical and self-correcting perspective of science, no matter how we might want to believe that the truth is at hand. Those who have taken up the theory only to abandon it after clinical trials might also find it useful to examine their own reasons for both accceptance and rejection. What was expected or demanded of the theory? Were these expectations appropriate? What can we require realistically of any formulation of the dying process, and what must we require directly of ourselves? No matter what base of external knowledge or what theoretical perspective we bring to the dying situation, there is no substitute for confronting and in some manner accommodating ourselves to the prospect of our own deaths—a central theme in the work of Kübler-Ross and most other pioneers in this field.

References

Feifel, H., ed. *The meaning of death.* New York: McGraw-Hill, 1959.

Glaser, B. G., and A. Strauss. *Awareness of dying.* Chicago: Aldine Publishing, 1965.

Kübler-Ross, E. *On death and dying.* New York: Macmillan, 1969.

Schulz, R., and D. Alderman. Clinical research and the "stages of dying." *Omega* 5:137–144, 1974.

HARVEY BLUESTONE & CARL L. McGAHEE

Reaction to Extreme Stress: Impending Death by Execution

There are many ways to die, and there are many ways of facing death. Terminal illness is not the only condition in which one knows that one's death is imminent. Capital punishment sets the individual the same task of preparing to die, but in an ignominious way. Unlike the case of the patient, there is no question of keeping the face of impending death from the prisoner and little or no social support to help him rationalize the fact of death. In a series of brief case histories, Bluestone and McGahee describe the development of characteristic coping mechanisms that serve to protect the prisoners from experiencing overwhelming anxiety or depression. Denial, projection, and obsessional concerns may have a specific content here, but the process of adjustment to stress is a familiar one.

We conventionally think of death as "the worst thing" that can happen to us. Knowing, as we all do, that we will die in some vague future does not impose any great stress. The man in the grip of a relentlessly fatal disease has to cope with much more severe stress. But mercifully, his death date is not fixed and he can always hope to see tomorrow's sun rise. Presumably, the greatest of stresses would be imposed on the man who knows he is going to be put to death—and knows just when that will be.

We have studied 18 men and one woman in the Sing Sing death house. Because of the inmates' utilizing opportunities for appeals for clemency or commutation there is adequate time for repeated psychiatric interviews and psychologic examinations.

These men are housed in an area detached from the rest of the prison. They have few visitors, though the authorities impose no restrictions on visiting. One might expect them to show severe depression and devastating anxiety, yet neither symptom was conspicuous among these 19 doomed persons. By what mechanisms did they avoid these expected reactions to such overwhelming stress? Do their emotional patterns change during a year or two in a death cell? And, do these defenses function to the moment of execution—or do they crumble toward the end?

Source: H. Bluestone and C. L. McGahee, "Reaction to Extreme Stress: Impending Death by Execution," *American Journal of Psychiatry,* Vol. 119, pp. 393–396, 1962. Copyright © 1962, the American Psychiatric Association. Reprinted by permission.

The 19 histories had certain features in common. All had come from deprived backgrounds. All but one came from homes where the father was missing (deserted, dead, unknown, or separated) during the childhood or adolescence. Practically all had been brought up (during their growing years) in institutions or foster homes. Not one had an education better than that of tenth grade. Some were illiterate. Their intelligence varied from an IQ of 60 to one with an IQ of 140. All had been convicted of murder. None of the murders was long planned: they were impulsive. Many were committed in connection with a felony. The world appeared as a hostile, dangerous, and menacing place, and they had reacted in their way—by aggression, suspiciousness, and cynicism.

The following are brief summaries of the reaction of some of these men to their imprisonment in the death house.

1. Age range of death house prisoners

18 or younger	1
19 or 20	2
21 through 25	5
26 through 30	3
30 to 35	5
over 35	3

2. Family background

Parents together during most of childhood	1
Father unknown or deserted	7
Father divorced or separated	10
Father and mother unknown	1

3. Highest school grade reached

Fourth or lower	4
Fifth or sixth	8
Seventh or eighth	2
Ninth or tenth	5

4. Intelligence quotient

60 through 69	2
70 through 79	5
80 through 89	7
90 through 119	4
120 through 140	1

5. Family status of prisoner as adult

Never married, but had common-law spouse	5
Never married, no regular consortium	11
Married, but separated	2
Living with wife	1

6. Psychological defense mechanisms used
   (*Totals more than* 19; *some used more than once*)

   Denial by isolation of affect 7
   Denial by minimizing the predicament 4
   Denial by delusion formation 1
   Denial by living only in the present 4
   Projection 7
   Obsessive rumination in connection with appeals .. 3
   Obsessive preoccupation with religion 2
   Obsessive preoccupation with intellectual or
      philosophical matters 5

1. This man has the longest residence in the death house of those in this study, approximately two years. An overt confirmed homosexual, he maintained a calm conviction that he would be ultimately pardoned. This belief remained bolstered throughout by an unchanging contention that he had been framed by the legal and medical authorities involved in his prosecution. Psychological testing showed a man of average intelligence with considerable withdrawal from real emotional interaction with others. Defense mechanisms of denial and projection were effective in warding off anxiety and depression despite prolonged incarceration in the death house.

2. This inmate is the only woman in this series. She is of dull intelligence, acts in a playful and flirtatious manner. She was usually euphoric, but became transiently depressed when she thought her case was going badly. She frequently complained of insomnia and restlessness. These symptoms quickly disappeared when she was visited by a psychiatrist whom she enjoyed seeing and talking to in a self-justifying and self-pitying manner. Psychological tests showed pervasive feelings of insecurity, repressive defenses, and an inability to handle angry and aggressive feelings in an effectual manner.

3. This inmate is a withdrawn, sullen, uncommunicative individual. When visited in the death house he would elaborately and slowly wash his clothes, ignoring examiners. He spends much of his time reading profound philosophical works which are beyond his comprehension. His intelligence is dull–normal. He has become progressively more suspicious and grandiose during his death house stay.

4. This man gives a long history of delinquent behavior. He is a litigiously minded individual who states that he can appeal his case for years. He is obsessed with his own power and is convinced that a law suit against the district attorney for lost automobile tools kept that official from being reelected. He has become progressively more angry and abusive, ultimately necessitating his physical isolation from other inmates. His IQ is 134. Projective tests show a chronically cold, withdrawn, narcissistically invested personality. Withdrawal, projection and denial are prominent defense mechanisms.

5. This man is at all times euphoric. He has shown little anxiety during

the full year he has spent in the death house. He has led a hedonistic life and has never been able to make future plans. His inability to see beyond the day seems quite effective in enabling him to avoid anxiety and depression.

6. This inmate showed during his early months of incarceration a contemptuous indifference toward the authorities and his own plight. Gradually, however, depression appeared and became progressively more intense. This was rather dramatically reversed when the inmate presented an apparent religious conversion, which seemed to both occupy his mind and also elevate him above the authorities and his situation. However, this defense was only partially successful for this individual who had a life-long history of discharging all tensions by immediate impulsive acting-out. Psychological testing showed dull–normal intelligence and a primitive, self-absorbed, hostility-ridden personality.*

8. This inmate related to examiners in an open and direct manner. He is mentally dull and preoccupied with thoughts of voodoo spells. His primary defense mechanism is denial of the possibility of being executed. This works poorly and he is chronically anxious and periodically depressed. His anger at his accomplice, who he is convinced is the cause of his difficulties, seems to relieve him of some of his unpleasant feelings. He amuses himself in working on a taunting poem which he proposes to recite when his accomplice is executed. This mechanism, too, is ineffectual and he reverts from these thoughts of revenge to a contemplation of his own plight.

9. This man is a moody individual who feels he is the victim of a Jewish plot since the judge, district attorney, and his own court-appointed lawyer are Jewish. He denied his guilt repeatedly during his early days in the death house, but became progressively more confused and a few days before his scheduled execution asked the examiner for truth serum so that he would know whether or not he committed the crime. He showed alternating use of introjection and projection. He would become depressed when news of his appeal was bad, and when a stay of execution was granted he became paranoid and grandiose. He managed in some obscure way to identify his impending death with that of Lumumba, who had recently been killed in the Congo, and felt that his own execution would make him a martyr in the cause of anti-imperialism.

10. This man stands out in the series as being the one who most successfully employed intellectualization as a means of defending against anxiety and depression. He elaborated a philosophy of life and values in which his own criminal career became not only justifiable, but even respectable. He rationalized his crimes by emphasizing the hypocrisy and perfidy of society on the one hand and by comparing himself with policemen and soldiers and others who live honorably "by the gun" on the other. This system was so effective for him

*Editors' Note: Number 7 was omitted in the original article, which has been exactly reprinted here.

that even when execution appeared imminent he maintained his hero's martyr role and disdained to request executive clemency.

11. This inmate is an illiterate, inadequate individual who was convicted as an accomplice to a robbery–murder. He has an overall IQ of 51. He showed primarily depression, withdrawal, and obsessive rumination over the details of the crime and conviction. He eventually evolved a poorly elaborated paranoid system whereby he supposedly was betrayed and framed by his girlfriend and one of the co-defendants. Despite the looseness of his persecutory thinking, it was accompanied by a clear-cut elevation in his mood and reduction of anxiety.

12. This inmate, also an accomplice to a robbery–murder, showed one of the most florid pictures of any in this series. Both grandiose and persecutory themes were prominent, but the latter predominated. He maintained that his arrest and conviction were malicious frauds, and he meticulously and obsessively combed through the court record to substantiate his contentions. His arguments were labored and illogical, hinging on such points as the use of words like "who" and "whom." The paranoid mechanisms seemed to mitigate, but not completely defend him against depression.

13. He is one of the two inmates in this series who uses religious preoccupation as his major defense mechanism. He repeatedly, in an almost word for word way, stated his situation as follows. "No one can understand how I feel unless it happened to you. Christ came to me and I know He died for my sins. It doesn't matter if I am electrocuted or not. I am going to another world after this and I am prepared for it." As his stay progresses he becomes increasingly more hostile and antagonistic, and his behavior progressively out of keeping with his professed religious ideas. In addition to obsessive rumination, projection and withdrawal are employed to ward off feelings of anxiety and depression.

Discussion

Faced with certain and ignominious death, a person would presumably be overwhelmed with anxiety or plunge into the depths of depression. Yet this does not happen. What defense does the human mind set up against intense anxiety or a paralyzing depression? We suggest, on the basis of our 19 case studies, that the defenses are of mainly three types—denial, projection, and obsessive rumination. The commonest form of *denial* is isolation of affect. "So, they'll kill me; and that's that"—this said with a shrug of the shoulders suggests that the affect appropriate to the thought has somehow been isolated. A second common form of denial is to minimize the gravity of the present situation and to take for granted that an appeal will be successful. The third and most extreme manifestation of denial, used by only one individual, was to delusionally believe that a pardon had been granted. Denial is also commonly used by persons dying of disease.

There is another phenomenon which deserves further explanation, since it may easily be confused with denial. Several cases impressed the examiners as being so immersed in the present moment as to virtually be insulated from any significant emotional relatedness with their own past or future. Thus, they do not have to deny anxiety since they do not experience it. This, incidentally, is the traditional profile of the "psychopath" who reacts only to present stimuli.

Projection is an obvious and not uncommon mechanism. Typically, it takes the form of persecutory delusions. At least three of our prisoners considered themselves persecuted by specific groups in the community. This mechanism converts dissolute criminals into martyrs. It is a comforting delusion. While it does not deny that death is just around the corner, it tries to lend it dignity and meaning. In some men there seems to be an almost quantitative reciprocal relationship between the use of projection and introjection so that they are either overly paranoid or depressed.

A third way of coping with painful affects is to *think furiously* about something else. Thus, the depressing thought is elbowed out of consciousness by the crowd of other ideas. We see this in a morbid obsessional concern about the preparing of appeals or pleas for clemency. One prisoner spoke to us for an hour about whether a pronoun in the appeal transcript should be "who" or "whom." To be sure, a meticulous concern with the appeal brief is rational; in these cases, however, the concern is obsessional, ruminative, and ineffective. Another type of obsession (two of the men showed this) is preoccupation with religion to the exclusion of everything else. The prisoners who developed this syndrome had involved their confederates in death sentences too, though neither accomplice had killed anyone. Presumably, this religious conversion served to blunt guilt feelings about involving the accomplices. This activity served two other purposes: it distracted them from anxiety, and it offered a route to a happy life in the hereafter. The third type of obsessive rumination is the intellectual: a dipping into philosophical thought by a man whose life had hitherto been devoted to hedonistic pursuits.

Some try desperately to mould a respectable image of themselves. This is certainly one sluiceway for draining out anxiety—as illustrated, for example, in the way in which one of the prisoners identified himself with Lumumba and the world-shaking events in the Congo.

The group support these men receive from fellow inmates is variable. Some are quite appealing and receive considerable emotional and even material support in terms of cigarettes and help with their correspondence. Others manage quickly to antagonize their fellows and are in turn ridiculed and tormented by them in a direct and sadistic manner. This is often true when a man gets the reputation of being a malingerer. The inmates are quite antagonistic to anyone they feel is falsifying religious beliefs or feigning mental symptoms.

Conclusion

Traditional ego defense mechanisms alleviate distress. They also mitigate anxiety and depression which would otherwise overwhelm the prisoner in a death cell. Some psychiatrists allege that the death fear (whether on the battlefield or in the death house) serves as an irrational surrogate for some other fear—such as castration. This oversimplified explanation does scant justice to the inescapable certainty shared by all, but anticipated only by man.

ANSELM L. STRAUSS & BARNEY G. GLASER

Awareness of Dying

The relationship between the individual's awareness of his or her own dying and the institutional response, as examined in the previous article for the atypical setting of a prison, is pursued by Strauss and Glaser for the more typical occurrence of hospital death. When dying occurs in a hospital, as is most often the case in North America, not only the family but also the hospital staff enter into a complex interaction with the dying person, often to maintain the fiction of nonterminal illness. In the following article, the authors describe the organizational strategies used to avoid confrontation with the patient and his or her death. The work of Strauss and Glaser has played a part in bringing about major change in institutional response toward dying patients, but the situations they identify still occur with some frequency.

Americans are characteristically unwilling to talk openly about the process of dying and death and are prone to avoid telling a dying person his prognosis. This is, in part, a moral attitude: life is preferable to whatever may follow it, and one should not look forward to death unless in great pain.

This moral attitude appears to be shared by the professional people who work with or near the patients who die in our hospitals. Although trained to give specialized medical or nursing care to terminal patients, much of their behavior toward the dying resembles the layman's. The training that physicians and nurses receive equips them principally for the technical aspects of patient care; their teachers deal only briefly or not at all with the management of the emotional response of patients to illness and death.

Similarly, students at schools of nursing are taught how to give nursing care to terminal patients, as well as how to give "post-mortem care," but only recently have the psychological aspects of nursing care been included in the nurses' training. Few teachers talk about such matters, and they generally confine themselves to a lecture or two near the end of the course, sometimes calling in a psychiatrist to give a kind of "expert testimony."[1]

Beyond the medical education experience, management of the dying patient in the hospital setting is quite naturally only in strictly technical medical and nursing terms. Staff members are not required to report to each other or to their superiors what they have talked about with dying patients; they are "accountable" only for the technical aspects of their work with the dying.[2]

Medical and nursing personnel commonly recognize that working with dying patients is upsetting and sometimes traumatic. Consequently, some

Source: Anselm L. Strauss and Barney G. Glaser, "Awareness of Dying," in *Loss and Grief: Psychological Management in Medical Practice.* Edited by Bernard Schoenberg, Arthur C. Carr, David Peretz, and Austin H. Kutscher. New York: Columbia University Press, 1970, 298–309.

physicians purposely specialize in branches of medicine that will minimize their chances of encountering dying patients; many nurses frankly admit a preference for those wards or fields of nursing in which death is infrequently encountered. Those who bear the brunt of caring for terminal patients understandably develop both standardized and idiosyncratic modes of coping with the inherent threats. The most standard mode is a tendency to avoid contact with those patients who, as yet unaware of impending death, are inclined to question staff members about their increasing debilitation. Also avoided are those patients who have not "accepted" their approaching deaths, and those whose deaths are accompanied by great pain. Staff members' efforts to cope with death often have undesirable effects on both the social and psychological aspects of patient care and their own comfort. Personnel in contact with terminal patients are always somewhat disturbed by their own ineptness in handling the dying.

The social and psychological problems involved in dying are perhaps most acute when the dying person knows that he is dying. For this reason, among others, American physicians are quite reluctant to disclose impending death to their patients, and nurses are expected not to disclose it without the consent of the responsible physicians. At the same time, personnel generally agree that a patient will usually discover the truth without being told explicitly. Some physicians maneuver conversations with patients so that disclosure is made indirectly. In any event, the demeanor and actions of a patient who knows or suspects that he is dying differ from those of a patient who is not aware of dying. The problem of "awareness" is crucial to what happens both to the dying patient and to the people who give him medical and nursing care.

From one point of view the problem of awareness is a technical one: Should the patient be told he is dying, and what exactly is to be said if he knows, does not know, or only suspects? But the problem is also a moral one. Is it really proper to deny a dying person the opportunity to make his peace with his conscience and with his God, to settle his affairs and provide for the future of his family, and to determine his style of dying, much as he determined his style of living? Does anyone, the physician included, have the right to withhold such information? And on whose shoulders should this responsibility of disclosure fall—the physician, the family, or the patient?

Both the human and the technical aspects of the awareness problem are becoming increasingly momentous. One reason for this is that most Americans no longer die at home. Fifty-three percent of all deaths in the United States in 1967 occurred in hospitals, and many more in nursing homes.[3] These people, then, pass through the dying process surrounded for the most part by strangers. Dying away from home is compounded by a noticeable and important medical trend—because medical technology has vastly improved, fewer people are dying from acute diseases and more from chronic diseases. Moreover, the usual duration of most chronic diseases has increased.

The public has become increasingly sophisticated regarding the implications of physical signs and symptoms and will not be put off by evasive or oversimplified answers to their questions. Inevitably, they will understand the truth. Therefore, it is predictable that the problem of awareness will become more and more central to what happens as people pass from life to death in American hospitals.

Awareness Contexts

There are specific "awareness contexts" revolving around the confrontation of patient and hospital personnel: for example, a patient may not recognize his impending death even though everyone else does, or he may also suspect what everyone else knows for certain. On the other hand, both patient and others may know that death is imminent yet pretend this is not so. Or they may all act on such awareness relatively openly. We shall refer to these situations as the following types of awareness: *closed awareness, suspected awareness, mutual pretense awareness,* and *open awareness.* The impact of each type of awareness context upon the interplay between patients and personnel is profound, for people guide their talk and actions according to who knows what and with what certainty. As talk, action, and the accompanying cues unfold, certain awareness contexts tend to evolve into other contexts.

Closed Awareness and Suspected Awareness

There are at least five important structural conditions which contribute to the existence and maintenance of the closed awareness context:

First, most patients have had little or no experience in recognizing the signs of impending death.

A second structural condition is that American physicians ordinarily do not tell patients outright that death is probable or inevitable. As a number of studies have shown, physicians proffer medical justifications for not disclosing the fatal prognosis to their patients.[4] For instance, one investigator[5] found that many physicians maintain that when one announces terminality to a patient, he is likely to "go to pieces"; one must therefore carefully judge whether or not to tell after sizing up the individual patient. In actual fact, this investigator notes, the "clinical experience" is not genuinely grounded experience but a species of personal mythology. The judgment was found to be based on one or two unfortunate incidents or even incidents recounted by colleagues.

Many physicians believe that patients really do not wish to know whether they are dying; if they did, then they would find out anyhow, so there is no sense telling them directly. Presumably some patients do not wish to know their fates, but there is no really good evidence that all wish to remain in blissful ignorance. There is, in fact, good evidence that they do wish to know.[6]

A third structural condition is that families tend to guard the secret, thereby confirming what the physician has announced. An interesting contrast is the practice in Asian countries, where the extended kin gather around the hospital death bed two or more days before death is expected, openly indicating to the patient that they are there to keep him company during his passage to death.

A fourth structural condition is that of the organization of hospitals and the commitments of personnel who work within them by which medical information is concealed from patients. Records are kept out of reach. Staff is skilled at withholding information. Medical talk about patients generally occurs in far-removed places, and if it occurs nearby it is couched in medical jargon. Staff members are trained to discuss with patients only the surface aspects of their illnesses, and, as we shall see, they are accustomed to acting collusively around patients so as not to disclose medical secrets.

A fifth structural condition, perhaps somewhat less apparent, is that ordinarily the patient has no allies who reveal or help him discover the fact of his impending death. Not only his family but other patients (if they know) withhold that information.

In her book, *Experiment Perilous,* Renée Fox has described a small research hospital whose patients recognized their own inevitable terminality.[7] Death was an open and everyday occurrence. Patients could talk familiarly to each other as well as to the staff members about their respective fatal conditions. Various consequences flowed from this *open* situation: patients could give each other support, and the staff could support the patients. Patients could even raise the flagging spirits of the staff! From their deathbeds, patients could thank the physicians for their unstinting efforts and wish them luck in solving their research problems in time to save other patients. They could close their lives with rituals such as letter writing and praying. They could review their lives and plan realistically for their families' futures. These consequences are, of course, not available to patients in the closed awareness situation. Instead, other consequences emerge. Since the unaware patient believes he will recover, he acts on that supposition. Thus he may convert his sick room into a temporary work-place, writing his unfinished book, telephoning his business partners, and in other ways carrying on his work somewhat "as usual." He carries on his family life and friendships with only the interruption necessitated by temporary illness. He plans as if life stretched before him. On the other hand, he may work less feverishly on his unfinished book than if he knew time was short and so fail to finish it. He may set plans into operation that in reality are useless and the plans will have to be undone after his death. The unaware patient may unwittingly shorten his life because he does not realize that special care is necessary to extend it, he may not understand the necessity for certain treatments and refuse them.

It is in some ways easier for the family to face a patient who does not know of his terminality, especially if he is the kind of person who is likely to die "gracelessly." And if an unaware person is suddenly stricken and dies, sometimes his family is grateful that "he died without knowing." On the other hand, when the kin must participate in a lengthy nondisclosure drama, they shoulder a tremendous burden. They suffer because they cannot express their grief openly to the dying person; this is especially true of husbands and wives who have always shared fully with each other.

> A dying man's wife had been informed of the prognosis by the doctor and had shared this information with friends, whose daughter told the patient's young son. The son developed a strong distrust for the doctor, and felt disinherited by his father since they had not (nor could they have) discussed the responsibilities that would fall to him in the future.

The closed context instituted by the physician permits him to avoid the potentially distressing scene that may follow an announcement to his patient, but such a closed context only subjects nurses to strain, for it is they who must spend the most time with the unaware patient, guarding constantly against disclosure. Nurses may sometimes actually be relieved when the patient talks openly about his demise and they no longer have to guard against disclosure. On the other hand, under certain conditions nurses prefer the closed context. Some do not care to talk about death with a patient, especially a patient who does not accept it with fortitude. An unaware person is sometimes easier to handle because he has not "given up." The closed awareness situation prevents staff members from enjoying certain advantages that accompany a patient's resigned—or joyous—meeting with death.

Important consequences of closed awareness also hold for the staff as a whole. Unaware patients who die quickly represent simply routine work for the staff. In contrast, the patient who moves explosively and resentfully from an unaware to a highly suspicious or fully aware state is disruptive.

The most crucial institutional consequence has already been mentioned: because American physicians generally choose not to tell patients of their terminal status, this burden falls squarely and persistently upon the nursing personnel. This considerable burden is built into the organization of the hospital services that deal with terminal patients. Another social structure condition intrinsic to the functioning of American hospitals also increases the nurse's burden, namely, the nurse's commitment to work relatively closely with and around patients. This structural condition can be better appreciated when seen in contrast to conditions in Asian hospitals, where the family clusters thickly and persistently around the dying patient, thus permitting the nursing personnel to remain at a relatively greater emotional distance from, and spend relatively little time with the patient. In addition, the enormously high patient-to-personnel ratio increases the probability of great distance and little contact.

Mutual Pretense Awareness and Open Awareness

The mutual pretense awareness context is perhaps less visible, even to its participants, than the closed, open, and suspicion contexts. A prime structural condition of this context is that unless the patient initiates conversation about his impending death, no staff member is required to talk about it with him. The patient may wish to initiate such conversation, but surely neither hospital rules nor common convention urges it upon him. Consequently, unless either the aware patient or a staff member breaks the silence by words or gestures, a mutual pretense rather than an open awareness context will exist.

The patient, of course, is more likely than the staff members to refer openly to his death, thereby inviting them, explicitly or implicitly, to respond in kind. If they seem unwilling, he may decide they do not wish to confront openly the fact of his death, and then he may, out of tact or genuine empathy for their embarrassment or distress, keep his silence.

Staff members, in turn, may give him opportunities to speak of his death without a direct or obvious reference. But if he does not care to act or talk as if he were dying, then they will support his pretense. In doing so, they have, in effect, accepted a complementary assignment of status—they will act with pretense toward his pretense.

Staff members may rationalize pretense by maintaining that if the patient wishes to pretend, it may well be best for his health. A second rationale is that perhaps they can give him better medical and nursing care if they do not have to face him so openly. A third rationale is that this sort of action is most tactful.

During the pretense episodes both sides naturally assume certain implicit rules of behavior. One rule is that dangerous topics should generally be avoided—the most obvious being the patient's death; another, the events that will happen afterward.

Talk about dangerous topics is permissible as long as neither party breaks down. The patient and the nurses may discuss daily events—such as treatments—as if they had implications for a real future, when the patient will have recovered from his illness. Some of the patient's brave, or foolhardy activities (as when he bathes himself or insists on tottering to the toilet by himself) may signify a brave show of pretense. The staff, in turn, permits his activity.

It is customary, then, that patient and staff focus determinedly on appropriately safe topics—daily routines of eating and sleeping; complaints and their management; minor personal confidences; events on the ward, and news events. Talk about the fatal illness is safe enough if confined to the symptoms themselves.

When something happens or is said that threatens to expose the fiction that both parties are attempting to sustain, then each must pretend that nothing has gone awry. Thus, a nurse may take special pains to announce herself before entering a patient's room so as not to surprise him at his crying. If she finds him crying, she may ignore it or convert it into an innocuous event with a skillful comment or gesture. A patient who cannot control a sudden expression of great pain will verbally discount its significance, while the nurse in turn goes along with his pretense. Clearly then, each party to the ritual pretense shares responsibility for maintaining it.

A mutual pretense context that is not sustained can only change to an open awareness context. The change may be sudden, temporary, or permanent. Or the change may be gradual: nurses, and relatives, too, are familiar with patients who admit to terminality more openly on some days than they do on other days, when pretense is dominant, until finally pretense vanishes altogether. Sometimes the physician skillfully paces his interaction with a patient, leading the patient finally to refer openly to his terminality and to leave behind the earlier phase of pretense.

Pretense generally collapses when certain conditions make its maintenance increasingly difficult, for example, when the patient cannot keep from expressing his increasing pain, or his suffering grows to the point that he must be kept under heavy sedation.

The pretense context can provide the patient with a measure of dignity and considerable privacy, although it may deny him the close relationship with his family that is created when he allows them to participate in his open acceptance of death. For the family—especially more distant kin—the pretense context can minimize embarrassment and other interactional strains; but for closer kin, openness may have many advantages. Oscillation between contexts of open awareness and mutual pretense is in itself a source of stress.

But whether staff or patient initiates the ritual of pretense, maintaining it creates a characteristic mood of cautious serenity throughout the ward. Even one such patient can set such an atmosphere. Denial in the patients of a cancer hospital (buttressed by staff silence), all of whom know the nature of the hospital, can be so strong that few patients talk openly about anyone's condition.

A persistent context of pretense profoundly affects the more permanent aspects of hospital organization as well. When closed awareness generally prevails, the personnel must guard against disclosure, but they need not organize themselves as a team to handle continued pretense and its sometimes stressful breakdown. Also a chief organizational consequence of the mutual pretense context is that it eliminates any possibility that staff members might "work with" patients psychologically on a professional basis. It is also entirely possible that a ward mood of tension can be set when a number of elderly dying patients continually communicate to each other their willingness to die, but the staff members persistently insist on the pretense that the patients are going to recover. On the other hand, the prevailing ward mood accompanying mutual pretense tends to be more serene—or at least less obviously tense—than when suspected awareness is dominant.

The context of open awareness does not eliminate complexity, and, in fact, certain ambiguities associated with two properties of the open awareness context are inevitable. Even when he recognizes and acknowledges the fact of terminality, the patient's awareness is frequently qualified by his ignorance or suspicion about other aspects of his dying. Thus, a patient who knows that he is dying may be convinced that death is still some months away. Staff members may then conceal their own knowledge of the time that death is expected to occur, even though they may refer openly to the fact that it is expected. Similarly, they may keep secret their expectation that the patient is going to deteriorate badly, so long as he is unaware of this contingency.

Of course, certain patients (such as physicians) may, as a matter of course, be aware of these subsidiary aspects of impending death. Patients who have the same disease are often kept together, so that each may observe a kind of rehearsal of his own fate by watching others who are closer to death.

The second ambiguous element of the open awareness context is the divergence in expectations about "appropriate" ways of dying which reflects in part the common tendency for staff and patients to come from different class and ethnic backgrounds. It also reflects deeply inculcated professional and institutional norms which differ from those of patients.

Once a patient has indicated his awareness of dying, he becomes responsible for his acts as a *dying* person. He knows now that he is not merely sick but dying. He must face that fact. Sociologically, facing an impending death means that the patient will be judged, and will judge himself, according to certain standards of proper conduct concerning his behavior during his final days and hours. At the same time, hospital personnel will be judged and will judge themselves in their responses to dying patients.

At first glance, the medical personnel's obligation to a dying patient seems obvious enough. If possible, they must save him; if not, then they must give proper medical and nursing care until he dies. But ethical and social, in addition to medical, judgments enter into questions such as when to try to save a patient and when to cease trying, whether to prolong life when death is certain or the patient is already comatose, and so on. These judgments, as well as less dramatic ones such as administering "better" care, depend in many instances, not on objective, but subjective criteria such as the "deserving" character of the patient.

Patients defined as less deserving risk the additional judgment that they are acting with purpose. If they know that they are dying, their improper behavior cannot be interpreted as a consequence of ignorance. Patients known to be aware of death have two kinds of obligation: first, they should not act to bring about their own death; second, there are certain positive obligations one has as a dying patient. There are no clear rules of behavior provided for the dying nor are there clear expectations on the part of the staff regarding his behavior.

Nevertheless, staff members do judge the conduct of dying patients by certain implicit standards. These standards are related to the work that hospital personnel do, as well as to some rather general American notions about courageous and decent behavior. A partial list of implicit canons includes the following: the patient should maintain relative composure and cheerfulness; at the very least, he should face death with dignity; he should not cut himself off from the world, turning his back upon the living, but should continue to be a good family member, and be "nice" to other patients; if he can, he should participate in the ward social life; he should cooperate with the staff members who care for him, and if possible he should avoid distressing or embarrassing them. A patient who does most of these things will be respected.

What the staff defines as unacceptable behavior in aware dying patients is readily illustrated. For instance, physicians usually honor requests for confirmatory consultations with other physicians but object to "shopping around" for impossible cures. Some patients do not face dying with fortitude but become noisy or hysterical. Other patients make excessive demands. Some patients wail, cry out in terror, complain, accuse the staff of doing nothing, or refuse to cooperate in their medical or nursing care. Perhaps the most unnerving are the patients who become apathetic or hostile and reproachful.

In general, then, the staff appreciates patients who exit with courage and grace, not merely because they create fewer scenes and cause less emotional stress, but because they evoke genuine admiration and sympathy, as well as feelings of professional usefulness. It is difficult to admire a patient who behaves improperly even though one can sympathize with his terrible situation. People cannot help judging him, even if by diverse and not altogether explicit standards. Occasionally a patient provides such a model of courage and fortitude that the staff remembers him with admiration long after his death. The reactions of staff members include not only respect for a great human being but also gratitude for being allowed to participate in the near-perfect drama of his dying.

A few points about the consequences of open awareness are worth emphasizing here. Awareness of impending death gives the patient an opportunity to close his life in the manner he chooses. He may finish important work, establish reconciliations, make satisfying farewells, give gifts to his friends, and leave detailed plans for his family and estate.

But open awareness has disadvantages for the patient, too. Other people may not approve of the patient's way of managing his death, and may attempt to change or subvert his management. A patient may not be able to close his life usefully and with dignity because he cannot face the dying process and death. An aware patient, therefore, may be unable to face death with equanimity, dying with more anguish and less dignity than he might if he were unaware of his terminality. For some patients there is the added stress of deciding whether to accept imminent death or to perhaps prolong life through surgery.

A patient who meets death with equanimity at the same time also makes this possible for his family. They will be able to share his satisfaction and they will treasure their experience for the remainder of their lives.

Notes

1. J. C. Quint and A. L. Strauss, "Nursing Students, Assignments, and Dying Patients," *Nursing Outlook* 12 (January 1964): 24.

2. A. L. Strauss, B. G. Glaser, and J. C. Quint, "The Nonaccountability of Terminal Care," *Hospitals* 38 (January 16, 1964): 73.

3. R. Fulton, "Death and Self," *Journal of Religion and Health* 3 (July 1964): 364.

4. H. Feifel, "Death," in *Taboo Topics*, ed. N. L. Farberow (New York: Atherton Press, 1963).

5. D. Oken, "What to Tell Cancer Patients: A Study of Medical Attitudes," *Journal of the American Medical Association* 175 (April 1, 1961): 1120.

6. Eighty-two percent of Feifel's sample of sixty patients wanted to be informed about their condition.

7. Renée Fox, *Experiment Perilous* (New York: The Free Press, 1959).

WILLIAM CARLOS WILLIAMS

To Waken an Old Lady

Though it is always a mistake to attribute the thoughts of a single writer to an age or a culture, individual thoughts do serve as windows to attitudes. Literary studies of death are often studies of life as well, with symbolic elements conveying much of the meaning. In his consideration of aging and awareness of mortality, William Carlos Williams develops a vignette that contrasts sharply in tone with Thomas's poem.

Old age is
a flight of small
cheeping birds
skimming
bare trees
above a snow glaze.
Gaining and failing
they are buffeted
by a dark wind—
But what?
On harsh weedstalks
the flock has rested,
the snow
is covered with broken
seedhusks
and the wind tempered
by a shrill
piping of plenty.

Source: William Carlos Williams, *Collected Earlier Poems.* Copyright © 1938 by New Directions Publishing Corporation. Reprinted by permission of the publisher.

VICTOR W. MARSHALL

Age and Awareness of Finitude in Developmental Gerontology

Noting the curious silence on the topic of death in the literature of developmental gerontology, Marshall seeks a cause. He presents research to identify the impact of aging on an individual's recognition of mortality. His findings suggest that though awareness of mortality, or finitude, is held to initiate processes of disengagement, self-focusing, and life review, age is less related to that precipitating awareness than are other social processes. Marshall underscores the value of sharing reminiscences in aging as a means of developing satisfaction and resolving conflicts of one's past life.

A reviewer of the social–psychological literature of gerontology might well conclude that death is not considered the inevitable termination of the life span. Despite the recent growth of the discipline of thanatology, the dying of the aged has little place in the research of gerontologists as they consider developmental issues. In this paper I seek to account for the lack of attention to the dying process in developmental research on aging. Then, relying most heavily on my own research in this area, I will attempt to give an account of the impact of the aging individual's recognition of his mortality on selected aspects of the aging process, arguing that in this case development is largely age-irrelevant (Baer 1970).

While certain European gerontologists have argued the importance of investigating the impact of awareness of finitude, in North America the debate between the activity theorists and disengagement theorists concerning the social relationships of older people has deflected attention from this concern. Activity theory completely ignores death or awareness of finitude in its formulations, because of its emphasis on continuing high levels of activity and usefulness. While the disengagement theorists argue that disengagement is triggered off by heightened awareness of finitude, this assertion has never been subjected to empirical test and, moreover, awareness of finitude has never been unambiguously defined. The reason for the failure of disengagement theory to adequately deal with awareness of finitude has been its emphasis in a manner not unlike that of activity theory, on an equilibrium state between the individual and his society. Gerontologists in both camps are concerned with social

Source: Victor Marshall, "Age and Awareness of Finitude in Developmental Gerontology," Omega 61 (1975).

relationships. The emphasis of disengagement theory research came to focus on social ties rather than any other concerns which might arise because of heightened awareness. In a rather simplistic fashion, disengagement theorists have argued that, in preparation for the total disengagement of death, the individual's major task is to smoothly sever his social relationships and say his good-byes, so as to maintain equilibrium (see the caustic remarks of Arnold Rose on this point, 1964). The individual is only considered to be *of interest* in his relation to his society; and he is considered to be *interested* only in his relationship to his society. Awareness of finitude is only one factor postulated as leading to "readiness for disengagement," along with perceived shrinkage of life space and decreased ego energy (Damianopoulos 1961), and as an instigator of disengagement has only once, and unsatisfactorily, been systematically examined, by Chellam. Finally, as I have defined the concept, awareness of finitude has only been considered as an independent, and never as a dependent or an intervening variable. It is this last point to which I now turn.

Awareness of Finitude as a Variable

As I have defined the concept, awareness of finitude has never been investigated as a dependent variable. Those few gerontologists who have used the concept or a related concept have taken it as non-problematic. Although they have argued that awareness of finitude leads to various psychological processes, they have never bothered to ask what leads to awareness of finitude.[1] The problem stems from an assumption that awareness of finitude is uniformly related to age, this assumption leading to a substitution of age as the independent variable when treating various propositions derived from theories such as disengagement theory.[2] This is evident, for example, in the empirical tests of aspects of disengagement theory reported by Havinghurst, Neugarten, and Tobin (1968; Neugarten, Havinghurst, and Tobin 1968). Moreover, any purported defense or critique of disengagement theory which uses age as a criterion variable for the appropriateness of disengagement (e.g., Maddox 1966; Lipman and Smith 1968) does not directly bear on the theory unless awareness of finitude is taken into account. Related attempts to test aspects of Butler's "life-review" theory (Falk 1970; Gorney 1968) fail to provide conclusive disconfirmation or to give support to the theory, because the life-review process is triggered off not, as these investigators assume, by age, but rather, Butler (1963) argues, by awareness of finitude. Finally, attempts to assess the utility of Erikson's conceptualization of the eighth identity crisis (Erikson 1963, 268–269) which rely on age (Gruen 1964; Rosen and Neugarten 1964; Lubin 1964) can be thought of as lacking in refinement, for although Erikson does not make the point explicit, the eighth identity crisis seems to be prompted by awareness of finitude (a point recognized by Cumming and Henry 1961, 225).

There is one common element in the above three approaches: all postulate a turning toward the self, a "stock taking" on one's life as a whole in relation to awareness of finitude, rather than in relation simply to age. I will first suggest that age and awareness of finitude are not uniformly related as has been presumed, and then offer some evidence of the focusing on the self which accompanies awareness of finitude. This focusing on the self is but one of several ways of experiencing death and dying, but it is an essential aspect of the experience of finitude, and hence of importance for a developmental theory of later life.

Awareness of Finitude as a Calculus

Do people as they age automatically become more aware of the shortness of the time remaining to them? Is the individual's anticipation of the time left to him an inverse function of his age? Data relevant to these questions were solicited from residents of a retirement village. Respondents were reasonably healthy middle-to-upper class white Americans who, for the most part, had attained educational levels of high school and college. Their socioeconomic and educational standing, as well as their community residence, undoubtedly affects their appreciation of their finitude (see Riley 1970). Generalizations to a wider sample are thus precarious. However, there are things we can learn from this group of persons between the ages 64 and 96, with average age 80.

The measure used in the following discussion is a fixed choice self-estimate of life expectancy utilized by Chellam (1964) as one component of her "awareness of death" scale. Following a series of questions concerning time perspective, the respondents were asked, "Which one of these would you say about your own future?"

1. I shall be around for some time yet; more than ten years.
2. I have a little while longer; oh, at least five to ten years.
3. Not too much longer; less than five years.
4. The end may be any time now.

Of 68 persons to whom this question was put, 50 gave codable answers. Collapsing the third and fourth categories into one yielded an array which correlated significantly with two other measures. One of these was Chellam's (1964) indicator which asks the respondent to place a mark on a line between the endpoints birth and death, so as to indicate where he feels he now is. The other was a direct question asking the respondent how many years he anticipated living. For reasons discussed elsewhere (Marshall 1972, 104–110) the fixed-choice indicator is the most satisfactory with these data at least, and is considered an operational measure of awareness of finitude.

Table 1 indicates that awareness of finitude is strongly related to age: the older an individual is, the less time he estimates is available to him before death. But age operates in a complex way in influencing awareness of finitude. Many individuals seem to perform a crude kind of calculus in estimating their own life expectancy; and this calculus rests heavily on the age to which family members, particularly parents, lived. Thus, in the words of a 65 year old

Table 1 | Awareness of Finitude in Relation to Age

	Age			
Respondent Anticipates Living an Additional	Young (64–75) %	Middle (76–84) %	Old (85–96) %	
10 or more years	50	28	10	
5 to 10 years	43	40	40	
less than 5 years	7	32	50	
TOTAL	100	100	100	
n =	14	25	10	49

Tau B = .340; sign. = .0003

respondent: "Up to now no men in my family have lived past 70. But a brother is going to be 72. But both parents died at 70. They say you die according to when your parents died." Another, aged 81, when asked how old he thought he would live to be, replied: "Ha! Ha! Very hard to say. To ninety. My father lived to 96; my mother to 72."

Table 2 indicates that awareness of finitude is strongly associated with a relationship of the respondent's own age to the age-at-death of his parents. If a person is still younger than the age at which both of his parents died, he is likely to give himself more years to live than if he has not exceeded the age-at-death of both his parents. By comparing the values of Tau (Kendall 1955), we can see that this comparison process is even more strongly related to awareness of finitude than is age itself. Although the numbers available for controls are small, the effects of the social comparison process remain highly significant (Tau B = -.540; sign. = .0001) within the middle age category, and appropriate trends appear within the other two age categories. This suggests that the process acts at least partially independently of age: a younger person who is now older than the age-at-death of both parents is more highly aware of finitude than an older person who has not yet surpassed the age of his parent's death.

Table 3 gives additional evidence for a social comparison process interpretation of the calculation of awareness of finitude. When an individual finds he has outlived all or most of his siblings, he becomes more highly aware that his own time of death draws nearer. That this is indeed a social comparison process is further suggested by the fact that placing oneself in relation to same-sex siblings is more strongly related to awareness of finitude than is comparison to siblings of opposite sex (as indicated in the Note to Table 3). A control for age failed to demonstrate that the comparison with sibling deaths acts independently of age (Marshall 1972, 120–121); the most that can be said for the social comparison process here is that it provides one explanation of the ways in which the aging experience effects the calculation of awareness of finitude.

Table 2 | Awareness of Finitude in Relation to Comparative Age at Death of Parents

Respondent Anticipates Living an Additional	Compared to the age at death of his or her parent, the respondent is now		
	Younger Than Age at Death of Both (%)	Younger Than Age at Death of One (%)	Older Than Age at Death of Both (%)
10 or more years	46	35	7
5 to 10 years	46	52	29
less than 5 years	9	13	64
TOTAL	101	100	100
n =	11	23	14	48

Tau B = −.426; sign. = beyond four places
Note: Controlling for sex, the following obtain
     males   Tau B = −.568; sign. = .008
     females   Tau B = −.390; sign. = .0003
     [a]Tau B = .175; sign. = .036
     [b]Tau B = .262; sign. = .004

Table 3 | Awareness of Finitude in Relation to Number of Siblings Dead

Respondent Anticipates Living an Additional	Number of dead brothers[a]		
	None %	One %	Two or More %
10 or more years	39	27	11
5 to 10 years	39	40	56
less than 5 years	23	33	33
TOTAL	101	100	100
n =	26	15	9	50

Respondent Anticipates Living an Additional	Number of dead sisters[b]		
	None %	One %	Two or More %
10 or more years	40	21	
5 to 10 years	40	36	67
less than 5 years	20	43	33
TOTAL	100	100	100
n =	30	14	6	50

Note: Controlling for sex, the following obtain
     males to brothers dead   Tau B = .396; sign. = .037
     males to sisters dead   Tau B = .289; sign. = .096
     females to brothers dead Tau B = .110; sign. = .166
     females to sisters dead   Tau B = .243; sign. = .016

The same interpretation can be offered for the effects of perceived health on this calculation. Not surprisingly, individuals who report that their health is only fair or poor (as opposed to excellent or good), and those who see their health as having changed for the worse (as opposed to change for better or no change), estimate fewer remaining years of life. These relationships are replicated as trends within the three age categories used, but the controlled relationships do not reach high levels of significance. That health factors do act as an added dimension to aging in the calculus of awareness of finitude is clear from the statements of respondents. However, at advanced age most people realize that their present state of health is not a good predictor of life expectancy. We may note the words of a lady who did in fact die of a stroke within three months of saying: "I have a feeling that as well as I am at 77, with my health I'm liable to go to 85 or so."

An additional way awareness of finitude is affected by social comparison processes is the death of friends. As one respondent said: "When you are up in the 60's and see all your friends around you going, you say, 'When am I due?'" Living in a retirement community, as these people, or in any residential setting for the aged can also affect the prediction of life expectancy (see Hochschild 1973, 83 for another account), for in the words of another respondent: "I suppose in a place like this—one thing I've had to get used to. . . . I see people about me with all sorts of ailments, people with sudden strokes and coronaries. People I know who die overnight. You have to wonder when it's going to happen to me."

Awareness of finitude is not, then, a simple function of age. Age is important in determining the estimate an individual makes of the amount of time remaining to him, but age itself takes on a meaning in relation to finitude in terms of the individual's perceived health and survivorship as compared to community members, friends and kin. Festinger (1954) argues that when objective criteria are not readily available for assessing the veridicality of opinions or abilities, individuals turn to a comparison of themselves with others similar to themselves. Awareness of finitude may be thought of as such a social comparison process. A major aspect of the underlying psycho-logic is presumably the conviction that longevity "runs in families."

While chronological age is a convenient ordering device for developmental theory, particularly in child psychology (Baer and Wright 1974) its classificatory use neglects the social and experiential dimensions (Baer 1970; Riegel 1973a, 1973b). Baer (1970) suggests that behavior change is less thoroughly ordered as age increases beyond childhood, but argues that "Late in life, age change may again take on a powerful function in correlating with behavior change; thus a developmental psychology, concerning this time of senescence again is possible." Riegel (1973a), however, has argued that ". . . we also need to comprehend development as a process of interactions. . . ." This suggests that Baer's advice should be applied throughout the life cycle.

Because these ways in which awareness of finitude develops are only indirectly related to age itself, we can infer both that an important aspect of the aging process has been neglected in gerontological research, and that research which substitutes measures of age for measures of awareness of finitude cannot provide adequate tests of theories incorporating awareness of finitude as a factor initiating developmental changes in the social psychology of aging. This last point will be developed illustratively in the following section in relation to the postulated changes in time perspective and focusing on the self which provide a common theme to disengagement theory, ego psychological approaches, and Butler's life-review formulation.

Awareness of Finitude and Reminiscence

Erikson has postulated that the final crisis in the developmental psychology of the individual is one involving the acceptance of one's life as a whole. Since failure to successfully adapt to this crisis is defined as the realization "that the time is short, too short for the attempt to start another life . . ." (Erikson 1959, 98), we can only assume that awareness of finitude is what precipitates this crisis. Resolution of this crisis may be thought of as a process, initiated by awareness of finitude, through which the individual assesses his past life as a whole, and during which he withdraws, at least to some extent, his attention from the outer world and focuses more on the self. This corresponds with the withdrawal from social relationsips and focusing on the self postulated as the disengagement process. A similar focusing on the self is postulated by Robert Butler (1963) to result from heightened awareness of finitude. In his theory, the life-review process is conceived as: ". . . a naturally occurring, universal mental process characterized by the progressive return to consciousness of past experience, and particularly, the resurgence of unresolved conflicts; simultaneously, and normally, these revived experiences and conflicts can be surveyed and reintegrated. Presumably this process is prompted by the realization of approaching dissolution and death. . . ."

Erikson and Butler offer only clinical evidence to warrant their arguments that awareness of finitude initiates the processes; Cumming and Henry are admittedly speculative; and Chellam did attempt to assess the impact of awareness, but confounded her measure. Studies directly attempting to test aspects of Butler's theory (Gorney 1968; Gorney and Tobin 1967, 1969; Falk 1970; Falk and Lieberman 1967, 1969; McMahon and Rhudick 1964), and related studies (Gruen 1964; Rosen and Neugarten 1964; Lubin 1964) have not employed direct measures of awareness of finitude. These studies provide little confirmation that the postulated focusing on the self is related to awareness of finitude (indeed, how could they!!). Thus Neugarten, Crotty, and Tobin (1964) were able to characterize only a small proportion of their sample as having "integrity," in an operationalization of Erikson's concept and, more important, they found those characterized as having integrity to range from ages 56–90, leading them to suggest a continuity between middle and old age.

The alternative hypothesis, implicit in Erikson's formulation, is for developmental change rather than stability: that age-related experiences lead some (but only some) individuals to become highly aware of impending death; and that those who are high in awareness of finitude focus more on the self. This hypothesis could not be tested by Neugarten, Crotty, and Tobin, because they had no measures of awareness of finitude.

In a similar vein, Gorney (1968, 119), while finding general support for Butler's formulation, noted as evidence calling the theory into question his finding that age has no interactive effect with reminiscence type in relation to other psychological attributes such as acceptance of the past. But the direct test would involve awareness of finitude and not age.

In a related study, Falk (1970, 124) summarizes her findings as follows: "The findings do not support theories postulating a universal task of life reviewing occurring with the approach of death. . . ." But Falk at least recognizes the possibility that she has not given the Butler theory (or the related Erikson formulation) an adequate test, for she notes (1970, 108): "It may be that theory and findings are not contradictory. The original perception that the self is mortal may act to heighten reminiscence activity, while factual imminence of death is associated with loss of reminiscence activity." By "factual imminence" Falk refers to the measure she employed of the distance the individual actually was from death. Not actual distance, of course, but awareness of finitude, is postulated as the initiator of the developmental changes in the Butler, Erikson, and Cumming and Henry formulations (though not, of course in all developmental formulations).

Were measures of awareness of finitude substituted for age in these and other empirical tests of hypotheses in these traditions, different findings would not necessarily emerge. The point is we can never know without measures of awareness of finitude. The data in the next section consider reminiscence and the focusing on the self in terms of awareness of finitude, and in general support the positions of Butler, Erikson, and, to some extent, Cumming and Henry. They also illustrate the usefulness of supplementing the age variable with experiential variables.

Illustrative Findings

In answer to a direct question, the majority of respondents attribute high levels of importance to their memories, regardless of awareness of finitude within the parameters I have measured. There is a slight indication that memories become more important for more people when they anticipate living no more than five to ten years, for only five percent of such respondents say their memories are not important. This indicates a shift from reasonably high importance attributed to memories for those who estimate living ten or more years (20 percent say memories not important) to even higher importance during the "middle awareness" category, followed by a decrease in the importance of memories (14 percent of those anticipating living less than five years say memories not important). The differences are small, and the data cross-sectional; however, they lend modest empirical support to the interpretation

Gorney makes from his data using age (instead of awareness of finitude) as an independent variable. Gorney (1968) postulated that a high level of introspection upon feelings during the 60's and 70's would be followed by a less-introspective stage following resolution of the life review. These data are complementary to those of Gorney in that they suggest that memories may become more important while the individual is engaged in the life review process, following which they may become somewhat less important.

If the life-review process is in fact a bringing to consciousness of past conflicts so that they might be resolved, then we should not expect individuals who are actively engaged in the life-review process to say that "memories are the most important thing I own." If Table 4(a) is read as a reflection of a developmental process, then we can interpret the increase in the proportion of people saying their memories are their most important possession as being due to the fact that these memories have now become, through the life-review process, happy memories.

Reminiscence has seldom been investigated as a *social* process (Marshall 1974). The unfortunate consequence of employing cross-sectional data is that any inferences as to direction of causation are most hazardous. In Table 4(b) we have evidence that people who anticipate living less than five years (i.e.,

Table 4 | Selected Indicators of Reminiscence in Relation to Awareness of Finitude

	Awareness of Finitude Respondent Anticipates Living an Additional			
	Ten or More Years %	Five to Ten Years %	Less Than Five Years %	
(a) Right now my memories are the most important thing I own				
Agree	14	10	36	
Disagree	86	90	64	
TOTAL	100	100	100	
n =	14	20	14	48
Tau C = −.177; sign. = .038				
(b) Do you often *talk* about things that have happened in your past life with anybody else?				
At least once a week	36	32	62	
Less frequently	64	68	39	
TOTAL	100	100	101	
n =	14	19	13	46
Tau C = −.208; sign. = .020				

Note: Number available for cross-tabulation varies because not all respondents answered all questions.

people high in awareness of finitude) are much more likely than those who anticipate living longer to engage in social reminiscence with others. It could be argued that individuals who have successfully completed the life review process will have more pleasant memories of their past, and as a result be more likely to share them with others. Alternately, it could be argued that it is only social reminiscence which allows the process to be successfully completed, with the consequence that the past is more readily accepted as pleasant.

Evidence (Marshall 1974) supports the second interpretation. Personalized or individualized reminiscence is most likely to occur during the middle awareness category. Here the individual is deeply engaged in bringing past conflicts to consciousness, reviewing them, and resolving his past life. During this stage the individual is likely to report that he has disappointments concerning his past life; he is less likely to desire to live his life over, if it were to be exactly the same; and he is less likely to say that, as he looks back on his past life, he is satisfied with it. During the stage of personalized reminiscence these subjects reported being more concerned with the past than the future, and more of them claimed to spend a great deal of time in thinking about the past. However, it was only when individuals reminisced about their past *with others,* supplementing personal reminiscence with social reminiscence, that the remembered past came to be accepted, and viewed as appropriate. It seemed as if individuals could get help from others in developing a conception of their past life as appropriate. In short, social reminiscence, which we have seen above is related to strongly heightened awareness of finitude, produced a view of the past which would be fairly called "integrity" in Erikson's definition of that term.

Conclusion

Gerontologists should attend more directly to awareness of finitude as a variable. Developmental processes which have been postulated by numerous gerontologists can in fact be investigated in relation to awareness of finitude, without having to use age as the measure of that which triggers the development changes. Whether future research employing direct measures of finitude disconfirms the postulates of disengagement theory, life-review theory, or development ego-psychology is of less concern than the desirability of submitting these theoretical approaches to the tests they deserve. It may even turn out that age itself, or actual distance rather than estimated distance from death (Riegel and Riegel 1972) acts in some mysterious manner, in initiating the various developmental changes catalogued in this paper, and that awareness of finitude bears a relatively unimportant and spurious relationship to these processes. However, the difficulties with any conceptualization of age acting alone to produce social–psychological changes have been noted elsewhere (Baer 1970; Baer and Wright 1974; Henry 1964, 417; Riegel, 1973a, 1973b, 1973c; Tallmer and Kutner 1969). I have shown that while awareness of finitude is indeed highly correlated with age, it is somewhat distinct. To the extent that it is correlated with age, awareness of finitude tells us something about the meaning of age; to the extent that it is distinct, awareness of finitude should be treated as distinct.

Notes

1. Teahan and Kastenbaum (1970) present a significant exception to this generalization, but for subjects ranging in age between 21 and 44. Their measure of life-expectancy was a direct question.

2. Tallmer and Kutner (1969) also fault investigators of disengagement theory for using age as their independent variable; their proposed substitute is not awareness of finitude: "It is not age which produces disengagement in our investigation but the impact of physical and social stress which may be expected to increase with age."

References

Baer, D. An age-irrelevant concept of development. *Merrill-Palmer Quarterly* 16:238–245 (1970).

Baer, D., and J. Wright. Developmental psychology. *Annual Review of Psychology* 25:1–82 (1974).

Butler, R. The life review: An interpretation of reminiscence in the aged. *Psychiatry* 26:65–76 (1963).

Chellam, G. The disengagement theory: Awareness of death and self-engagement. D.S.W. dissertation, Western Reserve University (1964).

Cumming, E., and Wm. Henry. *Growing old, the process of disengagement.* New York: Basic Books, 1961.

Damianopoulos, E. A formal statement of disengagement theory. In Cumming, E., and Wm. Henry, *Growing old, the process of disengagement.* New York: Basic Books, 1961.

Erikson, E. Identity and the life cycle. *Psychological Issues* 1, no. 1 (1959).

———. *Childhood and society.* 2nd rev. ed. New York: Norton, 1963.

Falk, J. M. The organization of remembered life experience of older people: Its relation to anticipated stress, to subsequent adaptation, and to age. Ph.D. thesis, Committee on Human Development, University of Chicago (1970).

Falk, J. M., and M. Lieberman. Cumulative life stress and adaptation in the very aged. Presented at 20th Annual Scientific Meeting of the Gerontological Society, St. Petersburg, Fla. (1967).

Falk, J. M., and M. Lieberman. The structure of personal history among the elderly: Its relation to anticipated stress, to subsequent adaptive capacity, and to age. Presented at 8th International Congress of Gerontology, Washington, D.C. (1969).

Festinger, L. A theory of social comparison processes. *Human Relations* 7:117–140 (1954).

Gorney, J. E. Experiencing and age: Patterns of reminiscence among the elderly. Ph.D. thesis, Committee on Human Development, University of Chicago (1968).

Gorney, J. E., and S. Tobin. Experiencing among the aged. Presented at 20th Annual Scientific Meeting of the Gerontological Society, St. Petersburg, Fla. (1967).

———. Experiencing and age: Patterns of reminiscence among the elderly. Presented at 8th International Congress of Gerontology, Washington, D.C. (1969).

Gruen, W. Adult personality: An empirical study of Erikson's theory of ego development. In Neugarten et al., *Personality in middle and late life, empirical studies.* New York: Atherton, 1964.

Havinghurst, R., B. Neugarten, and S. Tobin. Disengagement and patterns of aging. In Neugarten, *Middle age and aging.* Chicago: University of Chicago Press, 1968.

Henry, Wm. The theory of intrinsic disengagement. In Hansen, *Age with a future* (Proceedings of 6th International Congress of Gerontology). Philadelphia: F. A. Davis, 1964.

Hochschild, A. R. *The unexpected community.* Englewood Cliffs, N.J.: Prentice-Hall, 1973.

Kendall, M. *Rank correlation methods.* New York: Hafner, 1955.

Lipman, A., and K. J. Smith. Functionality of disengagement in old age. *Journal of Gerontology* 23:517–521 (1968).

Lubin, M., Addendum to Ch. 4. In Neugarten et al., *Personality in middle and late life, empirical studies.* New York: Atherton, 1964.

Maddox, G. L. Persistence of life style among the elderly: A longitudinal study of patterns of social activity in relation to life satisfaction. In Proceedings of 7th International Congress of Gerontology. Vienna: Verlag de Wiener Medizinische Akademie, 1966.

Marshall, V. W. Continued living and dying as problematic aspects of old age. Ph.D. thesis, Department of Sociology, Princeton University (1972).

Marshall, V. The life review as a social process. Presented at 27th Annual Scientific Meeting of the Gerontological Society, Portland, Oregon (1974).

McMahon, W. W., and P. J. Rhudick. Reminiscing: Adaptational significance in the aged. *Archives of General Psychiatry* 10:292–298 (1964).

Neugarten, B., B. Crotty, and S. Tobin. Personality types in an aged population, pp. 158–187. In Neugarten et al., *Personality in middle and late life, empirical studies.* New York: Atherton, 1964.

Neugarten, B., R. J. Havinghurst, and S. Tobin. Personality and patterns of aging. In Neugarten, *Middle age and aging,* Chicago: University of Chicago Press, 1968.

Riegel, K. An epitaph for a paradigm. *Human Development* 16:107 (1973a).

———. The recall of historical events. *Behavioral Science* 18:354–363 (1973b).

———. Dialectical operations: The final period of cognitive development. *Human Development* 16:346–370 (1973c).

Riegel, K., and R. Riegel. Development, drop, and death. *Developmental Psychology* 6:306–319 (1972).

Riley, J. W., Jr. What people think about death. In Brim, Freeman, Levine, and Scotch, *The dying patient.* New York: Russell Sage Foundation, 1970.

Rose, A. A current theoretical issue in social gerontology. *Gerontologist* 4:46–50 (1965).

Rosen, J., and B. Neugarten. Ego functions in the middle and later years: A thematic apperception study. In Neugarten et al., *Personality in middle and late life, empirical studies.* New York: Atherton, 1964.

Tallmer, M., and B. Kutner. Disengagement and the stresses of aging. *Journal of Gerontology* 24:70–75 (1969).

Teahan, J., and R. Kastenbaum. Subjective life expectancy and future time perspective as predictors of job success in the hard-core unemployed. *Omega* 1:189–200 (1970).

structured exercises

Before beginning these exercises, please read "Note to the Instructor" on page xxi.

1. List six problems that you think would be most likely to trouble you if everything in your life were as it is now except that yesterday you were told you have an inoperable advanced cancer. Then, on a separate sheet of paper, rank order the six problems from 1 (most important to you) to 6 (least important to you). Show your original (unranked) list to someone else (this can be done pairwise or by randomly redistributing the lists among the class) and have that person rank the list of problems according to their importance to him. Then compare the rankings together, discussing your reasons for agreeing or disagreeing with each other.*

   As a further attempt to understand others' perspectives on terminal illness, you could consider how the original list would change if:

   a. you were 20 years older or younger
   b. you were the other sex
   c. you were on welfare
   d. you had just learned that your two-year old son was mentally retarded
   e. your same-sexed parent had died of the same illness
   f. you were recently married

2. Try to look ahead to the time when you will actually die. Envision the ideal scene of your dying in some detail. Consider the following questions about how you would like your dying to be.

   a. How old would you be?
   b. Where would you be?
   c. What time of day would it be?
   d. What special objects would you see as you looked around you?

*Adapted from R. Koenig, "Counseling in Catastrophic Illness: A Self-Instructional Unit," *Omega,* 6 (1975), 227–241.

e. What music would be playing in the background?
f. What would you have been doing with your life just prior to this time?
g. Who would be with you?
h. What would you want to tell them?

In order to share the experience, the class could:

a. Write the answers to these questions on sheets of paper numbered from 1 to 8 and then, holding the sheets of paper in front of them, chest high, the students could walk around the room reading each other's comments. The reading should take place without conversation and involve only eye contact or other nonverbal communication. Once everyone has finished reading, class discussion of reactions can take place.
b. Each person can draw what he or she has imagined instead of writing it down. The drawings can be signed or left anonymous. They can be taped up around the room, the class can browse among them, and the group can discuss them.

3. Suppose you learned that a casual acquaintance had developed a terminal illness and was hospitalized. Would you visit the person? Why or why not?

a. Assume you did visit the person. What would you hope to accomplish with your visit? What hopes and fears would you confront as you anticipated the visit?
b. Assume now that you are hospitalized with a terminal illness and that you are expecting a visit from a casual acquaintance. What are your hopes and fears? What would you hope to accomplish during the visit?

questions

1. Define the following terms and give examples of each where approprite. Terms marked with an asterisk are psychological, sociological, or medical terms that the authors of the selections expect readers to know. If you are not familiar with the meanings of those terms, consult a dictionary, a medical dictionary, or an abnormal psychology textbook.

Pattison

living–dying interval
trajectory
crisis of the knowledge of death
existential denial
regression
sociological death
psychic death
biological death
physiological death

Kübler-Ross

denial
bargaining
depression
preparatory grief
acceptance
resignation

Kastenbaum

stage theory
*interrater reliability

Kastenbaum (continued)

*emphysema
*advanced renal failure
cognitive style
developmental level
sociophysical milieu

Bluestone and McGahee

*defense mechanism
*denial
*projection
*obsessive rumination

Strauss and Glaser

awareness context
closed awareness
mutual pretense awareness
open awareness
structural conditions
ritual pretense

Marshall

> developmental gerontology
> awareness of finitude
> activity theory
> life review
> disengagement theory
> calculus
> integrity
> social reminiscence
> social comparison process

2. Pattison defines the period between *knowledge of death* and *actual death* as the "living–dying period." What support does he suggest that the patient needs during this time? Using other selections in the chapter, list some of the factors that might make it difficult for the family to give the needed support.

3. a. Death-related research began with the study of relatively long-term illnesses with a terminal prognosis. How well do Pattison's "crisis model" and Kübler-Ross's stages fit the death row prisoners described by Bluestone and McGahee? To what extent do you think the concepts would apply to patients with a "suspended sentence," e.g., chronic hemodialysis, chronic cardiac disease, or emphysema?
   b. How might the stages of dying discussed by Kübler-Ross differ with family structure? Religious beliefs? Ethnic background? Type of illness?

4. Denial is a complex concept, more complex than this chapter indicates. Kübler-Ross has described denial as a result of interpersonal dynamics, but Strauss and Glaser have shown that it may be part of the social interaction process as well. What would you, as a helper, look for in deciding whether a patient's "denial" represented a serious inability to deal with significant facts of his illness, or an attempt to cope with what the patient perceived as others' inability to do so? What might you want to take into account in deciding whether, and how, to intervene?

5. Suppose the father in "Do Not Go Gentle into That Good Night" were admitted to a nursing home. What psychological supports would Pattison and Kübler-Ross recommend for the father? For the speaker in the poem?

6. Does final acceptance require that a patient work through all of the other attitudes? What is the difference between the acceptance of death and the resignation to death? Do you agree that acceptance as described by Kübler-Ross is a natural and desirable goal for all dying patients? Why or why not? How does age or "engrossment" in life as described by Kastenbaum affect potential acceptance?

7. Kübler-Ross and Pattison are writing about processes that occur in a person who is aware that he or she is dying. Having read these selections,

would you recommend withholding terminal diagnosis from a dying person? If so, under what circumstances? Survey the class on the following two questions:

a. If you had a terminal illness, would you want to be told?

b. If your mother (or father) had a terminal illness, would you want her (or him) to be told?

Using Strauss and Glaser, discuss your reasons for your answers. Consider both advantages and disadvantages of withholding the information from the point of view of the patient, of the hospital staff, and of the family.

8. a. In a way, the death row prisoner and the terminal cancer patient are both awaiting the execution of a death sentence. Compare and contrast the two situations, considering the origin of the death sentence, the amount of control held by various individuals in the setting, the psychological and social meaning of the "sentence," the relative determinancy of the "sentence," and the rationalizations available to the individual.

b. Considering cultural assumptions in North America, is it possible for death by execution to be considered an appropriate death? Under what conditions?

9. Marshall discusses social reminiscence as related to aging, but the symbolic deaths involved in new beginnings at any age may well trigger both personal and social reminiscence. Identify three such occasions in your own life and list elements of both personal and social reminiscence for each.

10. a. List as many people as you can whom you consider to be "aged." What criteria did you use in choosing them? To how many does the concept of "disengagement" seem to apply? What about the term "engrossment"? What do you think makes the difference?

b. Contrast your own life perspective with that of an aged relative. Can you do the same for a mother of teenaged children who is dying of cancer?

projects for further study

1. Psychiatrist Raymond Moody has reported in *Life After Life* (1975) accounts of "return from the dead." Using Moody's accounts and others (see, for example, R. Noyes, Jr., and D. J. Slymen, "The Subjective Response to Life-Threatening Danger, *Omega,* 9 [1978–79], 313–321), respond to the following questions:

   a. What features do the accounts have in common?

   b. What discrepancies are there in the "typical" features reported by the authors?

   c. Do you believe that such reports are evidence for "life after death," as some have claimed? If not, what do they tell us about phenomena of clinical death?

   d. What role do cultural factors play in the content of the reports?

   e. How do cultural variations in content affect the apparent validity of the reports in your mind?

2. Leo Tolstoy's novella *The Death of Ivan Illych* is often used by contemporary humanists to illustrate the needs of the dying and the failures of family, friends, and society to meet them. Read the short novel and identify situations that seem to fit the ideas presented in this chapter: the fears of the dying patient (Pattison), the stages/reactions of dying (Kübler-Ross), and the awareness context (Strauss and Glaser). In addition, it would be interesting to compare Ivan's transcendental experience with experiences reported by survivors of clinical death and cancer patients undergoing LSD therapy for pain reduction and conflict resolution.

3. Visit an elderly person. Interview that person about significant events in the past. Ask about such milestones as graduation, marriage, retirement. To what degree do these reminiscences reflect resolution?

for further reading

Brim, O. G., H. E. Freeman, S. Levine, and N. A. Scotch, eds. 1970. *The dying patient.* New York: Russell Sage Foundation.

Garfield, C. A. 1978. *Psychosocial care of the dying patient.* New York: McGraw-Hill.

Glaser, B. G., and A. L. Strauss. 1968. *Time for dying.* Chicago: Aldine.

Kübler-Ross, E. 1976. *On death and dying.* New York: Macmillan.

Lamerton, R. 1976. *Care of the dying.* Westport, Conn.: Technomic Publishing.

Levy, N. B., ed. 1974. *Living or dying: Adaptations to hemodialysis.* Springfield, Ill.: Charles C. Thomas.

Marshall, V. W. 1980 *Last chapters: A sociology of aging and dying.* Belmont, Calif.: Wadsworth.

Moody, R. A., Jr. 1975. *Life after life.* Simons Island, Ga.: Mockingbird Press.

National Cancer Institute. 1980. *Coping with cancer: A resource for the health professional.* Bethesda, Md.: National Institutes of Health.

Pritchard, E. R., J. Collard, B. A. Orcutt, A. H. Kutscher, I. Seeland, and N. Lefkowitz, eds. 1977. *Social work with the dying patient and the family.* New York: Columbia University Press.

Quint, J. 1967. *The nurse and the dying patient.* New York: Macmillan.

Shepard, M. 1975. *Someone you love is dying.* New York: Harmony Books.

CHAPTER | *three*

Grief, Mourning, and
Social Functions

*A*t *the same time the contemporary person has been deprived of his own death,* he has been similarly deprived of the right to mourn the dead. Philippe Ariès, surveying the reversal in social obligations attending death and mourning, has charged that "modern society deprives man of his own death, and . . . it allows him this privilege only if he does not use it to upset the living. In a reciprocal way, society forbids the living to appear moved by the death of others; it does not allow them either to weep for the deceased or to seem to miss them."

Psychiatry, however, has long recognized that grief is a natural and necessary—albeit complex—reaction accompanied by a range of contradictory emotions and apparently aberrant behaviors. Unpleasant and irrational as it may appear to many, the grief process cannot be safely bypassed. Freud recognized this in his key paper, "Mourning and Melancholia" (1917), which provides a theoretical framework for understanding reactions to loss, a framework that still underlies our conception of mourning today.

The Freudian model has led to the study of both the normal "symptomatology" of grief reactions and the pathological consequences of distorted grief. The condition of bereavement itself has been related to depression, suicide, psychosomatic disorders, and even to death from "natural" causes.

Styles of Grief

The understanding and consequent acceptance of grief results in the recognition of varied styles of mourning: the dynamics of grief will vary with the nature of the death. One mourns differently for a child than for an aged parent; the aftermath of a loved one's suicide differs from the aftermath of death in wartime. As the state of extended dying becomes common, anticipatory grief must be given more prominence. Preparatory mourning shared by the dying person with family members in a state of open awareness can attenuate the experience of grief by providing mutual support and an opportunity for gradual separation *during* the dying rather than after it.

Community

The shift from *intervention* to *prevention* in mental health care has been greatly influenced by the study of grief and bereavement. Now informal grief counseling, educational seminars on psychological and practical aspects of bereavement, and crisis intervention programs are often sponsored by churches, hospitals, and schools. Model programs, such as "Widow to Widow," begun by Phyllis Silverman at the Harvard Laboratory of Community Psychiatry, have given rise to community support groups throughout the country. Such groups seek to provide not only emotional support during the crisis of bereavement, but also to offer practical information to aid the bereaved in the social readjustment to life as a single person.

Appropriate Grief

If society's prohibition against mourning causes repression of grief, then it is incumbent on society to develop new cultural forms for the management of grief. As Ariès has emphasized, ritual has historically guided mourning. And although funeral rituals may appear to differ markedly from one culture to another, they traditionally serve the same functions of disposal of the body, support for the bereaved, and reaffirmation of the group identity of the living.

Modern pride in reason and practicality often leads to reactions against rituals: on the occasion of death, charges of exploitation, insensitivity, or simply irrelevance are frequently hurled at religious institutions or the funeral industry. Two factors may be at work in these reactions. First, as the distance from one's own death has increased and the right to mourn been obscured, the ability to "make sense" of death has broken down. Second, since rituals require individuals to return to a group identity by publicly proclaiming shared beliefs, they are bound to display dislocation at times when belief systems are being challenged. Consequently, the criticism of ritual may be not so much a rejection of the value of ritual itself as an indication that the awareness of the complexity of mourning exceeds the currently available social forms.

Overview of the Chapter

The readings in Chapter Three open with an examination of the nature of acute grief and the work of mourning over time; they then turn to a consideration of the rituals and social institutions that give shape to the experience of mourning. To illustrate theory with experience, the presentations on the nature of grief move from current research to literary manifestations spanning four thousand years. Our progression begins with a widow's experiencing such an overwhelming impact of loss that she questions her sanity. Cautioning against the pathological consequences of the refusal to mourn in "Symptomatology and Management of Acute Grief," psychiatrist Erich Lindemann establishes that the manifestations of acute grief are often so intense that the mourner needs reassurance of their validity. Lindemann's work, though developed at the close of World War II, remains central to the study of grief today; its timelessness is further attested by the Epic of Gilgamesh, the oldest known expression of grief in the Western tradition. There, the young king, Gilgamesh, rages in anguish at the death of his closest companion, Enkidu.

Painful as the period of acute grief may be, the full experience of mourning is an extended one. In "The Loss of a Spouse," British psychiatrist John Bowlby extends the treatment of grief through the first year of bereavement. Working largely within the tradition defined by Freud and Lindemann, Bowlby differs with them somewhat: Lindemann identifies emancipation from the relationship with the deceased as the essential part of grief work; whereas Bowlby insists that the original relationship continues to fill a central role in the emotional life of the bereaved, while undergoing redefinition during the mourning period.

Working from the vantage point of four months after the suicide of her close colleague, Maxine Kumin calls, "We're far from finished! I'm still/talking to you," as she gives expression to her powerful feelings with the extended image in "Splitting Wood at Six Above." The special grief reactions of the survivor of suicide are taken up in "Survivors of Suicide" by psychiatrist Albert Cain, who summarizes both the individual reactions and the interpersonal complications faced by those mourning a suicide.

The relationship between bereavement and culture in general is addressed in the next two readings. In "Bereavement and Mental Health," psychiatrist Edmund Volkhart, in collaboration with Stanley Michael, distinguishes between the inner experience of grief and the observable condition of bereavement. The two urge a scrutiny of such links between culture and individual behavior as social institutions, status, and roles. Inquiry into cultural orientations will, they hold, help realign the disjunction between personal experience and expected behavior. Then, using the example of a particular funeral tradition within black experience, Jean Masamba, a black African clergyman and pastoral psychologist, collaborates with psychologist Richard Kalish in a discussion of the factors (religious, psychological, and social) that influence the behavior of the bereaved. Though the authors draw their specific examples from a tradition within black experience (such as in their use of spirituals as reflections of death-related beliefs), many of the supportive elements they identify are found in other communities as well.

In the last reading of the chapter, psychohistorian Robert J. Lifton moves the discussion from funeral rituals to the more general concept of symbolic systems. The death of a significant other, he notes, assaults one's own sense of continued existence, forcing an examination of assumptions about immortality. In "The Struggle for Cultural Rebirth," Lifton moves the concept of immortality from its traditional theological context (outlined by Ariès in Chapter One) to several symbolic modes. In so doing, he outlines concepts of biological, theological, creative, natural, and transcendental immortality.

Such symbolic conceptions of immortality are vital to a community but, as the approaching Encounter demonstrates, they do not dull the edge of fresh loss.

encounter | *Grieving*

I knew Martin was dead, but somehow it took a long time for the reality to seep in, become part of me. I would go to the supermarket and think, "Oh, they have endive today. I'd better get some. Martin likes it so much." I would pick out an avocado for him, a fruit I've never really liked. Then I would realize, "My God! He is dead!" and put the avocado back as if it were burning me.

When something funny happened, I'd say to myself, "Oh, wait until I tell Martin about this tonight! He'll never believe it." There were times in my office when I would stretch out my hand to the telephone to call him, to chat. Reality always intervened before I dialed that disconnected number. . . .

One day when I was on the Fifth Avenue bus I spotted a man who looked like Martin. I pulled the cord and plunged after him. I knew it wasn't Martin, but I tried desperately to catch up with him. I couldn't. I lost sight of him and it made me very depressed, as if Martin had rejected me.

And I had dreams. I would dream that I heard the door open while I was in the kitchen getting the ice for our evening drink. It was Martin, home from work. I would be so happy to hear him come in. But I always woke up before I saw him.

I had a sense of Martin, of some quality of Martin that had filtered into me. A very real feeling that part of me was Martin.*

1. Lynn Caine reports a disturbing but frequent and natural reaction to a recent death. Can you recall similar experiences following per-

Source: Excerpts from pages 101 and 102 in *Widow* by Lynn Caine. Copyright © 1974 by Lynn Caine. By permission of William Morrow & Company.

sonal loss such as the death of a loved one, a divorce, or a separation? Describe three reactions to that loss.

2. Caine viewed the episodes in which Martin's presence continued to influence her behavior as part of her "crazy period." Have you ever tried to retain elements of a lost relationship in your own life? Is doing so necessarily maladaptive?

ERICH LINDEMANN

Symptomatology and Management of Acute Grief

The work of mourning is more complicated and more time consuming than most people expect or can easily accept. In the following article, Erich Lindemann places the anecdotal Encounter in a context for analysis. He defines grief as a "definite syndrome with psychological and somatic symptomatology." Presenting the sometimes distressing responses to recent death as natural and necessary, Lindemann emphasizes the need to mourn: denial of grief is a predisposing factor in both psychopathology and physical illness. Though written in 1944, a period of increased grief reactions due to war casualties, Lindemann's model of bereavement as a crisis period of increased vulnerability is one of the classic works in preventive community psychiatry.

Introduction

At first glance, acute grief would not seem to be a medical or psychiatric disorder in the strict sense of the word but rather a normal reaction to a distressing situation. However, the understanding of reactions to traumatic experiences whether or not they represent clear-cut neuroses has become of ever-increasing importance to the psychiatrist. Bereavement or the sudden cessation of social interaction seems to be of special interest because it is often cited among the alleged psychosomatic disorders. The enormous increase in grief reactions due to war casualties, furthermore, demands an evaluation of their probable effect on the mental and physical health of our population.

The points to be made in this paper are as follows:

1. Acute grief is a definite syndrome with psychological and somatic symptomatology.
2. This syndrome may appear immediately after a crisis; it may be delayed; it may be exaggerated or apparently absent.
3. In place of the typical syndrome there may appear distorted pictures, each of which represents one special aspect of the grief syndrome.
4. By appropriate techniques these distorted pictures can be successfully transformed into a normal grief reaction with resolution.

Our observations comprise 101 patients. Included are psychoneurotic patients who lost a relative during the course of treatment, relatives of patients

Source: Erich Lindemann. "Symptomatology and Management of Acute Grief." *American Journal of Psychiatry*, CI (1944), 141–148 (Vol. 101).

who died in the hospital, bereaved disaster victims (Cocoanut Grove Fire) and their close relatives, and relatives of members of the armed forces.

The investigation consisted of a series of psychiatric interviews. Both the timing and the content of the discussions were recorded. These records were subsequently analyzed in terms of the symptoms reported and of the changes in mental status observed progressively through a series of interviews. The psychiatrist avoided all suggestions and interpretations until the picture of symptomatology and spontaneous reaction tendencies of the patients had become clear from the records. The somatic complaints offered important leads for objective study. Careful laboratory work on spirograms, g.-i. functions, and metabolic studies is in progress and will be reported separately. At present we wish to present only our psychobiological observations.

Symptomatology of Normal Grief

The picture shown by persons in acute grief is remarkably uniform. Common to all is the following syndrome: sensations of somatic distress occurring in waves lasting from twenty minutes to an hour at a time, a feeling of tightness in the throat, choking with shortness of breath, need for sighing, and an empty feeling in the abdomen, lack of muscular power, and an intense subjective distress described as tension or mental pain. The patient soon learns that these waves of discomfort can be precipitated by visits, by mentioning the deceased, and by receiving sympathy. There is a tendency to avoid the syndrome at any cost, to refuse visits lest they should precipitate the reaction, and to keep deliberately from thought all references to the deceased.

The striking features are the marked tendency to sighing respiration; this respiratory disturbance was most conspicuous when the patient was made to discuss his grief. The complaint about lack of strength and exhaustion is universal and is described as follows: "It is almost impossible to climb up a stairway." "Everything I lift seems so heavy." "The slightest effort makes me feel exhausted." "I can't walk to the corner without feeling exhausted." Digestive symptoms are described as follows: "The food tastes like sand." "I have no appetite at all." "I stuff the food down because I have to eat." "My saliva won't flow." "My abdomen feels hollow." "Everything seems slowed up in my stomach."

The sensorium is generally somewhat altered. There is commonly a slight sense of unreality, a feeling of increased emotional distance from other people (sometimes they appear shadowy or small), and there is intense preoccupation with the image of the dereased. A patient who lost his daughter in the Cocoanut Grove disaster visualized his girl in the telephone booth calling for him and was much troubled by the loudness with which his name was called by her and was so vividly preoccupied with the scene that he became oblivious of his surroundings. A young navy pilot lost a close friend; he remained a vivid part of his imagery, not in terms of a religious survival but in terms of an imaginary companion. He ate with him and talked over problems with him, for instance, discussing with him his plan of joining the Air Corps. Up to the time of the study, six months later, he denied the fact that the boy was no longer with him. Some patients are much concerned about this aspect of their grief reaction because they feel it indicates approaching insanity.

Another strong preoccupation is with feelings of guilt. The bereaved searches the time before the death for evidence of failure to do right by the lost one. He accuses himself of negligence and exaggerates minor omissions. After the fire disaster the central topic of discussion for a young married woman was the fact that her husband died after he left her following a quarrel, and of a young man whose wife died that he fainted too soon to save her.

In addition, there is often a disconcerting loss of warmth in relationship to other people, a tendency to respond with irritability and anger, a wish not to be bothered by others at a time when friends and relatives make a special effort to keep up friendly relationships.

These feelings of hostility, surprising and quite inexplicable to the patients, disturbed them and again were often taken as signs of approaching insanity. Great efforts are made to handle them, and the result is often a formalized, stiff manner of social interaction.

The activity throughout the day of the severely bereaved person shows remarkable changes. There is no retardation of action and speech; quite to the contrary, there is a push of speech, especially when talking about the deceased. There is restlessness, inability to sit still, moving about in an aimless fashion, continually searching for something to do. There is, however, at the same time, a painful lack of capacity to initiate and maintain organized patterns of activity. What is done is done with lack of zest, as though one were going through the motions. The bereaved clings to the daily routine of prescribed activities; but these activities do not proceed in the automatic, self-sustaining fashion which characterizes normal work but have to be carried on with effort, as though each fragment of the activity became a special task. The bereaved is surprised to find how large a part of his customary activity was done in some meaningful relationship to the deceased and has now lost its significance. Especially the habits of social interaction—meeting friends, making conversation, sharing enterprises with others—seem to have been lost. This loss leads to a strong dependency on anyone who will stimulate the bereaved to activity and serve as the initiating agent.

These five points—(1) somatic distress, (2) preoccupation with the image of the deceased, (3) guilt, (4) hostile reactions, and (5) loss of patterns of conduct—seem to be pathognomonic for grief. There may be added a sixth characteristic, shown by patients who border on pathological reactions, which is not so conspicuous as the others but nevertheless often striking enough to color the whole picture. This is the appearance of traits of the deceased in the behavior of the bereaved, especially symptoms shown during the last illness, or behavior which may have been shown at the time of the tragedy. A bereaved person is observed or finds himself walking in the manner of his deceased father. He looks in the mirror and believes that his face appears just like that of the deceased. He may show a change of interests in the direction of the former activities of the deceased and may start enterprises entirely different from his former pursuits. A wife who lost her husband, an insurance agent, found herself writing to many insurance companies offering her services with somewhat exaggerated schemes. It seemed a regular observation in these patients that the painful preoccupation with the image of the deceased described above was transformed into preoccupation with symptoms or personality traits of the lost person, but now displaced to their own bodies and activities by identification.

Course of Normal Grief Reactions

The duration of a grief reaction seems to depend upon the success with which a persons does the *grief work,* namely, emancipation from the bondage to the deceased, readjustment to the environment in which the deceased is missing, and the formation of new relationships. One of the big obstacles to this work seems to be the fact that many patients try to avoid the intense distress connected with the grief experience and to avoid the expression of emotion necessary for it. The men victims after the Cocoanut Grove fire appeared in the early psychiatric interviews to be in a state of tension with tightened facial musculature, unable to relax for fear they might "break down." It required considerable persuasion to yield to the grief process before they were willing to accept the discomfort of bereavement. One assumed a hostile attitude toward the psychiatrist, refusing to allow any references to the deceased and rather rudely asking him to leave. This attitude remained throughout his stay on the ward, and the prognosis for his condition is not good in the light of other observations. Hostility of this sort was encountered on only occasional visits with the other patients. They became willing to accept the grief process and to embark on a program of dealing in memory with the deceased person. As soon as this became possible there seemed to be a rapid relief of tension and the subsequent interviews were rather animated conversations in which the deceased was idealized and in which misgivings about the future adjustments were worked through.

Examples of the psychiatrist's role in assisting patients in their readjustment after bereavement are contained in the following case histories. The first shows a very successful readjustment.

A woman, aged 40, lost her husband in the fire. She had a history of good adjustment previously. One child, ten years old. When she heard about her husband's death she was extremely depressed, cried bitterly, did not want to live, and for three days showed a state of utter dejection.

When seen by the psychiatrist, she was glad to have assistance and described her painful preoccupation with the memories of her husband and her fear that she might lose her mind. She had a vivid visual image of his presence, picturing him as going to work in the morning and herself as wondering whether he would return in the evening, whether she could stand his not returning, then, describing to herself how he does return, plays with the dog, receives his child, and gradually tried to accept the fact that he is not there any more. It was only after ten days that she succeeded in accepting his loss and then only after having described in detail the remarkable qualities of her husband, the tragedy of his having to stop his activities at the pinnacle of his success, and his deep devotion to her.

In the subsequent interviews she explained with some distress that she had become very much attached to the examiner and that she waited for the hour of his coming. This reaction she considered disloyal to her husband but at the same time she could accept the fact that it was a hopeful sign of her ability to fill the gap he had left in her life. She then showed a marked drive for activity, making plans for supporting herself and her little girl, mapping out the preliminary steps for resuming her old profession as secretary, and making efforts to secure help from the occupational therapy department in reviewing her knowledge of French.

Her convalescence, both emotional and somatic, progressed smoothly, and she had a good adjustment immediately on her return home.

A man of 52, successful in business, lost his wife, with whom he had lived in a happy marriage. The information given him about his wife's death confirmed his suspicions of several days. He responded with a severe grief reaction, with which he was unable to cope. He did not want to see visitors, was ashamed of breaking down, and asked to be permitted to stay in the hospital on the psychiatric service, when his physical condition would have permitted his discharge, because he wanted further assistance. Any mention of his wife produced a severe wave of depressive reaction, but with psychiatric assistance he gradually became willing to go through this painful process, and after three days on the psychiatric service he seemed well enough to go home.

He showed a high rate of verbal activity, was restless, needed to be occupied continually, and felt that the experience had whipped him into a state of restless overactivity.

As soon as he returned home he took an active part in his business, assuming a post in which he had a great many telephone calls. He also took over the role of amateur psychiatrist to another bereaved person, spending time with him and comforting him for his loss. In his eagerness to start anew, he developed a plan to sell all his former holdings, including his house, his furniture, and giving away anything which could remind him of his wife. Only after considerable discussion was he able to see that this would mean avoiding immediate grief at the price of an act of poor judgment. Again he had to be encouraged to deal with his grief reactions in a more direct manner. He has made a good adjustment.

With eight to ten interviews in which the psychiatrist shares the grief work, and with a period of from four to six weeks, it was ordinarily possible to settle an uncomplicated and undistorted grief reaction. This was the case in all but one of the 13 Cocoanut Grove fire victims.

Morbid Grief Reactions

Morbid grief reactions represent distortions of normal grief. The conditions mentioned here were transformed into "normal reactions" and then found their resolution.

Delay of Reaction

The most striking and most frequent reaction of this sort is *delay* or *postponement*. If the bereavement occurs at a time when the patient is confronted with important tasks and when there is necessity for maintaining the morale of others, he may show little or no reaction for weeks or even much longer. A brief delay is described in the following example.

A girl of 17 lost both parents and her boy friend in the fire and was herself burned severely, with marked involvement of the lungs. Throughout her stay in the hospital her attitude was that of cheerful acceptance without any sign of adequate distress. When she was discharged at the end of the three weeks she appeared cheerful, talked rapidly, with a considerable flow of ideas, seemed eager to return home and to assume the role of parent for her two younger siblings. Except for slight feelings of "lonesomeness" she complained of no distress.

This period of griefless acceptance continued for the next two months, even when the household was dispersed and her younger siblings were placed in other homes. Not until the end of the tenth week did she begin to show a true state of grief with marked feelings of depression, intestinal emptiness, tightness in her throat, frequent crying, and vivid preoccupation with her deceased parents.

That this delay may involve years became obvious first by the fact that patients in acute bereavement about a recent death may soon upon exploration be found preoccupied with grief about a person who died many years ago. In this manner a woman of 38, whose mother had died recently and who had responded to the mother's death with a surprisingly severe reaction, was found to be but mildly concerned with her mother's death but deeply engrossed with unhappy and perplexing fantasies concerning the death of her brother, who died twenty years ago under dramatic circumstances from metastasizing carcinoma after amputation of his arm had been postponed too long. The discovery that a former unresolved grief reaction may be precipitated in the course of the discussion of another recent event was soon demonstrated in psychiatric interviews by patients who showed all the traits of a true grief reaction when the topic of a former loss arose.

The precipitating factor for the delayed reaction may be a deliberate recall of circumstances surrounding the death or may be a spontaneous occurrence in the patient's life. A peculiar form of this is the circumstance that a patient develops the grief reaction at the time when he himself is as old as the person who died. For instance, a railroad worker, aged 42, appeared in the psychiatric clinic with a picture which was undoubtedly a grief reaction for which he had no explanation. It turned out that when he was 22, his mother, then 42, had committed suicide.

Distorted Reactions

The delayed reactions may occur after an interval which was not marked by any abnormal behavior or distress, but in which there developed an *alteration* in the patient's *conduct* perhaps not conspicuous or serious enough to lead him to a psychiatrist. These alterations may be considered as the surface manifestations of an unresolved grief reaction, which may respond to fairly simple and quick psychiatric management if recognized. They may be classified as follows: (1) *overactivity without a sense of loss,* rather with a sense of well-being and zest, the activities being of an expansive and adventurous nature and bearing semblance to the activities formerly carried out by the deceased, as described above; (2) *the acquisition of symptoms belonging to the last illness of the deceased.* This type of patient appears in medical clinics and is often labeled hypochondriasis or hysteria. To what extent actual alterations of physiological functions occur under these circumstances will have to be a field of further careful inquiry. I owe to Dr. Chester Jones a report about a patient whose electrocardiogram showed a definite change during a period of three weeks, which started two weeks after the time her father died of heart disease.

While this sort of symptom formation "by identification" may still be considered as conversion symptoms such as we know from hysteria, there is another type of disorder doubtlessly presenting (3) a recognized *medical disease,* namely, a group of psychosomatic conditions, predominantly ulcerative colitis, rheumatoid arthritis, and asthma. Extensive studies in ulcerative colitis have produced evidence that 33 out of 41 patients with ulcerative colitis developed their disease in close time relationship to the loss of an important person. Indeed, it was this observation which first gave the impetus for the present detailed study of grief. Two of the patients developed bloody diarrhea at funerals. In the others it developed within a few weeks after the loss. The course of the ulcerative colitis was strikingly benefited when this grief reaction was resolved by psychiatric technique.

At the level of social adjustment there often occurs a conspicuous (4) *alteration in relationship to friends and relatives.* The patient feels irritable, does not want to be bothered, avoids former social activities, and is afraid he might antagonize his friends by his lack of interest and his critical attitudes. Progressive social isolation follows, and the patient needs considerable encouragement in reestablishing his social relationships.

While overflowing hostility appears to be spread out over all relationships, it may also occur as (5) *furious hostility against specific persons;* the doctor or the surgeon is accused bitterly for neglect of duty and the patient may assume that foul play has led to the death. It is characteristic that while patients talk a good deal about their suspicions and their bitter feelings, they are not likely to take any action against the accused, as a truly paranoid person might do.

(6) Many bereaved persons struggled with much effort against these feelings of hostility, which to them seem absurd, representing a vicious change in their characters and to be hidden as much as possible. Some patients succeed in hiding their hostility but become wooden and formal, with affectivity and conduct *resembling schizophrenic pictures.* A typical report is this, "I go through all the motions of living. I look after my children. I do my errands. I go to social functions, but it is like being in a play; it doesn't really concern me. I

can't have any warm feelings. If I were to have any feelings at all I would be angry with everybody." This patient's reaction to therapy was characterized by growing hostility against the therapist, and it required considerable skill to make her continue interviews in spite of the disconcerting hostility which she had been fighting so much. The absence of emotional display in this patient's face and actions was quite striking. Her face had a mask-like appearance, her movements were formal, stilted, robot-like, without the fine play of emotional expression.

(7) Closely related to this picture is a *lasting loss of patterns of social interaction.* The patient cannot initiate any activity, is full of eagerness to be active—restless, can't sleep—but throughout the day he will not start any activity unless "primed" by somebody else. He will be grateful at sharing activities with others but will not be able to make up his mind to do anything alone. The picture is one of lack of decision and initiative. Organized activities along social lines occur only if a friend takes the patient along and shares the activity with him. Nothing seems to promise reward; only the ordinary activities of the day are carried on, and these in a routine manner, falling apart into small steps, each of which has to be carried out with much effort and without zest.

(8) There is, in addition, a picture in which a patient is active but in which most of his activities attain a coloring which is *detrimental to his own social and economic existence.* Such patients, with uncalled for generosity, give away their belongings, are easily lured into foolish economic dealings, lose their friends and professional standing by a series of "stupid acts," and find themselves finally without family, friends, social status or money. This protracted self-punitive behavior seems to take place without any awareness of excessive feelings of guilt. It is a particularly distressing grief picture because it is likely to hurt other members of the family and drag down friends and business associates.

(9) This leads finally to the picture in which the grief reaction takes the form of a straight *agitated depression* with tension, agitation, insomnia, feelings of worthlessness, bitter self-accusation, and obvious need for punishment. Such patients may be dangerously suicidal.

A young man aged 32 had received only minor burns and left the hospital apparently well on the road to recovery just before the psychiatric survey of the disaster victims took place. On the fifth day he had learned that his wife had died. He seemed somewhat relieved of his worry about her fate; impressed the surgeon as being unusually well controlled during the following short period of his stay in the hospital.

On January 1st he was returned to the hospital by his family. Shortly after his return home he had become restless, did not want to stay at home, had taken a trip to relatives trying to find rest, had not succeeded, and had returned home in a state of marked agitation, appearing preoccupied, frightened, and unable to concentrate on any organized activity. The mental status presented a somewhat unusual picture. He was restless, could not sit still or participate in any activity in the ward.

He would try to read, drop it after a few minutes, or try to play Ping-Pong, give it up after a short time. He would try to start conversations, break them off abruptly, and then fall into repeated murmured utterances: "Nobody can help me. When is it going to happen? I am doomed, am I not?" With great effort it was possible to establish enough rapport to carry on interviews. He complained about his feeling of extreme tension, inability to breathe, generalized weakness and exhaustion, and his frantic fear that something terrible was going to happen. "I'm destined to live in insanity or I must die. I know that it is God's will. I have this awful feeling of guilt." With intense morbid guilt feelings, he reviewed incessantly the events of the fire. His wife had stayed behind. When he tried to pull her out, she had fainted and was shoved out by the crowd. She was burned while he was saved. "I should have saved her or I should have died too." He complained about being filled with an incredible violence and did not know what to do about it. The rapport established with him lasted for only brief periods of time. He then would fall back into his state of intense agitation and muttering. He slept poorly even with large sedation. In the course of four days he became somewhat more composed, had longer periods of contact with the psychiatrist, and seemed to feel that he was being understood and might be able to cope with his morbid feelings of guilt and violent impulses. On the sixth day of his hospital stay, however, after skillfully distracting the attention of his special nurse he jumped through a closed window to a violent death.

If the patient is not conspicuously suicidal, it may nevertheless be true that he has a strong desire for painful experiences, and such patients are likely to desire shock treatment of some sort, which they picture as a cruel experience, such as electrocution might be.

A 21-year-old woman, whose 20-month-old son was accidentally smothered, developed a state of severe agitated depression with self-accusation, inability to enjoy anything, hopelessness about the future, overflow of hostility against the husband and his parents, also with excessive hostility against the psychiatrist. She insisted upon electric-shock treatment and was finally referred to another physician who treated her. She responded to the shock treatments very well and felt relieved of her sense of guilt.

It is remarkable that agitated depressions of this sort represent only a small fraction of the pictures of grief in our series.

Prognostic Evaluation

Our observations indicate that to a certain extent the type and severity of the grief reaction can be predicted. Patients with obsessive personality makeup and with a history of former depressions are likely to develop an agitated depression. Severe reactions seen to occur in mothers who have lost young children. The intensity of interaction with the deceased before his death seems to be significant. It is important to realize that such interaction does not have to be of the affectionate type; on the contrary, the death of a person who invited much hostility, especially hostility which could not well be expressed because of his status and claim to loyalty, may be followed by a severe grief reaction in which hostile impulses are the most conspicuous feature. Not infrequently the person who passed away represented a key person in a social system, his death being followed by disintegration of this social system and by a profound alteration of the living and social conditions for the bereaved. In such cases readjustment presents a severe task quite apart from the reaction to the loss incurred. All these factors seem to be more important than a tendency to react with neurotic symptoms in previous life. In this way the most conspicuous forms of morbid identification were found in persons who had no former history of a tendency to psychoneurotic reactions.

Management

Proper psychiatric management of grief reactions may prevent prolonged and serious alterations in the patient's social adjustment, as well as potential medical disease. The essential task facing the psychiatrist is that of sharing the patient's grief work, namely, his efforts at extricating himself from the bondage to the deceased and at finding new patterns of rewarding interaction. It is of the greatest importance to notice that not only over-reaction but under-reaction of the bereaved must be given attention because delayed responses may occur at unpredictable moments and the dangerous distortions of the grief reaction, not conspicuous at first, be quite destructive later and these may be prevented.

Religious agencies have led in dealing with the bereaved. They have provided comfort by giving the backing of dogma to the patient's wish for continued interaction with the deceased, have developed rituals which maintain the patient's interaction with others, and have counteracted the morbid guilt feelings of the patient by Divine Grace and by promising an opportunity for "making up" to the deceased at the time of a later reunion. While these measures have helped countless mourners, comfort alone does not provide adequate assistance in the patient's grief work. He has to accept the pain of the bereavement. He has to review his relationships with the deceased, and has to become acquainted with the alterations in his own modes of emotional reaction. His fear of insanity, his fear of accepting the surprising changes in his feelings, especially the overflow of hostility, have to be worked through. He will have to express his sorrow and sense of loss. He will have to find an acceptable formulation of his future relationship to the deceased. He will have to visualize his feelings of guilt, and he will have to find persons around him whom he can use as "primers" for the acquisition of new patterns of conduct. All this can be done in eight to ten interviews.

Special techniques are needed if hostility is the most marked feature of the grief reaction. The hostility may be directed against the psychiatrist, and the patient will have such guilt over his hostility that he will avoid further interviews. The help of a social worker or a minister, or if these are not available, a member of the family, to urge the patient to continue coming to see the psychiatrist may be indispensable. If the tension and the depressive features are too great, a combination of benzedrine sulfate, 5–10 mgm. b.i.d., and sodium amytal, 3 gr. before retiring, may be useful in first reducing emotional distress to a tolerable degree. Severe agitated depressive reactions may defy all efforts of psychotherapy and may respond well to shock treatment.

Since it is obvious that not all bereaved persons, especially those suffering because of war casualties, can have the benefit of expert psychiatric help, much of this knowledge will have to be passed on to auxiliary workers. Social workers and ministers will have to be on the look-out for the more ominous pictures, referring these to the psychiatrist while assisting the more normal reactions themselves.

Anticipatory Grief Reactions

While our studies were at first limited to reactions to actual death, it must be understood that grief reactions are just one form of separation reactions. Separation by death is characterized by its irreversibility and finality. Separation may, of course, occur for other reasons. We were at first surprised to find genuine grief reactions in patients who had not experienced a bereavement but who had experienced separation, for instance with the departure of a member of the family into the armed forces. Separation in this case is not due to death but is under the threat of death. A common picture hitherto not appreciated is a syndrome which we have designated *anticipatory grief*. The patient is so concerned with her adjustment after the potential death of father or son that she goes through all the phases of grief—depression, heightened preoccupation with the departed, a review of all the forms of death which might befall him, and anticipation of the modes of readjustment which might be necessitated by it. While this reaction may well form a safeguard against the impact of a sudden death notice, it can turn out to be of a disadvantage at the occasion of reunion. Several instances of this sort came to our attention when a soldier just returned from the battlefront complained that his wife did not love him anymore and demanded immediate divorce. In such situations apparently the grief work had been done so effectively that the patient has emancipated herself and the readjustment must now be directed towards new interaction. It is important to know this because many family disasters of this sort may be avoided through prophylactic measures.

Notes

Many of the observations are, of course, not entirely new. Delayed reactions were described by Helene Deutsch (1). Shock treatment in agitated depressions due to bereavement has recently been advocated by Myerson (2). Morbid identification has been stressed at many points in the psychoanalytic literature and recently by H. A. Murray (3). The relation of mourning and depressive psychoses has been discussed by Freud (4), Melanie Klein (5), and Abraham (6). Bereavement reactions in wartime were discussed by Wilson (7). The reactions after the Cocoanut Grove fire were described in some detail in a chapter of the monograph on this civilian disaster (8). The effect of wartime separations was reported by Rosenbaum (9). The incidence of grief reactions among the psychogenic factors in asthma and rheumatoid arthritis has been mentioned by Cobb et al. (10, 11).

References

1. Helene Deutsch, "Absence of Grief," *Psychoanalytic Quarterly* 6 (1937):12.

2. Abraham Myerson, "The Use of Shock Therapy in Prolonged Grief Reactions," *New England Journal of Medicine* 230 (Mar. 2, 1944):9.

3. H. A. Murray, "Visual Manifestations of Personality," *Journal of Abnormal and Social Psychology* 32 (1937):161–184.

4. Sigmund Freud, "Mourning and Melancholia," *Collected Papers*, IV, 288–317; 152–170.

5. Melanie Klein, "Mourning and Its Relation to Manic-Depressive States," *International Journal of Psychoanalysis* 21 (1940):125–153.

6. C. Abraham, "Notes on the Psycho-analytical Investigation and Treatment of the Libido, Viewed in the Light of Mental Disorder." Selected Papers.

7. A. T. M. Wilson, "Reactive Emotional Disorders," *Practitioner* 146:254–258.

8. S. Cobb and E. Lindemann, "Neuropsychiatric Observations after the Cocoanut Grove Fire," *Annals of Surgery*, June 1943.

9. Milton Rosenbaum, "Emotional Aspects of Wartime Separations," *Family* 24 (1944):337–341.

10. S. Cobb, W. Bauer, and I. Whitney, "Environmental Factors in Rheumatoid Arthritis," *Journal of the American Medical Association.* 113 (1939):668–670.

11. N. McDermott and S. Cobb, "Psychogenic Factors in Asthma," *Psychosomatic Medicine* 1 (1939):204–341.

12. Erich Lindemann, "Psychiatric Factors in the Treatment of Ulcerative Colitis," *Archives of Neurology and Psychiatry* 49 (1943):323–324.

selection from
Epic of Gilgamesh

Though Lindemann bases his study of mourning on research conducted in this century, the following selection demonstrates the timelessness of the reactions he identifies. In this oldest of Western literary fragments, dating from 2000 B.C. in Mesopotamia, Gilgamesh, the young king, mourns the death of his one dear friend, Enkidu. As he calls on all creation to mourn with him, Gilgamesh gives voice to the anger, despair, and excruciating pain of fresh loss.

This day on which Enkidu dreamed came to an end and he lay stricken with sickness. One whole day he lay on his bed and his suffering increased, a second and a third day; ten days he lay and his suffering increased, eleven and twelve days he lay on his bed of pain. Then he called to Gilgamesh, "My friend, the great goddess cursed me and I must die in shame. I shall not die like a man fallen in battle; I feared to fall, but happy is the man who falls in the battle, for I must die in shame." And Gilgamesh wept over Enkidu. With the first light of dawn he raised his voice and said to the counsellors of Uruk:

"Hear me, great ones of Uruk,
I weep for Enkidu, my friend,
Bitterly moaning like a woman mourning
I weep for my brother.
O Enkidu, the wild ass and the gazelle
That were father and mother,
All four-footed creatures who fed with you
Weep for you,
All the wild things of the plain and the pastures;
The paths that you loved in the forest of cedars
Night and day murmur.
Let the great ones of strong-walled Uruk
Weep for you,
Let the finger of blessing
Be stretched out in mourning.
O Enkidu, my brother,
You were the axe at my side,
My hand's strength, the sword in my belt,
The shield before me,

Source: From the *Epic of Gilgamesh*, trans. by N. K. Sandars (Penguin Classics, rev. ed. 1964), pp. 90–93. Copyright © N. K. Sandars, 1960, 1964.

A glorious robe, my fairest ornament.
Hark, there is an echo through all the country
Like a mother mourning.
Weep, all the paths where we walked together,
And the beasts we hunted, panther and tiger,
Lion and leopard, stag and ibex,
The bull and the doe.
The mountain we climbed where we slew the watchman
Weeps for you,
The river along whose bank we used to walk,
Weeps for you,
Ula of Elam, and dear Euphrates
Where once we drew water for the water-skins,
The warriors of strong-walled Uruk
Where the Bull of Heaven was killed,
Weep for you.
All the people in Eridu
Weep for you Enkidu.
The tillers and the harvesters
Who brought grain for you once
Mourn for you now.
The servants who anointed your body
Mourn for you now;
The harlot who anointed you with fragrant oil
Laments for you now;
The women of the palace, who brought you a wife
With the ring of your choice,
Lament for you now.
The young men your brothers
As though they were women
Go long-haired in mourning.
An evil fate has robbed me.
O my young brother Enkidu, my dearest friend,
What is this sleep which holds you now?
You are lost in the dark and cannot hear me."

He touched his heart but it did not beat, nor did he lift his eyes again. When Gilgamesh touched his heart it did not beat. So Gilgamesh laid a veil, as one veils the bride, over his friend. He began to rage like a lion, like a lioness robbed of her whelps. This way and that he paced round the bed, he tore out his hair and strewed it around. He dragged off his splendid robes and flung them down as though they were abominations.

In the first light of dawn Gilgamesh cried out, "I made you rest on a royal bed, you reclined on a couch at my left hand, the princes of the earth kissed your feet. I will cause all the people of Uruk to weep over you and raise the dirge of the dead. The joyful people will stoop with sorrow; and when you have gone to the earth I will let my hair grow long for your sake, I will wander through the wilderness in the skin of a lion." The next day also, in the first light, Gilgamesh lamented; seven days and seven nights he wept for Enkidu, until the worm fastened on him. Only then he gave him up to the earth, for the Annunaki, the judges, had seized him.

Then Gilgamesh issued a proclamation through the land, he summoned them all, the coppersmiths, the goldsmiths, the stone-workers, and commanded them, "Make a statue of my friend." The statue was fashioned with a great weight of lapis lazuli for the breast and of gold for the body. A table of hard-wood was set out, and on it a bowl of carnelian filled with honey, and a bowl of lapis lazuli filled with butter. These he exposed and offered to the Sun; and weeping he went away.

JOHN BOWLBY

The Loss of a Spouse

Where Lindemann identified the symptomatology and made recommendations for the management of acute grief, British psychiatrist John Bowlby writes on the extended work of mourning. Bowlby suggests that the original relationship with the deceased continues to hold a central position in the emotional life of the bereaved person; the work of grief is both affective and cognitive, requiring a gradual redefinition of the original relationship. From his clinical studies over a twenty-year period, Bowlby identifies a four-phased sequence in the mourning process.

Four Phases of Mourning

Observations of how individuals respond to the loss of a close relative show that over the course of weeks and months their responses usually move through a succession of phases. Admittedly these phases are not clear-cut, and any one individual may oscillate for a time back and forth between any two of them. Yet an overall sequence can be discerned.

The four[1] phases are as follows:

1. Phase of numbing that usually lasts from a few hours to a week and may be interrupted by outbursts of extremely intense distress and/or anger.
2. Phase of yearning and searching for the lost figure lasting some months and sometimes for years.
3. Phase of disorganization and despair.
4. Phase of greater or less degree of reorganization.

In what follows we concentrate especially on the psychological responses to loss, with special reference to the way the original relationship continues to fill a central role in a bereaved person's emotional life yet also, as a rule, undergoes a slow change of form as the months and years pass.[2] This continuing relationship explains the yearning and searching, and also the anger, prevalent in the second phase, and the despair and subsequent acceptance of loss as irreversible that occur when phases three and four are passed through successfully. It explains, too, many, and perhaps all, of the features characteristic of pathological outcomes.

In the descriptions of responses typical of the first two phases we draw especially on Parkes's study of London widows. In descriptions of the second two phases we draw increasingly on the findings of the Harvard (Glick et al. 1974) and other studies.

Source: From *Attachment and Loss*, Vol. III, *Loss: Sadness and Depression*, by John Bowlby. © 1980 by the Tavistock Institute of Human Relations. Reprinted by permission of Basic Books, Inc., Publishers.

Phase of Numbing

The immediate reaction to news of a husband's death varies greatly from individual to individual and also from time to time in any one widow. Most feel stunned and in varying degrees unable to accept the news. Remarks such as "I just couldn't take it all in," "I couldn't believe it," "I was in a dream," "It didn't seem real" are the rule. For a time a widow may carry on her usual life almost automatically. Nevertheless, she is likely to feel tense and apprehensive; and this unwonted calm may at any moment be broken by an outburst of intense emotion. Some describe overwhelming attacks of panic in which they may seek refuge with friends. Others break into anger. Occasionally a widow may feel sudden elation in an experience of union with her dead husband.

Phase of Yearning and Searching for the Lost Figure: Anger

Within a few hours or, perhaps, a few days of her loss a change occurs and she begins, though only episodically, to register the reality of the loss: this leads to pangs of intense pining and to spasms of distress and tearful sobbing. Yet, almost at the same time, there is great restlessness, insomnia, preoccupation with thoughts of the lost husband combined often with a sense of his actual presence, and a marked tendency to interpret signals or sounds as indicating that he is now returned. For example, hearing a door latch lifted at five o'clock is interpreted as husband returning from work, or a man in the street is misperceived as the missing husband. Vivid dreams of the husband still alive and well are not uncommon, with corresponding desolation on waking.

Since some or all of these features are now known to occur in a majority of widows, there can no longer be doubt that they are a regular feature of grief and in no way abnormal.

Another common feature of the second phase of mourning is anger. Its frequency as part of normal mourning has, we believe, habitually been under-estimated, at least by clinicians, to whom it seems to have appeared out of place and irrational. Yet it has been reported by every behavioural scientist, of whatever discipline, who has made grieving the centre of his research.

When such evidence as was then available was examined some years ago (Bowlby 1960, 1961) I was struck by the resemblance of these responses to a child's initial protest at losing his mother and his efforts to recover her and also by Shand's suggestion that searching for the lost person is an integral part of the mourning of adults. The view I advanced, therefore, was that during this early phase of mourning it is usual for a bereaved person to alternate between two states of mind. On the one hand is belief that death has occurred with the pain and hopeless yearning that that entails. On the other is disbelief[3] that it has occurred, accompanied both by hope that all may yet be well and by an urge to search for and to recover the lost person. Anger is aroused, it seems, both by those held responsible for the loss and also by frustrations met with during fruitless search.

Exploring this view further, I suggest that in bereaved people whose mourning runs a healthy course the urge to search and to recover, often intense in the early weeks and months, diminishes gradually over time, and that how it is experienced varies greatly from person to person. Whereas some bereaved people are conscious of their urge to search, others are not. Whereas some willingly fall in with it, others seek to stifle it as irrational and absurd. Whatever attitude a bereaved person takes towards the urge, I suggested, he nonetheless finds himself impelled to search and, if possible, to recover the person who has gone. In a subsequent paper (Bowlby 1963) I pointed out that many of the features characteristic of pathological forms of mourning can be understood as resulting from the active persistence of this urge which tends to be expressed in a variety of disguised and distorted ways.

Such were the views advanced in the early sixties. They have since been endorsed and elaborated by Parkes, who has given special attention to these issues. In one of his papers (Parkes 1970) he has set out evidence from his own studies which he believes supports the search hypothesis. Since this hypothesis is central to all that follows, his evidence is given below.

Introducing the thesis he writes: "Although we tend to think of searching in terms of the motor act of restless movement towards possible locations of the lost object, [searching] also has perceptual and ideational components . . . Signs of the object can be identified only by reference to memories of the object as it was. Searching the external world for signs of the object therefore includes the establishment of an internal perceptual 'set' derived from previous experiences of the object." He gives as example a woman searching for her small son who is missing; she moves restlessly about the likely parts of the house scanning with her eyes and thinking of the boy; she hears a creak and immediately identifies it as the sound of her son's footfall on the stair; she calls out, "John, is that you?" The components of this sequence are:

—restless moving about and scanning the environment
—thinking intensely about the lost person
—developing a perceptual set for the person, namely a disposition to perceive and to pay attention to any stimuli that suggest the presence of the person and to ignore all those that are not relevant to this aim
—directing attention towards those parts of the environment in which the person is likely to be found
—calling for the lost person.

"Each of these components," Parkes emphasizes, "is to be found in bereaved men and women: in addition some grievers are consciously aware of an urge to search."

Presenting his findings on the 22 London widows under these five heads Parkes reports that:

a. All but two widows said they felt restless during the first month of bereavement, a restlessness that was also evident during interview. In summarizing his own findings Parkes quotes Lindemann's classical description of the early weeks of bereavement: "There is no retardation of action and speech; quite to the contrary, there is a rush of speech especially when talking about the deceased. There is restlessness, inability to sit still, moving about in aimless fashion, continually searching for something to do" (Lindemann 1944). Nevertheless, Parkes believes the searching is by no means aimless. Only because it is inhibited or else expressed in fragmentary fashion does it appear so.

b. During the first month of bereavement 19 of the widows were preoccupied with thoughts of their dead husband, and a year later 12 continued to spend much time thinking of him. So clear was the visual picture that often it was spoken of as if it were a perception: "I can see him sitting in the chair."

c. The likelihood that this clear visual picture is part of a general perceptual set that scans sensory input for evidence of the missing person is supported by the frequency with which widows misidentify sensory data. Nine of those interviewed described how during the first month of bereavement they had frequently construed sounds or sights as indicative of their husband. One supposed she heard him cough at night, another heard him moving about the house, a third repeatedly misidentified men in the street.

d. Not only is a widow's perceptual set biased to give precedence to sensory data that may give evidence of her husband, but her motor behaviour is biased in a comparable way. Half the widows Parkes interviewed described how they felt drawn towards places or objects which they associated with him. Six kept visiting old haunts they had frequented together, two felt drawn towards the hospital where their husband had died, in one case to the point of actually entering its doors, three were unable to leave home without experiencing a strong impulse to return there, others felt drawn towards the cemetery where he was buried. All but three treasured possessions associated with their husband and several found themselves returning repeatedly to such objects.

e. Whenever a widow recalls the lost person or speaks about him tears are likely, and sometimes they lead to uncontrollable sobbing. Although it may come as a surprise that such tears and sobs are to be regarded as attempts to recover the lost person, there is good reason to think that that is what they are.

The facial expressions typical of adult grief, Darwin concluded (1872), are a resultant, on the one hand, of a tendency to scream like a child when he feels abandoned and, on the other, of an inhibition of such screaming. Both crying and screaming are, of course, ways by means of which a child commonly attracts and recovers his missing mother, or some other person who may help him find her; and they occur in grief, we postulate, with the same objective in mind—either consciously or unconsciously. In keeping with this view is the finding that occasionally a bereaved person will call out for the lost person to return. "Oh, Fred, I do need you," shouted one widow during the course of an interview before she burst into tears.

Finally, at least four of these 22 widows were aware that they were searching. "I walk around searching," and one, "I go to the grave . . . but he's not there," said another. One of them had ideas of attending a spiritualist seance in the hope of communicating with her husband; several thought of killing themselves as a means of rejoining theirs.[4]

Turning now to the incidence of anger amongst these widows, Parkes found it to be evident in all but four and to be very marked in seven, namely one-third of them, at the time of the first interview. For some, anger took the form of general irritability or bitterness. For others it had a target—in four cases a relative, in five clergy, doctors or officials, and in four the dead husband himself. In most such cases the reason given for the anger was that the person in question was held either to have been in some part responsible for the death or to have been negligent in connection with it, either towards the dead man or to the widow. Similarly, husbands had incurred their widow's anger either because they had not cared for themselves better or because they were thought to have contributed to their own death.[5]

Although some degree of self-reproach was also common, it was never so prominent a feature as was anger. In most of these widows self-reproach centered on some minor act of omission or commission associated with the last illness or death. Although in one or two of the London widows there were times when this self-reproach was fairly severe, in none of them was it as intense and unrelenting as it is in subjects whose self-reproachful grieving persists until finally it becomes diagnosed as depressive illness.

Within the context of the search hypothesis the prevalence of anger during the early weeks of mourning receives ready explanation. In several earlier publications it has been emphasized that anger is both usual and useful when separation is only temporary. It then helps overcome obstacles to reunion with the lost person; and, after reunion is achieved, to express reproach towards whomever seemed responsible for the separation makes it less likely that a separation will occur again. Only when separation is permanent is the anger and reproach out of place. "There are therefore good biological reasons for every separation to be responded to in an automatic instinctive way with aggressive behaviour; irretrievable loss is statistically so unusual that it is not taken into account. In the course of our evolution, it appears, our instinctual equipment has come to be so fashioned that all losses are assumed to be retrievable and are responded to accordingly" (Bowlby 1961). Thus anger is seen as an intelligible constituent of the urgent though fruitless effort a bereaved person is making to restore the bond that has been severed. So long as anger continues, it seems, loss is not being accepted as permanent and hope is still lingering on. As Marris (1958) comments when a widow described to him how, after her husband's death, she had given her doctor a good hiding, it was "as if her rage while it lasted had given her courage."

Sudden outbursts of rage are fairly common soon after a loss, especially ones that are sudden and/or felt to be untimely, and they carry no adverse prognosis. Should anger and resentment persist beyond the early weeks, however, there are grounds for concern.

Hostility to comforters is to be understood in the same way. Whereas the comforter who takes no side in the conflict between a striving for reunion and an acceptance of loss may be of great value to the bereaved, one who at an early stage seems to favour acceptance of loss is as keenly resented as if he had been the agent of it. Often it is not comfort in loss that is wanted but assistance towards reunion.

Anger and ingratitude towards comforters, indeed, have been notorious since the time of Job. Overwhelmed by the blow he has received, one of the first impulses of the bereaved is to appeal to others for their help—help to regain the person lost. The would-be comforter who responds to this appeal may, however, see the situation differently. To him it may be clear that hope of reunion is a chimera and that to encourage it would be unrealistic, even dishonest. And so, instead of behaving as is wished, he seems to the bereaved to do the opposite and is resented accordingly. No wonder his role is a thankless one.

Thus, we see, restless searching, intermittent hope, repeated disappointment, weeping, anger, accusation, and ingratitude are all features of the second phase of mourning, and are to be understood as expressions of the strong urge to find and recover the lost person. Nevertheless, underlying these strong emotions, which erupt episodically and seem so perplexing, there is likely to coexist deep and pervasive sadness, a response to recognition that reunion is at best improbable. Moreover, because fruitless search is painful, there may also be times when a bereaved person may attempt to be rid of reminders of the dead. He or she may then oscillate between treasuring such reminders and throwing them out, between welcoming the opportunity to speak of the dead and dreading such occasions, between seeking out places where they have been together and avoiding them. One of the widows interviewed by Parkes described how she had tried sleeping in the back bedroom to get away from her memories and how she had then missed her husband so much that she had returned to the main bedroom in order to be near him.

Finding a way to reconcile these two incompatible urges, we believe, constitutes a central task of the third and fourth phases of mourning. Light on how successfully the task is being solved, Gorer (1965) believes, is thrown by the way a bereaved person responds to spoken condolences; grateful acceptance is one of the most reliable signs that the bereaved is working through his or her mourning satisfactorily. Conversely, an injunction never to refer to the loss bodes ill.

It is in the extent to which they help a mourner in this task that mourning customs are to be evaluated. In recent times both Gorer (1965) and Marris (1974) have considered them in this light. At first, Marris points out, acts of mourning attenuate the leave taking. They enable the bereaved, for a while, to give the dead person as central a place in her life as he had before, yet at the same time they emphasize death as a crucial event whose implications must be acknowledged. Subsequently, such customs mark the stages of reintegration. In Gorer's phrase, mourning customs are 'time-limited,' both guiding and sanctioning the stages of recovery. Although at first sight it may seem false to impose customs on so intense and private an emotion as grief, the very loneliness of the crisis and the intense conflict of feeling cries out for a supportive structure.

Phase of Disorganization and Despair and Phase of Reorganization

For mourning to have a favourable outcome it appears to be necessary for a bereaved person to endure this buffeting of emotion. Only if he can tolerate the pining, the more or less conscious searching, the seemingly endless examination of how and why the loss occurred, and anger at anyone who might have been responsible, not sparing even the dead person, can he come gradually to recognize and accept that the loss is in truth permanent and that his life must be shaped anew. In this way only does it seem possible for him fully to register that his old patterns of behaviour have become redundant and have therefore to be dismantled. C. S. Lewis has described the frustrations not only of feeling but of thought and action that grieving entails. In a diary entry after the loss of his wife, H, he writes: "I think I am beginning to understand why grief feels like suspense. It comes from the frustration of so many impulses that had become habitual. Thought after thought, feeling after feeling, action after action, had H for their object. Now their target is gone. I keep on, through habit, fitting an arrow to the string; then I remember and I have to lay the bow down. So many roads lead through to H. I set out on one of them. But now there's an impassable frontier-post across it. So many roads once; now so many culs-de-sac" (1961, p. 59).

Because it is necessary to discard old patterns of thinking, feeling and acting before new ones can be fashioned, it is almost inevitable that a bereaved person should at times despair that anything can be salvaged and, as a result, fall into depression and apathy. Nevertheless, if all goes well this phase may soon begin to alternate with a phase during which he starts to examine the new situation in which he finds himself and to consider ways of meeting it. This entails a redefinition of himself as well as of his situation. No longer is he a husband but a widower. No longer is he one of a pair with complementary roles but a singleton. This redefinition of self and situation is as painful as it is crucial, if only because it means relinquishing finally all hope that the lost person can be recovered and the old situation re-established. Yet until redefinition is achieved no plans for the future can be made.

It is important here to note that, suffused though it be by the strongest emotion, redefinition of self and situation is no mere release of affect but a cognitive act on which all else turns. It is a process of "realization" (Parkes 1972), of reshaping internal representational models so as to align them with the changes that have occurred in the bereaved's life situation. Much is said of this in later chapters.

Once this corner is turned a bereaved person recognizes that an attempt must be made to fill unaccustomed roles and to acquire new skills. A widower may have to become cook and housekeeper, a widow to become the family wage-earner and house decorator. If there are children, the remaining parent has so far as possible to do duty for both. The more successful the survivor is in achieving these new roles and skills the more confident and independent he or she begins to feel. The shift is well described by one of the London widows, interviewed a year after her bereavement, who remarked: "I think I'm beginning to wake up now. I'm starting living instead of just existing . . . I feel I ought to plan to do something." As initiative and, with it, independence returns so a widow or widower may become jealous of the independence and may perhaps break off rather abruptly a supportive relationship that had earlier been welcomed. Yet, however successfully a widow or widower may adopt new roles and learn new skills, the changed situation is likely to be felt as a constant strain and is bound to be lonely. An acute sense of loneliness, most pronounced at night time, was reported by almost all the widows interviewed whether by Marris, by Hobson (1964), or by Parkes in England or by Glick or Clayton and their respective teams in the U.S.A.

To resume social life even at a superficial level is often a great difficulty, at least in Western cultures. There is more than one reason for this. On the one hand, convention often dictates that the sexes be present in equal number so that those who enjoy the company of the other sex find themselves left out. On the other are those who find social occasions in which the sexes are mixed too painful to attend because of their being reminded too forcefully of their loss of partner. As a consequence we find that both widowers and widows most often join gatherings of members of their own sex. For men this is usually easier because a work group or sports group may be ready to hand. For women a church group or Women's Institute may prove invaluable.

Few widows remarry. This is partly because suitable partners are scarce but at least equally because of a reluctance of many widows to consider remarriage. Plainly, the remarriage rate for each sample will depend not only on the widows' ages at bereavement but on the number of years later that information is gathered. In the studies reviewed here the highest rate reported is about one in four of the Boston widows; at the end of some three years fourteen had either remarried or appeared likely to do so. All of them, it should be remembered, were under 45 years when widowed. In the Marris study one in five of the 33 widowed before age forty had remarried. For older widows the proportions are much lower. By contrast, the proportion of widowers who remarry is relatively high.

Many widows refuse to consider remarriage. Others consider it but decide against it. Fear of friction between stepfather and children is given as a reason by many. Some regard the risk of suffering the pain of a second loss too great. Others believe they could never love another man in the way they had loved their husband and that invidious comparisons would result. In response to questions, about half the Boston widows expressed themselves uninterested in any further sexual relationship. Whilst half of the total acknowledged some sense of sexual deprivation, others felt numbed. It is probably common for sexual feelings to continue to be linked to the husband; and they may be expressed in masturbation fantasies or enacted in dreams.

A year after bereavement, continued loyalty to the husband was judged by Glick to be the main stumbling-block to remarriage in the case of the Boston widows. Parkes remarks that many of the London widows "still seemed to regard themselves as married to their dead husbands" (1972, p. 99). This raises afresh the issue of a bereaved person's continuing relationship with the person who has died.

Persistence of Relationship

As the first year of mourning draws on most mourners find it becomes possible to make a distinction between patterns of thought, feeling and behaviour that are clearly no longer appropriate and others which can with good reason be retained. In the former class are those, such as performing certain household duties, which only make sense if the lost person is physically present; in the latter maintaining values and pursuing goals which, having been developed in association with the lost person, remain linked with him and can without falsification continue to be maintained and pursued in reference to memory of him. Perhaps it is through processes of this kind that half or more of widows and widowers reach a state of mind in which they retain a strong sense of the continuing presence of their partner without the turmoils of hope and disappointment, search and frustration, anger and blame that are present earlier.

It will be remembered that a year after losing their husbands 12 of the 22 London widows reported that they still spent much time thinking of their husband and sometimes had a sense of his actual presence. This they found comforting. Glick et al. (1974) report very similar findings for the Boston widows. Although a sense of the continuing presence of the dead person may take a few weeks to become firmly established, they found it tends thereafter to persist at its original intensity, instead of waning slowly as most of the other components of the early phases of mourning do. Twelve months after their loss two out of three of the Boston widows continued to spend much time thinking of their husband and one in four of the 49 described how there were still occasions when they forgot he was dead. So comforting did widows find the sense of the dead husband's presence that some deliberately evoked it whenever they felt unsure of themselves or depressed.

Similar findings to those for the London and the Boston widows are reported also by Rees (1971), who surveyed nearly 300 widows and widowers in Wales, nearly half of whom had been widowed for ten years or longer. Of 227 widows and 66 widowers 47 percent described having had such experiences and a majority were continuing to do so. Incidence in widowers was almost the same as in widows and the incidence varied little with either social class or cultural background. The incidence tended to be higher the longer the marriage had lasted, which may account for its being higher also in those who were over the age of forty when widowed. More than one in ten of widows and widowers reported having held conversations with the dead spouse; and here again the incidence was higher in older widows and widowers than in younger ones. Two-thirds of those who reported experiences of their dead spouse's presence, either with or without some form of sensory illusion or occasionally hallucination, described their experiences as being comforting and helpful. Most of the remainder were neutral about them, and only eight of the total of 137 subjects who had such experiences disliked having them.

Dreams of the spouse still being alive share many of the characteristic features of the sense of presence: they occur in about half of widows and widowers, they are extremely vivid and realistic and in a majority of cases are experienced as comforting. "It was just like everyday life," one of the London widows reported, "my husband coming in and getting his dinner. Very vivid so that when I woke up I was very annoyed." Several of Gorer's informants described how they sought to hold the image in their minds after waking and how sad it was when it faded. Not infrequently a widow or widower would weep after recounting the dream.

Gorer (1965) emphasizes that in these typical comforting dreams the dead person is envisaged as young and healthy, and as engaging in happy everyday activities. But, as Parkes (1972) notes, as a rule there is something in the dream to indicate that all is not well. As one widow put it after describing how in the dream her husband was trying to comfort her and how happy it made her: "even in the dream I know he's dead."[6]

Not all bereaved people who dream find the dream comforting. In some dreams traumatic aspects of the last illness or death are re-enacted; in others distressing aspects of the previous relationship. Whether on balance a bereaved person finds his dreams comforting seems likely to be a reliable indicator of whether or not mourning is taking a favourable course.

Let us return now to a widow's or widower's daytime sense of the dead spouse's presence. In many cases, it seems, the dead spouse is experienced as a companion who accompanies the bereaved everywhere. In many others the spouse is experienced as located somewhere specific and appropriate. Common examples are a particular chair or room which he occupied, or perhaps the garden, or the grave. As remarked already, there is no reason to regard any of these experiences as either unusual or unfavourable, rather the contrary. For example, in regard to the Boston widows, Glick, Weiss, and Parkes (1974) report: "Often the widow's progress toward recovery was facilitated by inner conversations with her husband's presence . . . this continued sense of attachment was not incompatible with increasing capacity for independent action" (p. 154). Although Glick regards this finding as paradoxical, those familiar with the evidence regarding the relation of secure attachment to the growth of self-reliance will not find it so. On the contrary, it seems likely that for many widows and widowers it is precisely because they are willing for their feelings of attachment to the dead spouse to persist that their sense of identity is preserved and they become able to reorganize their lives along lines they find meaningful.

That for many bereaved people this is the preferred solution to their dilemma has for too long gone unrecognized.

Closely related to this sense of the dead person's presence are certain experiences in which a widow may feel either that she has become more like her husband since his death or even that he is somehow within her. For example, one of the London widows, on being asked whether she had felt her husband was near at hand, replied: "It's not a sense of his presence, he's here inside me. That's why I'm happy all the time. It's as if two people are one ... although I'm alone, we're sort of together if you see what I mean ... I don't think I've got the will power to carry on on my own, so he must be" (Parkes 1972, p. 104).

In accordance with such feelings bereaved people may find themselves doing things in the same way that the person lost did them; and some may undertake activities typical of the dead person despite their never having done them before. When the activities are well suited to the capabilities and interests of the bereaved, no conflict results and he or she may obtain much satisfaction from doing them. Perhaps such behaviour is best regarded as an example, in special circumstances, of the well-known tendency to emulate those whom we hold in high regard. Nevertheless, Parkes (1972, p. 105) emphasizes that in his series of London widows it was only a minority who at any time during the first year of bereavement were conscious either of coming to resemble the husband or of "containing" him. Moreover, in these widows the sense of having him "inside" tended to alternate with periods when he was experienced as a companion. Since these widows progressed neither more nor less favourably than others, such experiences when only short-lived are evidently compatible with healthy mourning.

Many symptoms of disordered mourning can, however, be understood as due to some unfavourable development of these processes. One form of maldevelopment is when a bereaved person feels a continuing compulsion to imitate the dead person despite having neither the competence nor the desire to do so. Another is when the bereaved's continuing sense of "containing" the person lost gives rise to an elated state of mind (as seems to have been present in the example quoted), or leads the bereaved to develop the symptoms of the deceased's last illness. Yet another form of unfavourable development occurs when the bereaved, instead of experiencing the dead person as a companion and/or as located somewhere appropriate such as in the grave or in his, or her, familiar chair, locates him within another person, or even within an animal or a physical object. Such mislocations as I shall call them, which include mislocations within the self, can if persistent easily lead to behaviour that is not in the best interests of the bereaved and that may appear bizarre. It may also be damaging to another person; for example, to regard a child as the incarnation of a dead person and to treat him so is likely to have an extremely adverse effect upon him. For all these reasons I am inclined to regard mislocations of any of these kinds if more than transitory as signs of pathology.

Failure to recognize that a continuing sense of the dead person's presence, either as a constant companion or in some specific and appropriate location, is a common feature of healthy mourning has led to much confused theorizing. Very frequently the concept of identification, instead of being limited to cases in which the dead person is located within the self, is extended to cover also every case in which there is a continuing sense of the dead person's presence, irrespective of location. By so doing a distinction that recent empirical studies show is vital for an understanding of the differences between healthy and pathological mourning becomes blurred. Indeed, findings in regard both to the high prevalence of a continuing sense of the presence of the dead person and to its compatibility with a favourable outcome give no support to Freud's well-known and already quoted passage: "Mourning has a quite precise psychical task to perform: its function is to detach the survivor's memories and hopes from the dead" (Freud, p. 65).

Notes

1. In an earlier paper (Bowlby 1961) it was suggested that the course of mourning could be divided into three main phases, but this numbering omitted an important first phase which is usually fairly brief. What were formerly numbered phases 1, 2, and 3 have therefore been renumbered phases 2, 3, and 4.

2. In concentrating on these aspects of mourning we are able to give only limited attention to the social and economic consequences of a bereavement, which are often also of great importance and perhaps especially so in the case of widows in Western cultures. Readers concerned with these aspects are referred to the accounts of Marris (1958) and Parkes (1972) for the experiences of London widows and to that of Glick et al. (1974) for those of Boston widows.

3. Traditionally the term "denial" has been used to denote disbelief that death has occurred; but "denial" always carries with it a sense of active contradiction. Disbelief is more neutral and better suited for general use, especially since the cause of disbelief is often inadequate information.

4. Behaviour influenced by an expectation of ultimate reunion is observed in many women with a husband who has deserted or whose marriage has ended in divorce. Marsden (1969) studied eighty such women, all with children, and dependent on the State for support, a great number of whom had not lived with their husband for five years or more. Remarking on the striking resemblance of the responses shown by some of them to responses seen after a bereavement, Marsden writes (p. 140): "The mother's emotional bonds with the father did not snap cleanly with the parting. Almost half the mothers, many of whom had completely lost touch with the father, had a sense of longing for him. . . . It was evident that a sizable minority of women persisted, in spite of evidence to the contrary and sometimes for many years, in thinking they would somehow be reunited with their children's father." After having moved into a new house three years earlier one of them had still not unpacked her belongings, unable to believe the move was permanent.

5. There is some evidence that the incidence of anger varies with the sex of the bereaved and also with the phase of life during which a death occurs. For example, findings of the Harvard study (Glick et al. 1974), which show an even higher incidence of anger among widows, show a lower incidence among widowers (see p. 43); and Gorer (1965) believes it to occur less frequently after the death of an elderly person—a timely death—than after that of someone whose life is uncompleted. The low incidence of anger reported by Clayton et al. (1972) may perhaps be a result of their sample being both elderly and also made up of one-third widowers.

6. Early in his work Freud (1916) had remarked on the way a dream can express incompatible truths: "When anyone has lost someone near and dear to him, he produces dreams of a special sort for some time afterwards, in which knowledge of the death arrives at the strangest compromises with the need to bring the dead person to life again. In some of these dreams the person who has died is dead and at the same time still alive . . . In others he is half dead and half alive" (p. 187).

References

Bowlby, J. 1960. Grief and mourning in infancy and early childhood. *Psychoanalytic Study of the Child* 15:9–52.

———. 1961. Processes of mourning. *International Journal of Psychoanalysis* 42:317–40.

———. 1963. Pathological mourning and childhood mourning. *Journal of the American Psychoanalytic Association* 11:500–41.

Clayton, P. J., J. A. Halikas, and W. L. Maurice. 1972. The depression of widowhood. *British Journal of Psychiatry* 120:71–8.

Darwin, C. 1872. *The expression of the emotions in man and animals*. London: Murray.

Freud, S. 1916. *The complete psychological works of Sigmund Freud*, Vol. 15, London: Hogarth Press.

Glick, I. O., R. S. Weiss, and C. M. Parkes. 1974. *The first year of bereavement*. New York: John Wiley, Interscience.

Gorer, G. 1965. *Death, grief, and mourning in contemporary britain*. London: Tavistock Publications.

Hobson, C. J. 1964. Widows of Blackton. *New Society* 24: September.

Lewis, C. S. 1961. *A grief observed*. London: Faber & Faber.

Lindemann, E. 1944. Symptomatology and management of acute grief. *American Journal of Psychiatry* 101:141–9.

Marris, P. 1958. *Widows and their families*. London: Routledge & Kegan Paul.

———. 1974. *Loss and change*. London: Routledge & Kegan Paul.

Marsden, D. 1969. *Mothers alone*. London: Allen Lane, Penguin Press.

Parkes, C. M. 1970. "Seeking" and "finding" a lost object: Evidence from recent studies of the reaction to bereavement. *Social Science and Medicine* 4:187–201.

Parkes, C. M. 1972. *Bereavement: Studies of grief in adult life*. London: Tavistock Publications; New York: International Universities Press.

Rees, W. D. 1971. The hallucinations of widowhood. *British Medical Journal* 4:37–41.

MAXINE KUMIN

Splitting Wood at Six Above

The shock and pain of grief cut deep, an ax blow at the heart of being. In the powerful image of splitting wood alone on a freezing, gray winter day, Maxine Kumin bodies forth the emotions of mourning. She wrote this particular poem in memory of her close colleague, poet Anne Sexton. It had been their custom to talk each day by telephone when large distances separated them. Kumin employs the personal image of the unfinished call—"I'm still/talking to you"—as a metaphor for the unresolved feelings of anger, yearning, and searching that Bowlby analyzed.

I open a tree.
In the stupefying cold
—ice on bare flesh a scald—
I seat the metal wedge
with a few left-handed swipes,
then with a change of grips
lean into the eight-pound sledge.

It's muslin overhead.
Snow falls as heavy as salt.
You are four months dead.
The beech log comes apart
like a chocolate nougat.
The wood speaks
first in the tiny voice
of a bird cry, a puppet-squeak,
and then all in a rush,
all in a passionate stammer.
The papery soul of the beech
released by wedge and hammer
flies back into air.

Time will do this as fair
to hickory, birch, black oak,
easing the insects in
till rot and freeze combine
to raise out of wormwood cracks,

Source: "Splitting Wood at Six Above," from *Our Ground Time Here Will Be Brief* by Maxine Kumin. Originally published in *The New Yorker*. Reprinted by permission of Viking Penguin Inc.

blue and dainty, the souls.
They are thin as an eyelash.
They flap once, going up.

The air rings like a bell.
I breathe out drops—
cold morning ghost-puffs
like your old cigarette cough.
See you tomorrow, you said.
You lied.

We're far from finished! I'm still
talking to you (last night's dream);
we'll split the phone bill.
It's expensive calling
from the other side.

Even waking it seems
logical—
your small round
stubbornly airborne soul,
that sun-yellow daisy heart
slipping the noose of its pod,
scooting over the tightrope,
none the worse for its trip,
to arrive at the other side.

It is the sound
of your going I drive
into heartwood. I stack
my quartered cuts bark down,
open yellow-face up.

ALBERT C. CAIN

Survivors of Suicide

Complex as the symptomatology of normal grief is, the mourning process for a survivor of suicide is infinitely more so. Albert Cain emphasizes the psychological vulnerability of the survivor, who is often tormented by feelings of personal responsibility in addition to the normal grief reactions of pain, anger, and guilt. Society offers no explanation or absolution for the death; rather it stigmatizes the mourner, depriving him or her of support.

The papers summarized in this book speak of and for the survivors of suicide, of their torment and their desperate need for psychological assistance. Seen at varying ages, individually or as a family, in different settings, at widely varying intervals following the suicide, in highly divergent forms of study or intervention, the survivors of suicides nevertheless spoke a story with many major convergences: The authors underline that there are qualitative and quantitative features in the stresses impinging upon the family survivors of suicide that range significantly beyond those typical of bereavement per se. They are struck by the severity of psychopathology found in the survivors, and by the intrinsic vulnerability of suicide survivors. They are not only aware of, but quick to insist upon the *multiplicity* of *pre-suicide* and *post-suicide* determinants of the survivor's personality and psychopathology. They are emphatic in balancing discussions of the obvious direct pathogenic impact of suicide itself with references to *preexisting* profoundly pathogenic influences (grossly evidenced, for instance, in the effects upon the family members of an eventual suicide's prior alcoholism, repeated desertions, acting out, borderline psychosis, depression, raw marital strife, and such—conditions often reported in the pre-suicide behavior of those who eventually commit suicide). So too do they spell out many powerful *post-suicide* secondary and tertiary pathogenic forces.[1] From these reports there evolves, frame by frame, a picture of the legacy of suicide that is simultaneously cognitive and affective, that captures the complex individual intrapsychic sequelae, placing these in turn within a powerful interpersonal and familial field of forces, and using a wide angle lens, within the larger social milieu of clan, neighbors and society.

The reactions portrayed, complex and individual as they are, can perhaps be clustered and capsuled as follows:

1. *Reality distortion*—massive, insistent use of denial and repression; tangled webs of evasions, contradictory beliefs, deliberate lies; concealment and anxiety-clouded confusion of memory, fantasy, and "imposed" rede-

Source: Albert C. Cain. *Survivors of Suicide.* Edited by Albert C. Cain. Springfield, Illinois: Charles C. Thomas, 1972. Copyright © by Charles C. Thomas. Used by permission.

finitions of reality . . . often elaborated into family myths, misconceptions, and varying disorders of reality linkage (feelings of unreality, derealization, weakened capacity for or commitment to reality testing, marked ego-splitting).

2. *Tortured object-relations*—desperate lonely neediness; disillusioned and doubt-filled distrust of human relationships; a hunger for, yet fear of closeness; a repetitive need to reenact separations, drive loved objects away, replay experiences of estrangement and reunion (or conversely, within the same dynamic configuration, ferocious determination to maintain crucial object-relations at any and all costs).

3. *Guilt*—visible quite directly, or in blaming and accusations, or in more symptomatic form; utterly irrational or painfully appropriate; focused variously on general anger and death wishes, specific acts, feelings that one could or should have prevented the suicide, a pervasive sense of complicity, or a sense of having been blamed by the suicidal individual for his despair; guilt variously fused with, displaced to or serving as screen guilt for other earlier guilts from myriad developmental sources.

4. *Disturbed self-concept*—compounded of a sense of shame, dishonor, and stigma; of having been cast away, abandoned, unwanted; of being worthless, unlovable if not bad or rotten; of being helpless, vulnerable; of being eternally unsure of self or others.

5. *Impotent rage*—intense yet admitting of little socially acceptable discharge; multiplied by the frequent sense of rejection and deliberate desertion, with its core narcissistic insult; fed by the social "branding" and at times ostracism, the intense frustration of ongoing needs, and the enforced facing of old and huge new burdens alone.

6. *Identification with the suicide*—often the result of a commingling of archaic introjective mechanisms and interpersonal tugs and pulls toward redefinition of self and family role;[2] masked or overt, accepted or fiercely defended against; the identification variously focusing upon personality features of the suicide, the threatening of suicide, the bodily sensations of the suicidal act, the committing of suicide—even the specific act of suicide itself in like manner, setting, or anniversary date.

7. *Depression and self-destructiveness*—bred of the guilt, shame, rage, unmet yearning and unresolved grief delineated above, depression in its many faces is paramount: in active self-hatred, in states of hollow emptiness and deadness; in apathy, withdrawal, and immobilization; in sadness and despair; these depressive processes, exacerbated by the identification processes noted, are visible in implacably self-destructive ways of life and a remarkable incidence of direct suicidal behavior—suicidal impulses, fantasies, threats, preoccupation,[3] repeated suicidal attempts and completed suicides.

8. *Search for meaning*—driven, endless repetitions and reconstructions of different versions of the events preceding the suicide, and a groping quest

for the "meaning" of the suicide. Spared temporarily for some by avoidance, suppression, flights into activity, spared for others by rigid, abrupt foreclosure of all but one unthreatening interpretation or construction; for many a struggle, too often alone, for a fixed sense of the specific suicidal events, the why of it, and the fit of the experience itself with the larger order of life. For too many this floundering search to construct a meaning, an interpretation of suicide, of *the* suicide, provides too few answers not colored with guilt, with perceived responsibility, with despair beyond redefinition or reparation.

9. *Incomplete mourning*—given the potent factors of denial, concealment, and evasion in the face of suicide, the shame and guilt-engendered avoidance of communication, and the mutual withdrawal of and from friends, neighbors and relatives (with consequent lack of opportunity for reassurance, reality testing, catharsis, shared grieving, and social support), the gradual working through of mourning is severely hampered if not made impossible; thus the survivor of suicide is peculiarly vulnerable to the crippling effects of unresolved mourning so richly described initially outside the realm of suicide (Bowlby 1961, 1963; Lindemann 1944).

It is also apparent from the studies presented here that these psychological processes neither originate nor evolve in an interpersonal vacuum.[4] Quite the contrary. They are often shaped by and amidst family interactions contorted by individuals too deeply preoccupied with their own grief to be helpful to each other, brimming with needs to blame and externalize, contending with newly erupted affects and problem behavior in themselves and each other, abruptly forced into significantly restructuring delicately intertwined family roles and sometimes required to learn utterly new roles and skills, caught between divergent if not conflicting patterns or pace of grief reactions among family members, urgently pressed to replace previous highly cathected modes of interpersonal relationship and sources of need-gratifications, buffeted as well by major practical problems which weigh toward further dissolution of the already harshly rent family structure.

These family processes are seen as still further contextually influenced by and infused with the prevalent values, constructions, taboos, and orientations toward suicide of a society whose proffered meanings of suicide tend to be at best ambiguous and fertile with the seeds of blame; a society whose attitudes toward suicide are basically punitive; a society which affords virtually no institutions or mechanisms for relieving the unique burdens bequeathed the suicide's bereaved. And ultimately a social milieu is portrayed which surrounds suicide and its survivors with the mark of *stigma;* stigma whose familiar accompaniments of shame, disgrace, social avoidance, and cloaked communication (if not forthright malignant blaming and ostracism) multiply the intrinsically formidable tasks of mourning and coping with the suicide death of a family member.

Notes

1. One can no more suggest that the substantial psychopathology seen is *purely* the product of, for example, parent suicide than one could claim that Oedipus' fall, torment, and commitment to self-destruction was purely or primarily the product of Jocasta's self-hanging!

2. Most vividly seen with the young children of suicides, whose surviving parent suddenly imposes identification—"mis-identification" in John Benjamin's fortunate term—with the dead parent upon them.

3. Reference here to suicidal preoccupation is not only to preoccupation with one's own suicide, but a pervasive interest in and often effort to involve oneself with suicidal individuals (evident in the number of survivors of suicide—family suicides or those of other intimates—who volunteer and often helpfully serve as lay staff in suicide prevention agencies).

4. It has been suggested that accumulating evidence of psychopathology in survivors of suicide attests to the validity of the concept that a primary motive of suicide is to damage others—blame them, accuse them, cause sorrow, regret and trouble. This concept is, of course, key to Adlerian approaches to suicidal behavior (Ansbacher 1970). "Revenge suicides" are well known and have been a normal social mechanism in a number of societies (Westermarck 1906; Jeffreys 1952; Murphy 1954; Noyes 1968). There are dramatic clinical cases of openly hostile, vengeful suicides on record, and many instances in which such motives and fantasies are not difficult to discern. In many others, however, no such motivation is apparent. But more to the point, it must be emphasized here that the "survivor" materials presented in this volume provide *no direct evidence* whatsoever as to the nature and meaning of the prior suicides per se. To infer from the effects on survivors simply and linearly to the suicides' *intention* is *a distortion of clinical inference and a misuse of survivor data.*

References

Ansbacher, H. L. 1970. Suicide as communication: Adler's concept and current applications. *Proceedings, Fifth International Conference for Suicide Prevention.* Vienna: International Association for Suicide Prevention, 222–225.

Bowlby, J. 1961. Childhood mourning and its implications for psychiatry. *American Journal of Psychiatry* 118:481–498.

———. 1963. Pathological mourning and childhood mourning. *Journal of the American Psychoanalytic Association* 11:500–541.

Jeffreys, M. D. W. 1952. Samsonic suicide or suicide of revenge among Africans. *African Studies* 11:118–122.

Lindemann, E. 1944. Symptomatology and management of acute grief. *American Journal of Psychiatry* 101:141–148.

Murphy, H. B. M. 1954. Suicide patterns in Singapore. *Medical Journal of Malaya* 9:1–45.

Noyes, R., Jr. 1968. The taboo of suicide. *Psychiatry* 31:173–183.

Westermarck, E. 1906. *The origin and development of the moral ideas.* London: Macmillan.

EDMUND H. VOLKHART with the collaboration of
STANLEY T. MICHAEL

Bereavement and Mental Health

Societies vary in their patterns of dealing with death. In the following cross-cultural study, Volkhart and Michael explore individual vulnerability to pathological grief reactions as a function of the cultural assumptions surrounding death. They conclude that the more significance a family structure places on a few individuals, the greater the impact of the loss of one of those individuals. In addition, the authors point out that conflict arises when personal reactions are at variance with social expectations.

Cultural Perspectives

A convenient place to begin is with the concept of culture, which is often regarded as the most important single concept in the social sciences. Although it may be defined technically in different words and used in slightly different ways, culture refers basically to the ideas, norms, values, practices, and beliefs which are historically shared by the members of an organized group or society. Each society has its own distinctive culture; and whereas at one level of abstraction there are certain universals common to all cultures, the specific content of various cultures are amazingly diverse.[1,2]

The concept of culture is significant in the present connection in that each individual is born into and develops within a specific cultural context. By example, precept, reward, and punishment he learns most of the culture to which he is exposed.[3]

Any sociocultural system may be envisaged as being composed of a series of organized groups, of what are sometimes termed "social institutions."[4] At one level of analysis these are specific and local—i.e., *a* family, *a* school, *a* church, and so on; at another level of analysis the specific units are combined into "type" institutions—i.e., *the* family, *the* school, *the* church, and so on, indicating a particular emphasis on the typical features of each.

Each such group, or institutional unit, in turn may be regarded as an organization of "positions" or "statuses." A family, for example, is composed of husband, wife, parents, children, brothers and sisters; each status being identified by its relation to another (i.e., husband–wife, parent–child, brother–sister, etc.). These positions are, of course, occupied by particular persons, but the behavior of the persons in their relation to each other is channeled by the

Source: Edmund H. Volkhart and Stanley T. Michael. "Bereavement and Mental Health." *Explorations in Social Psychiatry.* Edited by A. H. Leighton, J. A. Clausen, and R. N. Wilson. © 1957 by Basic Books, Inc., Publishers. Reprinted by permission of the publisher.

structure of the relationship itself. Mutual expectations arise, and the statuses of the relationships come to involve certain "roles" or role behaviors vis-à-vis each other. All of the principal social relationships, in any culture, may be regarded as interlocking roles.[5-7]

As soon as an individual is born, he begins to be a part of a social relationship (parent–child), in the setting of a particular situation (the family), which is composed, at least in part, of persons who have already been culturally trained. In their behavior toward the newcomer, much of their cultural learning will be manifest; and this is important because individual *self* will develop primarily in interaction with family members.[8,9] The individual self, in brief, is a social self, including the "reflected appraisals of others," such roles as have been internalized, and "the residue" of an individual's experiences within his institutional and cultural framework.[10,11]

From the standpoint of a given individual, his culture is experienced by the way in which his interactions are channeled in social relationships, within institutional settings, and by the various pressures, demands, responses, and expectations of others which make themselves felt in countless life situations. Thus each individual, consciously or unconsciously, comes to adopt most of the prevailing ideas, practices, norms, values and beliefs which parents, peers, and nonfamilial adults introduce to him. In this way he has available, for practically every life-situation, a culturally determined solution.

Thus far, then, culture has been shown to be linked to individual behavior[12] by means of a series of intervening concepts: social institutions, positions and statuses, roles, and the self. At this point some general implications of the concept of culture may be suggested.

In the first place, human death is a universal and recurring event. Every culture has its own values, ideas, beliefs, and practices concerning it. An individual learns the orientations of his culture toward death; and thus when he is faced with bereavement, one factor involved is his conception of the meaning of death. In this connection many, if not most, societies throughout the world do not regard the event of death as being an inevitable fact of life; rather, it is often construed as being the result of an accident, of negligence, or of malice on the part of magicians or sorcerers.[13] Similarly, the cultural orientation of many peoples toward death is that it represents a gain for the deceased, an improvement in his prospects and status, and that mourning for his loss of life is inappropriate.[14,15] These are in marked contrast to our own prevailing beliefs, for with us death is inevitable, and the fate of the deceased is by no means as clear and as certain as it may once have been in the Christian tradition.

If, then, we assume that beliefs can influence self-perceptions and self-reactions, the kinds of beliefs that are accepted and internalized will condition bereavement reactions. By the same token, the emotional displays of bereaved persons may also be learned responses and may have nothing to do with necessary and inherent feelings of grief. Conventional bereavement behavior varies widely from culture to culture, and whether it is genuine, "natural" emotional expression or mere ritual performance is in given cases often open to question.[16-18] In some cultures, for example, our conventional sign of grief—weeping—either is not manifest by the bereaved or is manifest in circumstances that we should regard as strange or is mingled with laughter as we understand it.

All of this raises the question, of course, as to whether the self is entirely social or whether it shares some deep-seated, indestructible fragments of humanity in general. Social science tends to hold the former view, whereas some branches of psychiatry tend to hold the latter. The issue cannot now be resolved, but it should be apparent that cross-cultural data can at least provide fresh perspectives on bereavement reactions and present viewpoints concerning them.

Moreover, it may not be amiss to note that cultural considerations may influence any attempt scientifically to analyze bereavement problems. Those who are familiar with, and sensitive to, cultural influences on behavior should first be wary of themselves and their work—i.e., the way in which they perceive, categorize, and explain behavioral events. For various implicit and explicit assumptions, biases, terminology and evaluations, all derived from the culture, can easily intrude upon the task at hand; they cannot all be erased, but they should at least be recognized for what they are: a curious blend of folk knowledge, rationalizations, beliefs, and ignorance. It may even be that some mental health problems we attribute to bereavement, by reason of proximity in time, have other and quite different sources.

The phenomena which we label "bereavement" and "grief" are embedded in a cultural frame of reference. Just as other peoples have their interpretation of death, and appropriate reactions to it, so, too, do we in Western civilizations; but our own implicit interpretation is not easy for us to recognize and make explicit as a cultural rather than scientific orientation simply because we have absorbed that orientation and perceive events accordingly.

Thus, as a cultural norm and idea we tend to define a given death as a "loss" to someone, especially to close members of the family of the deceased. Almost any behavior that they then manifest is regarded as "grief"; thus the term "grief" functions, culturally, both as a descriptive label and as a satisfying interpretation based on a presumably known "cause." Moreover, we tend to regard such "grief" not only as natural but also as desirable. A bereaved person *ought* to show grief, both as a token of respect for the dead and for the sake of his own mental health—expression of grief gets it "out of the system."

It is simply generally assumed that a bereaved person[19] will be grief-stricken; but whether these displays of grief stem from internal compulsions or external demands is not usually a matter of concern. Indeed, the very source of the behavior and the imputed feelngs is assumed to lie in what were satisfactory relationships with the deceased other, even though it is often well known that a given relationship, husband–wife or parent–child, fell far short of being satisfactory to one or both partners. At least in our culture there is a tendency to idealize the relationship which has been severed by death—and this, too, is culturally encouraged. "Don't speak ill of the dead."

In short, the behavioral phenomena characterized by the words "bereavement" and "grief" are heavily saturated with cultural assumptions. Moreover, any analyst, be he psychiatrist or social scientist, has absorbed many of these premises long before he has professed to be a scientist; to the extent that he has accepted and internalized them, his perceptions of events have therefore been previously structured, thus preconditioning the analysis through the uncritical use of conventional categories.

The point here, of course, is not the validity of the prevailing cultural interpretation of bereavement and grief, which may be correct in part or in whole, as other folk interpretations of events have been correct in the past. The point is that the cultural orientation is a matter for inquiry and verification rather than a priori, and often unwitting, acceptance.

Caution is therefore indicated. At best, words are slippery instruments of thought and expression, and this is especially true when familiar, and perhaps value-laden, terms are used.

Bereavement can be defined with sufficient precision to be useful. "Grief" on the other hand presents difficulties: the total reaction pattern of a bereaved person may be only partially an expression of grief (in the sense of felt loss), and the amount of grief anyone possesses is always inferential anyway. For these reasons, the phenomena that we usually label as "grief," "sorrow," and "mourning" will here be designated by the more colorless phrases "bereavement behavior" or "bereavement reactions." Such usage will not alter any of the distress of the experience or its poignancy, but it will remind us, perhaps, that more elements than sorrow or grief are involved, and it will also facilitate cross-cultural comparisons. "Behavior" can be observed and recorded, "grief" cannot. And it is essential that as much cross-cultural perspective as possible be gained, else the purported analysis may prove to be nothing more than a technical restatement of prevailing cultural premises.[20,21]

Bereavement, Family Structure, and the Self

Of all the social institutions, the family and kinship systems are of the greatest importance insofar as the study of bereavement is concerned. Indeed, their structure and the manner in which they emphasize some relationships rather than others supply initial reference points for the concept of bereavement itself. Always and everywhere some persons rather than others are considered to have a special interest in a given death; but who they are, and in what relationship they stand to the deceased, are matters of cultural variability.

In our society, for example, when a married adult dies, the prevailing definition of bereaved persons includes his parents and siblings (i.e., members of his family of orientation) and his spouse and their children (i.e., members of his family of procreation). The emphasis is placed on members of the immediate nuclear families as having suffered the main loss;[22-24] and if collateral relatives, such as cousins or aunts or uncles or "in-laws" are included, it is by special relationship rather than as part of the system. They are family members nominally, not functionally.[25]

By way of contrast, the Trobriand Islanders have a quite different scheme of family relationships and a correspondingly different concept of who constitute the bereaved.[26] Their emphasis is placed on persons related to the deceased through his mother— that is, his maternal kin of all kinds are considered to have been "closest" to the deceased and to have more of an interest in the event than any of the paternal relatives or even the spouse. A wife, for example, may "grieve" at the death of her husband, but this is usually ceremonial and obligatory rather than spontaneous, and she is not considered by others to be bereaved in the same sense as are the maternal kin.

These brief, contrasting examples of family systems indicate that, regardless of cultural variability, bereavement is an observable condition; it is not inferential; its definition, in cultural terms, can be determined. Further, bereavement is a formal status in which individuals either have or have not legitimate occupancy. It derives from family and kinship structures which place persons in necessary or preferred positions vis-à-vis each other. Thus, in some places a maternal aunt or a paternal uncle may be more important to the individual, socially and psychologically, than are his own biological or sociological parents. When they die bereavement is thrust upon him by the system.

Such considerations are important not only for purposes of initial orientation toward phenomena but also because they bear upon the development of the self in terms of to whom the individual will attach himself and in what manner. That is, although different family systems may have the same positions or statuses in the abstract (i.e., mothers, fathers, aunts, siblings, etc.) the psychological value of such positions in interpersonal relations is by no means always equivalent. Some positions may be singled out according to cultural principles of descent as more important than others; and their interpersonal value will also be influenced by the size of the family unit, together with the degree to which intrafamily relations are based on different ideas of authority, punishment, need satisfaction, and so on.

Thus, since the development of the self takes place primarily within the family context, that process will be influenced by the range, frequency, intimacy, and quality of the interactions provided by the family system. The number of "targets" for emotional attachment will vary accordingly, as will the particular statuses that will become targets. Such factors, in turn, will affect the number and kinds of identifications the self will make, the degree of dependency on others, and the general mode and strength of affective ties.[27]

If, then, the amount of self-involvement with another is a major variable in bereavement behavior, its sources must lie at least in part in the familial conditions of self-development. And if this is true, we should expect typically different bereavement behaviors in societies with different systems. There is some evidence for this interpretation, as the following examples will illustrate.

In his study of the Ifaluk people, Spiro[28] was puzzled by some features of bereavement there. When a family died, the immediate survivors displayed considerable pain and distress, which behavior was in accordance with local custom. However, as soon as the funeral was over, the bereaved were able to laugh, smile, and behave in general as if they had suffered no loss or injury at all. Their "grief" seemed to disappear as if by magic, and this too was approved by custom.

Several hypotheses might be offered to account for these events which contrast sharply with those we would expect. At one extreme, it might plausibly be argued that the brief, but intense, mourning period was sufficient to discharge all the implicated emotions (such as hostility, loss, guilt, etc.) and thus provided rapid reintegration of the self. This would assume object-relationships of a kind familiar to us but would not particularly account for the efficiency and timing of the observed behavior. At the other extreme,[29] it might be said that the displays were mere conventions, rituals, and, having little to do with emotional experience, could be turned off and on as learned. Or it might be suggested that the grief actually represented intense subjective feelings and that these persisted privately after the funeral but in a manner not easily detected by an observer.

Spiro's analysis, based on his knowledge of the total culture, is along the following lines, which involve the family system and socialization practices that prevail among the Ifaluk. There the developing child forms no exclusive emotional attachments to other family members. Child-rearing is not conducted solely in the home by parents and siblings but involves many other persons who are as important in an individual's life as are family members. The growing child and the mature adult have, therefore, diffused and dispersed their emotional ties among many persons rather than focused them on a few. Accordingly, the psychological significance of any single family member to any other family member is muted rather than intensified.

In terms of the thesis being developed here, the bereavement behavior of the Ifaluk suggest that their family system is such as to develop selves which are initially less vulnerable in bereavement than are the selves we are accustomed to. This can be explained by a consideration of how both social and psychological forces interact.

If we assume that any social relationship, mediated by physical and symbolic interaction, inevitably produces in the partners the feelings and conditions of love, ambivalence, hostility, identification, and dependence, then the Ifaluk develop selves in which these are relatively weak insofar as any given other person is concerned. The family relationships which impinge on self-development are such as to minimize personal dependence on any one person, to make a person's identifications multiple rather than exclusive, and to enable him to distribute his feelings of love and hostility more widely.

Another way of stating this is that in self–other relations among the Ifaluk, the other is not valued by the self as a unique and necessary personality. Functionally speaking, not only are the roles of others dispersed, but the roles themselves are more important psychologically than are the particular persons who play the roles vis-à-vis the self. Multiple and interchangeable personnel performing the same functions for the individual provide the individual with many psychological anchors in his social environment; the death of any one person leaves the others and thus diminishes loss.

In American society, of course, it is not so easy to describe *the* family system, for there are many sub-group variations. Nevertheless, some sociologists have discerned a trend toward the "small family system," particularly among middle-class urban populations.[30-33] To relate this system to the present problem involves considerable overgeneralization, yet for heuristic purposes it may be contrasted with the Ifaluk system.

The American small family system has several dimensions. In contrast to the extended family, it is one in which there are relatively few members and these few live together under one roof and somewhat apart from relatives and neighbors.

In terms of self-development, the small family system means a number of things. During a person's early years the range of his interactions is largely confined to his mother, father, and siblings, if any, and especially to his mother. Frequency and intimacy of contact are thereby channeled among the same few persons who become the only (and repetitive) targets for identification and dependency. Moreover, these same few sources provide the person with his most intense gratifications and frustrations, a condition that tends to maximize ambivalence as well as repressed hostility.[34] Guilt feelings are easily aroused in connection with authority figures—especially since the person knows that he is supposed to love them, yet cannot do so all the time because they punish and frustrate him.

In these circumstances, it is likely that the self develops strong emotional attachments to the family figures and has considerable affective investment in them. These self-feelings are, however, quite complicated. To the extent that one loves his family members (and this is inculcated as a cultural value), he may feel a corresponding loss when they die—a sentiment which is reinforced by the fact that, as a cultural norm, the death of a family member is socially defined as a loss. But, in addition to the love elements and those of dependency and identification, there are intertwined with them the self-feelings of ambivalence and hostility. In bereavement the self, therefore, faces not only the problem of replacing the loss but also the one of managing these feelings of guilt and hostility.

Moreover, the small family system tends to breed overidentification and overdependence. That is to say, intrafamily experiences are such as to make it difficult for the person to separate the parental activities toward him from the particular individuals who engage in those activities. The maternal role, for example, which aunts, older sisters, or other female adults could occupy and enact, is occupied continuously by the same woman, for in the small family system there are no other persons to act as substitutes and thus disperse the emotional investment. Emotional attachments to particular persons are thereby fostered, and the person becomes dependent on their unique personalities in addition to their roles.

Furthermore, other cultural values operate in the development of the self to influence the process similarly. Not only does the child experience the same persons in the roles of father and mother, but he is taught that he can have only one father and mother—that is, the particular persons who are thus labeled. Cultural training and actual experience thus reinforce each other in such a way that specific persons continually appear to be irreplaceable, and no one is psychologically prepared to accept substitutes.

By way of contrast, it is reported of the Murngin[35] that the death of a father creates few psychological problems for his children. All their lives they have called their paternal uncles "father," and their relationships with these uncles have not differed very much from their relationships with their father. When the self develops in such a system, there is less likelihood that it will become closely attached to a particular figure; thus the sense of loss is lessened and the relationship with that figure can be more readily transferred to substitute figures.

The inference to be drawn from all this is that familial systems, by their influence on the development of the self, can enhance or reduce the initial vulnerability of persons in bereavement. This vulnerability is increased to the extent that self-involvements with others are diffuse, thus minimizing the psychological significance of any one other.

In this connection, one further feature of the small family system should be noted. Typically, a married adult belongs to two families, the one of orientation and the one of procreation. In a sense this dual membership involves a dispersion of affect and self-involvement, for the person simply has more relationships: in addition to being son or daughter, brother or sister, he is now also husband and parent. His roles have multiplied.

But, although membership in the family of orientation is officially retained, residence in a separate household usually diminishes his opportunities for interaction and continued emotional investment in parents and siblings. There simply is not so much intimate association with them as there was when he lived under the same roof. He tends, therefore, to gain some release from whatever self-feelings he had toward them by increasing his physical, social, and psychological distance from them. Thus his vulnerability vis-à-vis these family members tends to be reduced.

At the same time, through marriage, children, and a separate residence, he is again enmeshed in a small family system, but with new personnel. Now his self-involvements tend to be directed toward spouse and children, and, because of the way his self developed in the small family of orientation, his relationships with these "new" persons tend to be of the same order as were the old—i.e., exclusive attachments.

In brief, membership in the two small families does not necessarily have the same psychological effect as continued residence in an extended family may have. Dispersion of affect need not occur. Rather, it is much more likely that one's emotional investments are merely redirected from one set of figures to another; and as vulnerability to bereavement in the family of orientation diminishes, vulnerability to deaths in the family of procreation may increase.

The preceding pages have attempted to sketch some of the ideal-typical relationships between family structure, self-development, and vulnerability in bereavement. From the two polar-type family systems that were used for illustrative purposes it is suggested that the meaning of bereavement to the persons involved can be modified. In one case the degree of self-involvement with others, and therefore vulnerability in bereavement, was minimal; in the other the degree of self-involvement with others, and therefore vulnerability in bereavement, was maximal.

High vulnerability in interpersonal relationships does not, however, mean the inevitable presence of mental health problems in bereavement. Psychic stresses and strains may be multiplied, to be sure, but if these have been fostered by some social and cultural conditions, there may be other social and cultural conditions which can help to ease them.[36,37] In brief, the course and outcome of high vulnerability in bereavement may be a function not only of itself but also of the requirements and taboos that exist within the bereavement situation. This can best be indicated by considering the importance and utility of the concept of "social role" as this is applicable to bereavement reactions.

Bereavement and Social Roles

It has previously been indicated that the category of bereaved persons, at a given death, is culturally defined. Some relationships in the family and kinship system are included and some are not, and the inclusions and exclusions vary from culture to culture; but whenever a death evokes that category, the persons in it come to occupy a formal, legitimate status in the eyes of others as well as in their own eyes. And as is the case with other statuses, the persons in it have a new social role to play—the social role of the bereaved person.

In cross-cultural terms, the specific content of the role varies widely: weeping, personal preparation of the corpse for burial, gashing one's body with knives or sharp sticks, protracted seclusion, fasting, wreaking vengeance on those responsible for the death, special religious obligations of prayer or sacrifice, sharp and humiliating alterations in dress and appearance, and so on.

In a given culture, some of these role behaviors may apply to all persons in the bereavement status, whereas others apply only to persons in specified relation to the deceased. For example, the widow may have some obligations which apply only to her, such as not to remarry or not to remarry within certain periods of time; or it may be that she is obliged to remarry with her next partner being culturally prescribed—e.g., a brother or cousin of the deceased husband.

Although there are great variations in the specific content of the social role of the bereaved person, one point is clear: whatever the obligations, proscriptions, or injunctions may be, they exist from his standpoint in the form of expectations, demands, and pressures from others. They are *social* obligations, immediate and potent, yet to fulfill them in a way that is both psychologically and socially satisfactory is by no means as obvious or as easy as is frequently assumed. Often the role requirements are painful in themselves, and it is also a difficult role to learn because it is not encountered frequently in the course of life and opportunities for rehearsal are scarce.

The import of this is to suggest that the conception of the bereaved person as having a social role to perform provides another perspective from which to examine mental health problems in bereavement. Such problems may be socially induced as well as psychologically induced—i.e., they may have their source in role deficiencies and difficulties as well as in the self–other relationship itself. Such a formulation suggests a number of possibilities that psychiatrists and social scientists might further explore.

The formulation, for example, opens up the possibility that some bereavement problems may be occasioned not by severe loss but by an awareness of one's inability to play the bereaved role properly.[38] If we assume that one of the role obligations is to express grief and loss and that these sentiments are imputed to the bereaved by others, the bereaved person who lacks these sentiments may be in a painfully dangerous situation as the result of guilty fear.

A hypothetical reconstruction, in terms of the present analysis, may illustrate the problem. A given role (husband, wife, mother, etc.) is culturally defined as involving considerable emotional investment in the partner who occupies the complementary role in the relationship. The role, in its ideal sense, is internalized by an individual, but his experience in the relationship contradicts the role. Inappropriate sentiments are developed—e.g., more hostility than love. Fearing the reactions of others, he remains in the relationship which, on the surface, does not deviate too far from the typical; but the hostility must be repressed and guilt over failure to meet the ideal is increased. Then, in bereavement, this individual is supposed to feel loss, and the social role he is expected to enact deals almost entirely with this imputed sentiment. He is expected to express grief. Such expectations and imputations are not congruent with his own self-feelings, and awareness of the discrepancy between self and role[39] increases guilt. There are also no socially sanctioned avenues for the release or displacement of the hostility. There is, in short, an accumulation of pressures which come to a climax in bereavement. In such a case, which is probably quite atypical, the bereavement experience, including the incompatible role that is imposed, precipitates and crystallizes mental health problems that were already incipient. Such a case can indicate the significance of situational pressures to adopt the proper role.

In American culture, it is difficult to consider the social role of the bereaved person in other than very general terms, but it appears to center around ideas of loss and the desirability of expressing that loss and grief. The language makes "bereavement" and "loss" interchangeable terms. Individuals learn to regard bereavement as meaning loss, and this sentiment is attributed to them by others when the bereavement situation actually occurs. Thus, to the extent that this evaluation of the event has been internalized, and to the extent that the self–other relationship as personally experienced makes it possible, the psychological sense of loss will be enhanced. When this happens, the bereaved person can more or less adequately play his required role—i.e., to have some sort of episodic breakdown, express his grief conventionally, and thus behave "normally."

However, this type of role, with its emphasis on loss, grief, and expression of them, may not always be psychologically functional. And here several possibilities appear.

For example, this particular type of role of the bereaved person may conflict with other roles he has—e.g., sex roles. In our society, females are generally permitted and encouraged to be more "emotional" than males in various life situations. To the extent that women internalize this segment of their sex role, it should be easier for them to meet the requirements of "expressing grief" in their social role of the bereaved person; it simply requires a reapplication of a lifelong pattern.

Men, on the other hand, are expected and encouraged to be more stoical and restrained than women in any life emergency.[40] The role of male in our culture does not encourage emotional displays. Thus, in bereavement males may experience a conflict between their lifelong training in their sex role and the immediate situational demand for emotional expression as a bereaved person.[41] It may be, therefore, that when bereaved males exhibit signs of psychic stress, in the form of intensities and distortions beyond expected levels, they are reflecting this conflict in addition to, or even instead of, the sense of loss and grief.

Our cultural emphasis on loss in bereavement, with its social role preoccupied with grief expression, provides still other problems. The social role, by concentrating on the feeling and expression of loss, thereby neglects to provide for other emotions and the needs they create. This can be formulated as follows: The emotions of a bereaved person, vis-à-vis the deceased other, consist of various degrees and intensities of the sense of loss, hostility, guilt, and the like. When these are minimal in strength, the bereaved person has a very low initial vulnerability to any mental health problems. When these are maximal and complicated, the person (unless he has a correspondingly high ego strength) has a high initial vulnerability to mental health problems in bereavement, for the stronger and more complex these self-feelings are, the greater is their tendency to create new personality needs. If a strong sense of loss is involved, there is a need for replacement; if there is much latent hostility, there is need for discharge; if guilt is strong, there is need for release or displacement. If all are present, as our family and cultural system tends to make probable, then the bereaved person is vulnerable unless his social role as a bereaved person adequately meets these needs.

In other words, the character of the self–other relationship conditions the level of initial vulnerability in bereavement. When this level is high, and new personality needs are therewith generated, the social role of the bereaved person may either lessen that vulnerability by meeting the needs or exacerbate it by failing to meet them.

From this standpoint, our preoccupation with loss and grief in bereavement may create special kinds of mental health problems of which we are only dimly aware. For example, as has been previously suggested, the significant other in our culture is significant in terms of his unique personality in addition to, or instead of, the functions he performs vis-à-vis the self. Thus, in bereavement, one loses not merely a role in his whole system of interaction but a particular person in the role. Thus, whereas we stress the sense of loss and recognize the need for replacement,[42] basically the culture creates conditions in which the deceased is irreplaceable because he cannot ever really be duplicated. The social role cannot contain a provision for "automatic replacement" because all our patterns of interpersonal relationships militate against such replacement.

In order for replacements to be accepted and acceptable, the role of the deceased must be regarded, culturally and personally, as at least equal in importance to the person who plays it. Other societies have handled this problem of replacement by the devices of obligatory remarriage[43,44] or adoption. Such arrangements, though, are not merely *ad hoc*, set up to take care of bereavement problems alone. Rather, they are basic ingredients of the way in which the sociocultural system operates, of the way in which interpersonal relations are perceived, valued, and practiced. Since the expectations of the partners in the social relationship do not come to include the absorption of the self in the other, it is possible for the social role of the bereaved person (i.e., as widow, widower, orphan, etc.) to include replacement of the other without particular psychic stress.

The fact that the social role of the bereaved person in our culture may not easily cope with the problem of replacement is, therefore, a local one. It is bound up in our system of interpersonal relations, the kind of selves we tend to develop, and is exaggerated by our cultural emphasis on loss. In this way the bereaved person has no automatic solution to the problem of replacement.

In the same manner, the social role of the bereaved person in our culture makes no real provision for the other emotions and the personality needs they create—i.e., hostility and guilt and their release, discharge, or displacement. At least, there are no obvious segments of the role which include socially approved devices for handling those residues of guilt, hostility, and ambivalence. With the person left on his own, so to speak, to handle them as best he can, it is not surprising that these feelings and the unmet needs they create appear in cases of "acute" or "distorted" grief in our society.

In many cultures prevailing mourning customs may be interpreted as providing role requirements which do meet some of these emotional needs. Opler,[45] for example, has shown how the ambivalence toward relatives, which is induced by the social structure of the Apache, finds socially sanctioned displacement in mourning rites and customs. Warner[46] indicates how the obligation of the bereaved to avenge the death of the deceased provides sanctioned means of ridding guilt feelings and hostility among the Murngin. And in anthropological literature there are many examples of the bereaved being required to inflict pain and disfigurement on their bodies—obligations which may be regarded as attempts to fasten the attention of the bereaved upon himself and therefore to hasten his emancipation from the deceased.

Such considerations lend some weight to the hypothesis that different cultures will select, from among all the possible involvements the self may have with the other, one or a few which will be dealt with in the social role of the bereaved person. Thus, if the bereavement problems of a given culture are adequately perceived, functionally adequate social roles for the bereaved may be devised which can blunt such vulnerability to breakdown as may appear. But to the extent that social and cultural conditions encourage interpersonal relationships in which overidentification, overdependence, sense of loss, hostility, guilt, and ambivalence are bred in profusion, and to the extent that the social role of the bereaved person does not take account of these feelings and the needs they inspire—to that extent bereaved persons may often be unintended victims of their sociocultural system. In our case, the sense of loss may be handled satisfactorily by the role which encourages expression of loss and grief; but the role does not, and cannot, adequately provide for replacement when this need is strong, and the added burdens of accumulated and unrelieved guilt, hostility, and ambivalence, when they are strong, can only increase vulnerability to psychic breakdown.

Notes

1. C. Kluckhohn, "Culture and Behavior," in *Handbook of Social Psychology*, ed. G. Lindsey (Reading, Mass.: Addison-Wesley, 1954), p. 922.

2. ———, "Universal Categories of Culture," in *Anthropology Today*, ed. A. L. Kroeber (Chicago: University of Chicago Press, 1953).

3. Strictly speaking, "learning" and "internalizing" should not be used as equivalents. One may "learn" a given idea or act, or how to act, without being impelled to so behave; he may simply learn that such is proper under certain circumstances. When something is "internalized," on the other hand, the implication is that the range of alternatives has been at least drastically restricted, if not eliminated. In other words, learning can be more superficial than internalization.

4. D. N. Mitra, "Mourning Customs and Modern Life in Bengal," *American Journal of Sociology*, 52 (1947): 309–311.

5. L. S. Cottrell, Jr., "The Adjustment of the Individual to His Age and Sex Roles," *American Sociological Review* 7 (1942): 618–625.

6. T. Parsons, *The Social System* (New York: The Free Press, 1951).

7. T. R. Sarbin, "Role Theory," in *Handbook of Social Psychology*, ed. G. Lindsey (Reading, Mass.: Addison-Wesley, 1952), Chap. 6.

8. G. H. Mead, *Mind, Self and Society*, ed. C. W. Morris (Chicago: University of Chicago Press, 1934).

9. H. S. Sullivan, *The Interpersonal Theory of Psychiatry*. (New York: Norton, 1953).

10. C. Kluckhohn, "Culture and Behavior," in *Handbook of Social Psychology*, ed. G. Lindsey (Reading, Mass.: Addison-Wesley, 1954), p. 922.

11. T. R. Sarbin, "Role Theory," in *Handbook of Social Psychology*, p. 224.

12. In a sense this can never be completely achieved to the satisfaction of psychology or psychiatry. Sapir's observations on this point are relevant: "problems of social science differ from

problems of individual behavior in degree of specificity, not in kind. Every statement about behavior which throws the emphasis . . . on the actual integral experiences of defined personalities or types of personalities is a datum of psychology or psychiatry rather than of social science. Every statement about behavior which aims, not to be accurate about the behavior of an actual individual or individuals or about the expected behavior of a physically and psychologically defined type of individual, but which abstracts from such behavior in order to bring out in clear relief certain expectancies with regard to those aspects of individual behavior which various people share, as an interpersonal or "social" pattern, is a datum . . . of social science." E. Sapir, "Why Cultural Anthropology Needs the Psychiatrist," *Psychiatry* 1 (1938): 12.

13. L. W. Simmons, *The Role of the Aged in Primitive Society* (New Haven: Yale University Press, 1945), pp. 217–220.

14. Ibid., pp. 223–224.

15. W. G. Sumner and A. C. Keller, *The Science of Society*, 3 Vols. (New Haven: Yale University Press, 1927), 2, pp. 943 ff.

16. Durkheim went so far as to write: "Mourning is not a natural movement of private feelings wounded by cruel loss; it is a duty imposed by the group. One weeps, not simply because he is sad, but because he is forced to weep. It is a ritual attitude which he is forced to adopt . . . but which is, in a large measure, independent of his affective state."

17. H. Gerth and C. W. Mills, *Character and Social Structure* (New York: Harcourt Brace Jovanovich, 1953), p. 20 and pp. 48 ff.

18. E. L. Hartley and R. E. Hartley, *Fundamentals of Social Psychology* (New York: Knopf, 1952), p. 210.

19. In one sense "bereavement" and "grief" can be defined in terms of each other, i.e., not one without the other. As will be indicated, however, clarity is gained if they are viewed independently.

20. C. Kluckhohn, "Culture and Behavior," in *Handbook of Social Psychology*, ed. G. Lindsey (Reading, Mass.: Addison-Wesley, 1954), p. 922.

21. E. Stainbrook, "A Cross-cultural Evaluation of Depressive Reactions," in *Depression*, ed. Hoch and Zubin (New York: Grune & Stratton, 1954).

22. T. D. Eliot, "The Adjustive Behavior of Bereaved Families: A New Field for Research," *Social Forces* 8 (1930): 543–549.

23. ———, "The Bereaved Family." *Annals of the American Academy of Political and Social Science*, March 1932, pp. 1–7.

24. W. Waller and R. Hill, *The Family* (New York: Dryden, 1951), Chap. 22.

25. T. Parsons, "The Kinship System of the Contemporary United States," *American Anthropologist* 45 (1943), pp. 22–38.

26. B. Malinowski, *Crime and Custom in Savage Society* (Atlantic Highlands, N.J.: Humanities Press, 1926), p. 26.

27. In a smaller vein, Sarbin writes that "we would expect different kinds of self-concepts in persons whose early socializing interactions were limited to one or two parent figures from those whose early socializing interactions were more extensive."

28. M. E. Spiro, "Ifaluk: A South Sea Culture," unpublished ms., submitted as a final report, Coordinated Investigation of Micronesian Anthropology, Pacific Science Board, National Research Council. Human Relations Area Files, Yale University, 1949.

29. E. Durkheim, *The Elementary Forms of Religious Life* (New York: The Free Press, 1947), p. 397.

30. J. H. S. Bossard, *Parent and Child* (Philadelphia: University of Pennsylvania Press, 1953).

31. A. W. Green, "The Middle Class Male Child and Neurosis," *American Sociological Review* 11 (1946) 31–41.

32. T. Parsons, "Certain Primary Sources and Patterns of Aggression in the Social Structure of the Western World," in *A Study of Interpersonal Relations*, ed. P. Mullahy (Nashville: Nelson, 1949), pp. 269–296.

33. ———, "The Kinship System of the Contemporary United States," *American Anthropologist* 45 (1943).

34. ———, "Certain Primary Sources and Patterns of Aggression in the Social Structure of the Western World," in *A Study of Interpersonal Relations*, ed. F. Mullahy (Nashville: Nelson, 1949), pp. 269–296.

35. W. L. Warner, *A Black Civilization* (New York: Harper, 1937).

36. L. W. Simmons, *The Role of the Aged in Primitive Society* (New Haven: Yale University Press, 1945), pp. 217–220.

37. M. E. Spiro, "A Psychotic Personality in the South Seas," *Psychiatry* 13:189–204, 1950, pp. 202–203.

38. This touches upon a problem raised by Rado.

39. This is in line with Sarbin's comment that "the self is what the person 'is,' the role is what the person 'does.' "

40. J. E. Anderson, "Changes in Emotional Responses with Age," in *Feelings and Emotions*, ed. M. L. Reymert (New York: McGraw-Hill, 1952), pp. 424–425.

41. Thus Lindemann observed men patients who, in bereavement, appeared unable to express their grief for fear they might "break down."

42. E. Lindemann, "Modifications in the Course of Ulcerative Colitis in Relationship to Changes in Life Situations and Reaction Patterns," in *Life Stress and Bodily Disease* (Baltimore: Williams and Wilkins, 1950), pp. 708–710.

43. As an illustration: "The heartbroken widow would be an object of curiosity; the widow mourns her husband in the prescribed manner with, it may be, genuine but very transient grief, and takes up life again just where she left it, but in the home of her next husband." A. T. and G. M. Culwick, *Ubena of the Rivers* (London: Allen & Unwin, 1936), p. 366.

Also: "In three deaths which I observed, the widows were married by levirate husbands on the third day after mortuary rites. In two of these the widows passed to the deceased's oldest brother; in the third, to his parallel cousin." A. R. Holmberg, *Nomads of the Long Bow*, Publications of the Institute of Social Anthropology, No. 10, Smithsonian Institute (Washington: Government Printing Office, 1950), p. 88.

44. W. G. Sumner and A. C. Keller, *The Science of Society*, 3 Vols. (New Haven: Yale University Press, 1927), 3, pp. 1841–1884.

45. M. E. Opler, "An Interpretation of Ambivalence in Two American Indian Tribes," *Journal of Social Psychology* 7:82–116, 1936.

46. W. L. Warner, *A Black Civilization* (New York: Harper, 1937), pp. 414–415.

JEAN MASAMBA & RICHARD A. KALISH

Death and Bereavement: The Role of the Black Church

In the following selection, Masamba and Kalish explore the beliefs and social practices surrounding death in a black community. Using various types of evidence—personal interview, observation, review of the literature, and analysis of spirituals—the authors recount the components of a black funeral they regard as typical. They argue that many of the components that are frequently criticized do, in fact, effectively assist the bereaved.

As the study of death and bereavement has become a matter of increasing academic and clinical concern, it is appropriate that some attention should be given to values, beliefs, expectations, individual behavior, and social practices regarding death in the Black communities. In the past few years, Kalish and Reynolds have reported on a three-year study of four groups (Black, Mexican-American, Japanese-American, Anglo) in the greater Los Angeles area and an earlier study by Pandey compared the death anxieties of Black and non-Black college students.[1-4] Other recent studies have explored the role of Black morticians[5] and death in Black writings,[6] and an analysis of death in Black Africa has been completed.[7] These have obviously just scratched the surface of this important topic.

In this paper, I[8] will explore the religious and psychosocial dynamics of bereavement in the Black experience and the implication of these phenomena for mental health. As a Black African clergyman and pastoral psychologist who has lived for several years in the United States, I can offer a combination of "the view from within" and "the view from without." The present paper discusses the patterns of religious, psychological, and social factors that influence behavior of the bereaved, with particular attention to the ways in which the church and church members cope with the dissolving powers of death.

Sources of Information

Sources of information for the present paper include:

1. *A literature review.*
2. *Personal experiences.* During my relatively brief stay in the United States, I have had fairly extensive experience with the dying and the bereaved in

Authors' Note: This project was funded by grants from NIMH and NICHD.
Source: Omega, 1976, Vol. 7 (No. 1), Baywood Publishing Co., Farmingdale, N.Y.

Black churches, where my involvement has been both that of parishioner and pastor. The junior author has drawn primarily on informal discussions, his academic background, and a research study he conducted several years ago.

3. *Direction of a ten-week seminar on death and bereavement for church deacons.*

4. *Interviews.* Ministers from selected congregations were interviewed on death and bereavement, and their views were compared. Key people in the churches, such as deacons and active members of the congregations, were also interviewed. Some interviews were also conducted with funeral directors.

5. *Field trips and participant observation.* I accompanied Black pastors on visits to hospitalized and bereaved parishioners, paying particular attention to relationships between the pastor and those he visited. I also attended a number of funerals where these same pastors officiated, observing the nature of eulogies, arrangement of the services, and social interactions. In addition, I participated in worship services and attended faith-healing sessions.

Death in Black Spirituals

The attitudes and expectations held by Black Americans concerning death have been extensively described in their spirituals and the blues. Through their songs, the Blacks have been able to ritualize and describe the emotional and religious contents of their relationships with life and death. Some of the major themes include:

1. death as a symbol for liberation,
2. death as an integral part of life,
3. death as the basis for fear,
4. death as cessation of this life, not extinction of all life, and
5. social extinction as the meaning of death without proper ceremonies or survivors.

Death Used as an Underground Symbol for Liberation Here and Now

Spirituals, according to Jackson, ". . . should be considered as a covert form of desire for freedom, with death simultaneously representing actual death and freedom—with the obvious realization that the only freedom most of the slaves would find was to occur with death" (p. 205).[6] The will to be free and to survive is expressed in death–rebirth metaphors. The Black who cries,

Oh Freedom, Oh Freedom, Oh Freedom over me
Before I'd be a slave
I'd be buried in my grave
And go home to my Lord
And be free.

is engaged in a battle of freedom and integrity that must be conducted until death. Death and the hereafter are only symbolic representations of the freedom and liberation in the here and now. The fear of death is therefore minimized as death becomes the symbol of courage, hope and liberation.

> Through all the sorrow of the Sorrow Songs there breathes a hope—a faith in the ultimate justice of things. The minor cadences of despair change often to triumph and calm confidence. Sometimes it is faith in life, sometimes faith in death, sometimes assurance of boundless justice in some fair world beyond . . . (p. 498).[9]

Death is therefore a positive symbol for freedom in the midst of social injustice and exploitation. This understanding of the meaning of death had influence on Black leaders in the 1950s and 1960s. King and Malcolm X were willing to die for their beliefs, if death is the price to be paid for freedom. Meredith believes that Black leaders contemplated death as one means of guaranteeing the legacy of their work.

> To understand the tenor of the '50s and '60s you have to understand the great importance of death. Death and the threat of death shadowed the life of every leader . . . It was a reality. In a sense, it was even a tactic, even a goal.
> Martin Luther King and Malcolm X, for example, wanted to die; for each of these men, their violent death was the only sure way to preserve their legacy (p. 157).[10]

In general, the Black's contact with the dead has been immediate, inescapable and dramatic. Struggle, violence, and aggression have been the Black American experience from the time of slavery to the present life in the ghetto, where sudden death is a reality. Violent death, sudden death, becomes a symbol of the ultimate justice to come. Death becomes an indication of things that are worse than death and against which the Black American needs to fight.[11] Thus, in the Black experience, death is most often a symbol of release from slavery without meaning release from life.[9] It sometimes was a welcome release from the burdens of this world, a means to be received in the kingdom of God.[12]

Death Recognized as an Integral Part of Man's Life

Being influenced by his African heritage, the Black American has a tendency to see death and life not as enemies but as partners.[7] Death is therefore personified. Because the reality of death was a part of their everyday experience, Blacks spoke of it in personal terms.

> Oh Deat' he is a little man,
> And he goes from do' to do',
> He kill some souls and he wounded some,
> And he lef' some souls to pray.
>
> Death he ain't nothin' but a robber, don't you see?
> Death come to my house; he didn't stay long,

I looked in de bed, an' my mother (father, sister, brother) was gone,
Death, he ain' nothin' but a robber, don't you see?

James Cone explains the historical basis that has given rise to this attitude of viewing death as part of life's experience:

> . . . black people were well acquainted with death, for they lived under its threat every moment. The slave owners, in particular, and white people in general were vivid reminders that life could not be taken for granted. It had to be defended all the time by all possible means. To stay alive in dignity was the essential task of the black slave community (p. 75).[12]

Death as the Basis for Fear

The impact of the community life of the slave era protected individual Blacks from mental exhaustion in response to violent death. Today, it seems that the presence of violent death in the Black ghetto induces fear as may be observed in the following history.

Mrs. A. is a young, married Black woman, mother of five children and an active member of her Baptist church; relationships with her own parents and with her sisters and one brother were apparently good. She expressed her feelings that she did not fear death itself, but was afraid of dying and of pain. "Being unaware of when death is going to get me bothers me, like being on an airplane and finding that in five minutes I'm going to die." She finds it threatening to contemplate dying without being prepared for it; in a similar vein, she finds lack of control over when and how she will die very threatening.

Mrs. A. says that natural death is acceptable to her and the pain associated with natural death is not especially disturbing. By natural death, she means dying in old age—at least 60—of causes that occur neither suddenly nor unexpectedly. She knows that drugs can calm pain. The experience of a friend of hers, an old lady who has been holding on to life during four years of suffering from terminal cancer, has helped Mrs. A. conquer her own fear of pain connected with natural illness and, thus, natural death. The anxiety Mrs. A. expresses over death that does not arise from natural causes may have its origins in the deaths of Blacks in the Vietnam War, and from the deaths of Black leaders such as Martin Luther King and Malcolm X:

> There is nothing for which I can sacrifice my own life, except saving the lives of my children. Whenever danger threatens my children, such as fire, police brutality, I'll run to save them even if it means losing my own life. This is where the unnatural death loses its sting. I am always afraid of unnatural death: violence, killings reported on radio . . . those police . . . they can kill even the innocent, I don't like to see the police wandering around because I don't know what they want. They can always kill you by mistake and no one will plead your case. I never dare a policeman to touch me. . . .

The fear of death has also been influenced by her relationships with her husband and children:

I cannot think of my husband dying. I will not look at him. When he is gone, I am gone too, I have no one else. I can stroke my child, though. I am stronger than the child. I don't like to talk about these things. I feel good that I can express these feelings. But I am always afraid that death might come in a very violent manner.

Not every Black thinks and talks freely about his own death. One interviewee expresses the need for dealing with his inner feelings:

I'm sentimental about death. I don't like to talk about it for several reasons. Mother died a couple of years ago. I don't know much about death, the life after death. Life is threatening when you think of physical pain about dying. You don't know what life over there looks like. People talk much about religion: don't drink, don't wear short dresses, don't sit with the ungodly people. All that scares me. I like Malcolm X because he talks about this earth as our heaven, instead of always talking about life over there. Religion is too legalistic and hell scares me.

Another person, forty-eight years old, explains his feelings of not wanting to deal with death in terms of his economic situation:

I take medicine every three hours. That keeps me going. I have a nice doctor, a Jew. He treats me often free. He does it because I'm a minority individual like he is. It is not easy to be poor and suffer, you know. I take it easy. The doctor does not tell me what I have, but I think I have cancer. Every time I go to the bathroom, white stuff come out. Probably my kidneys are very badly infected. I should go for another check-up. I drink a lot in order to forget it. I'm happy when I'm talking to people like you. But when I go to sleep, I start thinking about it. Nobody likes to die, you know. We want to live a little longer. I have obligations toward my family members and I like them. But it is not easy to be poor and sick. And the thought of dying bothers me because I don't know I'll have enough money to take care of all the expenses that go along with funerals and so on. That causes a lot of my anxiety. And when I am depressed because of the thought of dying without proper material preparation, I feel small and I dream about my own death and I become afraid.

Death Recognized as Cessation of This Life and Not as Extinction of Life

Death gives way to another quality of life with the Lord. The African concept of death as an extension of life was Christianized by Black Americans:

When I'm gone
When I'm gone . . .
Mother, don't you weep . . .
For I'm going to Heav'n above,
Going to meet the God I love,
O Mother, don't you weep when I am gone.

Death is therefore only a bridge between the hopeless and the hopeful life. As this is the case, one must die in dignity so that death is an unbroken bridge. Even today, death is referred to as "passing." The minister usually teaches that "we live unto the Lord and die unto the Lord. We weep because we care, not because we despair." That is why slaves wanted to die like Jesus.[12] To die in dignity is to experience the victory over injustice. This is why in the South the traditional procession to the cemetery was accompanied by songs of sorrow by the band, the procession back to the city was accompanied with songs of joy and victory. A sense of joy and purpose in living is experienced even after experiencing the death of a loved one. The following prayer, usually printed in the bulletin, is recommended for reading:

Prayer

O GOD! Great and Omnipotent Judge of the living and the dead! Before whom we are all to appear after this short life to render an account of our works. Let our hearts, we pray Thee, be deeply moved at this sight of death, and while we consign the body of the deceased to the earth, let us be mindful of our own frailty and mortality, that walking always in Thy Fear and in the ways of Thy Commandments we may, after departure from this world, experience a merciful judgment and rejoice in Everlasting Happiness, through Christ, our Lord.—Amen.

Social Extinction Feared

Social death has been described as the loss of social relationships, an event that often anticipates clinical death for those who are dying, taking place as friends, family members, co-workers, and others withdraw from social interactions.[13] Here we would like to postulate a parallel concept, that of social extinction, to be applied in situations where the individual ceases to have any earthly ties after his clinical death. When one dies and leaves no relatives behind, when he is without proper ceremonies, when he is no longer remembered, we can state that he suffers social extinction. Eventually, this will occur to everyone, although some may live in memories, record books, archives, and historical treatises longer than others.

Essentially, social extinction means that earthly immortality has ceased, according to the definition of the individual concerned. For a person to feel that social extinction will follow immediately upon his clinical death can be depressing. Death-related ceremonies and rituals can mitigate against this extinction. For devout Christians, the Resurrection probably provides a concrete basis for avoiding social extinction. It not only means that death does not extinguish self-aware existence, but that the death of the body itself is not a permanent phenomenon. The extent to which acceptance of such beliefs compensates for anxiety concerning social extinction, however, is not at all understood.

Burial insurance and the tradition of burial societies reflected not only the social, political, and economic experiences of the Black family, but also the religious meaning of the indivisibility of life and death, that is, the interpenetration of relationships between the living and the dead, when one dies and is buried with dignity. The religious attitude inherited from Africa was Christianized to fit the realities of Black American experience. To die without proper ceremonies, without the dignity of personhood, without the entourage of other human beings threatens a forgotten afterlife and the possibility of a distant relationship with God.

The world views, the theology of suffering and salvation have created institutional practices that have shaped Black perceptions in regard to death, dying, burial, bereavement, and have played a significant role in facilitating the spirit of Black nationalism.

Patterns of Support During the Crisis of Bereavement

Each person has his own mechanisms for coping with the process of bereavement. But it is also true that each culture has its own particular mechanisms that affect the emotional responses of the bereaved individual. If death is a biological reality, it seems that the anxiety connected with the personal event of death or the passing of a relative is a cultural phenomenon. This has some bearing on the stages through which the bereaved person passes. Black funeral practices, together with wake and other social services, provide a network of psychological mechanisms that facilitate grief work.

Psychological Dynamics of Black Funerals

The loss of a loved one through death gives rise to a variety of personal, social, and emotional needs, depending on the individual and on his social community or culture. For many, the church offers rituals and ceremonies that provide the bereaved the opportunity to fulfill many of their needs. Although Black Baptist churches are hardly unique in this matter, I will discuss what I have observed in that context.

There is little doubt that funeral services provide social support for bereaved persons in the Black community as in most others. I spoke with over two hundred members of Black Baptist churches concerning this and other matters, and I made a point of tabulating the responses. Although over three-fifths of those who had suffered a loss told me their family and friends gave support and sympathy, about four-fifths received support from their minister and members of their church. The religious funeral ritual is organized not primarily around the deceased person, but around the living. Even though flowers are brought, a eulogy is always part of the service, and an expensive casket is usually provided for the deceased, the survivors are at the center of the funeral service. A funeral rite is social par excellence. "Its ostensible object is the dead person, but it benefits not the dead, but the living" (p. 64).[14]

The wake services that precede or follow the funeral also offer a social support for the bereaved. The presence of many friends at the funeral and/or at the wake helps compensate for the sense of isolation caused by the death of a loved one. The social processes around the bereaved that often began in the hospital or nursing home continue at church, at the interment, and at home. At these places children as well as adults show their concern not only for the afterlife of the deceased, but for the psychological and material comfort of the survivors.

Many Black church members belong to societies within the church they attend. In the two Black churches I observed, these societies frequently organized a church banquet following the interment for the purpose of providing the survivors with emotional and social support. Although other church members may participate in preparing the dinner, the particular group or groups to which the dead person had belonged is responsible for leadership in planning and organizing. Sometimes funds are collected to meet some of the expenses of the funeral services. One pastor talked of the possibility of working out a program in the church community that would provide a substitute parent (or parents) for the surviving small children, and encourage new relationships for the bereaved adults.

The sense of an extended family becomes strong at the time of bereavement. In the family structure where people are not even related by blood, a feeling of being close to the bereaved transcends social services and obligations that one has to provide to the bereaved. In some of the funeral services that were under the directorship of Black morticians, I observed that a female chauffeur was provided whenever a woman lost her husband. This female chauffeur, dressed in black, remained with the widow during the service. She escorted her outside, brought her to the limousine, chauffeured her to the cemetery, and sat down with her at the interment service. This woman usually checked on the widow a few times during the week following the funeral service.

Although, according to one study,[2] Black Americans are less likely than Mexican or Japanese Americans to desire a mortician of their own race (39 percent did want a Black mortician, while 54 percent stated they were indifferent), given the actual situation—rather than a survey questionnaire—many Blacks undoubtedly feel that the Black funeral director is more sensitive to their needs and more trustworthy in his business dealings with the Black community. For example, at one of the wake services, people were quiet and subdued during the thirty minutes a White minister officiated, but they relaxed and resumed their normal talking, joking, and singing after he left.

Funeral Services as Channels for Emotional Catharsis

A major component of funeral services in Black churches is the opportunity for emotional catharsis. As one parishioner commented, "In times of anguish, the church has been a psychiatrist's couch. I can release my anxiety, anger, frustration, not only in the worship services where I am accepted even when I pass out, clapping my hands and shouting, but also in business meetings." One characteristic often attributed to Blacks is the capacity to express inner feelings of joy or sadness, anger or sympathy, without much inhibition. The blues, spirituals, trance experiences in church services, are expressions of such emotional expression.

Some of the factors that facilitate emotional discharge during funerals are the songs, the nature of the eulogy, and the visual confrontation with the body.

Songs Songs perform two kinds of functions for the survivors. First, the words of many songs seem particularly appropriate after a death has occurred, either because they recall the lost relationship or because they speak of the happiness and contentment of the dead. Secondly, for those Blacks who have shared church experiences with the dead person, the songs may bring back memories of being together in church singing the same songs.

Eulogy   The sermon is a memorial to the deceased, given in remembrance of him and supported with material from the Old and New Testaments. As might be anticipated, pastors tended to talk more about those persons whom they knew best. On some occasions, certain mourners gave brief testimonies, talking about the life and aspirations and deeds of the dead person. One pastor remarked that Black preachers make every deceased person into a saint, focusing solely on his positive attributes and exaggerating even these into a paean of glory. This tendency prevents the Black Baptist church from developing a theology of intercession that would permit pleading with God to intervene on behalf of the deceased. The lack of intercessory theology causes some bereaved persons, especially those who had knowledge of the moral and social inadequacies of the dead person, to wonder whether the service would be sufficient to provide entrance into eternal rest. One example of this was especially graphic. A middle-aged Black woman broke into violent crying when viewing her brother's body following the funeral. She later revealed to me her anxiety about his salvation because the minister did not plead on his behalf, and she was well aware that her brother's life was far from exemplary. This uncertainty created feelings of anger toward the minister and personal guilt for not having helped her brother to have lived a "Christian" existence.

The eulogy for another funeral, while hardly typical, is also worthy of note. The dead person was a twenty-year-old state university student who had been killed by a policeman on the campus. Objectively speaking, there was little or no basis for the shot having been fired, and the dead student had been student body president. The funeral was held late in the morning with three hundred and fifty to four hundred persons in attendance. The pastor's eulogy was particulary relevant:

> Jesus was a young man. He was a compassionate person. He tried not to do any harm to anyone. He loved children, "Let the children come to me." He loved his people. He talked about mercy, justice and truth. He had power to use violence, to use the power of heaven. But his power is seen in His voice of peace, "Blessed are the peacemakers for they shall see God." This boy was a leader—he was the president of a student body of twenty thousand persons. He suffered as an innocent one and was crushed. We have not gotten beyond the primitive drives of crucifying people. Anybody's son here can be next. Many young men who are being killed not only in Vietnam but also here, are Blacks. Why? How long, Lord, will it be until justice comes? How long will it be that we will react by saying, Father, forgive them for they know not what they do? Creative energies have to be used so that we can live in a better world. Are we going to be spectators and say that problems don't exist in our societies? Are we going to rise up and recognize that California is a new South? God knows how you feel because he lost his only

son on Good Friday. The spiritual and the body cannot be separated. (If God is interested in man's spiritual freedom, the body must also be free.)

At this funeral service emotion was easy to express. The emotional expression was accepted by the pastor and the rest of the congregation. It seems that violent death creates more overt emotional outburst and feelings of anger and rage than natural, suicidal, or accidental death. Two ladies fainted while viewing the remains. The pastor, parents, and many other people in the congregation cried.

Visual Confrontation   Black funerals generally call for visual confrontation of the dead body. On the bulletin of the order of service, the picture of the deceased person always appears. Of all the services attended, there were only two that did not have a picture printed on the order of service and these were under the care of a White funeral home. One member of a deceased person's family said that the printing of the picture on the order of service helped him accept the reality of loss as well as creating in him the feeling of "spiritual" presence of the deceased among the living.

The visual confrontation of the dead body is vivid when the remains are viewed by the living. In almost all the funerals I attended, caskets were closed from the beginning of the service to the end of the sermon when they were opened. Those present were asked by the representatives of the funeral home to view the body. (The body was cosmetized, dressed in regular clothes, using the best clothes the deceased person possessed while living.) It was observed that people had varieties of responses to the body. Some people stopped and looked at the body, touched it, talked to the deceased. Some people were unable to look at the body. Members of the family were always seated on the left side of the church and in the front row. They were the last to view the body. The body is brought closer to where they are seated so that they can see it without standing up.

The viewing of the body is the climax of the service, calling for overt expression of strong feelings. Sometimes the behavior exhibited is sufficiently vehement or involves so much physical movement that the pastor appears upset. When emotion is not expressed, it appears that one or more of the following may be the cause:

1. the feeling that emotional expression is an indication of personal or, more frequently, masculine inadequacy,
2. the belief that such emotions should not be expressed in front of people who are not family members or very close friends, and
3. the minister's beliefs that it implies a lack of acceptance of resurrection and hope in Christ.

Concluding Statement

In general, the Black church's handling of funeral services facilitates grief work as individuals are allowed to express their feelings. It is my personal hope that some of the practices, such as wake services, viewing the body, organizing banquets, will not be removed from people's experience as they tend to play a great role in the ways bereaved persons express their feelings and resolve guilt, frustration, isolation, and help the bereaved individual to experience a sense of community.

Notes

1. R. A. Kalish and D. K. Reynolds, 1973. Phenomenological reality and post-death contact. *Journal for the Scientific Study of Religion* 12:209–221.

2. R. A. Kalish and D. K. Reynolds, 1976. *Death and ethnicity: A study of attitudes.* Los Angeles: Andrus Gerontology Center Press.

3. D. K. Reynolds and R. A. Kalish, 1974. Anticipation of futurity as a function of ethnicity and age. *Journal of Gerontology,* 29:224–231.

4. R. E. Pandey and D. I. Templer. Use of the death anxiety scale in an inter-racial setting. *Omega* 3:127–130.

5. M. J. McDonald. The management of grief: A study of black funeral practices. *Omega* 4:139–148.

6. M. Jackson, 1972. The black experience with death. *Omega* 3:203–210.

7. J. Masamba, in press. The African concept of death. *Omega.*

8. The use of first person in this paper refers to the senior author, Jean Masamba.

9. J. Lovell, 1972. *Black song: The forge and flame.* New York: Macmillan.

10. J. Meredith. Black leaders and the wish to die. *Ebony.* May 1973, pp. 154–159.

11. H. Thurman, 1947. *The Negro spiritual speaks of life and death.* New York: Harper & Row.

12. J. R. Cone, 1972. *The spirituals and the blues: An interpretation.* New York: Seabury Press.

13. R. A. Kalish, 1965. Life and death: Dividing the indivisible. *Social Science and Medicine* 2:249–259.

14. R. Firth, 1964. *Elements of social organization.* Boston: Beacon Press.

ROBERT J. LIFTON

The Struggle for
Cultural Rebirth

The impetus to study death alternately throws one back to a reexamination of life and hurtles one forward to an exploration of the nature of immortality. Funerals reaffirm the shared sense of continuity, the concept of immortality established by particular belief systems. Throughout cultural history, myths have promoted belief in the solidarity of life and have insulated humankind from an overwhelming fear of death. In the following article, Lifton explores the reconstruction of modes of symbolic immortality during a time of historical dislocation such as the present. Lifton conducts his exploration of immortality on a number of levels simultaneously. He reaffirms the age-old pattern of death and rebirth in that every significant step in human existence involves some inner sense of death.

In times of relative equilibrium, the symbols and institutions of a society provide comforting guidelines, a prescribed life cycle, for our internal experience as well as our external behavior. But in times of severe historical dislocation, these institutions and symbols—whether having to do with worship, work, learning, punishment, or pleasure—lose their power and psychological legitimacy. We still live in them, but they no longer live in us. Or rather we live a half-life with one another.

The quest for images and symbols in new combination, for what might be called communal resymbolization, is precarious and threatening—so much so that it can itself be viewed as the cause for the cultural breakdown everyone senses.

Whether we acknowledge it or not, feelings of disintegration and loss permeate contemporary life. Consider, for instance, the widespread inclination to name and interpret man in our present situation not in terms of what he might actually be but rather in terms of what he has been, that is, what he has survived. We speak of man as post-modern, post-industrial, post-historic, post-identity, post-materialist, post-technocratic, and so forth. There are pitfalls in this way of naming the present (or the future) after what no longer is (or will be), but the terms have an authentic source in the sense of survivorship, present or anticipated, that so pervades our deepest image of ourselves.

In other writings I have emphasized the importance of holocaust in our symbolic vocabulary—of the recent past (Nazi death camps, Hiroshima and Nagasaki), the present (Vietnam), and the future (imagery of ultimate destruction by nuclear weapons, environmental pollution, or other means). Now we

Source: Adapted from *The Life of the Self* by Robert J. Lifton. Copyright © 1976 by Robert J. Lifton. Reprinted by permission of Basic Books, Inc., Publishers.

see the imagery of holocaust coming together with the experience of post-modern cultural breakdown: our loss of faith not so much in this symbol or that but in the entire intricate web of images, rituals, institutions, and material objects that make up any culture. The urgency of contemporary innovation stems from this sense of survival and loss at the most profound experiential level. I keep thinking of a (more or less) rhetorical question put to me recently by a thoughtful student: "Are four thousand years of human experience merely adding up to the capacity to repair a deficiency in a space ship several million light-years from home?"

In recent years we have witnessed the emergence of a "Protean" psychological style of flux and flow of the self, or self-process—of what the young call "goin' through the changes" in an interminable series of experiments and explorations of varying depth, each of which may be readily abandoned in favor of still another psychological quest. The Protean style is that of a survivor of the kinds of technological and cultural holocausts, real and anticipated, that swirl around us.

The Protean process is a product of a convergence of history and evolution. The two have always intertwined: Darwin's message was that man emerged from other species in a historical process; and there has been no lack of evolutionary interpretations of history. But we tend to view evolution as prehistorical, and history as post-evolutionary. The separation has been based upon our assumption of radically differing time scales in their impact upon man: during a historical unit of a decade or century, man was rarely changed in a fundamental way—an evolutionary unit of a millennium or more was required for that to be accomplished. But our present revolutionary technology and unprecedented historical velocity cast doubt upon that distinction. We sense, uneasily, our capacity to eliminate man in evolution no less than in history, and short of that to alter man—whether genetically or through organ exchange or mind influence—as never before.

Like so many of our boundaries, that between history and evolution is obscured rather than eradicated. As history and evolution converge, innovators embrace our new access (made possible by technology) to all forms ever known to human culture. Poised at a confusing and liberating psychic brink, ready to plunge wildly ahead in an unknowable process devoid of clear destination, man suddenly finds, swirling about him, the total array of images created over the full course of his historical and evolutionary past. These images become an elusive form of psychic nutriment, to be ingested, metabolized, excreted, and, above all, built upon and recombined in a process of organic growth.

Richard Sennett has observed that when a machine's parts wear down, the machine cannot operate. "But," Sennett continues, "the essence of human development is that growth occurs when old routines break down, when old parts are no longer enough for the needs of the new organism. This same kind of change, in a larger sphere, creates the phenomenon of history in a culture."

Death and loss can occasion profound research, recreation, and renewal. But for such transformation to occur, the relationship of man to machine and of man to work must be altered in the direction of organic growth.

This is Lewis Mumford's principle of transition from mechanism to organism. But something more is involved as well: social arrangements that permit and encourage technology to become part of a larger principle of imaginative transcendence.

Modes of Symbolic Immortality

Everywhere, men and women band together to confront the pervasive sense of "living deadness" emanating from holocaust, undigested change, large technobureaucracy, and above all the image of the machine. They seek new forms of connection, movement, and integrity around which to build new communities for living and working. One way to probe some of the fundamental dimensions of this process of communal resymbolization is to view it within a framework of shifting modes of symbolic immortality.

Symbolic immortality is an expression of man's need for an inner sense of continuity with what has gone on before and what will go on after his own limited biological existence. The *sense* of immortality is thus more than mere denial of death, and grows out of compelling, life-enhancing imagery of one's involvement in the historical process. This sense of immortality may be expressed *biologically*, by living on through one's sons and daughters and their sons and daughters, extending out into social dimensions (of tribe, organization, people, nation, or even species); *theologically*, in the idea of a life after death or of other forms of spiritual conquest of death; *creatively*, through "works" and influences persisting beyond biological death; *naturally*, through identification with nature, with its finite extension into time and space; or *transcendentally*, through a feeling-state so intense that time and death disappear.

Historical change itself can be understood in terms of shifts in these modes, or in combinations of these modes. Darwinism, for instance, became the center of a shift (always gradual and partial) from the theological to the biological and natural modes. Or the Chinese Revolution of the twentieth century can be understood as a shift from the biological mode (the socio–religious principles of family continuity and filial piety) to a form of "revolutionary immortality" that embodies aspects of all the modes. I believe that the significance of contemporary social experiments can best be grasped within this larger quest not just for change but for a change in enduring connectedness and commitment, in relationship to contemporary paths to immortality.

The biological–biosocial mode is at issue in the new kinds of families and familylike structures now taking shape. A wide variety of experimental communal arrangements press toward new forms of biosocial continuity—toward new "tribes," a new "people," or at least new forms of community. These groups (sometimes but not always called communes) concern themselves with root psychobiological matters—organic food, greater sexual freedom, collective child-rearing, and spontaneity of mental and physical expression.

Observe the altered definitions of manhood and womanhood taking shape not only in such experimental enclaves but throughout much of society. Within a single generation we have seen the virtually exclusive American male ideal of the tough (even brutal), tight-lipped, fist-ready, physically powerful, hard, anti-artistic, no-nonsense, highly competitive sexual conqueror give way to the gentle, open, noncombative, physically unimpressive, soft, aesthetic-minded, indirect and associative, noncompetitive, sexually casual self-explorer—with a variety of types in between. Similarly, the feminine ideal of the soft, compliant, self-sacrificing, family-oriented helpmate has given way to that of the aggressive, physically and psychically strong, self-expanding, liberation-oriented feminist. Much of the original hippie and Women's Liberation movements can be understood as explorations in broadened definitions of sex roles, so that one can be soft and tentative while still manly, hard and assertive while still womanly. This kind of experiment on the part of any of these groups must inevitably include excesses and absurdities. But in reaching for both the center and periphery of maleness and femaleness there is a groping toward fundamental alteration of the bio–social mode of immortality.

There is, in other words, a biological base to Protean experimentation. And the theme of community—of quest for bio-social continuity—becomes fundamental to all contemporary transformation. The struggle for "community control" is often a struggle for community formation. It is an effort to reassert authority over the most fundamental aspects of life, to combine autonomy with lasting human connection.

Protean efforts at transformation are very active in the theological—or, more accurately, religious or spiritual—mode, as is evident in experiments with both social–activist and experiential–meditative forms of Christianity and Judaism, as well as with Buddhist, Hindu, and other Eastern religions. One can also point to revived interest in various premodern religious-like rituals and superstitions—Eastern and Western astrological charts, the Chinese Book of Changes (*I Ching*), and tarot cards and other forms of fortune-telling.

Most commentary emphasizes the antirational nature of this embrace of seemingly primitive spirituality, which can indeed be present, especially for those who develop a preoccupation with charts and cards or feelings and vibes that excludes ideas, growth, and change. More characteristic, I believe, are the people who make forays in and out of these varied spiritual alternatives, as experiments in both knowing and feeling, in which one absorbs a fragment here, an image there, and maintains a sense of flow that is more consistent (more "stable") than the involvement with any one of them.

John S. Dunne, the distinguished Catholic theologian, posits as the new religion of our time "a phenomenon we might call 'passing over' . . . a going over to the standpoint of another culture, another way of life, another religion . . . followed by an equal and opposite process we might call 'coming back,' coming back with new insight to one's own culture, one's own way of life, one's own religion." The process, and the new religion itself, are epitomized not by Jesus or any other founder of a world religion but by Gandhi, who followed such a trajectory from Hinduism to Christianity (and even to some extent to Islam) and then back to Hinduism. But even Gandhi, in the very focus of his faith, has a certain nostalgic ring for us. Could it be that the holy man of our time has only just begun to invent himself, that he will not merely "pass over" and "come back" in that relatively orderly sequence but will do so in a sustained, repeated, perhaps even endless process, in which spiritual depth no longer depends upon exclusive doctrine of any kind and realization combines "the principle of permanence" with that of continuing open search?

Whatever form our next prophet may take, we can be certain that we will be witnessing great waves of religious feeling. For what we call religion directs itself, at least at its best, to precisely the kinds of altered relationships to death and the continuity of life that occur during any historical turning point. But lest contemporary priests misunderstand the stirrings within their churches and temples (and the much stronger religious expressions outside of them), this kind of renewed religious feeling presses not toward the stability of denominations and orders but toward their overthrow, not towards orderly worship within existing social arrangement but towards forms of worship—of celebration and immortalization—that subvert the numbing pseudoritual of "normal religion" in favor of newly immortalizing visions.

The third mode of symbolic immortality, that of immortality via man's works, has been a crucial area of social preoccupation. Involved here is the disorganized but powerful critique now under way of all major social institutions: those within which one learns, is governed, judged, or punished, and, above all, finds significance. In the fundamental questions now being raised about universities and schools, political and judicial arrangements, intellectual disciplines and professional practices, there is a common overriding theme: the quest for significant work experience, both in immediate involvement and in a sense of the work's contribution to the continuing human enterprise. For what we call work is a uniquely important boundary between self-process and social vision. Perhaps for the first time in history very large numbers of men and women are beginning to demand harmony and meaning at that boundary; to demand a reasonable equation between work and "works."

This fundamental relationship between work and symbolic immortality is typified in the passions of the "work commune" movement—the creation of small communities that permit poolings of professional, political, and psychobiological experiments. In these and such related groups as radical institutes and radical caucuses in all the professional disciplines, there is not only a powerful transformative element but a conservative one as well: a determination to confront and thereby preserve a particular social or intellectual tradition—rather than dismiss or ignore it—in a spirit critical both of the tradition itself and of its conventional applications.

This task of resymbolization, traditionally the mission of great innovators, has now become something close to a mass experience. Large numbers of people, in one way or another, move (in Daniel Berrigan's phrase), "toward the edge" of their profession or craft, not necessarily because they originally plan to but because their situation evokes altered relationships and judgments—involving the lost ethical and hypertrophied technical components of work and profession, the separation of work and life, and the nature of the society and culture in and for which one works. All this is part of a largely inchoate yet profound quest for newly immortalizing combinations of human influence. We may suspect that the structures and institutions that emerge will have to build into their own evolving tradition the expectation of the unexpected, the capacity to engender a stability in equilibrium with periodic transformation—which may, indeed, be the only form of true stability possible.

The natural mode of immortality has obvious relationship to ecological passions and to general fears about destruction of the environment, fears all too appropriate. But there is also a more positive impulse toward nature among many innovators as exemplified by the rural commune movement. Many have ridiculed this movement and have looked upon it as nothing more than a pathetic form of pastoral romanticism, a regression to a discredited myth that is particularly misdirected in our present urban–technological society. There is no doubt that many of these communal efforts *have* been romantically envisioned and poorly planned. Moreover there is pathos and error in the claim, occasionally made, that they are *the* answer to our urban–technological dilemmas. But what is often missed in these exchanges is the psychological significance of reclaiming a relationship to nature as part of a more general psychic renewal. When young Americans create a rural commune in New Mexico or New Hampshire, they approach nature with contemporary sensibilities. They seek to bring nature back into the human imagination. They embrace nature in an experiment with the self. The ramifications of that experiment may yet make their way into the most urban minds.

The final mode, that of experiential transcendence, differs from the others in being a psychic state per se. It includes various forms of ecstasy and rapture associated with the Dionysian principle of excess, and with the mystical sense of oneness with the universe Freud referred to as the "oceanic feeling." Mystics speak of a state of awareness where, totally unencumbered by any particular idea or image, one is able to perceive the entirety of the larger universe and of one's own being within it.

This is the "high" one can get from drugs or from various forms of intense encounter; the "trip"; the state of being "stoned." The terms are interesting. "High" implies elevation of psychic state in the direction of transcendence. "Trip" implies being in motion but something briefer and more temporary than, say, a "journey," and having the implicit suggestion of return. "Stoned" implies an absolute intensity (the smoothness, hardness, solidity, and finality of stone), in this case intensity of feeling, ecstasy—but also the numbness, insensitivity, or deadness of a stone (stone blind, stone deaf, stone dumb, stone cold, stone dead). The duality may be appropriate; one undergoes a "small death" (of more or less ordinary feeling) in order to open oneself up to a "new life" (to feeling on a different plane of intensity), to a sense of transcendence. One becomes impervious to the prosaic idea of mortality and feels oneself so exquisitely attuned to—indeed merged with—the universe as a whole that the issue of life versus death is no longer of consequence. Should the process fail, whether because of depending too much upon the technology of becoming "stoned" (the drugs themselves) or for other reasons, one is left in a state of perpetual numbing (stone dumb, stone cold, etc.).

In a wide variety of experiments—sexual, political, aesthetic—there is a powerful insistence upon making the quality of "awareness" or transcendence basic to the act. Indeed, there is a very real sense in which experiential transcendence is the key, the baseline, for the other four modes. That is, one requires some form of ecstasy and oneness—whether all-consuming or of a more gentle variety—in order to experience oneself as living on in one's children, works, spirituality, or relationship to nature. And that level of experience is also required for the inner psychological reordering necessary to individual transformation.

structured exercises

Before beginning these exercises, please read "Note to the Instructor" on page xxi.

1. This exercise is designed to synthesize the information about funeral customs provided by the readings in Chapter Three. The exercise can serve as a basis for further investigation of the function of funerals or for a fuller exploration of students' feelings about funerals.

   a. Imagine that you have died with everything in your life as it is right now. Design a personalized funeral or memorial service for yourself. Describe in detail the arrangements you would like: the time the service would be held; the kind of gathering it would be; the setting where it would be held; who would be there; what would occur during different parts of the gathering; whether there would be music and flowers, and if so, what kind; and so on. Even if you want a traditional religious funeral, describe the details; there are still many options such as choice of hymns or prayers which personalize such a service.

      This exercise could be written up before class discussion, or it could be done in class as a visualization exercise once the class is familiar with what goes on at a funeral. In class discussion, try to compare and contrast the themes that emerge from the different descriptions as well as focusing on the personal feelings of loss.

   b. The eulogy is the traditional funeral oration which reviews the life of the deceased and represents a formal farewell from the community. Assume that everything in your life is as it is right now and write your own eulogy. How would you sum up your life at this point?

      In order to share the experience with the class, you could form small groups to read the completed eulogies, either by passing them around to be read silently, or by reading them aloud to the group. A second alternative for sharing the eulogies would be to have each person take turns at lying on a table, eyes closed, imagining a funeral setting in as much detail as he or she wishes, while his or her eulogy is read aloud.

After all the eulogies have been read, discuss your reactions both to composing the eulogy and then to hearing it read. What has the process told you about yourself and your goals?

c. The epitaph is the brief statement placed on a memorial marker. What would yours be? Explain your choice to the class. Do they agree with its appropriateness for you?

2. To enable the student to explore his or her personal reactions to loss, have each student respond to the following exercises. Picture the most important person in your life. Suppose he or she were to die tomorrow. Take ten minutes to decide on responses to the following questions. Use a worksheet to make notes if you wish.

a. What would you miss most about that person?
b. What one thing do you wish you had had a chance to tell that person?
c. What one thing do you wish you could have heard from that person?
d. What one thing would you have wanted to change in the relationship?
e. What was the happiest moment you recall sharing with that person?
f. What was the most painful moment, before now, the two of you shared?
g. What circumstances (time, place, event) do you expect to bring the most painful memories?

When everyone has completed the questions, you may share the responses either as a class or in smaller groups. During this part of the exercise, you may discuss your reactions to actually doing the exercise, how you selected the person you chose, and what you learned from the experience.

questions

1. Define each of the following terms used in this chapter. Terms marked with an asterisk are concepts that the authors of the selections expect readers to know. If you are not familiar with the meanings of those terms, consult a dictionary.

Lindemann

 *traumatic experience
 *syndrome
 normal grief reaction
  (grief syndrome)
 *psychoneurotic
 grief work
 *identification
 *conversion symptom
 anticipatory grief

Bowlby

 phase of numbing
 phase of yearning and searching
 phase of disorganization and despair
 phase of reorganization

Cain

 *object-relations
 incomplete mourning
 *stigma

Volkhart and Michael

 *culture
 *norm
 *value
 *social institution
 *self
 *status position
 *social role
 *socialization

Lifton

 "Protean"
 resymbolization
 symbolic immortality
 biological–biosocial mode
 theological mode
 creative mode
 natural mode
 transcendental mode

2. a. When Lynn Caine found herself as a new widow, she quickly became aware of a new role expectation. She was determined to be the "ideal American widow," full of courage and restraint. Outline the character-

istics of the admired American widow. How does the role expectation differ for a widower?

b. Volkhart and Michael describe how the cultural role expectation can be at odds with the experience of the mourner and result in pathology. In what ways does the American stereotype provide support for the widow? In what ways does it block expression of her needs?

3. a. Lindemann lists identification as a part of normal grief that in its extreme forms may indicate pathology. Compile a list of different kinds of behavior that might be considered identification, beginning with the examples given by Lindemann and Albert Cain.

b. Do the same with Bowlby's phase of yearning and searching.

4. Lindemann and Albert Cain describe in detail how the mourning process can fail to resolve loss. What different forms can "pathological grief" take? What kinds of behavior might indicate to you that a bereaved person was reacting in a psychologically unhealthy manner? What factors would you need to take into account in making your determination?

5. a. As expected death after a long illness becomes more frequent in our country, family and friends are more likely to begin an anticipatory grief reaction before death occurs. Recalling the discussions of Kübler-Ross and Lindemann, outline the benefits and the dangers involved in beginning to mourn while the terminally ill patient is still alive.

b. Under these circumstances, the needs of the mourner would no longer be met by the social role demands of the bereaved. Contrast the kinds of role behavior that would be appropriate following sudden unexpected death with those following a long terminal illness. How might the funeral rites be changed to reflect these differences in needs?

6. In discussing funeral practices, Masamba and Kalish make several generalizations. Examine the article closely to identify some of those generalizations and suggest in each case a procedure by which you could test the validity of the assertions they make.

7. Consider the war novel as a literary subgenre. Using war novels you know, identify attitudes toward death that are expressed directly or indirectly. What examples of guilt do you find when characters confront the death of another?

8. Bereavement after suicide is considered an especially high-risk grief period. What special supports do the survivors of suicide need? How could you provide for their particular reactions?

9. Lifton explains that every step in life involves an inner sense of death. Many rituals celebrate the beginning of a new life and the "death" of a former existence. How is the death–life progression evident in the rituals for baptism, bar mitzvah, graduation, marriage, divorce, the birth of a child, a job promotion?

projects for further study

1. Lynn Caine poignantly portrays the feelings of helplessness of the widowed, whose needs are too often overlooked. Investigate the "Widow to Widow" program described by Phyllis Silverman in *Helping Each Other in Widowhood*. What supports are offered in your community? What specific services would be helpful to the widowed? Try to interview three widows (perhaps through a church group) on their experience of bereavement in order to generate a specific list of problems and needs.

2. a. Although the funeral is one of our most conservative rituals, it is subject to change, as is any social institution. Interview some older relatives on funeral customs they recall from their youth. How have funeral customs changed over the last fifty years? Have attitudes toward funeral customs also changed? Why?

   b. Not only the social customs but the ritual itself also changes. Study the new funeral liturgies both in the church and in the secular funeral. For example, the funeral industry is developing the "Life Centered" funeral; ideas for personalized services are suggested in Ernest Morgan's *A Manual of Death Education and Simple Burial*. Compare and contrast the orientation, the symbols, and the styles of the newer liturgies with the more traditional.

3. Writers such as Jessica Mitford, in *The American Way of Death*, and Ruth Mulvey Harmer, in *The High Cost of Dying*, cite examples of financial abuses in the funeral industry. To protect the "consumer" from unnecessary expenses, they advocate the development of nonprofit memorial societies. Visit a funeral home to investigate the typical funeral costs in your area. If there is also a memorial society in the area, compare the services offered by each and their costs. The following resources may be useful in gathering information.

   Information in various forms about traditional funerals is available from

the National Funeral Director's Association, 135 W. Wells Street, N.W.,
Washington, D.C. 20036.

Information about memorial societies is available from the Continental
Association of Funeral and Memorial Societies, Inc., 1146 19th Street,
N.W., Washington, D.C. 20036.

4. a. Social immortality is one of the most common forms of symbolic im-
      mortality. Identify as many examples as you can during a one-week
      period. (Consider physical memorials, dedications, memorial events,
      donations, endowed programs, etc.) Discuss the degree to which social
      immortality is valued in our society.

   b. In the nineteenth century the word *cemetery* began to replace the
      traditional generic terms, *graveyard* or *burial ground*. The shift reflected
      the fact that the cemetery had become a cultural institution. Visit a local
      cemetery to see how death is presented: identify as many different
      representations of death as you can, both individual symbols (e.g.,
      ornaments and headstones) and the symbolism of the place itself (e.g.,
      the setting and the architectural styles). Where you find inscriptions on
      the headstones, collect representative examples of different styles of
      epitaphs. What different themes do you find? What information is
      typically given about the deceased? Besides serving as a disposition site
      for bodies, what other social, religious, or personal functions does a
      cemetery serve?

for further reading

Beane, W. C., and W. G. Doty, eds. 1975. *Myths, rites, symbols: A Mircea Eliade reader*. New York: Harper & Row.

Freud, S. 1966. Mourning and melancholia. In *The complete psychological works,* ed. J. Strachey, Vol. 14. London: Hogarth.

Fruehling, J. A., ed. 1982. *Sourcebook on death and dying*. Chicago: Marquis Professional Publications.

Goody, J. 1962. *Death, property, and the ancestors*. Palo Alto, Ca.: Stanford University Press.

Gorer, G. 1965. *Death, grief, and mourning*. New York: Doubleday.

Grollman, E. A., ed. 1974. *Concerning death: A practical guide for the living*. Boston: Beacon Press.

Habenstein, R. W., and W. M. Lamers. 1960. *Funeral customs the world over*. Milwaukee: National Funeral Directors Association.

Kalish, R. A., ed. 1980. *Death and dying: Views from many cultures*. Farmingdale, N.Y.: Baywood.

Lamm, M. 1972. *The Jewish way of death and mourning*. New York: Jonathan-David.

Lifton, R. J. 1970. *History and human survival*. New York: Random House.

Lopata, H. Z. 1979. *Women as widows: Support systems*. New York: Elsevier North-Holland.

Lynch, J. L. 1977. *The broken heart: The medical consequences of loneliness*. New York: Basic Books.

Margolis, O. S., et al., eds. 1981. *Acute grief: Counseling the bereaved*. New York: Columbia University Press.

Morgan, E. 1980. *A manual of death education and simple burial*. Rev. 9th ed. Burnsville, N.C.: The Celo Press.

Parkes, C. M. 1972. *Bereavement: Studies of grief in adult life*. New York: International Universities Press.

Pincus, L. 1975. *Death and the family*. New York: Pantheon.

Schoenberg, B., A. Carr, D. Peretz, and A. Kutscher, eds. 1970. *Loss and grief: Psychological management in medical practice.* New York: Columbia University Press.

Silverman, P. R. 1981. *Helping women cope with grief.* Beverly Hills, Calif.: Sage Publications.

Wass, H., ed. 1979. *Dying: Facing the facts.* New York: McGraw-Hill.

CHAPTER *four*

Death and the Child

*A*s *recently as the sixteenth century,* Montaigne could write to a friend in terms that surprise the modern reader: "I have lost two or three children in infancy," he explained, "not without regret, but without great sorrow." With the probability that several children born to any one family would die before reaching the age of majority, it was argued, families could not allow themselves to become too attached to children whose hold on life was still fragile.

In twentieth-century America, decreased infant mortality, control of childhood diseases, and vastly improved health conditions have rendered the death of a child a rare tragedy: at once a senseless waste, an affront to pride in medical progress, and a haunting intimation of mortality. The child is not only regarded as a person from the moment of birth (or conception as is often evidenced in arguments against abortion), the child is often seen as the center of the family unit, the natural recipient of extensive care, and the tangible representation of the hopes of those around him or her. There is considerable variety in contemporary styles of child rearing, but, common to most, is the dedication of adults to protect their children from all that is harmful. And, as one might have predicted from studies of adult attitudes, the discussion of death has most often been considered as something harmful, something to protect children from. Indeed the taboo against the discussion of death with children has been so effective that Simon Yudkin, a physician, has observed that children today know more about their origin than about their end.

More than parental tenderness, however, restrains the discussion of death with children and makes even less likely the discussion of the child's own death. Such a discussion poses a threat to one's own hold on life. Faced with the death of a parent or a friend, a person recognizes the possibility of his or her own death, but when confronted with the death of a child (someone who has shared fewer years), the arbitrary power of death becomes unavoidable. The person is forced to concede not only that he or she *will die at some time,* but that *he or she might die at any time.*

Current Research

Thus, it comes as no surprise that widespread study of children and death followed well after studies of the dying adult were conducted. Recent work on the subject of children and death has taken three forms: research in the social sciences directed to an understanding of children's conceptions of death and their mourning reactions, studies oriented to advancements in the treatment of terminally ill children, and popular children's literature and films that have been designed to bring their presentations of death to children into line with the best available research.

Research in the Social Sciences

As developmental psychology has moved from a normative to a structural approach, beginning with renewed interest in the work of Jean Piaget, considerable research into the child's formation of the concepts of *life* and *death* has followed. Sylvia Anthony, observing school-age children's play and fantasy, found death a common theme and the child's discovery of death to be simply an incident in the normal day-to-day process by which a child explores his environment. Maria Nagy, working in Hungary, traced a developmental sequence in children's theories concerning the nature of death. Nagy found that the child who at the age of four might pour water on a dead animal to "make it alive," grows into the six-year-old telling tales of the boogeyman, and then becomes the nine-year-old at once forced to accept the inevitability of death and ready to mock it with jokes and gestures.

But to say that the child's discovery of death in the abstract is more exploratory than emotional is not to suggest that children feel little emotional response to particular deaths. On the contrary, when a child loses a significant person in his or her life, warns child psychiatrist Benjamin Shambaugh, "every defense will be mobilized to ward off the impact and . . . every new object relationship as it develops will be influenced by the fact that an earlier one was lost." Agreement on the child's capacity to mourn, however, is not unanimous. According to Martha Wolfenstein, young children, though they may be aware of death, are not developmentally ready to begin the work of mourning. She suggests that adolescence, a period when individuals come to see time as irreversible and when they give up a major love object, their parents, is a trial mourning period and a necessary precondition to actual mourning. John Bowlby, however, suggests that mourning can be divided into three phases—protest, despair, and detachment—and that it may occur, at least in its first phase, as early as six months of age. The research into the child's understanding of death and capacity to mourn has been joined recently by a growing number of observations of the dying child and his or her family in the hospital environment.

The Dying Child

The care of the dying child, or adolescent, presents a doctor with one of his or her most difficult tasks. Yet, as recently as 1968, William Easson, a child psychologist, noted that in most cases "the physician or physician-to-be was given little understanding of the management of the dying child." Though new research on the dying child is still scant, beginning in 1960 a small number of psychiatrists and pediatricians began documenting the dying child's awareness of impending death. In addition, they recognized that the child's awareness of his or her death was often accompanied by withdrawal and denial of the diagnosis on the part of both parents and hospital staff. Currently, research into the support systems needed by the dying child and his or her family has burgeoned, resulting in a text on the subject and a hefty, internationally edited volume in child psychiatry.

Literature and Film

The past quarter century, which has been so productive in studies of child development, has been equally abundant in children's literature. At one time the subject of death was presented primarily to motivate children through fear to good behavior. Later it was avoided altogether.

> A little child
> That lightly draws its breath
> And feels its life in every limb
> What should it know of death?
> *Wordsworth*

It has more recently been presented in a realistic manner that acknowledges the child's understanding of death and often reflects the complexities of his or her reactions to it.

Some works such as *Charlotte's Web* portray death as a necessary part of the cycle of nature; others like *Annie and the Old One* and *My Grandpa Died Today* present death within the family unit. A smaller number present the death of a child, for example, *A Taste of Blackberries, The Brothers Lionheart,* and *Sadako and the Thousand Paper Cranes.* Interest in the presentation of death to children has not been confined to books, for both film and television portrayals have appeared in the past few years. So great has been the activity in this field, in fact, that the danger of exploitation of emotion, always present in marketing for children and equally likely in presentations of death for any audience, lurks dangerously close. To identify those works that will be most conducive to understanding, we must seek enduring simplicity, those books that Paul Hazards notes will "distill from all kinds of knowledge, the most difficult and the most necessary—that of the human heart."

Overview of the Chapter

The readings in Chapter Four begin with an examination of the developmental growth in the child's understanding of death, then move to the presentation of death in a variety of contexts. The opening Encounter begins with a series of children's anecdotal accounts, a methodology not uncommon with early researchers like Nagy. Building on the work of Anthony and Nagy, though using a more structured method, Gerald Koocher, a psychologist, questions some of their findings. In "Talking with Children About Death," he reports on a study in which the differing conceptions of death held by children ranging in age from six to fifteen were matched with their cognitive level. Koocher closes with recommendations for discussing death with children who have suffered loss. Next, the brief selection from James Agee's Pulitzer Prize–winning novel *A Death in the Family* presents an interesting counterpoint to Koocher's theoretical study. In Agee's novel, two children of different ages reveal their own assumptions about death as they try to make sense of the explanations adults have given them of their father's death.

A somewhat different resolution is reached in Joan Fassler's *My Grandpa Died Today,* where a young boy discusses his grandfather's approaching death and then must face life without him. Fassler's work is an example of the growing emphasis within children's literature on themes of aging, separation, and death.

The growing acceptance of the appropriateness of discussing death with children raises related issues. While most would now agree that the natural fact of death should be discussed openly with children, there is considerably less agreement as to the appropriate treatment of large-scale disasters, particularly when massive death is the work of human beings. In "Telling Your Children About the Holocaust," Irving and Blu Greenberg, the former a rabbi and professor, the latter a lecturer and writer, present a specific example that raises more general value-laden questions. They outline the program they followed to make their own children knowledgeable and continually conscious of the fact of the extermination of Jews during World War II. That historic fact, the Greenbergs hold, cannot be excised from contemporary Jewish identity. Increasingly, children of all heritages are becoming conscious of the potential for full-scale nuclear holocaust. The impact of living with the threat of nuclear war is explored by psychologist Milton Schwebel. In "Effects of the Nuclear War Threat on Children and Teenagers: Implications for Professionals," Schwebel reports on studies involving 3,500 students who ranged from second grade to the second year of college. Schwebel documents widespread awareness of the nuclear threat, identifies several responses to it, and makes recommendations for people dealing with youth.

The final readings in the chapter approach the most threatening region: the child's awareness of imminent personal mortality and the impact of the death of a child. In "Children's Awareness of Fatal Illness," Eugenia Waechter, a professor of nursing, analyzes the extent to which a dying child is likely to realize his or her condition. Waechter, too, ends by underscoring the extensive awareness that children possess. In "Portrait of Jen: Memories from the Children's Cancer Ward," a father eloquently traces his growing awareness that a routine hospitalization has suddenly become his daughter's last day.

As we begin, the Encounter offers five brief statements of elementary school–age children recalling the first time somebody they knew died.

encounter | The First Time Somebody I Knew Died

The statements below are the recollections (reproduced as written) of elementary school children asked to write about the first time somebody they knew died.

"I remember when I was five years old my uncle died. Then a lot of people came to the funeral and there was many flowers inside the box and outside too. I got to tuch him and he was very cold then my mother told me why he was that cold. He was cold because some people take out al there things from inside. I went to tell someone els and he told me the same thing. And know I had believed her. Everybody was cring that my tears came out. Sins that time I did not want to go to a funeral ever again."

"When my granmather died I died too."

"My father went to Vietnam and he was Berly to go in the jungle and he step om pungy stikes and I was very sad sow they gave me all of his guns begde boots and his very owm money everybody loved him in the force so my mother crying and she told me that I was the man for the house."

"My Great grand father died when he was having a heart attack. My Great Grand mother was very sad and had to marry again."

"After a person is buride He will always be with you. And if you will not belief me ask your parents."

Thinking back on your own childhood, when was the first time you encountered the death of somebody close to you? Picture the time, recalling who died. Was it a person or a pet? How old were you at the time? What did you think was the cause of death? Did that death make you worry about your own health or safety?

Source: Contributed by children at St. Toribius, Annunciation, and St. Emydius Schools in Los Angeles, California.

GERALD P. KOOCHER

Talking with Children About Death

The selections in the preceding Encounter were written by children between the ages of nine and twelve, the time when children begin to understand death as an irreversible and inevitable occurrence. The children's responses are typical in their simple realism, their puzzled efforts to understand what death means, and their ultimate reliance on parental authority.

Gerald Koocher surveys the research on the developmental theories concerning death and reports on a study of seventy-five children between the ages of six and fifteen. In his study, children were identified in relation to Piaget's stages of cognitive development and their responses to four questions about death matched to those stages. The results, in several instances, validate the conclusions Maria Nagy reached in an earlier classic study. Koocher did not find the personification of death that Maria Nagy reported but instead found that American children seem to employ an abundance of specific detail as a control mechanism.

Many volumes have been written on the meaning of death, and its psychological concomitants. Many authors have attempted to describe the ways in which man learns about death and tries to cope with this universal phenomenon. Most of the recent literature on death and dying tends to focus on those confronting their own death, or those attempting to cope with the loss of people close to them. These works focus on adults for the most part, and are thus subject to a common fallacy that goes something like this: "Children look like grown-up people only smaller; therefore they probably think like grown-ups about most things." In point of fact, the opposite is the case. Children are far from being miniature adults when it comes to the quality of their thought processes. The adult literature on death and dying is simply not relevent to the child, in most cases.

Physicians, theologians, educators, and psychologists are often called upon for advice about how best to explain death to children, and many have taken up the challenge through books and magazine articles. For all of the writing that has been done in this area, however, there is embarrassingly little in the way of empirical research. That is to say, few of these authors have taken the time to talk extensively with children about death, and to report the

Source: Gerald P. Koocher, "Talking with Children About Death." *American Journal of Orthopsychiatry*, Vol. 44, No. 3, April 1974, pp. 404–411. Copyright © 1974 by The American Orthopsychiatric Association, Inc. Reproduced by permission.

children's answers. Whatever the reason for this state of affairs, the lack of empirical data in this area leaves a significant void. Virtually all professionals who work with children are aware of the need for accurate information on how their ideas about death develop. The purpose of this paper is to begin to fill the void caused by our ignorance of this area.

In her book on children's attitudes toward death, Mitchell [1] points out that very little research has been done on the development of these attitudes, although well before age six most children have discovered death in fact or conversation and are very interested in finding out more about it. Mitchell also notes that most of the research in this field is of the "opinion poll" variety, and there has been little effort to refine or improve on this. In the now classic studies by Anthony [2] and Nagy,[3] data is interpreted in ways that credit the child with superordinate levels of abstractive ability; Anthony's subjects were chiefly her own siblings.

In the present study, children were to be asked four questions, the answers to which were to be analyzed in developmental terms. The questions were: "What makes things die?" "How do you make dead things come back to life?" "When will you die?" and "What will happen then?" Answers were grouped according to the child's level of cognitive development, in order to best understand the reasoning that went into the answers. It was anticipated that answers to these four questions would vary predictably according to the developmental stage of the child.

Subjects

The subjects were 75 children ranging in age from six to fifteen years. They were drawn from among participants in various summer recreation and school enrichment programs in a midwestern university community. The sexes were approximately equally represented, and roughly 20% of the sample was nonwhite. The median socioeconomic status of the sample was three on a five-point scale devised by Hollingshead and Redlich,[4] and might be described as "middle class."

Measures

To obtain an estimate of intellectual level of each subject, the Similarities Subtest of the Wechsler Intelligence Scale for Children was used. It is comparatively simple to use, and yields good estimates of a child's verbal concept formation, abstract reasoning, and general intellectual level. Children who did not obtain at least average scores on this subtest (scaled score of 10) were not included in the study.

Criteria suggested by Phillips [5] formed the basis for classifying the children according to their level of cognitive functioning. Each child was tested with three conservation tasks (i.e., mass, number, and volume) and one task in hypothesis formation. If the child failed one or more conservation tasks, he was placed in the "preoperational" group. If he passed all three of those, but failed the hypothesis formation task, the child was classified as "concrete-operational." If the child dealt with all four tasks successfully, he was classified as "formal-operational."

Procedure

The examiner introduced himself to prospective subjects as a person who is interested in finding out what children think about different things, and in seeing how well they can solve certain puzzles. Each child was told in advance that he would be rewarded with a candy bar "for spending the time to tell us what you think about these things." Each child was then tested to determine his cognitive development and estimated intellectual level. During the same session the questions on death were asked verbatim, with no elaboration aside from the probes, "Anything else?" or, "Can you tell me any more about it?" When in doubt, the children were encouraged to guess or, "Just give the best answer you can think of."

Although this procedure involved three separate parts: the similarities subtest, the cognitive development tasks, and the death questions, no distinction as such was made to the child. In this way the whole procedure took on a unity as a questioning and problem solving activity. Thus, any potential stress associated with the impact of bringing up the discussion of death was minimized. It was one way of communicating to the child the message that, "All of these questions are important, and all should be approached as puzzles to solve or phenomena to explain."

The examiners were prepared to follow-up with psychological assistance any children who appeared anxious or upset following the questioning; however, this proved to be unnecessary. One child did not want to estimate when he might die, and was not pressed further once he declined to answer; this child was willing to answer the other questions asked. Most of the other children seemed very interested in making their ideas about death known, and were quite willing to elaborate on them in great detail. A frequent response when the children were allowed to choose their candy bars following the procedure was, "Is that all you wanted to know?" This finding was in marked contrast to the feelings of a few parents and teachers who expressed reservations about allowing their children to participate in the study. Often these adults would refer incidentally to their own experiences with death, and recall their own anxiety. Contact with parents following the interviews confirmed the initial observation that the children showed little or no adverse reaction to being interviewed on this topic. Some of the parents volunteered that they were pleased someone had talked with their children about this.

The examiners who administered and scored the tests were all graduate students in clinical psychology. All were unaware of the major hypotheses of the study. All had completed one full year of graduate study, including practicum courses in the administration of objective and projective psychological instruments.

Results

From the outset it should be noted that no statistically significant differences attributable to the race or sex of the subjects were found.

What Makes Things Die?

The answers to this question were found to be of three different varieties, ranging on a continuum from the very concrete to the very abstract. While not mutually exclusive, the categories are appropriately descriptive of children's thinking on the subject. The categories, with actual examples, are listed below.

Category 1: This group includes fantasy reasoning, magical thinking, and realistic causes of death that are marked by egocentric reasoning as demonstrated in one or more special cases. This sort of response is characteristic of the "preoperational" child. Often these explanations are closely tied to the child's individual experiences. In the examples listed, the examiner's comments are bracketed.

> CAROL (age 7.3): "They eat poison and stuff; pills. You'd better wait till your mom gives them to you. [Anything else?] Drinking poison water and stuff like going swimming alone."

> NAOMI (age 6.5): "When they eat bad things, like if you went with a stranger and they gave you a candy bar with poison on it. [Anything else?] Yes, you can die if you swallow a dirty bug."

> DAVID (age 7.8): "A bird might get real sick and die if you catch it. [Anything else?] They could eat the wrong foods, like aluminum foil. That's all I can think of."

> BRIAN (age 8.2): "Poison, marijuana, not heroin, because that's the same as marijuana. [Anything else?] You could die from styrofoam cups and wood [How?] If you swallow a whole bunch and get sick."

These responses are fairly typical of the children under age eight. It should be remembered, however, that the categories described here are not mutually exclusive and span many ages. That is to say, a primitive response, such as those listed above, might well be given as a partial answer by an older child. In addition, the answers of some children will include items from one or more categories.

Category 2: This group includes specific means of inflicting death, with or without intention. Naming specific weapons, poison, or other means including assaultive acts are all included here. This category of response is most typical of the child at the "concrete-operational" stage of development.

> JEFF (age 10.3): "The fact that they stop living. Diseases can kill you or you can get stabbed or use a gun; there are millions of ways. Do I have to tell you all of them?

[As many as you want to tell.] You could crash their brains out or shoot them, there are millions of ways."

DEBRA (age 12.0): "Accidents, cars, guns, or a knife. Old age, sickness, taking dope, or drowning. [Anything else?] Nope."

TODD (age 7.5): "Knife, arrows, guns, lots of stuff. Do you want me to tell you all of them? [As many as you want.] Hatchets and animals, and fire and explosions too."

KENNY (age 9.5): "Cancer, heart attacks, old age, poison, guns, a bullet, or if someone drops a boulder on you. [Anything else?] That's all."

This type of response was the most common and spanned the broadest age range, from about seven to twelve. Children in this group generally addressed the question, "What makes things die?," in terms of specific causes of death rather than general processes. Older children would also list specific causes of death, but often paired these with the more abstract responses typical of Category 3.

Category 3: This group includes relatively abstract clusters of more specific possibilities. The idea of physical deterioration, naming classes of potential causes, or the recognition of death as a natural process are all included in this group. The responses in this category are typical of those offered by the "formal-operational" children.

ED (15.7): "Death in a physical sense? [Yes.] Destruction of a vital organ or life force within us."

GEORGE (age 13.5): "They get old and things, and their body gets all worn out, and their organs don't work as well as they used to."

DEAN (age 10.2): "When someone gets too old. You could also die of a sickness, or if you couldn't have enough to eat. [Anything else?] Well, when you get old you can just wear out eventually."

PAULA (age 12.2): "When the heart stops, blood stops circulating, you stop breathing and that's it. [Anything else?] Well, there's lots of ways it can get started, but that's what really happens."

Most of the children interviewed who were over age twelve gave this sort of response, but so did some children as young as nine or ten. One exceptionally bright example was Tina, age 8.5, who noted:

"Sometimes they just die when they don't have the things they need to live, like food and water or clean air."

How Do You Make Dead Things Come Back to Life?

According to Piaget,[6] children at the "preoperational" stage of cognitive development, generally age seven and below, might be expected to describe one or more means to accomplish this feat. Kübler-Ross[7] agrees somewhat, stating that the child does not develop a realistic conception of death as a permanent biological process until age nine or ten. At the "preoperational" stage, the child is unable to share the experiences of others to a significant degree, and is not fully able to distinguish animate from inanimate objects. Since he has had no personal experience with death (i.e., he himself has never died), the child at this level might not be expected to regard death as permanent.

Eight children in the present study did tell ways in which they thought the dead might be revived. These eight children ranged in age from 6.0 to 7.1 years, and all were found to be "preoperational" in terms of Piaget's[6] description. These eight also gave Category 1 answers to the question, "What makes things die?" Although no children under age six were included in this study, it seems reasonable to conclude that they would also tend to view death as reversible. Typical responses included:

> "You can't revive them unless you take them to the emergency room and get them doctored up. Then they'll be okay."

> "Help them, give them hot food, and keep them healthy so it won't happen again."

> "No one ever taught me about that, but maybe you could give them some medicine and take them to the hospital to get better."

> "If you know a lot of science, and give them some pills, you can do it."

Older children considered the question seriously, but recognized death as a permanent condition. Some representative responses included:

> "If it was a tree you could water it. If it's a person you could rush them to the emergency room, but it would do no good if they were really dead already."

> "By thinking about them; then they can live in our mind, but you can't really make them come alive again."

> "Maybe some day we'll be able to do it, but not now. Scientists are working on that problem."

When Will You Die?

In answer to this question, all but one of the 75 subjects were willing to make an estimate. These ranged from a low of seven by a six year old, to a high of 300 years by a nine year old. When the subjects are grouped by age and cognitive development, however, some interesting variations can be observed. Once again it must be remembered that the "preoperational" child, as described by Piaget,[6] is unable to make use of the experiences of others to his advantage. Thus, such children (i.e., approximately age seven and below) would be expected to base their estimates more on fantasy than on reality and the observation of others.

The children's responses to this question are summarized in Table 1. Although the average estimates of all three age groups fell quite close together, the variability of these estimates was quite diverse. As indicated in Table 1, variance of these estimates decreases significantly ($p < .001$) as the subjects'

Table 1 | Children's Estimates of When They Will Die (Age)

Age Group	Number of Subjects	Mean Estimates	Standard Deviation	F
6–8 [preoperational]	20	86.6	66.01	
9–11 [concrete-operational]	35	81.3	12.68	27.10[a]
12–15 [formal-operational]	20	81.4	9.54	478.85[a]

[a]Indicates that F is significantly different from the 6–8 age group beyond the $p<.001$ level. The 9–11 and 12–15 group did not differ significantly, producing an F of only 9.54.

ages move beyond eight. That is to say, there was a very wide range or variance of estimates in this youngest group of children that was significantly greater than the range of variance of estimates by the two older groups. The older groups did not differ from each other on this measure to a significant degree. This change occurs, rather predictably, at the point when the child first becomes capable of using the observed experience of others in his own mental problem solving.

What Will Happen When You Die?

A wide variety of responses to this question was obtained. Answers were grouped in non-exclusive categories, with response rates as follows: references to being buried were given by 52% of the children; references to being judged, going to heaven or hell, or other hints at any sort of afterlife by 21%; references to having a funeral by 19%; specific predictions of how death would occur by 10%; references to some aspect of sleep by 7%; references to being remembered by others by 5%; references to reincarnation by 4%, and references to cremation by 3%. A sampling of responses follows:

LARRY (age 9.5): "They'll help me come back alive. [Who?] My mother, father, and grandfather. They'll keep me in bed, and feed me, and keep me away from rat poison and stuff."

WILLIE (age 8.1): "You go to heaven, and all that will be left of you will be a skeleton. My friend has some fossils of people. A fossil's just a skeleton."

DEBBIE (age 13.3): "It will be an accident, and I'll be rushed to the hospital, and I'll die of a piece of bone in my blood stream. They'll perform an autopsy, and then cremate me."

BOYD (age 11.3): "I'll feel dizzy and tired and pass out. Then they'll bury me and I'll rot away. You just disintegrate, and only your bones will be left."

MARK (age 12.0): "I'll have a nice funeral, and be buried, and leave all my money to my son."

META (age 10.8): "If I tell you then you'll laugh. [No, I won't, I want to know what you really think.] I think I'm going to be reincarnated as a plant or animal; whatever they need at that particular time."

GEORGE (age 14.9): "I'll rot. You just decay and then turn back into material like the earth. That's it."

Discussion

Kübler-Ross[7] provides an eloquent context for discussing the findings of this study. She writes:

> The most meaningful help that we can give any relative, child, or adult, is to share his feelings before the event of death and allow him to work through his feelings, whether they are rational or irrational. (p. 180)

It is apparent that children's ideas about death are quite different at different age levels. These differences assume dramatic proportions when the death of a relative, or even a pet, forces an adult into the awkward and uncomfortable position of explaining to a child what has happened. Yet, it seems imperative that we help the child to understand what has happened and share his feelings of loss in a way that will help him to adapt and grow appropriately.

The present data lead to some suggestions for discussing death with the child who has suffered a loss. First, the reactions of the children to the questioning procedure suggests that there should be no "unspoken barriers" to this topic of conversation. Children are capable of talking about death, and seem to want to do this. They are pleased by the attention of understanding adults. Silence teaches them only that the topic is taboo; it cannot help them to cope with their feelings of loss. Second, the data in the present study suggest that the best explanations for children, especially those under age seven or eight, will be those that are simple, direct, and draw as much as possible from the child's own experiences. In this way the relative concreteness of the younger child will produce the least possible distortion.

Still another suggestion follows from an examination of the more magical answers given by younger children to the questions, "What makes things die?" and "How can you make dead things come back to life?" Those adults who would undertake explaining death to a young child would also be wise to ask the child to explain back again what he has been told. This would offer the opportunity to detect and correct any gross distortions or misperceptions on the part of the child. From the variety of causes of death that children are apt to think about, one can conclude that it is far better to explore and attempt to respond to the child's ideas, than to allow magical or unspoken fears to play upon the child's imagination.

Keeping in mind the fantasies that childhood reasoning might lead to regarding the permanence of death is also important. For some children in this study there were ways in which ". . . you can make dead things come back to life." By implication, death need not be permanent if someone will only look after the corpse properly. This view could easily give rise to guilt and anxiety when the child learns that the body has been buried rather than nurtured back to health.

While no data were gathered on church affiliation or parental theism, it seems a bit surprising that little in the way of detailed religious concepts of death and its concomitants was elicited. In fact, only seven percent of the children in the study used the word "god" in answering the questions. Another 21% referred to this somewhat indirectly, mentioning heaven, hell, judgment, or some unearthly afterlife, but still this may seem rather low. There are many possible explanations, not the least influential of which might be media portrayals of death, including cartoons, comic books, television westerns, televised accounts of war news, etc. The weight of religious content in all of these is minimal. One might also think in terms of the growing disillusionment with religion as a mode of coping with death. This might be particularly reflected in the population for this study, because of the prevalence of this point of view in the university community.

Along these same lines it is worth comparing the present findings with those of Nagy.[3] She noted that Hungarian children between five and nine years old generally personify death. That is to say, they speak of death as if it were a person, and in this way keep it at a safe distance since, "Only those die whom the death-man carries off." Kübler-Ross[7] also notes that children of this age group tend to ". . . regard death as a bogey-man who comes to take people away" (p. 179). Not a single child in the present study gave a personification type response when discussing what might happen at the time of death. This finding probably reflects cultural differences, but certainly suggests a different sort of coping mechanism than Nagy found in her sample. Kübler-Ross cites Nagy as a reference and reports no new data. This might lead one to suspect that she has not looked for any cultural differences, but is simply repeating Nagy's assertions.

In the present study, answers to the question, "What will happen when you die?" are more difficult to interpret than are the others. While most children mentioned the idea of being buried, some giving graphic details of the interment process, there was a wide range of responses. It is particularly interesting to note that only 5% discussed their death in terms of how others might react. Rather, most of the subjects focused on concrete or stereotyped accounts of what would happen, such as detailed accounts of their funerals or of "rotting away" in the grave.

Perhaps the "coping mechanism" used instead of personification is hinted at in these findings. In the present sample, even children who were capable of above-average levels of verbal abstraction were consistently specific and concrete in their replies. Perhaps American children are more inclined to use specificity of detail as a means to mastery and hence "control" over death, rather than personification. That is to say, "If I know what is going to happen to me when I die, then I won't have to worry about it now." If this is indeed the case, then seeing that death is talked about with children becomes especially important.

References

1. M. Mitchell, *The Child's Attitude to Death* (New York: Schocken Books, 1967).

2. S. Anthony, *The Child's Discovery of Death* (New York: Harcourt, Brace, 1940).

3. M. Nagy, "The Child's Theories Concerning Death," *Journal of Genetic Psychology* 73 (1948): 3–27.

4. A. Hollingshead and E. Redlich, *Social Class and Mental Illness* (New York: John Wiley, 1958).

5. J. Phillips, *The Origins of Intellect: Piaget's Theory* (San Francisco: W. H. Freeman, 1969).

6. J. Piaget, *The Child's Perception of the World* (Patterson, N.J.: Littlefield, Adams, 1960).

7. E. Kübler-Ross, *On Death and Dying* (New York: Macmillan, 1964).

JAMES AGEE

selection from
A Death in the Family

In the following selection, two children work to understand the sudden death of
their father, a tragedy that has effectively disordered their universe. The children mull over the explanations given them by adults and pool their own reflections to conclude that God, the death-man, has carried off their father. In the
discussion between the children and their Aunt Hannah, Catherine typifies the
response of a young child as she listens to all the explanations and yet denies
the finality of death with her question, "When is Daddy coming home?" Rufus,
for his part, moves toward a more mature understanding of death as physical
cessation when he realizes that it was not God but a concussion that killed
his father.

Catherine did not like being buttoned up by Rufus or bossed around by him,
and breakfast wasn't like breakfast either. Aunt Hannah didn't say anything
and neither did Rufus and neither did she, and she felt that even if she wanted
to say anything she oughtn't. Everything was queer, it was so still and it seemed
dark. Aunt Hannah sliced the banana so thin on the Post Toasties it looked
cold and wet and slimy. She gave each of them a little bit of coffee in their milk
and she made Rufus' a little bit darker than hers. She didn't say, "Eat"; "Eat
your breakfast, Catherine"; "Don't dawdle," like Catherine's mother; she
didn't say anything. Catherine did not feel hungry, but she felt mildly curious
because things tasted so different, and she ate slowly ahead, tasting each
mouthful. Everything was so still that it made Catherine feel uneasy and sad.
There were little noises when a fork or spoon touched a dish; the only other
noise was the very thin dry toast Aunt Hannah kept slowly crunching and the
fluttering sipping of the steamy coffee with which she wet each mouthful of dry
crumbs enough to swallow it. When Catherine tried to make a similar noise
sipping her milk, her Aunt Hannah glanced at her sharply as if she wondered if
Catherine was trying to be a smart aleck but she did not say anything.
Catherine was not trying to be a smart aleck but she felt she had better not
make that noise again. The fried eggs had hardly any pepper and they were so
soft the yellow ran out over the white and the white plate and looked so nasty
she didn't want to eat it but she ate it because she didn't want to be told to and
because she felt there was some special reason, still, why she ought to be a good

Source: From *A Death in the Family* by James Agee. Copyright © 1957 by The James Agee Trust.
Used by permission of Grosset & Dunlap, Inc.

girl. She felt very uneasy, but there was nothing to do but eat, so she always took care to get a good hold on her tumbler and did not take too much on her spoon, and hardly spilled at all, and when she became aware of how little she was spilling it made her feel like a big girl and yet she did not feel any less uneasy, because she knew there was something wrong. She was not as much interested in eating as she was in the way things were, and listening carefully, looking mostly at her plate, every sound she heard and the whole quietness which was so much stronger than the sounds, meant that things were not good. What it was was that he wasn't here. Her mother wasn't either, but she was upstairs. He wasn't even upstairs. He was coming home last night but he didn't come home and he wasn't coming home now either, and her mother felt so awful she cried, and Aunt Hannah wasn't saying anything, just making all that noise with the toast and big loud sips with the coffee and swallowing, *grrmmp*, and then the same thing over again and over again, and every time she made the noise with the toast it was almost scary, as if she was talking about some awful thing, and every time she sipped it was like crying or like when Granma sucked in air between her teeth when she hurt herself, and every time she swallowed, *crmmp*, it meant it was all over and there was nothing to do about it or say or even ask, and then she would take another bite of toast as hard and shivery as gritting your teeth, and start the whole thing all over again. Her mother said he wasn't coming home ever any more. That was what she said, but why wasn't he home eating breakfast right this minute? Because he was not with them eating breakfast it wasn't fun and everything was so queer. Now maybe in just a minute he would walk right in and grin at her and say, "Good morning, merry sunshine," because her lip was sticking out, and even bend down and rub her cheek with his whiskers and then sit down and eat a big breakfast and then it would be all fun again and she would watch from the window when he went to work and just before he went out of sight he would turn around and she would wave but why wasn't he right here now where she wanted him to be and why didn't he come home? Ever any more. He won't come home again ever any more. Won't come home again ever. But he will, though, because it's home: But why's he not here? He's up seeing Grampa Follet. Grampa Follet is very, very sick. But Mama didn't feel awful then, she feels awful now. But why didn't he come back when she said he would? He went to heaven and now Catherine could remember about heaven, that's where God lives, way up in the sky. Why'd he do that? God took him there. But why'd he go there and not come home like Mama said? Last night Mama said he was coming home last night. We could even wait up a while and when he didn't and we had to go to bed she *promised* he would come if we went to sleep and she promised he'd be here at breakfast time and now it's breakfast time and she says he won't come home ever any more. Now her Aunt Hannah folded her napkin, and folded it again more narrowly, and again still more narrowly, and pressed the butt end of it against her mouth, and laid it beside her plate, where it slowly and slightly unfolded, and, looking first at Rufus and then at Catherine and then back at

Rufus, said quietly, "I think you ought to know about your father. Whatever I can tell you. Because your mother's not feeling well."

Now I'll know when he *is* coming home, Catherine thought.

All through breakfast, Rufus had wanted to ask questions, but now he felt so shy and uneasy that he could hardly speak. "Who hurt him?" he finally asked.

"Why nobody hurt him, Rufus," she said, and she looked shocked. "What on earth made you think so?"

Mama said so, Catherine thought.

"Mama said he got hurt so bad God put him to sleep," Rufus said.

Like the kitties, Catherine thought: she saw a dim, gigantic old man in white take her tiny father by the skin of the neck and put him in a huge slop jar full of water and sit on the lid, and she heard the tiny scratching and the stifled mewing.

"That's true he was hurt, but nobody hurt him," her Aunt Hannah was saying. How could that be, Catherine wondered. "He was driving home by himself. That's all, all by himself, in the auto last night, and he had an accident."

Rufus felt his face get warm and he looked warningly at his sister. He knew it could not be that, not with his father, a grown man, besides, God wouldn't put you to sleep for *that,* and it didn't hurt, anyhow. But Catherine might think so. Sure enough, she was looking at her aunt with astonishment and disbelief that she could say such a thing about her father. Not in his *pants,* you dern fool, Rufus wanted to tell her, but his Aunt Hannah continued: "A *fatal* accident"; and by her voice, as she spoke the strange word, "fatal," they knew she meant something very bad. "That means that, just as your mother told you, that he was hurt so badly that God put him to sleep right away."

Like the rabbits, Rufus remembered, all torn white bloody fur and red insides. He could not imagine his father like that. Poor little things, he remembered his mother's voice comforting his crying, hurt so terribly that God just let them go to sleep.

If it was in the auto, Catherine thought, then he wouldn't be in the slop jar.

They couldn't be happy any more if He hadn't, his mother had said. They could never get well.

Hannah wondered whether they could comprehend it at all and whether she should try to tell them. She doubted it. Deeply uncertain, she tried again.

"He was driving home last night," she said, "about nine, and apparently something was already wrong with the steering mech—with the wheel you guide the machine with. But your father didn't know it. Because there wasn't any way he could know until something went wrong and then it was too late. But one of the wheels struck a loose stone in the road and the wheel turned aside very suddenly, and when . . ." She paused and went on more quietly and slowly: "You see, when your father tried to make the auto go where it should, stay on the road, he found he couldn't, he didn't have any control. Because something was wrong with the steering gear. So, instead of doing as he tried to make it, the auto twisted aside because of the loose stone and ran off the road into a deep ditch." She paused again. "Do you understand?"

They kept looking at her.

"Your father was thrown from the auto," she said. Then the auto went on without him up the other side of the ditch. It went up an eight-foot embankment and then it fell down backward, turned over and landed just beside him.

"They're pretty sure he was dead even before he was thrown out. Because the only mark on his whole body," and now they began to hear in her voice a troubling intensity and resentment, "was right—here!" She pressed the front of her forefinger to the point of her chin, and looked at them almost as if she were accusing them.

They said nothing.

I suppose I've got to finish, Hannah thought; I've gone this far.

"They're pretty sure how it happened," she said. "The auto gave such a sudden terrible jerk"—she jerked so violently that both children jumped, and startled her; she demonstrated what she saw next more gently: "that your father was thrown forward and struck his chin, very hard, against the wheel, the steering wheel, and from that instant he never knew anything more."

She looked at Rufus, at Catherine, and again at Rufus. "Do you understand?" They looked at her.

After a while Catherine said, "He hurt his chin."

"Yes, Catherine. He did," she replied. "They believe he was *instantly* killed, with the one single blow, because it happened to strike just exactly where it did. Because if you're struck very hard in just that place, it jars your whole head, your brain so hard that—sometimes people die in that very instant." She drew a deep breath and let it out long and shaky. "Concussion of the brain, that is called," she said with most careful distinctness, and bowed her head for a moment; they saw her thumb make a small cross on her chest.

She looked up. "Now do you understand, children?" she asked earnestly. "I know it's very hard to understand. You please tell me if there's anything you want to know and I'll do my best to expl—tell you better."

Rufus and Catherine looked at each other and looked away. After a while Rufus said, "Did it hurt him bad?"

"He could never have felt it. That's the one great mercy" (or is it, she wondered); "the doctor is sure of that."

Catherine wondered whether she could ask one question. She thought she'd better not.

"What's an eight-foot embackmut?" asked Rufus.

"Em-bank-ment," she replied. "Just a bank. A steep little hill, eight feet high. Bout's high's the ceiling."

He and Catherine saw the auto climb it and fall backward rolling and come to rest beside their father. Umbackmut, Catherine thought; em-*bank*-ment, Rufus said to himself.

"What's instintly?"

"Instantly is—quick's that"; she snapped her fingers, more loudly than she had expected to; Catherine flinched and kept her eyes on the fingers. "Like snapping off an electric light." Rufus nodded. "So you can be very sure, both of you, he never felt a moment's pain. Not one moment."

"When's . . ." Catherine began.

"What's . . ." Rufus began at the same moment; they glared at each other.

"What is it, Catherine?"

"When's Daddy coming home?"

"Why good *golly,* Catherine," Rufus began; "Hold your tongue!" his Aunt Hannah said fiercely, and he listened, scared, and ashamed of himself.

"Catherine, he *can't* come home," she said very kindly. "That's just what all this means, child." She put her hand over Catherine's hand and Rufus could see that her chin was trembling. "He died, Catherine," she said. "That's what your mother means. God put him to sleep and took him, took his soul away with Him. So he can't come home . . ." She stopped, and began again. "We'll see him once more," she said, "tomorrow or day after; that I promise you," she said, wishing she was sure of Mary's views about this. "But he'll be asleep then. And after that we won't see him any more in this world. Not until God takes us away too.

"Do you see, child?" Catherine was looking at her very seriously. "Of course you don't, God bless you"; she squeezed her hand. "Don't ever try too hard to understand, child. Just try to understand it's so. He'd come if he could but he simply can't because God wants him with Him. That's all." She kept her hand over Catherine's a little while more, while Rufus realized much more clearly than before that he really could not and would not come home again: because of God.

"He would if he could but he can't," Catherine finally said, remembering a joking phrase of her mother's.

Hannah, who knew the joking phrase too, was startled, but quickly realized that the child meant it in earnest. "That's it," she said gratefully.

But he'll come once more, anyway, Rufus realized, looking forward to it. Even if he *is* asleep.

"What was it you wanted to ask, Rufus?" he heard his aunt say.

He tried to remember and remembered. "What's kuh, kuh-kush, kuh . . .?"

"Con-cus-sion, Rufus. Concus-sion of the brain. That's the doctor's name for what happened. It means, it's as if the brain were hit very hard and suddenly, and joggled loose. The instant that happens, your father was—he . . ."

"Instantly killed."

She nodded.

"Then it was that, that put him to sleep."

"Hyess."

"*Not* God."

Catherine looked at him, bewildered.

JOAN FASSLER

My Grandpa Died Today

Though the subject of death appeared in children's literature of the eighteenth and nineteenth centuries, it was usually presented as a prod to moral behavior. Frequently, children were urged to behave well in life in order to avoid eternal punishment thereafter. In recent years, however, death has returned to children's literature as a subject for realistic presentation and open consideration. Often in works such as *Charlotte's Web,* it is an animal that dies, but the following piece by Joan Fassler demonstrates that even the death of a family member can be presented to children so as to allay rather than arouse fears. In *My Grandpa Died Today,* the child who serves as the narrator describes his feelings of loss and grief as well as his personal means of honoring his grandfather's memory.

My grandpa was very, very old. He was much,
much older than me. He was much older than
my mother and father. He was much older
than all my aunts and uncles. He was even a
little bit older than the white haired
bakery-man down the block.

My grandpa taught me how to play checkers.
And he read stories to me. And he helped me
build my first model. And he showed me how
to reach out with my bat and hit a curve ball.
And he always rooted for my team.

One day, grandpa and I took a long slow walk
together. Grandpa stopped to rest awhile.
"David," he said, "I am getting very old now.
And surely I cannot live forever." Then
grandpa put his arm around my shoulders and
went on talking in a soft voice. "But I am not
afraid to die," he said, "because I know that
you are not afraid to live." And I nodded my
head in a thoughtful way, even though I did
not understand what grandpa meant.

Source: Joan Fassler. *My Grandpa Died Today.* New York: Human Sciences Press. © 1971.

Just two days later grandpa sat down in our
big white rocking chair. And he rocked
himself for a little while. Then, very softly,
very quietly, grandpa closed his eyes.

And he stopped rocking.
And he didn't move any more.
And he didn't talk any more.
And he didn't breathe any more.
And the grownups said that grandpa died.

My mother cried and cried. And my father
cried and cried. And many people came to
our house. And they cried, too. And they
took grandpa away and buried him.

More people kept coming to our house. And
they pulled down all the window shades. And
they covered all the mirrors. And our whole
house looked as if it was going to cry. Even
the red shingles on the roof. Even the white
shutters at the windows. Even the flagstone
steps going up to the door. And everyone was
very sad.

I was sad, too. I thought about my grandpa
and about all the things we used to do
together. And, in a little while, I discovered a
funny, empty, scary, rumbly kind of feeling
at the bottom of my stomach. And some tears
streaming down my cheeks.

Somehow, I didn't feel like sitting in the
living room with all the gloomy grown-ups. So
I walked quietly into my own room, and I
took out some of my favorite toys. Then I did
two jig-saw puzzles and colored three
pictures. And I rolled a few marbles very
slowly across the floor.

The grownups didn't mind at all. They came
in and smiled at me. And someone patted me
gently on my head. It was almost as if they all

knew that grandpa and I must have had some very special talks together.

The next day was still a very sad day at our house. Late in the afternoon, I heard a soft knock at the door. My best friend, Bobby, wanted to know if I could play ball. And again the grownups didn't seem to mind. So I left our sad, sorry house. And Bobby and I walked slowly down to the park.

Almost too soon, it was my turn at bat. I looked around and saw that the bases were loaded. Then I took a deep breath, and tried to forget about the rumbly feeling at the bottom of my stomach. I planted my feet firmly on the ground. I grasped the bat with two steady hands. I watched the ball whizz towards me. And, SMACK, I hit it high and far.

And then I ran. I ran with every bit of strength and power and speed inside my whole body.

And it was a grand slam home run!

And somehow, right there on the field, in the middle of all the cheers and shouts of joy, I could *almost* see my grandpa's face breaking into a happy smile. And that made me feel so good inside that the rumbles in my stomach disappeared.

And the solid hardness of the ground under my feet made me feel good inside, too. And the warm touch of the sun on my cheeks made me feel good inside, too.

And, it was at that very moment, that I first began to understand why my grandpa was not afraid to die. It was because he knew that there would be many more hits and many more home runs for me. It was because he knew that I would go right on playing, and reading, and running, and laughing, and growing up.

Without really knowing why, I took off my cap. I stood very still. I looked far, far away into the clear blue sky. And I thought to myself, "Grandpa must feel good inside, too."

Then I heard the umpire calling, "Batter-up!" And we went on with the game.

IRVING & BLU GREENBERG

Telling Your Children About the Holocaust

The desire to present facts truthfully to children may be at odds with protective
instincts. But the historical reality of the Holocaust is so much a part of contemporary Jewish identity that the Greenbergs argue for continued observance
of its impact even for children. Though the Greenbergs present a specialized example, every parent or teacher is, at some time, confronted with the conflicting
values of knowledge and protection.

On Wednesday morning, November 15, 1978, the *New York Times* front page
featured an aerial photo of a large open-deck sea transport filled to capacity
with human cargo. These were Vietnamese refugees, 2,500 men, women, and
children waiting to gain entry to any country that would offer a temporary
haven.

I have always felt that to be a Jew is to see the world with Jewish eyes, to
hear the world with Jewish ears, and to do it effortlessly, unconsciously,
sometimes almost against one's will. Like many other Jews who read the paper
that morning, I was reminded of another picture, another story—1939: the
Struma, the *St. Louis,* 100 other refugee ships laden with Jews shunted from
one country to another, confirming the darkest suspicions of their passengers
that no one in the whole world cared about or wanted Jews. My memory
recalled distant, deeply embedded descriptions of month-long voyages,
crowded, unsanitary conditions, passengers who carried unbelievable tales of
terror, trauma, loss, and separation.

I did not summon these images; they were simply there. Nor did I share
them with our children, who also read the article that Wednesday morning. I
was convinced that they had read it without all the layers of associated
memories that I had, and on one level I was relieved.

On another level, however, I felt that I should use the opportunity to get
across one more "Jewish connection." But I let it pass. Almost perfunctorily I
said, "We should do something about it; we should write a letter to Carter
telling him to help these Vietnamese." But I did not give voice to the feelings
that I felt and feel, the anger at the world that did nothing while Jews' lives were
at stake. Why burden the children with this pain?

On the following Monday morning it was snowing. A beautiful pristine

Source: Irving and Blu Greenberg, "Telling Your Children About the Holocaust." *Kosher
Home's Jewish Living,* March/April, 1979, © 1979, Adar Communications Company, New York,
New York.

279

Greenberg &
Greenberg
Telling Your
Children About
the Holocaust

snow, not yet turned to slush. The children were elated. Our daughter Goody was ahead of the rest of us and was standing at the window with her nose pressed against the cold pane. She stared dreamily outside at the falling flakes. Talking to no one in particular, she prattled on about how she was going to go sledding after school, that she would bring some friends home, was there hot chocolate in the house, and maybe (dream of dreams) school would have to close early. After a moment of silence I heard her say, "I wonder how Renee Ostry feels when it starts snowing." (Renee, our good friend, is a survivor of Auschwitz.)

"What do you mean, Goody?" I asked.

"Well," she said, "the snow must remind her of Gehenna [hell], and for me it's fun and play." For a moment, the sight of emaciated prisoners dressed in rags in the freezing snow shivered through my mind, as it did through hers. I gave her a little hug and said, "You're right, Goody," and pursued it no further. But it took my breath away, the incredible sensitivity of an 11-year-old.

Three days after that, our daughter Deborah was writing a letter to President Carter protesting the U.N.'s backing of the P.L.O. As she read it over to us, we heard these words: ". . . and I see by your act of taking in the Vietnamese refugees that you learned your lesson from the Holocaust." This time, I couldn't resist pursuing it further. "Did you discuss that in school, Deb?" "No," she answered. "Then what made you think of that?" "Well, I just thought about it when I saw the boats in the *New York Times* and it reminded me of the *St. Louis.*" . . .

We share these incidents with you because we have learned from them that our children have a deeper sense of the Holocaust than we ever imagined, and that they have the ability to make sophisticated connections and associations and draw certain inferences on their own.

The Holocaust is a central event in our lives. It comes up naturally in our conversation—sometimes daily, sometimes not for long periods of time. It has never seemed to us that we are doing a hard-sell job on the subject. Rather, our children have learned about the Holocaust almost by osmosis—from their relationships with people, from their home and school environments, and from communal events.

There are many events in the Jewish community that seem to be unrelated to the Holocaust, yet are, in fact, intimately connected. The underlying sense of all those rallies for Soviet Jewry to which we take our children is that never again will anyone do to us what Hitler did. The birth of Israel conveys a similar message. We have never been to a Yom Haatzmaut parade or celebration where the theme of nationalism was half as important as the theme of rebirth. As we pushed strollers and bought balloons and sang with the marchers, or later took pictures as our children marched past us in the parades, we gradually began to realize that these celebrations were another facet of our children's Holocaust education. Here they were learning not facts, but rather the basic lesson: We are one people, we are responsible for each other, we will not stand idly by as the world once did.

Another important factor in our children's understanding of the Holocaust has been our friendship with many survivors. The Holocaust does not automatically come up in our conversations together. In fact, many survivors feel that no one wants to hear about the Holocaust and are reluctant to discuss their experiences. But each and every survivor's life is a miraculous gift and a precious resource to the Jewish community. They have suffered for all of us, and we must be ready to hear the whole story each witness has locked up inside him. At times, our children have seen us, our eyes glistening, in quiet conversation with our friends. Sometimes they would overhear; sometimes they would ask later; sometimes we offered without their asking. We have always told them the tales we felt they could bear to hear.

The personal stories of people they know are certainly the most potent means of conveying to our children the essence of the Holocaust. And in a certain unspoken way, a survivor who has managed to put together a normal second life, despite the memories and nightmares, must surely represent to our children, as to us, a symbol of hope. Perhaps, too, our children will become sensitive to the special needs and problems of survivors' children and grandchildren, and to their emotional wounds, which the rest of the community must help to heal.

Every year, our synagogue, the Riverdale Jewish Center, marks Yom Ha-Sho'ah, a day of remembrance of the Holocaust. When it first began, some 15 years ago, only a handful came, all adults. Ironically, most of them were survivors.

Now the children come. They even take part in the program. Two years ago, the fourth-grade class of SAR (Salanter Akiba Riverdale) Academy was asked to participate in the synagogue memorial. Several students spoke of family members who had died in the Holocaust. We listened as Sharon Moerdler, a fair-skinned, freckle-faced, ten-year-old redhead, spoke of her family. Up until that moment, we did not know that her father, Charles Moerdler, a one-time New York City Commissioner of Housing, had escaped Germany as a boy. But he had paid a terrible price. His father, who had arranged for the wife's and son's escape, had to stay behind. "We still don't know what happened to my grandfather," said Sharon.

Another ten-year-old, Pamela Shamir of Israel, talked about her great-grandmother, dead at age 45 in Auschwitz. As Pamela spoke, she fingered a small silver brooch and said, "This is all that I have of hers." Everyone in the synagogue was moved to tears.

Through a subtle process, Yom Ha-Sho'ah has become increasingly child-oriented. The genius of the rabbis of ancient times is that they structured many of the holiday mitzvot as pedagogic devices for the young. The Passover seder and the Chanukah lights are perfect examples. It seems as if, almost instinctively, we are moving in that direction today with Yom Ha-Sho'ah.

While we have tried to do many things as a family and with the community, we have to say that a major part of the children's knowledge of the Holocaust has come through the yeshiva day school they all attended. The SAR Academy places great emphasis on both the Holocaust and Israel in its curriculum. Not only the facts are taught, but also their implications for Judaism and human relations. And for our three older children, this process has been continued at the Manhattan Hebrew High School.

In addition to an extensive Yom Ha-Sho'ah program, SAR also marks the anniversaries of the Warsaw Ghetto uprising and Kristallnacht [The Night of Shattered Glass, November 10, 1938: the beginning of a massive pogrom against the Jews of Germany] with special activities. This year, for Kristallnacht, a parent who had lived through it described the event to the students of grades four through eight.

But it is not only at these special times that the connection is made. In their final term the eighth-graders work on an independent research paper. They may choose any topic relating to the Holocaust. And recently, in response to the Guyana tragedy, the school showed a film on mind control to the seventh and eighth grades. In the discussion that followed, the issue was raised as to whether or not the German people had been subjected to mind control—as in fact had been the plea of many Nazi war criminals.

Thus, the school has made our task as parents infinitely easier. Even more important, the fact that our children have experienced some of the trauma alongside their friends and peers has made it that much easier for them. But what if your children's school doesn't have such a program? We believe that almost any school or youth-centered program can duplicate the SAR model. Parents who want their children to come to grips with Sho'ah, yet are unsure of how to approach it themselves, would be wise to prod their schools—parochial and public—to institute Holocaust teaching as part of the standard curriculum.

Fieldston, a private school in New York City, has inaugurated such a program. It all began with Sondra Wald, a 17-year-old senior. Sondra's young grandmother, a still stunning blue-eyed blonde, barely escaped Germany in 1939 along with her new husband, who had just been released from a concentration camp. They spent the next six years desperately trying to bring to America some of the large family they had left behind. But they had little success—only five of five score survived. Two years ago, Sondra approached the social studies teacher at Fieldston about scheduling a Holocaust program. Many of the students and faculty were unaware even of the meaning of the word.

As Sondra and her teacher talked, the idea developed from having a single hour-long assembly into setting aside a Holocaust commemoration week. Sondra's mother and grandmother were called upon as resource people, as were many others in the area. The local newspapers covered it, and it was an educational experience for the entire community.

Programs like this can be—and are being—duplicated across the country with but a little initiative from interested parents. And how valuable it would be to have, along with these school programs, a Holocaust memorial in every major U.S. city, for Jewish and non-Jewish children alike. The Holocaust should no longer be the private, painful secret of the Jewish people.

In contrast to barely a decade ago, there is now a large body of Holocaust books and films available, geared to children at different levels. The most widely used and most powerful literary encounter for children, as well as for adults, still remains Elie Wiesel's *Night*. Wiesel manages to convey a sense of the enormity of the catastrophe in a manner that even the young mind can grasp. Each of our children read this work at a different age (the youngest was ten); for each it was a very powerful experience. They all read Anne Frank's *The Diary of a Young Girl*, another classic text. There are certain weaknesses in the diary; in particular, the Holocaust is kept rather distant. But one cannot be a purist here. The fact that the book is readily available—and very moving— makes it a most useful text. A more direct account of the ruptures in a young child's life, and of the losses in the Holocaust, can be found in Marietta Moskin's *I am Rosemarie*.

Two years ago, a publisher sent us a review copy of Milton Meltzer's book, *Never to Forget*. The book lay around for a while unreviewed. Several weeks later, as we came to tuck in Goody, we noticed she was reading it. She had been reading a few pages every night before falling asleep. It's not exactly what we would have prescribed as bedtime reading for a nine-year-old. But this was what she had done on her own, and we simply observed how she handled it. Several times, she had to read through her tears; but every night she would once again pick up the book. *Never to Forget* gives an accurate, factual account with hardly any rhetoric. It is history, not a novel; yet it held our daughter's interest until she finished it. Since that time, another historical work accessible to children has appeared: *Hitler's War Against the Jews*, an adaptation of Lucy Dawidowicz's prize-winning *The War Against the Jews*.

Other material has caught the children's eye—the collections of poetry of children in the camps, such as *I Never Saw Another Butterfly*, or Hannah Senesh's *Diary*. We never push specific books on them, but we have noticed the power of environmental learning: what is around, and appropriate for their level, has a fairly good chance of being looked at; even if they don't read it, they know such a work exists.

Many Holocaust documentaries have been shown on television. These include *Night and Fog*, a 30-minute presentation; *The 81st Blow*, a devastating hour-long documentary; *Genocide*, a unit of the BBC's history of World War II; and *Let My People Go*, a description of the Holocaust and the emigration to Israel that followed. Having the family view these films together is an effective way of sharing the experience. Afterward, there is a natural opportunity to talk over and assimilate the film.

After watching a television program on the Holocaust last spring, Goody and J. J. had the following conversation:

Goody: "If Grandpa hadn't come to America when he did, that would have been us."

283

Greenberg &
Greenberg
*Telling Your
Children About
the Holocaust*

J. J.: "You're wrong, Goody [his favorite phrase]. If Grandpa hadn't come to America, we would never have been born."

One of the ways in which we thought that our children's perception would differ from ours is that they would never say, "There but for the grace of God go I," that they would never feel that their very lives were intertwined with the events of the Holocaust. We thought that even with all they had learned at school and at home, they would never be able to bridge the gulf of time. It took the power of the visual media to bring to them a new and deeper level of understanding. Now, for the first time, we knew that they understood that the Holocaust meant that whole family lines were cut off, that there but for the grace of God. . . .

Many questions have been posed to us about teaching the Holocaust to children. What we have found to be true for our family may not be true for another. Still, we can offer some reassurance. Children are not as fragile or as vulnerable as we often think they are. They can feel pain, and they can overcome.

At what age to begin? The Holocaust is so horrifying an event that if one could, one would postpone indefinitely telling one's children about it. But the Holocaust is fact, it is our heritage; we can't make it go away by ignoring it.

Each of our children encountered the Holocaust at a different age and in a different way. When Moshe was five, he spent a Shabbat with his grandparents in Far Rockaway. On Sunday, he returned home, the same old Moshe, full of fun and mischief. After he had been home several hours, he paused in the middle of his usual high jinks and asked, "Is it true what Saba [grandfather] said—that there was an enemy worse than Pharoah, worse than Haman, that he killed all the Jews, that his name was Hitler?" "Yes," we said. Back came Moshe, who had obviously mulled over the question in his five-year-old mind, "Then why wasn't there a Moshe Rabbeinu (Moses our teacher) to save the Jews?"

David and Deborah were probably closer to nine or ten. For David, it was learning about the great-uncle after whom he was named and reading Wiesel's *Night* that brought forth the questions. For Deborah, it was her fascination with Hannah Senesh. By the time she was ten, she had already read five different books on or by this heroine. J. J. and Goody, while they had heard a good deal of the word Holocaust, and had associated it with a tragedy, did not really begin to comprehend the event until the family visited Yad Vashem, the Holocaust memorial in Jerusalem. J. J. was then nine and a half, Goody, eight.

When Moshe and David were quite young (seven and eight), we took them to a Yom Ha-Sho'ah service at the synagogue. The film they showed that year was *Camps of the Dead,* a stark documentary. In retrospect, we had made a mistake in bringing them. But no harm was done. They immediately tuned out and started to fool around. We simply took them right out. They had let us know indirectly, but in no uncertain terms, that the film was not for them at that stage of their lives.

One thing we have learned is that there are no hard and fixed rules. At about the time a child begins to comprehend evil in the world, he can begin to understand the Holocaust. Common sense dictates that a parent start with the bearable—not with the Mengele medical experiments, for example. But when dealing with the Holocaust, one soon runs out of bearable facts.

We rather suspect that those of our children who now seem to be less sensitive to the Holocaust will later do what many Jewish college students and adults do—go through a period of intense encounter, reading Holocaust literature voraciously for months on end—and then go through a period of distancing, of disengagement, a period of healing emotional wounds, until their Holocaust consciousness stabilizes and becomes a natural component of their lives as Jews. This, in fact, is what happened to both of us.

How will our children be affected? Will they have nightmares? Will they feel threatened and disturbed by the sheer horror? We have always been caught in this dilemma—between the feeling that our children must be told and the problem of how to tell them effectively without scarring them emotionally.

Last year, when our son David balked at going to a Yom Ha-Sho'ah program because he had a big test the next day, we simply said to him, "This comes first. This is what we do as a family. Change out of those sloppy jeans. You are coming." Our big compromise was that he could wear his old sneakers and flannel shirt to the synagogue. We have often suspected that David resists because he cannot bear the pain of the Holocaust. Are we wrong in forcing him to come? We will never know, since he certainly manages to cope. At the least, he understands how important it is to us to have him share this experience.

When Goody saw the rape scene on NBC's "Holocaust," she burst into tears. Yet she did not become morbid or withdrawn. In fact, the next day she and her friend discussed the scene and their fright—probably a much healthier way of handling it than that of most grown women, who no doubt felt equally threatened by the scene.

Some psychologists have suggested that if children are exposed to morbid material during certain stages of development, it can retard their emotional growth. Our general impression is that the chance of this happening is quite small. The response to the Holocaust is itself developmental; it is a gradual process. Children will be guided by their own level of emotional and psychological maturation; they generally know how to protect themselves.

And are not some of the responses that we fear—tears, anger, nightmares—in fact protective devices? How many times have we ourselves put down a book after only a few pages, unable to withstand any more pain? How many nights have we, as adults, awakened with Holocaust nightmares? Perhaps it is these nightmares that allow some catharsis and enable us to function normally, happily, during our waking hours.

The absorptive capacity of young children is quite amazing. If a child is not otherwise emotionally disturbed, he will manage to absorb what he can handle—and then some—and still remain psychologically intact. Children, while highly impressionable, seem to be as capable as adults of assimilating the

285

Greenberg &
Greenberg
Telling Your
Children About
the Holocaust

At What Age?: A Conversation

Jewish Living *recently asked Yael Danieli, a clinical psychologist and founder and director of the Group Project for Holocaust Survivors and Their Children, to discuss her views on teaching the Holocaust to children. Following is an excerpt from the interview, which was conducted by Jacob Helfman, himself a child of survivors.*

JEWISH LIVING: At what age do you think it's appropriate to teach a child about the Holocaust?

YAEL DANIELI: I think children of three, four, and five don't have the equipment to comprehend or make sense of the Holocaust in terms of their own world. A child should be at least seven, eight, or nine. However, the way you convey the material to children is really more important than whether you convey it. If you want real learning to take place, you have to address yourself to the age group. I think eleven is a very important age to teach it because that's also the age of identity crisis.

JL: What are the roles of the school and home in teaching the Holocaust?

YD: Ideally, knowledge of the Holocaust should start at home, like most intimate and important teaching. It should be done while everybody in the family is together. Then the child won't feel totally lonely with the stories. The parent shouldn't just hand the child a book to read. Parents should be available to discuss it, to talk about the feelings.

But there are also great advantages in school teaching, especially if there's a curriculum, because the school can cover many more aspects than a parent is competent to cover. However, the teacher doesn't replace the parent. When the child has a nightmare, it's Mommy who will take him in her arms, not the teacher.

JL: What would you tell parents who want to start talking about the Holocaust with their seven-year-old?

YD: You know your child best. If you listen to your child, are intimate with him, you will know how to talk about the Holocaust better than any expert. Better than I. I don't know your child.

Be responsible about learning the Holocaust for yourself; so when your child asks a question, you can answer knowledgeably. If you can't handle talking about the Holocaust, then don't, because you'll just confuse the child. Don't share only fantasies and fears with the child, because then he's faced with having to take care of you.

horrors of the Holocaust. Our children know quite a lot about the Holocaust, a thousand times more than we knew at their ages, yet they are all as happy and fun loving as any other normal child. The difference is that they have this little pocket of consciousness that can be summoned forth when necessary.

How can a child handle it as a Jew? If Passover, Sukkot, Chanukah, and Purim all teach us of God's special love for the Jewish people, what can we answer the child who asks why God let the Holocaust happen? Or worse, what can we say to the child who does not ask but who privately wonders: perhaps God does not exist; perhaps God no longer loves His people.

We personally reject the notion that the Holocaust was God's punishment of the Jews for their sins. We feel that within the framework of the Holocaust this classic response is inappropriate.

A child can intuitively understand that one can be a Jew of faith and commitment, with love for God and the Jewish people, even while wrestling with questions that have no answers, questions that trouble parents as much as their children. Equally important, a child can gain from the Holocaust a new sense of the unity of the Jewish people, of love for all its members and of the primacy of ethical responsibility.

Children experience all the redemptive joy of Passover, Purim, and Chanukah. They can travel to Israel—the modern Exodus experience. Thus feeling God's presence in their lives and experiences, they are better able to struggle with God's silence at Auschwitz.

Paradoxically, a child's knowledge of the Holocaust can lead to a feeling of hope and pride and even to a sense of great security as a Jew. We have survived such terrible destruction. We are alive and creative, we have a restored homeland and a hopeful future. What greater testimony can there be to the original promise that we would survive into eternity? The incredible resurgence of life spirit with which the Jewish people responded to the Holocaust has led to a reborn Israel and to the rebuilding of hundreds of yeshivot. Our daughter Deborah wants to learn Yiddish. Moshe and David stayed up all night on Yom Ha-Sho'ah last year to study the Torah.

Two years ago on a B'nai Akiva Simchat Torah retreat, after a discussion of the Holocaust, the children began to sing and dance to the song "Am Yisrael Chai"—the people of Israel live! Then they went into the chant: Mi Anachnu? Israel! Who are we? Israel!

When his turn came, our son began to chant: After Auschwitz? Israel! After Hitler? Israel! We will never forget his final words: Until the Messiah? Israel!

The fundamental statement of the Jewish people, that hope is not lost and that the promise will be kept, will surely find its place in the fertile, searching minds and souls of our young.

MILTON SCHWEBEL

Effects of the Nuclear War Threat on Children and Teenagers: Implications for Professionals

Using material gathered from interviews of 3,500 students ranging from the second grade to the second year of college, psychologist Schwebel suggests that continuing nuclear threat is a contributing factor to anxiety and other disorders noted among these youths. Characterizing the collective response of the youths as one of resentfulness and helplessness, Schwebel urges professionals to help young people become informed about the dangers and consequences of the threat of nuclear war and to deal with their reactions.

Mental health and education professionals, confronted with behavior that all too often is inexplicable, cannot help but wonder about the influence of the threat of nuclear war. Having hung over the heads of several generations of children during years which saw an increase in family disruption, drug abuse, and heightened loneliness, as well as a decline in the quality of behavior and scholastic performance in the nation's schools, the threat must be considered as a possible contributor to those costly changes in contemporary life. The studies reported here represent only preliminary attempts to inquire about that relationship.

After the height of the Berlin crisis in 1961, but while it was still very much part of the daily news, some 3,000 students were queried about the threat of war and about civil defense.[1] During the first week of the Cuban crisis in 1962 about 300 high school students were the subjects of a parallel study.[1] They were asked to write answers to the following questions: Do I think there is going to be a war? Do I care? Why? What do I think about fallout shelters? In the wake of the Three Mile Island nuclear plant accident in 1979, the responses of 368 elementary and secondary students, addressing parallel questions, were obtained.[2]

Source: Milton Schwebel, "Effects of the Nuclear War Threat on Children and Teenagers: Implications for Professionals." American Journal of Orthopsychiatry, Vol. 52, No. 4, October 1982, pp. 608–613. Copyright © 1974. The American Orthopsychiatric Association, Inc. Reproduced by permission.

In sum, these young people said that in the event of a nuclear war they would have the most to lose. Time and again, in response to questions about nuclear conflict, they said—and they said it bitterly—that they would pay the biggest price. They would be denied a chance to live, to love, to work, to bear children and raise a family. They would lose, they felt, the largest portion of their lives, and they would miss the opportunity to enjoy the pleasures they had hardly even begun to taste.

This is what came from some 3,500 students in response to questions. They were female and male; black, Hispanic, Oriental, and white; urban, suburban, and rural; and they were, at the time of questioning, in the second grade to the second year in college, though most were from fourth through twelfth grades and, in fact, in junior and senior high school.

The Responses

When young people were asked what they expected if there were to be a nuclear war, many of the responses were eloquent in their simplicity: "I will die." "We will all die." Most of those who had any hope that perhaps they themselves might live, nonetheless felt that their fate would be as bad as death because, as one said:

> If I was in school when the bomb was dropped and I hid under some wall or something, and I came out alive and came home and found my family gone, disappeared with everything, who'd want to live anyway?

But even when they thought that there might be a chance that they and their families would be fortunate enough to survive, they saw through that, too; they did in the early 1960s, and they do now. Even though they were confused and sometimes talked about wanting to be safe and hoping that they would be safe, and maybe there would be bomb shelters that would save them, nonetheless they said:

> Supposing my family was lucky enough, even if we lived, we couldn't last. Animals and plants would be destroyed, and if they weren't, they'd be radioactive. Who could eat them?

The younger subjects are especially vulnerable. In a recent study on the reaction of children to nuclear plant accidents, those in the intermediate grades were more fearful than the older students. The fourth graders dreaded the dangers of nuclear plant accidents more than the senior high students did, and were more insistent that the nuclear plants be closed. Understandably, the younger ones are even less informed about the nature and behavior of radioactivity than the older ones, and their comments reveal their naïvete. For example, they gave such responses as these, in connection with the consequences of nuclear plant accidents: "We'd probably have to run fast to stay ahead of the radioactivity." Or: "We should kill it, we should shoot it with a shotgun." But naive as these statements are, their images convey the terror these children associate with nuclear perils.

The ignorance of some of the older students just comes in more sophisticated packages. For example: "Bomb shelters should be available for us all." Sometimes the older student is speaking not so much out of ignorance about the dangers—ignorance about the possibility of survival—as out of an effort to deny the threat by postponing its likely occurrence to a distant future. "A nuclear war could break out," said one senior high school student, "in the far future."

The use of denial appeared in an interesting way some 20 years ago. When young people were questioned within the first three days after President Kennedy addressed the nation at the very height of the Cuban crisis in 1962, the world was teetering on the brink. Their responses about the expectation of nuclear war, compared with those of students a year earlier after the Berlin crisis had abated, revealed the use of denial under circumstances of helplessness in the face of great danger. Whereas after the Berlin crisis, in comparable groups of junior high school students, almost 50% expected there would be a nuclear war, now, a year or so later, during the Cuban crisis week at this time of great peril, fewer than 25% expected that there would be a nuclear war. The heightened threat of annihilation, it seems, nourished an irrational optimism, an insistent need to believe that there would be no war, nourished, that is, a denial of the obviously greater possibility of war.

When they were asked if they cared about the nuclear threat, their answers were emphatic:

Anyone who doesn't is insane.

Anyone who doesn't care is inhuman.

It's insulting even to be asked such a question.

It's a naive question.

Of course I care. Sometimes I cry when I think of it.

It keeps me awake at night.

It's so terrible I try not to think about it.

Generally they deal with their anxiety by trying one means or another to deny the existence of the threat:

If I allowed myself to think about it, I'd be miserable.

But when the thought of it, the knowledge of it, penetrated into their consciousness, then their reactions were manifold. They expressed bitter resentment against what some young people called the "old men who have lived and who control our government," and against adults in general for putting them in this position—bitter resentment against those who had had a full life and didn't really care about the young. For many of them knew what price they would have to pay. One high school student asked, "If I live, dare I bear children?" A sixth-grader in Tucson, which is ringed by missiles, said recently, in answer to the question about personal feelings: "I'm scared and mad."

Besides resentment, they feel helpless: "I'm outraged that the leaders can consider the world's population expendable," one high school junior said, "and there's just nothing I can do about it." The powerlessness that teenagers feel, at a time when they should be developing a sense of identity and a sense of mastery, came through frequently, no matter in what part of the country these questions were asked. The mix of emotions brings to mind a statement that Eleanor Roosevelt made many years ago: "War's greatest evil is the degradation of the human spirit."[3]

Living with the nuclear threat, feeling resentful, bitter, and helpless, are degrading to the spirit. They erode the hopes for a future. The feelings may well emanate from a form of double jeopardy. It is burden enough for human beings to discover, when we are young, that we have to die some day. We don't like it, we deal with it in many kinds of ways, but we have to face it. And we are reassured by the knowledge that we could really live a long life, by the fact that there are after all—and there always are—a lot of old people around. We are reassured even when some young children die. It's too much to deny children that reassurance—to expect them to accommodate to the threat of sudden extinction without paying a great price. One student said:

> It makes me start to think that the end of my time in life may not be as far off as I would like it to be.*

In order to deal with the anxiety, to deal with a life of double jeopardy, in a land, they feel, whose leaders and even adults don't care, they resort to different forms of accommodation. One of them is immediate gratification. If there's no tomorrow, they say, let me live for today:

> I'm constantly aware that any second the world might blow up in my face. It makes living more interesting.

Another one put it this way:

> It's terrifying to think that the world may not be here in a half-hour, but I'm still going to live for now.

We could ask what another adolescent, the victim of an actual Holocaust, would have said were she alive today. Anne Frank, living in a hideout with her own and another family—including the young man Peter, aged 17—wrote in her diary[5] after she had embraced Peter for the first time:

> Oh, Anne, how scandalous! But honestly, I don't think it is; we are shut up here, shut away from the world, in fear and anxiety, especially just lately. Why, then, should we who love each other remain apart? Why should we wait until we've reached a suitable age? Why should we bother?

*This and several other student comments were taken from a recent study of Beardslee and Mack.[4] The rest, from the author's studies, were obtained in 1961, 1962, 1979, and 1982.

A high school student, echoing Anne's thoughts, said in 1979:

> Sometimes, when I think that there may be no future at all, I feel just like letting myself go. Why wait?

Another response to the weight of anxiety that they carry reflects an illusion of power. We're not that much in danger, this point of view goes, because we'll win or we're smart enough to do them in before they get us. This macho attitude, which was hardly apparent in the early 1960s, and is even now the expression of only a small group of males, is very disquieting, especially after the Air Florida crash in Washington [1982]. In excerpts reported by the *New York Times* it was evident that the officers, especially the copilot, were acutely anxious about the ice on the wings. They laughed and joked as men do trying to mask their fears before combat. The copilot seemed to be suggesting that they leave the take-off line-up, and said, among other things:

> Boy, this is a losing battle here on trying to de-ice those things, it [gives] you a false sense of security, that's all that does.

On that afternoon another crew decided to leave its place on the take-off line to be de-iced again, but not this one. Would it have been unmanly to acknowledge and be guided by the fear? Would it have been weakness? To some of the subjects in our several studies, it seems, it is unmanly to show that one is frightened, to suggest that we are at an impasse, in a "no-win" situation, unmanly to hold any but a superior, controlling position, and trigger-ready to use our arms first. The illusion appears in the responses of some but not many sophisticated and academically able high school students. Still it is chilling to have them say:

> We have the intelligence to use the bombs only when absolutely necessary.

Another form of response to nuclear anxiety is a narcissistic one. A small but distinct portion of the 1979 sample of students exhibited this quality by responding in a noticeably different way from the 1960 sample. In the 1960s, in frequent responses, the young people would say in effect: We find it abhorrent that people should suggest that you keep a rifle in your bomb shelter so you can kill anyone who wants to come in. Over and over, with only rare exception, they found this suggestion terribly immoral. But today, in response to questions about nuclear plant accidents, shortly after one at Three Mile Island, there were some—a minority, but still too many—who said, "Why should I care? It didn't happen in New Jersey, it happened in Pennsylvania." Or: "Why should I care if something like this happens in California?" It is possible, of course, that the difference is simply the result of a sampling bias, either in the 1960 studies or the recent one. On the other hand, perhaps this indifference to the welfare of others reflects a wider social change in the past 20 years evidenced also by a self-interested disregard for others, first highlighted in connection with the Genovese murder which many witnessed but did not report to the police out of fear of "becoming involved."

The final reaction to the nuclear threat is what some students refer to as nervousness, tension, and pressure. In considering the sources of these symptoms, one is aware that a nuclear threat hardly exists in isolation. It coexists with a diversity of international and domestic conflicts, involving economic and political power, and personal ones as well. The threat is in fact a product of these conflicts and, again, contributes to them; yet because of its extraordinary nature, it seems likely to have a major impact on mental condition. In commenting about the world of the future, some juniors and seniors in New Jersey, in individual interviews, talked about problems at home and with relationships and said the following:

> I don't look forward to the future. We're all antsy these days. There's too much tension, too much hassle. I hope there will be a lot less unhappiness in the future. Maybe people will be more caring, but not until we have a terrible upheaval. There's so much tension now from the uncertainty in the world, maybe if there were no threats of war people would have friendlier interactions.

And one high school student in Massachusetts said:

> I refuse to bring up children in a world of such horrors and dangers of deformation.

For years many of us believed that sustained unemployment had a profound effect on mental health. This was no more than a hypothesis, however, until Brenner[6] in 1973 reported substantial evidence of the association between unemployment and such dire human consequences as suicide, mental hospital admissions, alcoholism, and, in fact, general mortality. It is knowledge such as this that leads us to wonder about and investigate the consequences of the sustained threat of nuclear disaster.

Collectively, then, young people tell us that the nuclear threat is too terrible to contemplate; when they do think about it, they feel resentful and helpless. They learn to cope with life today either by living for the moment, by persuading themselves that they are on the winning side—the surviving side, that is—by postponing the nuclear holocaust to a far-distant future, by putting hope in bomb shelters, by expecting part of this country and its people to survive, and, probably most of the time, by keeping the nuclear threat out of mind.

The Role of the Professional

Knowledge about the needs of school-aged children and adolescents is persuasive that the role of professionals (mental health specialists, educators, clergy, etc.) is first and foremost to reassure children in the most formidable way, by actions in support of reducing the nuclear threat, wherever they perform their role: in school or college; in church, synagogue, or mosque; in clinic, agency, or mental health center; in newspaper, publisher's, or TV programmer's office, trade union, art studio, and at home; wherever, the young need to know that there are adults struggling to see that reason prevails in human affairs—strong adults, whom they can depend upon, who will give them the feeling of caring about them, adults who can serve as models, adults who care as much about the nuclear threat as their children do, and who let them know that they're afraid and that they care and that they mean to do something about it. In other words, adults who don't themselves deny the peril, who have courage enough to work to change some prevailing practices in their own organizations—a tough job to do in most, if not all, organizations—and to include the nuclear threat as an issue central to their professional activity. The role means that they help young people acquire the knowledge and skills necessary for effective participation in community affairs.

What in particular should they learn? What attitude is constructive? What might be set as the criterion against which to evaluate the effectiveness of adult effort? To answer that, I want to highlight one particular feature that separates a small portion of the young whom I have studied from the rest. This group finds the arguments for nuclear armament incredible, and while they know the threat of a holocaust is very real, they find it so extraordinarily absurd that it too seems incredible. To their great advantage they are perceptive enough to recognize the perilous delusions; they understand that we are being victimized by claims that the world can tolerate a little nuclear war, and that we are more secure when we have the capacity to destroy the enemy ten times or a hundred times over rather than once. In terms of self-efficacy they are fortunate because they have not been deceived—have not allowed themselves to be deceived. Yet it is painful to realize that some of one's leaders and some adults are mad, just as it is terribly painful to discover that one's parents are mad. But not so painful as being caught up oneself in the irrationality, powerlessness, and accompanying degradation. It is better by far, because then one can come to understand what keeps the threat of a nuclear holocaust alive, and one can do something reasonable and effective about it.

People's inability or refusal to credit their senses is not new; others before us have resisted allowing themselves to make the unthinkable thinkable. Paul Fussell,[7] in his book on the First World War, commented that

> ... the problem for the writer trying to describe the elements of the Great War was its utter incredibility.

The world had never known industrialized mass trench warfare with its efficient mechanized butchery day in and day out over a few feet of land. The world had never known that form of absurdity. Writers could not assimilate what their senses were experiencing; it was too incredible to accept as real.

The more one resists accepting the absurd as an acceptable reality, in fact, the more one can resist the madness. Anne Frank wrote about the incredibility of the world she experienced. By contrast with the nuclear holocaust, and the carnage perhaps of billions, hers was a "minor" holocaust since only six million died, but it still leaves us stupefied with disbelief. Her diary entry[5] of

May 3, 1944, written three months before she was arrested and sent to Bergen-Belsen, contains the following:

> Yes, why do they make still more gigantic planes, still heavier bombs and, at the same time, prefabricated houses for reconstruction? Why should millions be spent daily on the war and yet there's not a penny available for medical services, artists or for poor people? Why do some people have to starve, while there are surpluses rotting in other parts of the world? Oh, why are people so crazy?

During the Cuban crisis, a few students asked how grown people, leaders, could be "so crazy," could bring the people of the world to the abyss. Referring to Hiroshima, one said in 1979:

> I remember feeling sad and bitter belonging to a race that would do such things.

For more than 35 years, since the Allied troops liberated the concentration camps, many people have asked themselves time and again: Why did we ignore the Holocaust? Why did the world sit it out? Surely professionals have been among them. If they are to serve young people in connection with the psychological effects of the nuclear threat, they would have to stop beating their breasts and wringing their hands because there is nothing that can be done about that Holocaust but study and remember it and assist the surviving victims. It can't be reversed, and we hardly wish, by example or other form of instructions, to encourage children to be obsessed with reversing the irreversible. However, we can abort the one that's in the making, as millions of people are seeking to do; and as professionals, we had better not be timid about it. A "limited" nuclear war is as mad and immoral as a limited Nazi Holocaust. To say it forcefully again and again, and to give young children the opportunity to see that for themselves, will validate their impulses and give them strength.

Despite differences among professional groups that work with the young, the similarities are considerable, and the principles proposed here are generally applicable. In brief they are:

1. Professionals see to it that they themselves are well-informed about the dangers, the potential consequences, their own reactions to the threat of nuclear war, and those of children and adolescents.
2. Professionals set as their goal that young people be informed, and be helped to deal with their reactions, through knowledge about adult action to protect them and the world from nuclear war, and about actions they might take appropriate to their age.
3. Professionals work at improving the methods of serving the young in this connection, among others in detecting those most in need of adult intervention.

To concretize these principles, we can start with the school setting and examine a number of actions that those working in the schools can take (and insofar as the particular measures permit, students and parents could profitably be involved): Get the professional organizations to include nuclear threat as one of their professional concerns incorporated in meeting agendas and in committee activities. Obtain support for in-service programs for school board members, school administrators, and teachers to acquaint them with the physical, biological, and psychological consequences of the threat. Encourage PTAs to institute programs of their own. Seek to establish, as a minimum, at least a two-week unit of work in science and social science for the program of every child in junior high schools to insure that they have the opportunity to learn the basic facts about the bombs and the threat. (Though it is difficult to estimate the extent to which those facts are already incorporated in programs in schools, one expert opinion[8] is that in all probability at most five percent, and more likely one percent of young people get some organized and systematic instruction in them—other than a current events discussion—but primarily in elective courses in the senior high school and usually for students who have other opportunities to learn about those matters.) Organize committees of teachers to consider ways of integrating material into the curriculum and to make some of the work interdisciplinary in nature. Include nuclear threat issues in auditorium programs, calling on organizations such as Physicians for Social Responsibility for appropriate resources. Work at the state level as well to develop interest in both experimental and collaborative programs on a state-wide basis. Work with publishers in connection with school texts; surely they need that. Use the arts related to peace and the threat of nuclear war, perhaps dances, rock concerts, and exhibits of graphic art. Develop a system to get acquainted with the new resources that are rapidly becoming available, such as those through organizations like Educators for Social Responsibility.*

The role of the educator in exposing social realities is, to make a gross understatement, not a simple one. There are many objections to educating children about the nuclear threat. First is the tendency to deny the threat. It hasn't happened so far, one adult reassured himself, forgetting, or perhaps just ignorant of the effort that had gone into preventing it from happening during past crises; countless people had worked at controlling the situation. Second, there will be claims that it will arouse the anxieties of the young. One student, when asked about that, said:

> We *should* be anxious. We've been lucky so far. How long can that go on? I put it out of mind, I guess we all do. We shouldn't.

Of course children are anxious, or at least they are made anxious when crises occur and when the news reports, if not the anxieties of adults themselves, set off their own alarm responses.[10] Third, there will be resistance on the grounds that there is no room in the curriculum. Recently, a student in a private secondary school that prides itself on the quality of its programs, said she

*See, for example, *The War Game,* a movie simulation of a nuclear attack on London; also, the Facing History and Ourselves Project, for access to information about events in history usually unavailable to students; both, and other materials, available through Educators for Social Responsibility, Box 1041, Brookline Village, Mass. 02147. Some general guiding principles in bringing information on nuclear dangers to children have been published previously.[9]

would really like to discuss the issues but her teachers explained there wasn't the time if they were to cover all the work. Anyone acquainted with the history of the American school since World War II can genuinely sympathize with the argument that we have dumped on schools every conceivable social problem, reduced the time available for the established curricula, and then blamed them for the declining student performance. We can hardly expect the schools to solve the problems of the nuclear threat. However, this topic is not some unrelated extra. It *is* the curriculum; it's science and history, literature and economics and drama. It's their life experience, a source of relevance and of motivation for students. The fourth objection is that the children are too young to comprehend anything about the nuclear threat, a strange objection considering that third and fourth graders have some horrible images about the dangers, even if distorted ones. However, we have reason to believe that any topic, no matter how complex, can be treated at a level appropriate to almost any age group.[11] Of course, as far as the early elementary grades are concerned, we would be particularly sensitive to their anxiety and would convey to them what efforts we are making to protect them. The fifth objection is an important one: it is unpatriotic to raise questions or encourage reading and discussion that lead students to find the policies of some of their government leaders to be irrational and indefensible. In fact, the contrary is correct; if our children are to develop as reasonable people and intelligent citizens, they need to be able to be critical. This, we must assert and insist, is the American way in its best tradition.

Children can be helped immeasurably by learning about competition and cooperation and, in particular, the psychological knowledge about what enhances a cooperative relationship. It is important for them to learn how essential it is to be able to appreciate the perspective of the other person, the other side, not only in international relations but in family relations as well, in relations between people, in relations between the sexes; to develop trust through social interaction, to have a stake in the other's welfare, a husband and a wife, as well as the Soviet Union and the United States.

So far applications have been made from the perspective of the school. There are obvious counterparts in other settings, e.g., the child, youth, and family serving organizations where mental health professionals can also make the nuclear war threat an ongoing agenda item at staff and association meetings and a consideration in assessing the sources of unaccountable anxiety. Professionals can also give special attention to the research necessary to identify those types of children who are particularly vulnerable to the periodic crises of brinkmanship. Some studies[10,12] are helpful in indicating the stressfulness of the early years when children feel particularly helpless, and in identifying conditions that appear to contribute to susceptibility to the deterioration of functioning, and those influences and conditions that seem to establish the capacity to cope with the environment and stress. Other studies[13] are suggestive of temperamental differences that may account for vulnerability. And some propose ways of training individuals in the use of coping skills.[14] (In addition, an early study by Escalona[15] addresses related issues.)

The application of the principles enumerated above, about addressing the psychological consequences of the nuclear war threat, is nowhere needed more than on television, that major educational force in the lives of children: and television, which is filled with so much brutality, need show no timidity concerning the brutality of programs devoted to nuclear war and the nuclear threat—only care that the programs explore the issues in rational ways with sound information and with no false hopes. But with realistic hope—hope based on ongoing programs of education for the people of our country, ongoing programs unrelentingly pursued. For if we survive, the nuclear threat that each new generation inherits is going to be a factor in the forseeable future. Instead of it being a source of terror and trauma, it can, with adult assistance and with adults as models, be transformed into social learning experiences that help rather than impede children's developing sense of identity, their mastery and strength.[16] That action could give them more reason to expect and to plan for a future, more desire to be an adult.

The young people who voice hope for survival, and who say they want to live and make a better world, echo the words Anne Frank[5] wrote the month before she was taken. She talked then about her circumstances, which were such as to shake anyone's ideals:

> It's really a wonder that I haven't dropped all my ideals, because they seem so absurd and impossible to carry out. Yet I keep them, because in spite of everything I still believe that people are really good at heart. I simply can't build up my hopes on a foundation consisting of confusion, misery, and death. I see the world gradually being turned into a wilderness. I hear the ever-approaching thunder, which will destroy us too. I can feel the sufferings of millions and yet, if I look up into the heavens, I think that it will all come out right, that this cruelty too will end and that peace and tranquility will return again.

Anne had only the heavens to look to, and a memorable work to write. We professionals must do more than look to the heavens.

References

1. M. Schwebel, "Nuclear Cold War: Student Opinion and Professional Responsibility," in *Behavioral Science and Human Survival*, ed. M. Schwebel (Palo Alto, Calif.: Behavioral Science Press, 1965).

2. M. Schwebel and B. Schwebel, "Children's Reactions to the Threat of Nuclear Plant Accidents," *American Journal of Orthopsychiatry* 51 (1981): 260–270.

3. E. Roosevelt, Introduction, in *The Diary of a Young Girl*, A. Frank (New York: Pocket Books, 1953).

4. W. Beardsley and J. Mack, "The Impact on Children and Adolescents of Nuclear Development," in *Psychological Aspects of Nuclear Development, Task Force Report #10* (Washington, D.C.: American Psychiatric Association, 1981), 64–93.

5. A. Frank, *The Diary of a Young Girl* (New York: Pocket Books, 1953).

6. M. Brenner, *Mental Illness and the Economy* (Cambridge, Mass.: Harvard University Press, 1973).

7. P. Fussell, *The Great War and Modern Memory* (New York: Oxford University Press, 1975).

8. J. Nelson, Professor of Social Education, Rutgers University, personal communication.

9. M. Schwebel, "Students, Teachers, and the Bomb," *National Education Association Journal*, in *Behavioral Science and Human Survival*, ed. M. Schwebel (Palo Alto, Calif.: Behavioral Science Press, 1963).

10. L. Murphy and A. Moriarty, *Vulnerability, Coping, and Growth* (New Haven, Conn.: Yale University Press, 1976).

11. J. Brunner, *The Process of Education* (Cambridge, Mass.: Harvard University Press, 1960).

12. E. Anthony, C. Koupernick, and C. Chiland, eds., *The Child in His Family* (New York: John Wiley, 1978).

13. A. Thomas and S. Chess, *Temperament and Development* (New York: Brunner/Mazel, 1977).

14. D. Meichenbaum and R. Cameron, "Stress-Inoculation Training: Toward a General Paradigm for Training Coping Skills," in *Stress Prevention and Management*, ed. D. Meichenbaum and M. Jarenko (New York: Plenum Press, 1982).

15. S. Escalona, "Children and the Threat of Nuclear War," in *Behavioral Science and Human Survival*, ed. M. Schwebel (Palo Alto, Calif.: Behavioral Science Press, 1965).

16. A. Bandura, *Social Learning Theory* (Englewood Cliffs, N.J.: Prentice-Hall, 1977).

EUGENIA H. WAECHTER

Children's Awareness of Fatal Illness

We can no longer accept the rationalization that since children do not understand the meaning of death they are unaware of its approach. In order to determine the extent of terminally ill children's awareness, Eugenia Waechter administered a standardized anxiety scale to sixty-four hospitalized children between
the ages of six and ten. Her findings indicate that despite efforts to shield a
child from knowledge of the seriousness of his or her illness, the anxiety of
those close to the child is likely to alter the emotional climate in the family to
such a degree that the child will develop suspicions and fears about his or her
condition. Often children will feel that their awareness of their condition is
knowledge they are not supposed to have, so the silence of those nearby isolates
children from needed support. Waechter dismisses the much-debated question
of whether a child should be told if a condition is terminal, as she argues that
the seriously ill child should be able to discuss any concerns or questions he or
she has.

No one's emotions are left untouched by the death of a patient, but the death of
the very young is particularly poignant because it speaks silently of unfulfilled
promise and destroyed hopes. To defend ourselves, we may unconsciously
avoid children with fatal illness and leave them largely alone to deal with their
fears and anxieties at a time when comfort, nearness, and sympathetic understanding are most important to them.

Researchers have been reporting that fatally ill children do not, as a rule,
experience or express anxiety about death until after the age of ten. And
they infer that until then, children are not aware of what is happening to
them.[1-4]

I didn't believe them.

To test my own hypothesis I set up a study based on the assumption that,
despite widespread efforts in our society to shield children with fatal illness
from awareness of their diagnoses or prognoses, the anxiety of meaningful
adults is conveyed to them through the false cheerfulness or evasiveness of
those around them. The child might believe that if he expresses fear of death
openly, he may risk loss of human contact. Therefore, research that relies on a
child's overt expression of anxiety or fears about death, mutilation, or separation might get an incomplete or distorted picture of the actual concerns of the
seriously ill child.

The subjects for my study were 64 children between the ages of six and ten, divided into four groups matched for age, race, social class and family background. In one group were three children with leukemia, six with neoplastic diseases, six with cystic fibrosis, and one with progressive septic granulomatosis. In the second group were children with a chronic disease, but good prognosis; in the third, children with a brief illness. These groups were tested in the hospital. Testing of the fourth group, non-hospitalized children, was carried out at an elementary school selected after the data had been completed for the three groups of hospitalized children.

A General Anxiety Scale for Children that measured concerns in many areas of living was administered to each hospitalized child.[5] Each child was also shown a set of eight pictures and asked for stories about the pictures to elicit indirect and fantasy expression of the child's concerns related to present and future body integrity. Four of the pictures were selected from the Thematic Apperception Test and four were specifically designed for the study.[6]

The General Anxiety Scale for Children

1. When you are away from home, do you worry about what might be happening at home?
2. Do you sometimes worry about whether your body is growing the way it should?
3. Are you afraid of mice or rats?
4. Do you ever worry about knowing your lessons?
5. If you were to climb a ladder, would you worry about falling off it?
6. Do you worry about whether your mother is going to get sick?
7. Do you get scared when you have to walk home alone at night?
8. Do you ever worry about what other people think of you?
9. Do you get a funny feeling when you see blood?
10. When your father is away from home, do you worry about whether he is going to come back?
11. Are you frightened by lightning and thunderstorms?
12. Do you ever worry that you won't be able to do something you want to do?
13. When you go to the dentist, do you worry that he may hurt you?
14. Are you afraid of things like snakes?
15. When you are in bed at night trying to go to sleep, do you often find that you are worrying about something?
16. When you were younger, were you ever scared of anything?
17. Are you sometimes frightened when looking down from a high place?
18. Do you ever worry when you have to go to the doctor's office?
19. Do some of the stories on radio or television scare you?
20. Have you ever been afraid of getting hurt?

21. When you are home alone and someone knocks on the door, do you get a worried feeling?
22. Do you get a scary feeling when you see a dead animal?
23. Do you think you worry more than older boys and girls?
24. Do you worry that you might get hurt in some accident?
25. Has anyone ever been able to scare you?
26. Are you afraid of things like guns?
27. Without knowing why, do you sometimes get a funny feeling in your stomach?
28. Are you afraid of being bitten or hurt by a dog?
29. Do you ever worry about something bad happening to someone you know?
30. Do you worry when you are home alone at night?
31. Are you afraid of being too near fireworks because of their exploding?
32. Do you worry that you are going to get sick?
33. Are you ever unhappy?
34. When your mother is away from home, do you worry about whether she is going to come back?
35. Are you afraid to dive into the water because you might get hurt?
36. Do you get a funny feeling when you touch something that has a real sharp edge?
37. Do you ever worry about what is going to happen?
38. Do you get scared when you have to go into a dark room?
39. Do you dislike getting in fights because you worry about getting hurt in them?
40. Do you worry about whether your father is going to get sick?
41. Have you ever had a scary dream?
42. Are you afraid of spiders?
43. Do you sometimes get the feeling that something bad is going to happen to you?
44. When you are alone in a room and you hear a strange noise, do you get a frightened feeling?
45. Do you ever worry?

The author marked the "yes's," counted them, and compared the scores of dying children with two control groups of hospitalized children. Dying children showed twice as much anxiety.

Source: Adapted from Sarason, S. B., and Others. *Anxiety in Elementary School Children.* New York: John Wiley & Sons, 1960.

Interviews with the parents of each hospitalized child were tape recorded to gather data on the variables that I believed would influence the quality and quantity of fatally ill children's concerns related to death. These were the child's previous experience with death, the religious devoutness within the family, the quality of maternal warmth toward the child and the opportunities the child had had to discuss his concerns or the nature of his illness with his parents, professional personnel, or other meaningful adults.

In one of the projective tests to elicit the fantasies of dying children ages six to ten the author asked them to tell stories about these pictures. They often gave the characters their own diagnosis and symptoms, and 63 percent related their stories to death.

Analysis of the results of the General Anxiety Scale showed that the total scores of the children with fatal illness were twice as high as the scores of the other hospitalized children, supporting the prediction that although only two of the 16 children had been told their prognoses, the generalized anxiety was extremely high in all cases.

Children with poor prognoses told substantially more stories relating to threat to body integrity than did the comparison groups, indicating that they were more preoccupied with death, and suggesting that the denial may not be an effective or complete defense in blocking awareness and in minimizing fear and anxiety in such an extreme situation.

Those children who were threatened with death discussed loneliness, separation, and death much more frequently in their fantasy stories, although none of them did so directly either to me or to other hospital personnel.

A most striking finding was the dichotomy between the child's degree of awareness of his prognosis, as inferred from his imaginative stories, and the parent's belief about the child's awareness. As mentioned previously, only two of the 16 subjects in the fatally ill group had discussed their concerns about death with their parents, yet the proportion of stories related to death told by these children was 63 percent. The children often gave the characters in the stories their own diagnoses and symptoms; they frequently depicted death in their drawings; and occasionally they would express awareness of their prognoses to persons outside their immediate family. This dichotomy suggests that knowledge is communicated to the child by the change in affect which he encounters in his total environment after the diagnosis is made and by his perceptiveness of other nonverbal clues. It also implies a deepening of isolation when the child becomes aware of the evasiveness which meets expression of his concern.

I found a highly significant correlation between the total score on the projective test and the degree to which the child had been given an opportunity to discuss his fears and prognosis. This supports the prediction that giving the child such opportunity does not heighten death anxiety; on the contrary, understanding acceptance and conveyance of permission to discuss any aspect of his illness may decrease feelings of isolation, alienation, and the sense that his illness is too terrible to discuss completely.

The degree of awareness, as influenced by the opportunities the child has had to discuss his illness with his parents, is influenced by the immediacy of the threat of death, or the chronicity of the disease, and by the extent to which the cooperation of the child is necessary in the treatment regimen. The immediacy to parents of the threat of the child's death affects both the intensity of anxiety communicated to the child and the quality of his particular concerns. Children with illnesses which run a fairly rapid course are not often allowed to learn of their diagnoses (adults consider this a protective measure), whereas children with cystic fibrosis or other chronic handicapping conditions may become more aware of and knowledgeable about both their medical regimens and their ultimate prognoses.

Many parents are deeply troubled about the best procedure to follow with their child. Frank discussion with their child about the possibility of imminent death would arouse, they believe, feelings they couldn't cope with. Although my purpose in the interview with the parents was to elicit specific information, it also gave parents an opening to discuss their feelings and concerns about their child's prognosis. Many parents asked for further interviews. They needed to discuss these questions with an empathetic counselor.

The data about religious instruction and previous experience with death lacked a variability suitable for drawing conclusions about specific effects of either. Trends, however, indicated that both influences do affect the response of children with fatal illness. The religious devoutness of parents does not seem to affect the quantity of anxiety as expressed by children, but does influence the quality of their concerns and the manner in which they cope with their fears. Previous experience with death may also influence children's fantasy about their own future, depending on the manner in which they were supported during the former incidents.

Some illustrations from the data may highlight these children's awareness of their diagnoses and prognoses and their fears of the future.

One six-year-old boy in the terminal stages of leukemia had discussed his illness with his parents in terms of "tired blood." He told me the following story after looking at a picture of a woman entering a room with her face in her hands:

> This is about a woman. She's somebody's mother. She's crying because her son was in the hospital, and he died. He had leukemia. He finally had a heart attack. It just happened . . . he died. Then they took him away to a cemetery to bury him, and his soul went up to heaven.
>
> This woman is crying. But she forgets about it when she goes to bed. Because she relaxes and her brain relaxes. She's very sad. But she sees her little boy again when she goes up to heaven. She's looking forward to that. She won't find anybody else in heaven—just her little boy that she knows.

This story illustrates this boy's awareness of the present and probable future, the influence of religious instruction on this fantasy and ways of dealing with his concerns, and the quality of loneliness and separation he is experiencing. His sense of helplessness to alter events and certainty about an inevitable future are apparent.

One eight-year-old girl with cystic fibrosis told the following story after examining a picture of a small child in bed with a nurse standing nearby:

> One girl was reading a book in the hospital. The nurse was over by the bed. The girl's name was Becky. She had the bad coughing. She had trouble with her lungs. She had lung congestion. The nurse is looking at her chart. Becky is thinking they're going to do an operation. Becky is only eight years old. She thinks they're going to hurt her and she doesn't want it. And they did give the operation. They gave her a sleeping shot. She didn't like shots. The same nurse always came in, because she knew what to do. Becky died. Then her mother came to see her and they told her she died. But the mother didn't like to hear that.

This story illustrates further the identification which was apparent as the children viewed the pictures, and in this case, the child's projection of her feelings onto the mother. In many instances, though the clues were purposely vague, the children attributed their own diagnoses and symptoms to the characters in their story and thus communicated their concerns and fears. Again, a sense of helplessness is apparent in this story—of inability to alter events, fear of mutilation and pain, certainty about an inevitable future, sadness and separation, yet reliance on those in her environment as giving the only assistance available to her.

Some comments in the stories not only indicated the helplessness a child may feel, but also reflected the view of an environment which is nonsupportive and on some occasions actively hostile, punishing, and impeding anxiety reduction and recovery of a sense of body integrity. A seven-year-old boy with cystic fibrosis commented in a story:

The little boy had to stay in the hospital because the doctor wanted it. He got a shot in the back; a big needle. He was scared of shots, and didn't want it. And the doctor did it hard. His lungs are gone—he can't breathe. His lungs got worse and he didn't get well. He died and he was buried with a big shovel.

These statements also communicate the child's fear, his perspective regarding treatment procedures, his sensing that body integrity and intactness cannot be regained, and his feeling of incompleteness in body image. Despondency regarding the future is poignant and loneliness is apparent in the concluding sentence.

In other stories, this boy made statements such as "They [hospital personnel] put a tent on him and freeze him, too," "The nurse turned off the lights and the door was closed, and he was lonesome and scared," "The little boy's very sick—he's mad too, because he wanted to go home." Statements like these illustrate some children's real concern about what they see as unsupportiveness in an environment they are incapable of escaping. They may not appreciate the therapeutic intent of hospital personnel and are preoccupied with fear, loneliness, and anger. Other statements this boy made, such as, "The boy is thinking he hopes he gets well—he's thinking he might not get well and die," highlight very real anxiety about nonbeing, though he had never discussed this overtly with anyone. When coupled with the loneliness he also expressed, it is possible to imagine his fear that he might die in an alien and hostile environment, separated from all those who care about him.

The sense of loneliness is accentuated because of the young child's sense of time as stretching interminably between parental visits. One six-year girl commented, "She has to be in the hospital for long days and never gets to see her Mommy and Daddy. She's very lonesome." She also said in one of her stories that the child character "got sick by not coughing up the mucus," which tells us not only that she has received instruction about her condition (cystic fibrosis), but also that young children often assume responsibility for the causality of their illness whether warranted or unwarranted and may feel guilt in addition to their fears.

Strong feelings of anger and hostility may also accompany the loneliness associated with the question, "Why did this have to happen?" And these feelings may be accentuated by sensed prohibitions against revealing suspicion or knowledge of the diagnosis. An eight-year-old girl who had very recently been diagnosed as having a malignant tumor of the femur and whose mother was determined that she should never be told the diagnosis, nevertheless indicated preoccupation with death in all eight of her stories, angrily concluding almost every story with the death of the main character and remarking, "And nobody cared—not even her mother!" Another story ended with the statement, "She was very lonesome before she died because nobody cared." Such statements give us insight into the manner in which evasiveness or uneasy cheerfulness may be interpreted by children. That this girl was aware of the meaning of the alterations in the emotional climate surrounding her can be seen in this story:

She's in the hospital, and the doctor is talking to her mother and father. She's sick—she's got cancer. She's very, very sick. She's thinking she wishes she could go home. She had an operation at the hospital, but she didn't want it because she wanted to get out of the hospital. This little girl dies—she doesn't get better. Poor little girl. This girl at the hospital—she has cancer. Her hip is swollen and her bone's broken. This little girl in the picture died, and then they buried her. And then she went up to heaven. She didn't like it there—because God wasn't there.

Conclusion

It seems clear that frequently denial or the protectiveness of adults may not be entirely effective in preventing children with fatal illness from experiencing anxiety or in keeping awareness of their diagnoses and probable prognoses from them. The question of whether a child should be told that his illness is fatal is meaningless; rather questions and concerns which are conscious to the child threatened with death should be dealt with in such a way that the child does not feel further isolated and alienated from his parents and other meaningful adults. There should be no curtain of silence around his most intense fears. These feelings of isolation may also be relieved by efforts designed to keep the child closer, both spatially and emotionally, to others on pediatric wards.

Support must also be made available for them during and following actual encounters with death on pediatric wards. They need support that allows introspective examination of attitudes and fears related to death in general and to the death of children in particular.

Notes

1. A. G. Knudson and J. M. Natterson. "Participation of Parents in the Hospital Care of Their Fatally Ill Children," *Pediatrics* 26 (Sept. 1960): 482–490.

2. J. R. Morrissey. "Death Anxiety in Children with a Fatal Illness," in *Crisis Intervention*, ed. H. J. Parad (New York: Family Service Association of America, 1965), pp. 324–338.

3. J. M. Natterson and A. G. Knudson. "Observations Concerning Fear of Death in Fatally Ill Children and Their Mothers," *Psychosomatic Medicine* 22 (Nov.–Dec. 1960): 456–465.

4. J. B. Richmond and H. A. Waisman. "Psychologic Aspects of Management of Children with Malignant Diseases," *American Journal of Diseases of the Child* 89 (Jan. 1955): 42–47.

5. S. B. Sarason et al. *Anxiety in Elementary School Children* (New York: Wiley 1960).

6. H. A. Murray. *Thematic Apperception Test* (Cambridge, Mass.: Harvard University Press, 1943).

ROBERT A. BECKER

Portrait of Jen:
Memories from
The Children's
Cancer Ward

This concluding selection examines the death of a child from a parent's vantage point. Becker lays bare intensely personal reactions as he reconstructs his young daughter's struggle with cancer and recounts the events of what, suddenly, became Jennifer's last day of life. His account evokes for the reader the powerful emotions associated with this most threatening of all deaths: the death of one's child.

A nurse on the floor ushered us to a room and handed me a small, open-backed gown for Jen to wear.

"Leave my clothes on," the child insisted. "I want my shirt on. Don't take my shoes off." Jen was terrified. It was our seventh visit to Children's Hospital in three weeks, visits which invariably began in the outpatient clinic on the first floor with a technician pricking her finger for a blood sample, followed by a doctor's probings and palpations. The more recent trips, like this one, often turned into a two- or three-day stay in the hospital, much to Jen's growing dismay.

Ten months earlier, when Jennifer was 20 months old, her mother and I noticed a lump on her side after lifting her from the tub one Sunday night. She had been lethargic for a couple of weeks before that, but the pediatrician said she was probably anemic and prescribed iron pills. After the swelling appeared, though, we took her to Alexandria Hospital where they operated and discovered neuroblastoma, the most common form of solid-tumor cancer that strikes infants and toddlers.

In the months that followed, we had taken her to a private oncologist for chemotherapy every other week, and to the radiologist every day for the first two months. We were lucky. The combination of drugs and radiation had worked and produced what the doctors said was "complete remission," which simply meant there was no trace of the disease. It was not to be confused with a "cure."

Still, we had begun to allow ourselves the luxury of believing she just might be cured anyway, when suddenly the lethargy, the failing appetite, the constant crying from the discomfort—and the tumor—all reappeared. A relapse.

Realizing there was little he could do, the oncologist, a rather large man with an air of determined detachment, arranged for Jen's admission to the fourth floor of Children's Hospital—the children's cancer ward.

But before Jen's first appointment at Children's, this bitter, abrupt change started me on the last stretch of a psychic marathon, a race known to countless families of the cancer-stricken—The Miracle Chase. I am talking now of hope and fear. Sunrise, sunset, the dread remains, the hope remains. I placed phone calls all around the country to leading hospitals and clinics. Was there any new treatment, any drug that looked hopeful? Desperate for help, I found none. Most likely, there was none then to be found. There still isn't.

The fourth floor at Children's brims with activity, at least during the day. Youngsters on short, spindly legs waddle along the length of the hallway like small penguins. Assorted toys, mostly the bulky wooden types found in pediatricians' waiting rooms, litter the hall at odd intervals, abandoned by youngsters whose interests have been diverted or who have been taken elsewhere for treatment.

At her insistence, I carried Jen up and down the long hallway pointing out other youngsters in their beds and trying to coax her with, "Look how that little boy is resting in his bed; wouldn't you like to take a little rest, too?"

"No, I want you to carry me," she shot back.

As a concession to get her to stay in bed, my wife Carolyn and I spent most of the day reading Jen's favorite books to her over and over. Periodically, someone would come in either to prick her finger, take her temperature or check the intravenous fluid tube that had been inserted once we got her settled down. By late afternoon, Jen finally fell asleep and a nurse offered to stay with her while we went downstairs to get something to eat. But we did so reluctantly, knowing Jen was never receptive to strangers in the first place and fearful of losing any time with her in the second.

When we returned about a half-hour later, there was Jen in the woman's arms, feebly smiling up at her. The whole scene went through us like a knife. Jen wanted so much to be near someone. She was so frightened at being alone that, surprisingly, she found comfort in this kindly stranger and actually asked the nurse to hold her. Happily, the nurse had the good sense and kindness of heart to pick her up, I.V. and all, and rock her—a gesture we would never forget.

That night Carolyn and I slept in shifts, watching over Jen when she woke to throw up bile. She didn't really have the strength to do anything more than simply turn her head. So we had to watch her carefully and occasionally slide a small stainless steel bowl beside her mouth to avoid soiling the bedsheets.

During the night, a thought kept recurring to me. It was something one of the doctors had said some nine or ten months ago, back in Alexandria Hospital. I had asked him why it was that Jen didn't seem to complain very much about her discomfort and pain. He said, "Children are often the easiest patients to treat simply because small youngsters in these circumstances, those with severe and sometimes painful illnesses like Jennifer's, don't know enough about life to complain. For them, this is what life is all about: they haven't yet experienced enough to know that life is not all pain. This is part of life and they just accept it."

The next morning, I sat on the edge of the bed and started to read a new book I had picked up, Gay Talese's *The Kingdom and the Power,* while Carolyn slipped downstairs for a quick breakfast and Jen slept. I read only enough that morning to learn that *New York Times* reporter Tom Wicker's 106-paragraph on-the-spot report of the assassination of John F. Kennedy would be saved "by hundreds, perhaps thousands of readers" and that students and historians would be reading it again and again a half-century later. I wondered if 50 years from now anyone would give a damn that Jen died of cancer or even that she had lived at all.

But my thoughts were interrupted by our doctor who came into the room at that point to examine Jen. She was awake now and lay quietly as he breathed on his stethoscope and briskly rubbed it on his jacket to warm it before he touched her chest with it. For the first time, I thought I noticed some irregularity in her breathing as he bent over her; he stared at the wall as he listened.

"There's something in her lungs," he said. He wanted to put her in an oxygen tent. While the oxygen equipment was brought in, he wanted to have her X-rayed to see what that "something" was.

I wasn't prepared for all this. "Now wait a minute," I said. "She's really pretty uncomfortable. I don't see what an X-ray is going to accomplish."

The doctor tried to reassure me he only wanted to take a look to see if anything was obstructing her breathing.

This was all a little too sudden for me, but I reluctantly agreed.

Jen was difficult for them to handle in the X-ray department. They asked me to sit her up, turn her on her side and hold her head. Jen didn't want any part of this. "Daddy, my tummy hurts," she cried.

I was getting angry and impatient with the technicians. "Look, I'm sorry, but she can't sit up. You're not going to get her to sit up. Try something else. Let's get this over with."

I felt my eyes start to burn as I spoke now and I fought to hold back the tears. "She's dying," I said feebly. It was 10:30 A.M.

When we returned to the room, the oxygen tent was in place, draped over the top of the bed. An oxygen bottle was installed at the head of the bed.

To try to make Jen happy and comfortable, I read her a book, "Raggedy Ann and Fido." She paid close attention to the story, watching the pictures intently as I read. Midway through the story, she said, "Daddy, you hold me." That request has haunted me ever since she said it. I was terribly torn. There wasn't anything I wanted to do more than to pick her up. But I hesitated. I thought about the I.V. and the oxygen tent. It was supposedly doing her some good. So I didn't pick her up. Like a damn fool I went on with the story, trying to divert her attention.

She watched me read and looked at the pictures again as I held the book up for her. She even mumbled, "Uh-huh," or "Uh-uh," to questions I'd ask her about the story. Or I'd leave out key words in sentences and she'd fill them in.

I again noticed her starting to have trouble breathing. I reached under the tent and tried to elevate and arch her back and maybe turn her on her side to face Carolyn. I cranked the bed up a bit, hoping that by raising her head slightly, it might ease her breathing. Nothing helped.

"I'm going to get the doctor to make sure there's nothing wrong with her," I said to Carolyn on my way out.

I saw our doctor talking to nurses halfway down the hall, near the nurses' station. "Hey, Doc," I called. "Come here quick." He turned and started for me at a quick trot and followed me into the room. "Doc, she's not breathing right. What's going on?"

He examined her with his stethoscope but I couldn't detect any show of concern on his face. I don't remember exactly what he said, but I think he must have known what was happening.

Carolyn was standing right behind me and I began to talk to Jen. I held her right arm, the one with the I.V. still plugged into it, and stroked her forehead.

I kept telling her, "Daddy's going to make you feel better, baby. Everything's going to be all right." I thought perhaps she was getting upset or excited: her breathing became even more irregular. Then her attention turned away from me. She had been looking at me, but now she looked straight ahead. Her breaths began getting shorter and closer together, like gasping.

I still wasn't quite fully aware of how serious things were at this point. Somewhere along the line, the doctors had told us that we would be told when Jen entered the terminal phase.

I looked across the bed at the doctor. He wasn't doing anything. Just standing there looking at her. I looked back down at Jen and she was struggling for breath now.

Excited now, I shouted, "Hey! Hey, man! Doc!" I was waving my arms at him, directing him to the door. "Go get something. Go, man. Right now!"

He started for the door, then he stopped and started to say, "Well, Mr. Becker . . ." and then started to leave again.

Before he got past the foot of the bed, though, I motioned him back. I knew there was nothing he could do and I wanted him to stay there. I guess I was half hoping there might be some last-minute thing he could do. Maybe, too, I expected some help from him, for me.

There was a sound in Jen's throat. I felt Carolyn's fingers grasp my shoulders. Small flecks of saliva seeped through her teeth, and she gritted her teeth. Her gaze was still fixed ahead.

That tore me. "This is it," I thought, "Holy good God, man, this is it!" I could feel everything slipping away.

I began to plead, "No, no, Jen. Don't. No, no, Jen. . . ." I looked up at the doctor. "Doc, what's happening?" He had a deadpan look on his face. A nurse must have heard the commotion because I thought I heard the door shut.

Carolyn was vigorously patting my shoulders, trying to calm me down. She was saying something, but I didn't hear her.

I felt the sting in my eyes. "No, Jen. Don't. Don't go, Jen. Stay with me now. Don't go." And then her eyes rolled back. There was silence for a couple of seconds. Then a sudden tensing of her features, almost like shivering from a chill. Then she relaxed. In that split second, I looked up and asked the doctor what time it was.

"Eleven twenty-five," he replied.

"I want to remember that."

For a few minutes, it was totally quiet in the room. None of us said a word. We all just looked at Jen.

Inside, a monologue was going on, telling all the other parts about what had just happened.

"Man, this really happened," the voice said. "She's gone. That's the end of the line." Then it all began to cave in, all at once.

Carolyn was crying now, and I was coming unglued. I started talking to Jen again, quietly, almost whispering. "Jen, Jen. Come on, Jen. Jen . . ." Her lips were only slightly parted. Her eyes were half open. They were different, though. Not like the eyes of people who are alive. There was no contraction of the pupils. There was absolutely nothing.

"This is my child," I kept thinking. "How the hell does this happen? It's unbelievable something like this could really happen."

The thought of death had never completely registered in my mind; the finality of it, I mean. It's something the mind blocks out on its own. We had become accustomed to dealing with life on a minute-to-minute basis, almost totally without regard to what had passed or what lay ahead. But now, suddenly in the past few moments, all was very different and it all came rushing in on us, crushing us, that it has happened. This is it.

The doctor had left the room unnoticed by either of us until we finally stood up. Carolyn held my arm with both hands and helped me to stay calm long enough to say a prayer at the foot of the bed.

We left to call the family while the nurses unplugged the I.V. and tried to make Jen look comfortable. Everyone reacted predictably, crying at first, then trying to comfort us and finally saying they'd all come down together the next day.

After the calls we went back to the room. The nurses were still there.

"Say, look," I said to their somber faces. "I'm really sorry about coming unglued. I guess I really wasn't quite prepared."

"Oh, please don't apologize, Mr. Becker," said one nurse. "You have to do whatever you feel." She was right.

We stayed with Jen for the next three hours. Strangely, it seemed just like minutes. Neither of us was tense any longer. We were comfortable with Jen now. We were no longer anxious about the tumor spreading or causing pain and discomfort. She didn't murmur or cry out or turn from side to side hoping to avoid the nagging pain. She just rested comfortably now.

Shortly after 3 P.M., we left the hospital. I looked up at the fourth floor window of Jen's room.

"I'm leaving her up there," I thought. "We're leaving her behind." And it was very strange for me, suddenly, going somewhere without Jen. I looked over at Carolyn and knew from the tears that she sensed the same loneliness. I imagined what Jen would feel being left like this. Even before she got sick, we rarely went out without her. She had a great fear of being separated from Carolyn.

When we got home, Carolyn went into our room to lie down while I went to Jen's room. I began to hear Carolyn crying softly, the sound muffled by the pillow. I hung my head over Jen's crib and let it all out, sobbing. Carolyn heard me and came in to comfort me. It was odd. Neither of us wanted the other to grieve. It hurt each of us to see the other cry.

Sun and moon. Time goes. Four years have passed since Jen died. The sorrow sears less. But an intense need to keep her memory alive remains. I dread that one day she might fade from memory and the incidents of her life and death drift into haziness. Recollections have already become clouded with the subsequent births of Krista, now three, and Kathleen, just turned three months. Krista, it seems, is an extension of Jen. The two are virtually indistinguishable in photographs. She delights in the same games we played with Jen so long ago, though Krista is a good deal more aggressive and certainly more bold about life than Jen.

And, as I watch Krista and her sister grow and pass through the stages of maturity Jen had before them I'm constantly reminded of a clipping someone handed me shortly after Jen died. I never found where it came from, but it was by a Richard J. Needham writing about relationships between parents and their children.

He said: "My favorite philosopher, George Santayana, had many distinguished friends, among them the Marchesa Iris Origo. When her little boy died, he wrote to her: 'We have no claim to any of our possessions. We have no claim to exist; and as we have to die in the end, so we must resign ourselves to die piecemeal, which really happens when we lose somebody or something that was closely intertwined with our existence.'

"This would seem a wise attitude to take toward children. They are not possessions, we have no claim on them, they owe us nothing. They are lent to us, you might say, and are taken away by death or, more commonly, by the natural process of growing up."

structured exercises

Before beginning these exercises, please read "Note to the Instructor" on page xxi.

1. A class session can be devoted to children's literature. Bring a large selection of children's books that deal with death or have students each bring two books they have read. Divide the class into groups of five. Circulate the books within each group so each person can read all the books in the group. Allow twenty minutes for reading them, and have the groups discuss their reactions to the books. Did they find them enjoyable? Realistic? Was the dialogue realistic? Were the characters credible? How threatening was the death? Was there any resolution for the grief? Would students read the book to a child? Why or why not? Did they agree with the conception of death?

2. Five members of the class can role play the following situation before the rest of the class:

The parents of a seven year-old leukemic boy are meeting with a health care team consisting of the child's physician, nurse and social worker. The child has reentered the hospital in the terminal phase of his painful illness; he has previously experienced three spontaneous remissions and returned home, only to fall dangerously ill and return to the hospital each time. A fourth remission is not expected. The group must decide whether to begin the child on an expensive new experimental treatment. Although the treatment is not expected to be able to control the disease for the child, it might keep him alive for up to six months longer, and its use in this case would add to medical knowledge and possibly improve the survival rate of other sick children. However, the parents and the two younger brothers of the child have prepared themselves for his death at each return to the hospital. The emotional strain of the dramatic recoveries is reflected in the worsening relationship between the parents and in behavior problems in the

313

children. The father is working a second job to help pay the medical bills. The mother alternates between wanting to keep her child alive at all costs and wanting to release him from pain. The doctor is committed to saving and prolonging life if at all possible, especially in the case of a child. The nurse has cared for the child during each hospitalization and considers herself to have the primary responsibility for caring for the child. The social worker has given the parents financial counseling and has tried to give them psychological support during the long illness.

The five students are to reach a group decision as to whether to prolong the child's life. After the decision has been made, each should describe to the class how he or she felt about his or her role as the discussion progressed. Then the class as a whole should discuss their reactions, answering the following questions:

    a. What criteria did the group use to reach the final decision?
    b. What additional information would you have liked to have had?
    c. Should anyone else have been included in the decision making?
    d. What factors contributed most to the difficulties in making the decision?

questions

1. Define the following terms. Those marked with an asterisk are terms that the authors of the selections expect readers to know. If you are not familiar with the meanings of those terms, consult a dictionary.

Koocher

    Wechsler Intelligence Scale for Children
    preoperational stage
    concrete-operational stage
    formal-operational stage
    *conservation task
    personification
    magical thinking

Agee

    *concussion

Greenberg and Greenberg

    Holocaust

Schwebel

    nuclear anxiety
    narcissism

Waechter

    *anxiety scale
    *Thematic Apperception Test
    *cystic fibrosis
    *neoplastic disease

Becker

    *oncologist
    neuroblastoma
    *remission

2. a. The children's statements, "The First Time Somebody I Knew Died," that appear at the beginning of this chapter represent individual attempts to make sense of death. Examine each selection, separating accurate from inaccurate information, and hypothesize how the ideas were formed.

   b. Find evidence that would lead you to classify the children's ideas about death into one or another of Koocher's categories.

3. As Aunt Hannah's attempts at explanation demonstrate, the child is likely to misinterpret statements in a way that may be carried into later life either as factual errors or, more subtly, as attitudes. List euphemisms that parallel the child's notion of death (a) as reversible, (b) as sleep, and (c) as a person.

4. a. *A Death in the Family* and *My Grandpa Died Today* both portray a young boy faced with the death of a close family member, a father in the former and a grandfather in the latter. Though this chapter presents only a small part of *A Death in the Family,* much of the mourning process is depicted. Compare and contrast the grief reactions of the boys in the two works. Consider the degree of loss, the practical implications of the loss, the "appropriateness" of the death, the information each boy has been given about the death, and each boy's efforts to cope with his loss.

   b. Using the information from this chapter, write a brief explanation to (i) Rufus and (ii) Catherine explaining that their father has died.

5. Recalling the discussion of grief and mourning by Lindemann and by Bowlby in Chapter Three, list the factors in the manifestations of grief that you would expect to differ in the case of a child mourner. What systems of support would you suggest?

6. The professionals represented in this chapter advocate honesty with children about death, even with those children who are terminally ill. Yet these professionals do not necessarily equate honesty with a decision to inform a child of his or her terminal diagnosis. Outline the factors to be considered and the kind of information to be given if a child is to be informed of a terminal diagnosis.

7. Eugenia Waechter discusses a number of reactions that terminally ill children express either verbally or nonverbally. List these reactions and compare them to the reactions of a dying adult as outlined by Kübler-Ross in Chapter Two.

8. a. To what extent should the Holocaust, the nuclear threat, and related topics be part of the elementary school curriculum? Outline a classroom unit for one such topic, using information presented by Milton Schwebel and Blu and Irving Greenberg.

   b. Consider arguments against such instruction. What issues do you think are involved?

9. a. Re-read Robert Becker's account of his young daughter's death in "Portrait of Jen." Identify as many concepts and behaviors as you recognize from your study of articles in this and earlier chapters.

   b. List the ways in which the death of a child challenges our notions of appropriate death.

projects for further study

1. Interview three children on the subject of the death of a favorite pet. Allow their discussion to range freely, and ask questions only when necessary to continue the discussion. Analyze each set of interview responses in terms of the developmental stages outlined by Gerald Koocher.

2. Using the card catalog of your local children's library, compile a bibliography of children's literature in which the primary subject is death. Expand the bibliography through annotation: include such details as date of publication, developmental level of audience, point of view from which the story is told, conceptualization of death, religious or cultural setting, object of death, portrayal of the mourning reaction.

3. Much as attitudes about death and dying are rooted in childhood, so are attitudes toward the aging process and the aged shaped at an early age. To explore children's attitudes toward aging, ask five or six children, "Who is the oldest person you know?" and "What do they most like to do?" Then have each child draw a picture of that person involved in his or her favorite activity. Ask each child to tell you about the picture. Compare the pictures and the oral reports that you gather from the children. Note both the similarities and the differences in their accounts and suggest possible reasons for each.

for further reading

Anthony, E. J., and C. Koupernik, eds. 1973. *The child in his family*. Vol. II: *The impact of disease and death*. New York: John Wiley.

Anthony, S. 1972. *The discovery of death in childhood and after*. New York: Basic Books.

Bowlby, J. 1969, 1972, 1980. *Attachment and loss*. Vol. I: *Attachment*. Vol. II: *Separation*. Vol. III: *Loss*. New York: Basic Books.

Coerr, E. 1977. *Sadako and the thousand paper cranes*. New York: Putnam.

Furman, E. A. 1974. *A child's parent dies: Studies in childhood bereavement*. New Haven, Conn.: Yale University Press.

Grollman, E. A., ed. 1967. *Explaining death to children*. Boston: Beacon Press.

Kübler-Ross, E. 1983. *On children and death*. New York: Macmillan.

Lindgren, A. 1975. *The brothers Lionheart*. Leicester, England: Brockhampton.

Miles, M. 1971. *Annie and the old one*. New York: Little, Brown.

Mills, G. C., R. Reisler, Jr., A. E. Robinson, and G. Vermilye. 1976. *Discussing death: A guide to death education*. Homewood, Ill.: ETC Publications.

Romero, C. E. 1976. Children, death and literature. *Language Arts* 53:674–678.

The School Counselor. 1977. ("Special Issue on Death") 24(5) 305–384.

Smith, D. B. 1973. *A taste of blackberries*. New York: Thomas Y. Crowell.

Stein, S. B. 1974. *About dying*. New York: Walker and Co.

Wolf, A. 1973. *Helping your child to understand death*. New York: Child Study Press.

Wass, H., and C. A. Corr. 1982. *Helping children cope with death: Guidelines and resources*. Washington, D.C.: Hemisphere Press.

Wolfenstein, M., and G. Kliman, eds. 1965. *Children and the death of a president*. New York: Doubleday.

CHAPTER *five*

Choices and Decisions in Death

Given an extended period of dying, would you prefer to be at home or in a hospital? Would you want to be maintained on life-extending machinery? To what extent? What do you want to happen to your body after death? Can you imagine any cause that might motivate you to sacrifice your life in martyrdom or that would motivate you to sacrifice your life in an altruistic act? Are there any conditions under which you might choose to end your own life? How would you like to spend your last decade?

The discovery of the role of decision in death is not recent, but the range of possible choices is continually expanding, as is the range of choices for improving the quality of life. Treatments of the element of personal decision in death in earlier centuries occasionally included references to martyrdom, but most often they were limited to a discussion of suicide, an option that was rarely considered responsible.

Suicide

Apart from isolated accounts of honorable death, as in battle, both Greek and Roman culture generally opposed suicide on ethical grounds. In Athens, for instance, those who attempted suicide were punished with the removal of one hand, generally the hand that had been instrumental in the attempt. The milder Roman censure of suicide was strengthened with the influx of the Christian tradition, which judged suicide an offense against the commandment "Thou shalt not kill."

From the Middle Ages through the eighteenth century, penalties against suicide continued in the form of confiscation of property, degradation of the corpse, and prohibition against burial in consecrated ground. Though the legal sanctions against suicide have fallen into disuse, the social censure against a suicide attempter or the bereaved "survivor" of a suicide continues.

Not until the nineteenth century was suicide studied as a medical problem, often as a form of insanity. In 1897, Emile Durkheim began to study suicide within the context of societal disorganization and alienation. More recently, psychology has taken the study of suicide into an investigation of the nature of personal motivation and levels of intention, thereby expanding the study of self-murder into one of self-destructive behaviors.

Elective Death

The debate over the role of decision in death extends far beyond the issue of suicide and frequently centers on the right of the dying patient to determine the manner of his or her own death. Euthanasia, which once meant simply "the good death," is now associated with elective death in the face of imminent natural death. In this context, the ethical dilemmas that were posed with the issue of suicide are multiplied; with euthanasia, in the sense of voluntary death, the responsibility for decision usually extends beyond the dying person to those around him or her.

Implicit Choice

Choices related to death are made regularly both in the social context and in the personal realm. In the larger framework of society, the decision to enter a war, no matter how just the cause, to impose the death penalty on a convicted criminal, or even to accelerate the progress of environmental pollution is an exercise of choice. Likewise, the personal decision to undertake a rescue operation in spite of personal hazard or even to persist in a life-endangering behavior challenges mortality.

Reverence for Life

Decisions in death, and their counterpart, reverence for life, force a reexamination of ethical principles. The abilities to create living organisms under laboratory conditions, on the one hand, and to terminate prenatal life through abortion, on the other, call for an evaluation of responsibility in the generation and termination of life. Ethical issues that once may have been reserved for the philosopher have entered the domain of the scientist and press with immediacy on us all. Confronted with the intubation of the helpless who, if conscious at all, seem aware only of pain and hopelessness, how is one to weigh the relative merits of the quality of life against its quantity, or, as some have suggested, against its costs—both psychological and financial? Any study of elective death must draw freely on the best available information in all disciplines. In the future, the number of choices associated with death is destined to increase, and a continued study of death and dying can make implicit choices *explicit.* Continued examination is not without its hazards, however. We might ask what the effects of an intellectual familiarity with death will be. Will the study of death and dying be popularized to the point of defeating its purpose by exploiting innate fears? Or, in taming death, will we regularize decisions with mundane practicality and rob death of its mystery? And, finally, will the study of death enrich living?

Overview of the Chapter

Chapter Five brings together readings from moral philosophy, psychology, and literature in a review of the range of life and death decisions an individual may encounter. The Encounter presents a news account of an elderly couple facing one such decision. Technological progress has certainly multiplied the number of choices a given individual is likely to confront, but as the opening selection drawn from Plato's *Apology* illustrates, estimating the worth of a life without freedom was a task Socrates faced in 399 B.C. Joseph Fletcher, a medical ethicist, takes up the task of evaluating life in "Elective Death," with the question, "If we have a right to initiate a life deliberately, may we not terminate one?" He develops his case in the context of temporal existence, warning that his results may be at odds with those who begin with a belief in life as the gift of a Creator rather than as a human right. As Fletcher articulates his views clearly, noting qualifications at each step, he provides a framework for a discussion of *chosen dying*.

Though essentially individual choices, many of the decisions have implications for public policy. Philosopher Michael Bayles expands the discussion in "The Value of Life—By What Standard?" He moves the discussion from the hypothetical mode back to the experiential world as he extracts implicit value statements from examples of current medical decisions. Addressing nurses as the professionals who can make a significant impact on the qualities that give value to closing life, Bayles argues that life is not intrinsically valuable. He focuses on the nexus formed by the sometimes conflicting standards for quality as defined by doctor, patient, and hospital staff. In speaking to the interpretation of existing standards for nursing practice, Bayles provokes much-needed discussion as the contemporary individual recasts enduring values in a form responsive to the potential afforded by new technologies.

Having taken consideration of the choices available at the societal level, Anne Sexton, a modern American poet, draws the focus back to the individual's facing a specific choice—that of suicide. In "Suicide Note," the persona explores from the inside the decision to die, questioning the purity of motives and trying, at all costs, to evade narcissism.

It is not clear that the choice of death can ever be entirely objective. Edwin Shneidman, a thanatologist known for his work in suicide prevention, argues against the romanticization of death and suicide. In "The Enemy," he expands his consideration from the conscious choice of suicide to include a range of subintentioned deaths where unconscious motivation may result in the truncation of life. Shneidman questions not only the choice made but also the basis on which it is made.

Life and death choices imply a range of alternatives, a broader range than is normally considered. This chapter closes with two approaches to living and dying, each offering a contrast to the study in earlier chapters. Concern over the quality of life in the final stages has led to the rapid development of the hospice movement. In "Hospice: A Caring Community," hospital administrator Kenneth P. Cohen describes the growth of alternative models for terminal care. Although the original British Hospice was a separate demonstration facility, Cohen shows how the hospice philosophy has penetrated mainstream medical care to the point that hospice units are now being frequently established within acute care hospitals, the very institution the hospice movement was designed to counterpose. Finally, in "Exit and Existence: Alternative Scenarios," psychologist Robert Kastenbaum examines society's unwritten script for old age and death. He traces two scenarios, extrapolating from the ways society has answered the question of what value there is in being an old, a dying, or a dead person.

Common to each life or death decision is a moral intricacy that puts to the test all that a person believes and feels. The following newspaper account recounts the complexity of one such instance.

encounter | *Suicide Pact*

Dr. and Mrs. Henry P. Van Dusen, leaders in American theological life, swallowed overdoses of sleeping pills last month in the bedroom of their Princeton, N.J., home in an effort to carry out a suicide pact.

Mrs. Van Dusen died. Dr. Van Dusen vomited up the pills and died 15 days later on Feb. 13, apparently of a heart ailment, in the Carrier Clinic in Belle Meade, N.J.

Dr. Van Dusen, the former president of Union Theological Seminary, and his wife—both members of the Euthanasia Society and advocates of an individual's right to terminate his or her own life—had entered into the pact rather than face the prospect of debilitating old age.

Mrs. Van Dusen was 80 years old when she died on January 28. Her husband was 77. Although reportedly depressed, the Van Dusens were convinced that their suicide attempt carried no burden of sin but rather the promise of after-life.

Friends and associates had known of the couple's suicide effort, but details about the incident did not become widely known until yesterday.

In a letter they left behind, the Van Dusens said there were many old people who would die of natural causes if not kept alive medically and expressed the resolve not to "die in a nursing home."

The Van Dusens, whose prominence peaked while Dr. Van Dusen served as president of the seminary from 1945 until his retirement in 1963, said that they had led "happy lives" but that poor health no longer permitted them to "do what we want to do."

Source: Kenneth A. Briggs. "Suicide Pact Preceded Deaths of Dr. Van Dusen and His Wife." *New York Times*, February 25, 1975. Copyright © 1975 by the New York Times Company. Reprinted by permission.

A worsening arthritic condition had made Mrs. Van Dusen lame. Five years ago, Dr. Van Dusen suffered a severe stroke which limited his physical activity and prevented him from speaking normally. For the vigorous, articulate Presbyterian scholar and his active wife, the setbacks were serious impediments to living the kind of useful, productive lives to which they had become accustomed.

1. The Van Dusens' act highlights the issue of the individual's right to choose death. Do you believe that this right exists? Under what circumstances?
2. Had you been in circumstances similar to the Van Dusens' would you have made the same choice?
3. Consider the person discovering the Van Dusens within a reasonable period after they had taken the sleeping pills. Would that person have a moral obligation to revive them? Would the obligation be any different for a friend, relative, or family doctor?

PLATO

Apology:
The Death Scene

In Athens when the Court pronounced Socrates guilty of impiety and of cor-
rupting the youth with his teachings, the law required him to propose his own
penalty as an alternative to the death penalty. Refusing to compromise his principles, Socrates proposed, somewhat facetiously, that he be honored by the
State as a distinguished citizen. In the final section of the *Apology*, he explains
that it is irrational to fear death since the experience of death is unknown. Socrates goes on to assess the choice between a death of unknown value and a life
without value.

[After Socrates is condemned to death.]

For no great thrift in time, my fellow citizens, you will have from those
who wish to vilify the City the name and blame of having put to death the wise
man, Socrates; for they will call me wise, even if I am not, they who would
defame you. If only you had waited for a little while, the thing would have
occurred for you in the course of nature; for you can see my age, that I am far
along in life, and near to death. I say this, not to all of you, but only to those
who voted for my death. And to them I have also to say this as well. It may be,
Gentlemen, that you think I lost my cause for lack of arguments of the sort with
which I might have won you over, if I had thought that I ought to say and do all
things in order to escape the verdict. Far from it. I lost for a lack, but not of
arguments; it was for lack of impudence and daring, and for not being ready to
say to you the sort of thing it would have given you most pleasure to hear—me
weeping and wailing, and doing and saying any and every sort of thing that I
hold to be unworthy of me, but you are accustomed to hear from the rest. No, I
did not then believe that, to avoid a danger, I ought to do anything unseemly in
a freeman, nor do I now regret my manner of defence. No, far rather would I
choose this manner of defence, and die, than follow that, and live. Whether in a
court of justice or in war neither I nor any other man should seek by using every
means conceivable to escape from death; for in battle you very often see that if
you throw away your weapons and beg those who are pursuing you for mercy,
you may get out of dying. Indeed, in every sort of danger there are various ways
of winning through, if one is ready to do and say anything whatever. No,
Gentlemen, that is not the hard thing, to escape from death; ah no, far harder is

Source: Reprinted from *Plato on the Trial and Death of Socrates: "Euthyphro," "Apology,"
"Crito," "Phaedo,"* translated by Lane Cooper. Copyright © 1941 by Lane Cooper. Used by
permission of the publisher, Cornell University Press.

it to escape from sin, for sin is swifter than death. And so I, being old and slow, am overtaken by the slower enemy; while my accusers, who are strong and swift, have been caught by the swifter, namely wickedness. And so I now depart, by you condemned to pay the penalty of death; and they, by the truth convicted of a base injustice. And as I abide the payment, so do they. Who knows? Perhaps it had to be so, and I think that things are as they ought to be.

Touching the future, I desire to make for you who voted to condemn me, a prediction; for I am at the point where men foresee the future best—when they are soon to die. Let me tell you then, you men who have condemned me, that after I am gone there will straightway come upon you a chastisement far heavier, by Zeus, than the death you have set for me. You have now done this in the belief that you have freed yourselves from giving any reckoning for your life; but I tell you the result will be the very opposite for you. There will be more inquisitors to sift you, men whom I now hold in check without your knowing it. And they will be more critical as they are younger, and will annoy you more; for if you think that by putting men to death you will prevent the slur from being cast at you that you do not live aright, you are in error. This way of getting freedom is neither very sure nor fine; no, the finest and readiest way is this, not to interfere with other people, but to render oneself as good a man as possible. There is the prophecy I make for you who voted to condemn me. And of them I take my leave.

With those of you who voted to acquit me I should be glad to talk about this thing that has occurred, while the magistrates are busy and it is not time for me to go to the place where I must die. So, Gentlemen, please wait with me as long as that. There is nothing to keep us from talking to each other as long as it is allowed. To you as to friends I wish to explain the real meaning of what has just happened to me.

Justices, for when I call you that I am naming you aright, the thing that has come to me is wonderful.

My customary warning, by the spirit, in previous times has always, up to now, come to me very often to oppose me, even when a matter was quite unimportant, if ever I was going to do something amiss. But to-day, as you yourselves have witnessed, that thing has happened to me which anybody might suppose, and which is considered, to be the uttermost of evils. Yet neither did the sign from god oppose me when I left my house this morning, nor at the point when I ascended here to the tribunal, nor in my speech at anything I was about to say; though often when I have been talking elsewhere it has stopped me in the middle of a speech. But to-day, with reference to the whole procedure, not once did it oppose me in a thing I did or said. What, then, do I take to be the cause of this? No doubt this thing that has happened to me is good, and it cannot be that our supposition is correct when any of us think that death is a misfortune. For me, the proof of this is telling: it cannot be but that the customary sign would have opposed me, if I had not been about to do a thing that was good.

Let us view in another way how ample are the grounds for our hope that death is a good. To be dead is one of two things. Either it is a sort of non-existence, and the dead man has no feeling about anything whatever, or else, as people say, the soul experiences a shift and a migration from here into another place. Now if there is no feeling, if death is like a sleep in which one does not even dream, what a wonderful gain it would be! I believe if a man were to take that night in which he slept so deeply that he did not have a single dream, and compared it with the other nights and days of his life; if he had to say, upon reflection, how many days and nights, all told, in his life, he had passed better and more sweetly than that night; I believe that every one, not merely any private citizen, but the Great King himself, would find them easy to count up in comparison with all the others. So if death is a sleep like that, I say it is a gain; for thus all time appears to be no more than a single night. If, on the other hand, death is like a journey from here to another place, and if what they say is true, that everybody who has died is there, then, Justices, what greater good than this could there be? If, on arriving in Hades, one could be freed from those who here pretend that they are Justices, and there find those who by report deal real justice, Minos, Rhadamanthus, Aaecus, and Triptolemus, and all the rest of the demigods who were just in their lives here, what a small thing would that journey seem! Or, again, to be with Orpheus and Musaeus, with Hesiod and Homer, what price would not any of you pay for that? I would gladly die repeatedly, if all that is true. To me it would be a wonderful way to pass my time, there where I could meet with Palamedes and with Ajax son of Telamon, and any one else among the ancients who died through an unjust decision. To compare my lot with theirs, methinks, would not be so un-pleasant; and most important of all would be to go on sifting people there, as here, and finding out who is wise, and who thinks he is so, but is not. What would not anybody give to examine, Justices, the leader of that mighty expedi-tion against Troy, or else Odysseus, or Sisyphus, or a myriad of others one might mention, men and women too? There to talk with them, consort with them, examine them, would be a happiness beyond compare! Surely there, I take it, they do not put a man to death for doing that; for, happy in all else, people are happier there than here in that henceforth they are immortal, at all events if what is said is true.

But, Justices, you also it behoves to have good hope with reference to death, and this one thing you must bear in mind as true, that, living or dead, to a good man there can come no evil, nor are his affairs a matter of indifference to the gods. Nor has my destiny now come about by chance; rather, it is clear to me that it was better for me now to die and to be released from my troubles. That is why the sign did not at any point deter me, and why I am not very bitter at those who voted to condemn me, or at my accusers. It is true they did not have this notion in condemning and accusing me; no, they thought to injure me, and therein they merit blame.

One thing, however, I do beg of them. When my sons grow up, then,

Gentlemen, I ask you to punish them, you hurting them the same as I hurt you, if they seem to you to care for money, or aught else, more than they care for virtue. And if they pretend to be somewhat when they are nothing, do you upbraid them as I upbraided you, for not regarding as important what they ought to think so, and for thinking they have worth when they do not. If you do that, I shall have received just treatment from you, and my sons as well.

And now the time has come for our departure, I to die, and you to live. Which of us goes to meet the better lot is hidden from all unless it be known to God.

JOSEPH FLETCHER

Elective Death

In choosing their time of death, the Van Dusens took a stand on a long-debated issue: the issue of whether or not an individual has the right to terminate his or her life. Though some major writers (Epicurus, Thomas More, John Donne, and Montaigne among them) have presented the arguments in favor of the individual's right to choose his or her dying, the main current of Western thought has held that the proprietary right over human life rests with divine authority, or with the state (often seen as the earthly representative of the divine order), rather than with the individual.

In the following selection, Fletcher argues that human needs validate human rights, so that in certain situations a person has the right to end his or her own life. Fletcher bases his views on what he terms a "pragmatic situation ethic" and urges that the issue of when to terminate life be examined in the context of changing conditions.

> Vex not his ghost: O, let him pass! He hates him
> That would upon the wrack of this tough world
> Stretch him out longer.
>
> *Shakespeare*

Since we shoulder our responsibility for birth control, a feature of every civilized culture, can death control be far behind? If we have a right to initiate a life deliberately, may we not terminate one? Depending, of course, upon the circumstances?

There are really two questions here, one factual and one moral. In what follows, the thrust is toward answering both of them in the affirmative. To a certain extent these questions are mutually penetrating. In actual fact the practice of death control is increasing, due to medical pressures and human needs so great that they provide their own moral justification. And as the practice is further justified by the situation, it is more easily and sensibly encouraged and disinhibited. It is exactly in this sense that I use the term *right*—as something justified pragmatically by the situation. These who entertain any notion that there are some rights which are simply given in the very nature of things, above and beyond circumstances or human needs, will not be happy about everything I am about to say, and they ought to be alerted.

What is to be said to a nurse who is upset and suffers an acute anxiety reaction, unable to carry out her duty, because an intern, on instructions from a staff surgeon and a resident, has told her that a patient in the recovery room is

Source: Joseph Fletcher. "Elective Death." *Ethical Issues in Medicine.* Edited by E. Fuller Torey. Boston: Little, Brown and Company, 1968.

to be "let go," and that she is to turn off the intravenous fluids and the oxygen? (Often only the slower strategy of starvation is used, without suffocation.) What is a man to do whose father has been lying virtually unconscious for four years in a hospital bed, following a massive cerebral hemorrhage? The patient cannot eat or speak; is incontinent, shows no neurological evidence of interpersonal communication and is kept going with tube feeding by around-the-clock private nurses. The patient's son would feel guilt about suggesting that the doctors bring it to a close, yet he also feels guilty about the expense ($40,000 a year), the wasted resources that other things and people need, and his father's distressingly subhuman status. After all, is the patient anymore his father?

Years ago, in 1954, I wrote that there is a logical contradiction in the Hippocratic Oath, subscribed to by the medical profession. As I saw it then, the Oath illogically promises two incompatible things, both to relieve suffering and, as I put it, to "prolong and protect life."[1] But I was mistaken. Actually, there is not a word in that pious old apprenticeship agreement about either relieving suffering or prolonging life. Instead, the promise is to seek the "benefit of the sick," leaving the meaning of "benefit" unstipulated. The vitalistic idea that preserving life is the *summum bonum* of medicine appears nowhere in the Oath, except eisegetically (i.e., when read into it). On the contrary, making life sacrosanct was more likely a Pythagorean taboo, different from the empirical temper of Hippocrates and his case-minded approach. In place of such moral metaphysics, he said, in a famous maxim, "Life is short and art is long, the occasion fleeting, experience fallacious and judgment difficult." He knew the relativity of ethical decision. In fact, some of his disciples engaged in direct euthanasia on the same grounds that Plato, Socrates, Epicurus, and the Stoics approved it.[2]

In any case, what appeared to be ethical to whomever it was who wrote the Oath is not an eternal verity. Almost certainly it was not Hippocrates, as Edelstein has now made abundantly clear.[3] There is no reason to take that unknown moralist's understanding of right and wrong or good and evil as a permanent model of conscience for all times and all conditions. What is right or good does not transcend changing circumstances; it arises out of them.

When biologists predict that by, let us say, the year 2100, men will be free of hunger and infectious diseases, able to enjoy physical and mental life to the age of 90 or 100, replacing defective parts of the body as need develops, cyborg fashion, we can hope that the frequency of treatment situations posing the question of elective death will be cut down. But sooner or later it will arise for many patients, no matter what the longevity norm may become. Paradoxically, modern medicine's success in prolonging life has itself directly increased the incidence of death control decisions in the chronic and terminal ills of the American people. Those over 65 are expected to increase from 18.5 million in 1966 to 24.5 million in 1980—something in the order of one out of every eight persons.

Novels in the classic tradition have drawn a picture of the deathbed scene where the elderly "pass on," surrounded by their families and friends, making their farewell speeches and *meeting* death instead of being overtaken or snatched by it. This model of death has become almost archaic. Nowadays, most of the time, death comes to people (even the young and middle aged) in a sedated and comatose state; betubed nasally, abdominally, and intravenously; and far more like manipulated objects than like moral subjects. A whole fascinating array of devices—surgical, pharmacological, and mechanical—is brought into play to stave death off clinically and biologically. Yet ironically, by their dehumanizing effects these things actually hasten personal death, i.e., loss of self-possession and conscious integrity. They raise in a new form the whole question of "life" itself, of how we are to understand it and whether the mere minimum presence of vital functions is what we mean by it.

For many people contemplating modern medicine's ability to prolong life (or, perhaps, to prolong death), death itself is welcome compared to the terrors of senility and protracted terminal treatment. Patients actually look for doctors who will promise not to allow them to "go through what mother did" or "lie there as Uncle John was made to." They are beginning to ponder ways of *escaping* medical ministrations; the white coats of our doctors and their paramedical attendants are taking on a grimmer hue, a new and less benign image. This is bound to increase as medicine's victories continue. It is a success problem, not a failure problem! The predominant illnesses become degenerative and chronic, not acute or infectious. Disorders in the metabolic group, cardiovascular ills, renal problems, and malignancies—these fill our hospital beds.

Death: Enemy and Friend

In all talk of elective death—that is, chosen or moral dying rather than fatal or amoral dying (*moral* always means the voluntary as against the involuntary or helpless)—the basic issue is whether human beings are always to regard death as an enemy, never as a friend. Is death never to be welcomed? May we never choose to go out and meet it? Dr. Logan Clendenning years ago, in his popularizing effort to make knowledge a part of the public's weaponry against illness, thought of it as being sometimes a friend. He wrote, "As I think it over, death seems to me one of the few evidences in nature of the operation of a creative intelligence exhibiting qualities which I recognize as mind stuff. To have blundered onto the form of energy called life showed a sort of malignant power. After having blundered on life to have conceived of death was a real stroke of genius."[4]

The logic of this is to either fight off or make an ally of *mortis,* as it happens to suit human needs. This is exactly what all medicine does; it either uses or outwits all biological forces for the sake of humanly chosen ends. Medicine is, at bottom, an interference with blind, brute nature. Three hundred years ago Thomas Sydenham called it "the support of enfeebled and the coercion of outrageous nature." Medicine refuses to "leave in God's (nature's) hands what must be" in everything else but death. Why should it stop there? Maurice Maeterlinck was sure that "there will come a day when science will protest its errors and will shorten our sufferings."[5] And that day is at hand, precisely because of the achievements of medical science and the pressures such achievements create to rethink our values and our view of man.

Medicine's primary *raison d'être* is, in Albert Schweitzer's phrase, "reverence for life." Life is its business. This, however, is very far from absolutizing the vital spark regardless of human personality and its claims. To subordinate every other consideration to bare sentience is to make biological life, as such, an idol. It is the vitalistic error. Respiration, circulation, reflexes, and the like, are not ends in themselves. Can it not be that life in its fullest meaning includes death, and that, since death is certain to come whether it does so constructively or willy-nilly, the only real question open to us is how it comes, as a good death ("euthanasia") or a bad death ("dysthanasia")?

Dr. David Karnofsky, who did so much for the Sloan-Kettering Institute, put the point of view of radical vitalism very clearly, at a meeting of the American Cancer Society in 1961. He opposed letting the patient go under any circumstances, arguing that the practice of keeping the patient alive is endorsed by "state planners, efficiency experts, social workers, philosophers, theologians, economists and humanitarians." Apart from this being a pretty wild *omnium gatherum* (practically everybody in the helping professions), the accusation is symptomatic of the embattled, almost paranoid mentality of many physicians. Karnofsky's main professed reason for preserving life by any and all means as long as possible was the old statistical absurdity about "something might turn up at the last minute, some new discovery or an inexplicable remission." But what is more irresponsible than to hide from decision making behind a logical possibility that is without antecedent probability?

As an example of "ethical" medicine, Dr. Karnofsky cited a patient with cancer of the large bowel. After a colostomy followed by recurrence, x-ray treatment was used; radioactive phosphorus checked abdominal fluids, and an antibiotic stopped broncho-pneumonia. Metastases ended liver function in spite of innumerable delaying actions, stupifying or traumatic, until the end "came." The patient was kept alive for ten months, but might otherwise have died in a matter of days or weeks. Was it right or wrong to add ten months? Was it more life or more death that was added? Who was benefited? What were the benefits? For Dr. Karnofsky, the obligation to maintain biological function or "life" was not a question of weighing benefits and forfeits. For him what is right or good was intrinsic; and life as such, per se, was precious—of greater value than anything else. This is the fundamental question in all cases of ethical concern, not only in life and death. Is the worth or desirability of thing or action inherent and intrinsic, regardless of the situation; or do right and good depend contingently and extrinsically upon the situation? If you take the intrinsic position, then some if not all obligations are absolute and universal; if you take the extrinsic view, all are relative. Karnofsky, like many others, was

an absolutist. I am not. On the absolutist view some things are never open to
responsible decision and choice; in "situation ethics" everything is.

Important Distinctions

It is at this point that we need to pause to make distinctions of some
practical importance. In the management of terminal illness there are two
distinct moral problems, closely related but by no means the same. One is the
classic issue over *euthanasia;* the other, and by far the more pressing in its
frequency, is "letting the patient go" or, as I have called it, *antidysthanasia.*[6]
The classic debate was about "mercy killing," i.e., doing something directly to
end a life graciously when it would otherwise go on (active euthanasia, it is
sometimes called). The more pressing and more common issue is whether one
may graciously refrain from procedures, not *doing* something but *omitting* to
do something, so that death will come (in some circles this is called *passive
euthanasia*). This second problem is the one that our success with prolongation
and resuscitation forces upon us daily in hospitals all around the world.
Possibly the best way to put the distinction with its various sides is to speak of
euthanasia in four terms:

1. *Direct voluntary,* as when a patient consciously chooses to end it all, with
   or without medical intervention. Such is the case of the patient who sneaks
   an overdose or is left one within reach, or who swallows a Kleenex or pulls
   out a tube. It is deliberately done and consciously willed by the patient.
2. *Indirect voluntary,* as when a patient before reaching an unconscious or
   comatose state (while still competent and with a *mens sana* even if not *in
   corpore sano*) gives leave to his medical servants to use discretion about
   letting death come. This, too, the patient has willed, yet his death is not
   directly done but indirectly by ceasing opposition to it. Such is the case of
   those who, after consultation, "pull the plug" at some point of diminish-
   ing returns.
3. *Indirect involuntary,* as when a patient's wishes are not known and yet
   doctors and/or family and friends *choose for him* to stop fighting off
   death. Such is the case when the pain, subhuman condition, irreversibility,
   cost, injustice to others, and the like, combine to outweigh the benefits of
   keeping him alive. This third form is far and away the most typical and
   frequent situation—indirect euthanasia, without the patient's past or
   present opinion in the account, except as it might be presumed.
4. *Direct involuntary,* as when a patient's wishes are not known, yet in the
   judgment of physicians, family, or friends it seems better to them to end
   his life by a "mercy killing" than to let it go on, as it will. Such a case
   would be a decerebrated person, perhaps one whose cerebral cortex has
   been shattered in an auto accident, in "excellent health" biophysically, fed
   by indwelling nasal tubes, unable to move a muscle, suffers no pain but
   only reacts by reflex to a needle prick. I know one such, a young man (who

now looks like a little child), and his mother says. "My son is dead." Another case would be an obstetrician's decision not to respirate a monster at birth, or a "blue baby" deoxygenated beyond tolerable limits of cyanosis or brain suffocation.

Some moralists have tended to put great store by the distinction between "direct" and "indirect" actions, Roman Catholics, for example. They argue that it is one thing morally to *do* an act such as ending a life by "bare bodkin" (as Shakespeare put it), and another thing altogether to *permit* a life to end by starvation, as when an intravenous therapy is discontinued. To others this seems a cloudy and tenuous distinction. Either way the intention is the same, the same end is willed and sought. And the means used do not justify the end in one case if not the other, nor are the means used anything that *can* be justified or "made sense of" except in relation to the gracious purpose in view. Kant said, as part of his practical reason, that if we will the end, we will the means. Whether euthanasia is direct or indirect, voluntary or involuntary, is ethically something that *depends upon the facts in the situation,* not upon some intrinsic principle regardless of the realities. This is the shape of the tension between empirical and metaphysical moralities.

Curiously enough, in view of the religious and philosophical differences which divide moralists and ethicists, this matter of an alleged obligation to make the maintenance of a patient's life the supreme obligation is one around which moralists are pretty well united against the publicly professed opinion of the medical profession. (Note, I say "publicly.") That is, we find that Catholic, Protestant, Jewish, and humanist teachings all have a place for euthanasia in one form or another. Archbishop Temple,[7] the Anglican theologian, once said of pacifism what can be said of Karnofsky's radical vitalism, that it "can only rest upon a belief that life, physiological life, is sacrosanct. That is not a Christian idea at all; for, if it were, the martyrs would be wrong. If the sanctity is *in* life, it must be wrong to give your life in a noble cause as well as to take another's. . . . Of course, this implies that, *as compared to some things,* the loss of life is a small evil; and, if so, then, *as compared to some other things,* the taking of life is a small injury."

Catholic moralists, and most orthodox Jews and most orthodox Protestants, are opposed to euthanasia in forms # 1 and # 4 (see previous list); i.e., they rule out as immoral any direct methods of ending a life in order to end suffering and waste. But they allow forms # 2 and # 3, the indirect strategies. Catholic theologians refuse to call the indirect forms "euthanasia," and they add a further *caveat* or limitation. Pius XII[8] and his interpreters have restricted even the indirect forms (both of which they justify) to permission to cease and desist from the use of "extraordinary" treatments only, where there is no reasonable hope of benefit. All ordinary treatments must continue without letup. Usually, *extraordinary* procedures are taken to be those that are expensive, painful, or inconvenient.[9]

The difficulty with this is, like so much else, due to the rapid advance of medical science and of the medical arts. Ordinary and extraordinary are very relative terms as the weaponry of health and control of nature's pathologies sweeps on. Look at how quickly penicillin ceased to be extraordinary, and also sulpha drugs and electronic cardiac devices such as the pacemakers. In no time prosthetic implants will be old hat. There is no way to establish a consensus (even if desirable) as to the defining features of an extraordinary treatment. Is it mortality rate, pain, inconvenience, expense, effectiveness, competence, subject's life expectancy (a lung removed in a child is not the same as in an old person), frequency, or what? And so it goes.

Those who live by situation ethics, and this includes many liberal Jews and Protestants and humanists (this writer being one), are ethically prepared to employ euthanasia in all four forms, depending in every actual case upon the circumstances. Nevertheless, no matter what rhetoric and doctrine are used at the theoretical level, there can be no doubt that in practice there is an increase of responsible situational decision making in proportion to the increase of the problem's occurrence in our hospitals. By now, due to greater longevity and medical know-how, it is an everyday, almost routine thing. Considerations of income and experience, especially in teaching hospitals, may tend to soft-pedal the issue and discourage it, but profit, training, and research are only brakes; they do not stop the trend to elective death. The frightening pressures of population only add to it. Sooner or later we shall be forced back on "statistical" morality. Speaking of a situation not unlike ours in America, the British medical journal *Lancet*[10] says: "If the average length of a patient's stay in a hospital is two weeks, a bed in that hospital occupied for a year could have been used by 26 other patients . . . In a country without a surplus of hospital beds, an irrevocably unconscious patient may sometimes be kept alive at the cost of other people's lives."

Objections

In *Morals and Medicine*[1] I have identified and thoroughly discussed ten different objections to euthanasia. I will not attempt to retrace all of that ground but there are some elements in the traditional opposition to euthanasia (we can call it *elective death*, if we prefer) that keep cropping up. The objection that it is suicide is only an epithet which is not really in question. The objection that it is murder only begs the question, since the problem is precisely whether a *felo de se* for medical cause is to be held an unlawful killing or not. When people cite the Ten Commandments they often fail to note that the decalogue prohibits murder, not killing as such, and this too ties in with the whole question of licit and illicit dying and killing. Obviously the Jews, as well as their Christian cousins, have not been in any significant numbers vegetarians or pacifists or opposed to capital punishment.

Once a bishop castigated me for saying that by wanting to release those caught in a painful and incurable condition I was ignoring the theologically alleged benefit spiritually ("the redemptive effect") of suffering, as in Jesus' crucifixion. The bishop himself ignored the fact that sacrificial suffering is voluntary and chosen and conscious. There is nothing redemptive going on *in most instances* of terminal misery and loss of human functions. And when it is said that given the right to choose death too many would do it impulsively or connive and encourage it in others for selfish reasons (e.g., "to get the deed to the old home place"), what reply is needed other than *abusus non tollit usum,* the abuse of a thing does not rule out its use? Otherwise we should always have to repress any research, innovation, and development which enlarges our human control over the conditions of life, since all such power can be used for ill as for good.

Some say that if our society and culture tolerated suicide in such cases as we have mentioned the result would be a cheapening of life and weakening of our moral fiber.[11] They seem to think that all interest would be lost, for example, in intensive care units, and nobody would respond to emergency Code 90 calls! If there is danger of becoming hardened by the practice of death control, by the same token there is danger of becoming hardened by the constant practice of prolonging life beyond any personal or human state. Pope's lines on vice cut two ways: "Yet seen too oft, familiar with her face, We first endure, then pity, then embrace." It is at least possible that euthanasia could not have half the demoralizing influence of stockpiling and planning to use weapons of mass extermination, even "tactical" bombs, and the total war of modern military technology. Besides, not every human being cries, *Timor Mortis conturbat me* (the fear of death confounds me); there are the pure in heart who fear not. "It is safe," said C. S. Lewis, "to tell the pure in heart that they shall see God, for only the pure in heart want to."[12] The fear of the hereafter, among religious believers and skeptics alike, is nearly gone except for primitives and a few doctrinaire incorrigibles.

Perhaps the most anomalous stance in the whole developing discussion is the official or formal position of the medical fraternity, as taken in the American Medical Association and similar groups, that what they are opposed to only is making euthanasia *legal*. That is, they want to use their own discretion, as they are already doing, but they do not want any public acknowledgment that they have any such discretion or ever use it. The fact is, of course, that even in the case of euthanasia in form #3, doctors are vulnerable to malpractice suits ("failure to do what is of average competence and practice"). Hence the essentially scared and "phony" discussion in medical circles, and a tightly bound fraternal refusal to testify in court adversely to a fellow physician no matter what the charge or the facts. In this matter as in so many others, the law, and the conventional wisdom, are hopelessly antediluvian when seen in the light of medicine's progress. But the day is coming when doctors will recognize that just as they are slowly accepting the morality of terminating some lives at the beginning (abortion) for therapeutic reasons of mental, emotional, and social well-being, so they should be terminating for these reasons some lives at the ending, i.e., therapeutic euthanasia.

It would be unfair to the morally muscle-bound and false to the facts to urge the case for euthanasia in any of its forms as if there were no difficulties. The finest diagnosticians and prognosticians are sometimes baffled. At best the safest way to describe a professional person, whatever his field, is as an educated guesser. We cannot be "sure" that the "hopeless" case is really hopeless. Resuscitation procedures now have greatly increased our chances of reviving drowned people or frozen people who not long ago were beyond help. So also with cardiac arrests, anoxia, some cerebral vascular lesions, spontaneous hypoglycemia, and the like. The exciting thing about medicine is that even though it magnifies the problem of medical initiative in death for the aged and the chronic, it reduces it for the young and the acute. Yet there is no escape from the necessity of decision, case by case. This is as true for "ending it all" or "letting him go" as for whether to operate or not. Nothing is certain but death itself, on its own terms or ours. But if in the face of man's finite knowledge and understanding of health, life, and death, even our physicians cannot make good "*guess-timates,*" then we are indeed trapped in a merely fatalistic web. But if they have a truly creative competence, as I believe they have, then why refuse them the initiative late and not early? What does it mean to "have" a doctor?

What Is Death and When?

Back and behind this very human and crucial question of when death is to be accepted lies the question, "When *is* death?" And, in a way, *what* is death? Even the most pragmatic value problems presuppose profound philosophical or theological commitments. The outmoded legal definition of death nearly completely misses the mark in these days of biochemistry and death control, and of genetic control. Almost certainly the heart-and-lungs definition, by which life is supposed to be present if there is clinically detectable breathing or heartbeat, will have to go. We cannot use mad Lear's test of Cordelia's corpse: "Lend me a looking glass; If that her breath will mist or stain the stone, Why then, she lives."

The philosophy of elective death turns its advocates in the direction of determining death as present, or life gone, when a patient's EEG (electroencephalographic tracing) has remained flat for say 24 hours, regardless of other criteria such as respiration or heartbeat.[13] This is certainly a long enough anoxia or cessation of the bioelectric activity of the brain to establish cerebral death, *and cerebral death is death.* This is reported to have been adopted by the French Academy of Medicine, and neurologists everywhere (e.g., Clarence Carfoord of Sweden) advocate it.

The point to note is that modern medical thinking, using a conceptual apparatus drawn from scientific method, no longer regards life and death as *events.* They are seen and understood now as points along a biological continuum. This makes nonsense of much of the old-fashioned abortion debate about when conception occurs, at insemination or fertilization or development of the embryo to certain stages, and so on along the pregnancy line. In the same way it undercuts the argument about when death "occurs," because death is a *process,* not an event. And the core of it is not sentience of the body or some arbitrary minimum of vital functions; *it is the person, and mental function.* When mind is gone, in the degenerative process, and with it the homeostasis of the organism, then life is gone: death has come. Then, at least, if not before, let the battle stop.

It is this problematic character of both life and death, medically regarded, that lends so much interest to a suggestion from Dr. Charles K. Holling[14] of the College of Medicine in the University of Cincinnati: "Hospitals of the future may well have 'death boards.' Applications for permission to discontinue the artificial measures by which life is being maintained might be made to such boards either by the patient who is in possession of his mental faculties or by his next-of-kin." Such review boards could well have an ombudsman, an intelligent lay participant. Dr. Holling is using a model from the "TA" boards of hospitals, those that make decisions in cases of therapeutic abortion.

Bernard Shaw has Sir Patrick say, in *The Doctor's Dilemma,* "All professions are conspiracies against the laity." The old gambit of writing prescriptions in Latin to keep patients from knowing what they say will not work any longer. Medicine is not a "mystery" any more, and its practitioners no longer have a craft of which everybody else is totally ignorant. This is the age of science, and that means a unity of knowledge and freedom of exchange. Repressed knowledge does not stay repressed, as the growing membership of the Nuclear Nations Club attests. Among other things this means that the doctors are no longer alone or isolated in their decision making. In situation problems about terminal cases the physician does not have to cast his own vote alone and uncounted with others. Nor, given medicine's great gains, is the range of decisions as narrow as it once was. When we have to reckon with death, we need not always only glimpse it over our shoulder as we run. Indeed, if we run we are lost.

Fatality or Integrity

There are deep-rooted psychic inhibitions which prevent us from seeing our problem in a rational and responsible perspective. There is, or has been, too much *mystique* and superstitious metaphysics about it. But now it presents itself as a challenge to human control, as distinguished from supernatural or natural and fatalistic control. It is a question of responsible control of life, not merely of health and well-being but of being itself. It is time we confronted theology's blanket denunciation of suicide and medicine's uncritical opposition to death.[15]

In the final analysis there are three postures we can assume. The one with the most tradition is absolutist. In its theological form it has been expressed in terms of a divine monopoly theory of life and death. It says that God is the creator of each person ("soul") and reserves to himself the right to decide when life shall come (as against birth control) and when death shall come (as against euthanasia). A much studied treatise in this old tradition says death control is "a violation of the property rights of Jesus Christ."[16] If the absolutist posture takes a nontheological shape it becomes radical vitalism or a sort of naturalistic mystique about life as the highest good and death the worst evil, regardless of the situation. It is the first posture, the absolutist one, which lends itself to accusations of "playing God" when elective death is discussed.

The second posture is the one of stoic indifference or anomie. Because it finds no meaning in existence, it assigns no real value to it and can as easily embrace endurance of life at its worst as repudiation of life at its best.

In between these two extremes of absolutism and adiaphorism lies the pragmatic situation ethic. It finds life good sometimes, and death good sometimes, depending upon the case, the circumstances, the total context. In this view life, no more than any other good thing or value, is good in itself but only by reason of the situation; and death, no more than any other evil, is evil in itself but only by reason of the situation. This is the method by which medicine makes decisions, and there is every reason why it should do so from first to last.

Notes

1. J. Fletcher, *Morals and Medicine* (Princeton: Princeton University Press, 1954).

2. G. Williams, *The Sanctity of Life and the Criminal Law* (New York: Alfred A. Knopf, 1957).

3. L. Edelstein, *The Hippocratic Oath* (Baltimore: Johns Hopkins University Press, 1943).

4. L. Clendenning, *The Human Body*, 3rd ed. (New York: Alfred A. Knopf, 1941).

5. G. W. Jacoby, *Physician, Pastor and Patient* (New York: Paul B. Hoeber, 1936).

6. J. Fletcher, Death and medical initiative. *Folia Medica* (Tufts University) 7:10, 1962.

7. W. Temple, *Thoughts in War Time* (London: Macmillan & Co., 1940).

8. Pope Pius XII, *Acta Apostolicae Sedis* 49:1027, 1957.

9. G. Kelly, *Medico-Moral Problems* (St. Louis: Catholic Hospital Association, 1958).

10. The prolongation of dying. Editorial. *Lancet* 2:1205, December 8, 1962.

11. E. Shils, The sanctity of life. *Encounter* 28:39, 1967.

12. P. S. Rhoads, Management of the patient with terminal illness. *Journal of the American Medical Association* 192:611, 1965.

13. H. Hamlin, Life or death by EEG. *Journal of the American Medical Association* 190:112, 1964.

14. C. K. Holling, Terminal decisions. *Medical Opinion and Review* 2:1, 1966.

15. J. Hillman, *Suicide of the Soul* (New York: Harper & Row, 1964).

16. A. Koch and A. Preuss, *Handbook of Moral Theology* (St. Louis: Herder, 1924).

MICHAEL D. BAYLES

The Value of Life—By What Standard?

Philosopher Michael Bayles moves the theoretical discussion of choosing death to the immediate decision making of patient and medical staff. Arguing that the value of life is not intrinsic, Bayles urges attention to the potentially conflicting standards for a life with value in a hospital setting.

The treatments they do or do not order may give physicians more absolute control over how long a patient's life may be extended, but nurses provide the constant human care that can make the difference between a life that is valuable and meaningful to the last, and one that ends in humiliation, deprivation, and suffering. More than most people, nurses need a deep and reflective view of the value and quality of life.

In developing a philosophical conception of the value of life, one must consider whether life itself is intrinsically valuable. I maintain that it is not.

Suppose you were told that you would live until the age of 90, but that after 70 you would be unconscious and have no physical movement except for such vital functions as breathing. Would those last 20 years of life be of any value to you? Would it make any difference to you whether you survived to 90 or died two days after lapsing into the coma? If the answer to these questions is no, as I think it would be for most of us, then life is not intrinsically valuable to the possessor of it. Instead, it is the quality of *conscious* life that is important.[1]

Such characteristics as pleasure, physical movement, and relations of personal affection are what give life value. Life is a necessary condition for these characteristics, but in itself or by itself life does not have value.

If life is not intrinsically valuable, the basic question to be considered is, "What characteristics or qualities render life valuable to the one who lives it?"

Ancient Greek ethical theories introduced two types of standards for judging the value of life: perfectionist standards and a utilitarian standard.

According to perfectionist standards, a minimum number of specific qualities is necessary for a life that is valuable or worth living; the more such qualities one has or exercises, the greater the value of life.

The qualities valued vary. Plato used the proper balance of the three elements of the soul: reason, desire, and the spirited element. Aristotle used the exercise of distinctively human characteristics and defined reason as the most distinctive. Self-actualization theories are species of perfectionist views.

Source: Copyright © 1980, American Journal of Nursing Company. Reproduced with permission from *American Journal of Nursing,* December, Vol. 80, No. 12.

Immanuel Kant developed a perfectionist standard of reason and autonomy or free will. Many contemporary theories that use perfectionist standards
are closely tied to the concept of personhood; these theories often specify such
qualities as self-awareness, memory, love, communication, conceptual thinking, and physical mobility as essential. Perfectionists usually consider happiness as an aspect of a good or valuable life that accompanies essential qualities,
but do not consider happiness *per se* as one of the qualities for a valuable
life.

Utilitarian standards are based on the net utility (degree of utility minus the
degree of disutility) experienced at a moment. There are at least two variations
of this standard.

The hedonist variant considers only pleasure and pain as utility and
disutility: the valuable life is characterized by the presence of pleasure and the
absence of pain. A second variant counts the fulfillment and nonfulfillment of
desire as utility and disutility.

For simplicity, the terms happiness and unhappiness will be used here to
include both variants: pleasure and pain as well as the fulfillment and nonfulfillment of desires.

By the utilitarian standard, life is valuable if happiness exceeds unhappiness; it is bad when unhappiness exceeds happiness.

Applying a Standard

The value of life is likely to be similar by both utilitarian and perfectionist
standards because the presence of essential qualities (perfectionist standard)
often increases happiness (utilitarian standard). In judging the value of continued life, three indicators are predominant: mental capacity, physical capacity, and pain.

Proponents of euthanasia usually emphasize pain as a primary indicator
for terminating life. Such an emphasis suggests a utilitarian pleasure/pain
value. But on a perfectionist standard, pain does not make life worthless unless
the pain interferes unduly with essential qualities of life, such as mental
functioning. On the other hand, mental or physical incapacity may indicate
that life is no longer worth living, even in the absence of pain.

For example, in an English court case, on which the play *Whose Life Is It
Anyway?* is based, a sculptor injured in an automobile accident sued to refuse
life-sustaining treatments. He was paralyzed from the neck down, and though
he retained full mental capacity, he viewed his future life as not worth living.

Applying a utilitarian criterion of total happiness, one might say that if the
sculptor had strong unfulfillable desires for sculpting and other activities
requiring physical mobility, his life would have more unhappiness than happiness and would not be worth living.

On the other hand, one might propose that the sculptor could lose these
desires and develop new ones that could be fulfilled, so that, after a transition

period, his life would have more happiness than unhappiness. By this standard, his life, vis-à-vis life-sustaining measures, would be worth continuing.

On a perfectionist criterion, if physical mobility of more than the head is a necessary condition for a life worth living, even if the paralyzed sculptor could develop a new set of desires and become happy, his life would not be worth living.

Which version of these standards for judging the value of continued life should one adopt? Frankly, I have no general argument to show that one is preferable to another. Indeed, I'm not sure how to argue for one of them over the others. Ethical principles are not capable of strict proof or demonstration the way some logical principles are. At least one can become clear about what different values involve and determine which value one prefers.

However, even if one cannot demonstrate which criterion is appropriate in each clinical case, one need not despair. In many cases, one will arrive at the same judgment no matter which criterion is used. More importantly, one may often permit the individual whose life is in question to judge the value of its continuance.

After all, the point of all the standards is to determine when life is valuable to the person who lives it, and that largely depends upon his values and circumstances. If he finds his life worthwhile, it is. Especially important are his standards on the value of life.

Thus, the nurse should use the standard of the particular competent adult patient.

However, one must be very careful not to impose one's own standard as a test of a person's competency. Consider the following.

A woman with metastasized breast cancer began to fail. The resident ordered a blood transfusion. The patient refused it. The resident claimed that because of changes in her blood chemistry, which a transfusion would correct, the patient was not rational.

The resident did a cutdown and started a transfusion. After the transfusion, the resident claimed the woman wanted the treatment continued, although the family and the nursing staff believed that either she did not understand the question, or, due to the stress of the transfusion, she had lost her competency. After complications occurred, the physician finally removed the intravenous apparatus.[2]

Although an altered blood chemistry can affect mental status, it is not a criterion of rationality. Since this was the only criterion cited by the resident, one suspects that she declared the woman irrational because the woman refused the transfusion, and that the physician was imposing her standard of the value of life as a criterion of rationality.

Deciding for Incompetent Patients

While one can and should apply the standard of value of life that a competent adult patient holds, problems arise with incompetent patients. One approach is to try to determine what standard each of these patients held before becoming incompetent.

With infants, even this approach is ruled out, because they never had views on the subject. Others must choose a standard for judging the value of the infant's life. Which standard is most appropriate?

Again, there are cases in which it makes no difference which standard is used. For example, an anencephalic infant does not have a life of value by either utilitarian or perfectionist standards.

By utilitarian standards, the life of such an infant is of no value since, not being conscious, the infant cannot feel pleasure or pain or have desires. Similarly, consciousness is one of the qualities required for life to be worthwhile by all perfectionist standards.

For mentally retarded infants, utilitarian and perfectionist standards may have different implications.

Consider the Johns Hopkins Hospital case of an infant born with Down's syndrome and duodenal atresia. The parents refused permission for the relatively simple operation to remove the obstruction, and after 15 days the infant died of dehydration and starvation. Should this infant's life have been prolonged?

On a utilitarian standard, one would be hard pressed to show that such children have more unhappiness than happiness and, so, the answer might be yes. Retarded Down's children do not appear to be unhappy, except perhaps due to their treatment by society. They do not suffer overwhelming anxiety about their condition, and they appear to take pleasure in many simple activities.

Yet, on some perfectionist standards, their lives may not be of value. The degree of retardation varies, but many persons with Down's syndrome lack competence to live on their own in society, even with support from various agencies. The more severely retarded an infant is, the less likely it will have a life of value on a perfectionist standard since most perfectionist standards attach considerable importance to mental capacity.

Reasonable-Person Test

Some scholars and some courts have suggested using a reasonable-person test to decide the value of continued life for those incapable of making their own judgments.[3] Life is no longer of value if most reasonable people would judge that it is not. The difficulty with this test is determining what reasonable people would decide. It is doubtful that a majority or even a substantial plurality of reasonable people would opt for any one criterion.

Ordinary vs. Extraordinary Means Test

Some scholars believe that such cases as that at Johns Hopkins can be settled without considering the value of the life. Instead, they focus on the means used and distinguish between ordinary and extraordinary means

A common definition of ordinary means is those which "offer a reasonable hope of benefit, and which can be obtained and used without excessive expense, pain or other inconvenience."[4] However, such subjective qualifiers as "excessive" and "reasonable hope" void this definition in hard cases.

For example, many physicians believe that the operation for duodenal atresia is an ordinary one if performed on an otherwise normal infant, but an extraordinary one if performed on an infant with Down's syndrome. Obviously, as Richard McCormick has argued, one must consider the value of life in order to determine whether the means are ordinary.[5] Whether a treatment offers hope of benefit depends on whether the life prolonged is worth living; for if it is not worth living, prolonging it does not provide any benefit.

Killing vs. Allowing to Die

Another important issue arises in the Johns Hopkins case. Should the infant have been killed in some painless way once the decision not to operate had been made?

The slow death by starvation may have been painful for the infant, which would make its life for those 15 days of little value on any of the standards. Moreover, the presence of the infant was a great strain on the medical personnel, especially the nursing staff.

In general, once decisions are made not to prolong a life and, as in that case, one is sure the person will not survive more than a couple of weeks, is there any important moral difference between killing him and allowing him to die? Society generally says there is. But, philosophically, one can claim that there is no intrinsic moral difference between killing and allowing to die by ceasing or not initiating treatment, when both actions have the same motive, and the same consequences are equally probable.[6]

Suppose a man whose family has been killed by Idi Amin comes upon him, unconscious and trapped under a burning car. Amin's guards and driver have been killed. The man could rescue Amin before the car explodes. But for revenge and the good of humanity he desires Amin's death.

Does it make any difference to the rightness or wrongness of the man's conduct whether he watches Amin blown up by the exploding car or shoots him in the head? The motive, consequences, and certainty appear the same in either case.

Note that the example is independent of whether the man acts rightly or wrongly. If it is wrong for Amin to die, is the wrong done any more serious if he is shot? If it is right, is it any better if he is blown up or shot?

Some people would say killing is worse because it lessens one's moral integrity. But that argument is unsound. One does not become morally worse by killing than by allowing to die, *unless* killing is a greater wrong. One has to decide whether killing is a greater wrong before one can use the effect on moral integrity as a reason for claiming it makes one morally worse.

If one concludes that there is no intrinsic moral difference between killing and allowing to die, two cautions are needed. First, the point cuts both ways. If it is permissible to allow someone to die, it is also permissible to kill him; by the same logic, if it is wrong to kill him, it is also wrong to allow him to die.

Second, the argument of no intrinsic moral difference between killing and allowing to die applies only when the consequences, probability, and motives are the same. Usually, there is a difference in one or more of these factors. For example, the probability is usually greater that someone will die if one shoots him than if one merely fails to rescue him.

Sometimes allowing a person to die may be worse than killing him. Suppose, for the sake of argument, that we accept that the life of the infant in the Johns Hopkins Hospital case was not worth living. Allowed to die, the infant and the medical personnel suffered for 15 days. Had the infant been killed, all would have been spared this suffering. Not killing the infant involved the cruelty of not alleviating two weeks of a miserable existence and imposed suffering on the medical staff.

Nursing Practice Standards

A useful place to begin examining how various standards of the value of life relate to nursing practice is the ANA *Code for Nurses*. The introduction states, "Nursing encompasses the promotion and restoration of health, the prevention of illness, and the alleviation of suffering."[7] The "alleviation of suffering" suggests a utilitarian standard of the value of life.

Part of interpretive statement 1.6 on the dying person provides further guidance:

> The nurse . . . [works] with the client and others to arrive at the best decisions dictated by the circumstances, the client's rights and wishes, and the highest standards of care. The measures used to provide assistance should enable the client to live with as much comfort, dignity, and freedom from anxiety and pain as possible.[8]

This statement emphasizes the patient's rights and wishes in the circumstances, which accords with using the competent adult patient's standard in making decisions about the value of life. The emphasis on maximizing comfort, dignity, and freedom from anxiety and pain is appropriately compatible with either utilitarian or perfectionist standards of the value of life.

Other passages could be cited, but the point here is that according to the *Code*, the patient's standard of the value of life, at least if the patient is a competent adult, should be a primary guide in determining the nursing care provided.

Using a competent adult patient's standard of the value of life is a rather gratuitous gesture unless it may make a difference in the care provided. In other words, using a patient's standard rather than that of healthcare professionals is significant only if it may result in different treatment and care.

Perhaps the easiest way to consider whether differences in standards may affect treatment is to examine the ANA *Standards of Nursing Practice*.[9]

Standard I, pertaining to the collection of data, should be understood to emphasize discovering the patient's standard of the value of life. The assessment factors on health status include such items as cultural, religious, socioeconomic background, and health goals. This nonbiological information may help one to determine a patient's standard of the value of life.

One cannot directly ask most patients for their standard, because few people have an easily expressible, reflective view on the matter. Moreover, it is likely that they will not even have a purely consistent view. Thus, a nurse can expect inconsistent and even contradictory signals from patients as to the characteristics they attribute to a valuable life.

The point of collecting such data, as Standard II indicates, is to develop a nursing diagnosis. In doing so, the standard of the value of life may be very important. The first and second assessment factors suggest comparing the client's status with the norm and thus determining his capabilities and limitations. However, an appropriate diagnosis is not based solely upon deviation from norms.

Whether deviations or limitations are significant partly depends on the patient's standard of the value of life. For example, physical incapacity in a limb may be a highly significant handicap to a physically oriented person, such as a truck driver or an athlete, and a less significant inconvenience to an intellectually oriented person, such as an English professor.

According to Standard III, the purpose of a diagnosis is to derive goals for a plan of nursing. In formulating goals, the patient's standard of the value of life will be most significant in the functional capabilities he chooses to maximize. A patient who has a utilitarian standard of the value of life may be quite willing to receive heavy sedation in order to alleviate pain. Yet, a patient with a perfectionist standard that emphasizes intellectual alertness may object to sedation except to alleviate the most excruciating pain.

Standard V pertains to the autonomy of the patient in directing, so far as he is capable, his own care. Assessment factor 2 makes the nurse responsible for providing the patient and his family with information needed to make decisions and choices. With a competent patient, the best way to have medical and nursing care contribute to a valuable life is to let the patient make informed choices in light of his standard of value of life. In order to do so, the patient needs as much information as possible concerning his condition and treatment. Nurses can be valuable in providing patients with realistic appraisals of their condition.

Finally, with slight emendation, Standard VI may be the most important standard. "Nursing actions assist the client/patient to maximize his health capabilities." I would change this to read "maximize the value of his life."

The health capabilities of dying patients are limited. Further, they may be willing, congruent with their standard of the value of life, to sacrifice some health for other qualities.

For example, a patient may tire himself and perhaps risk more rapid deterioration or death by long periods of conversing with others. If he is informed of the risks and wishes to spend his final days relating to others, even at the expense of further life, there is no reason to forbid it. There is no gain in prolonging a patient's life if it is of no or minimal value to him.

Nurses are in frequent and long contact with patients. This puts them in the best position of all healthcare personnel to discover the patients' standards of the value of life. But, when physicians undertake treatments which nurses believe are detrimental to the value of patients' lives, to what extent should they intercede on behalf of patients? The extent to which the nurse is an advocate for the patient is one of the most difficult ethical issues of nursing practice.

Consider, for example, the case of Anna Henderson. Anna was a diabetic who had an above-the-knee amputation. The stump would not close, and she developed other post-operative complications.[10] With infection and poor nutrition, she physically deteriorated and mentally withdrew. She was listed as a "no code," yet when she had a gastrointestinal bleed, the physicians decided to send her to surgery. At this point, one should ask whether the treatments and surgery contributed to a life the patient found valuable or merely prolonged one she found a burden.

In Anna's case, one nurse took a strong stand against surgery. "If you want her in surgery," he said, "I'll give you the forms, and you can send her yourself. I won't do it. It's not right." This strong stand appears to have been effective.

But what should the nurse have done had the physicians determined to go ahead anyway? To make matters more complicated, suppose the patient's standard of the value of life differed from that of the nurse?

To what extent should a nurse be an advocate for the patient and to what extent should a nurse's own standard of the value of life be the basis of his action? In short, are there any limits to the extent to which a nurse's conduct should be guided by a patient's judgments of the value of life?

This is perhaps the hardest issue of the ethics of nursing care, for it poses the conflict between the nurses' personal values and goals and the responsibilities of being a professional nurse.

References

1. Jonathan Glover, *Causing Death and Saving Lives* (New York, Penguin Books, 1977), 45–46.

2. M. A. Cawley, "Euthanasia: Should It Be a Choice?" *American Journal of Nursing* 77 (May 1977): 859–860.

3. *Matter of Quinlan*, 70 N.J. 10, 355 A.2d 647 (1976).

4. "Pope Pius XII." *New York Times* Nov. 25, 1957, 1.

5. R. A. McCormick, "To Save or Let Die: The Dilemma of Modern Medicine." *Journal of the American Medical Association* 299 (July 8, 1974): 173–174.

6. M. D. Bayles, "Euthanasia and the Quality of Life," in *Medical Treatment of the Dying: Moral Issues,* ed. by M. D. Bayles. (Cambridge, Mass., Schenkman Publishing Co., distributed by G. K. Hall, 1978), 128–152.

7. American Nurses' Association. *Code for Nurses, with Interpretive Statements* (Kansas City, Mo., The Association, 1976), 2.

8. Ibid., 6.

9. American Nurses' Association, *Standards of Nursing Practice* (Kansas City, Mo., The Association, 1973).

10. Priscilla Johnson, "The Gray Areas—Who Decides?" *American Journal of Nursing* 77 (May 1977): 856–858.

Suicide Note

While Michael Bayles raised the question of the price of life in the hypothetical or philosophic mode, Anne Sexton's poem reminds the reader that the answer is given in terms of personal experience. The speaker in the following work asserts that "everyone has a death,/his own death,/waiting for him." The right of the individual to choose the best route is proclaimed amidst a tense struggle that provides the central dynamic of the poem.

 Suicide notes are typically unrevealing, perhaps because the act of ending one's life requires such concentrated psychic effort. Sylvia Plath's final note, for instance, was stark in its brevity: "Please call Dr. ———," with a phone number following. Yet, the poetry preceding her death stands as an articulate testimony to her increasing preoccupation with self-destruction. In like manner, the final poems of Anne Sexton analyze the decision to die.

You speak to me of narcissism but I reply that it is a matter of my life.

                Artaud

At this time let me somehow bequeath all the leftovers to my daughters and their daughters.

                Anonymous

Better,
despite the worms talking to
the mare's hoof in the field;
better,
despite the season of young girls
dropping their blood;
better somehow
to drop myself quickly
into an old room.
Better (someone said)
not to be born
and far better
not to be born twice
at thirteen

Source: Anne Sexton. "Suicide Note." *Live or Die.* Boston. Houghton Mifflin Company, 1966.   *351*

where the boardinghouse,
each year a bedroom,
caught fire.

Dear friend,
I will have to sink with hundreds of others
on a dumbwaiter into hell.
I will be a light thing.
I will enter death
like someone's lost optical lens.
Life is half enlarged.
The fish and owls are fierce today.
Life tilts backward and forward.
Even the wasps cannot find my eyes.

Yes,
eyes that were immediate once,
Eyes that have been truly awake,
eyes that told the whole story—
poor dumb animals.
Eyes that were pierced,
little nail heads,
light blue gunshots.

And once with
a mouth like a cup,
clay colored or blood colored,
open like the breakwater
for the lost ocean
and open like the noose
for the first head.

Once upon a time
my hunger was for Jesus.
O my hunger! My hunger!
Before he grew old
he rode calmly into Jerusalem
in search of death.

This time
I certainly
do not ask for understanding
and yet I hope everyone else
will turn their heads when an unrehearsed fish jumps
on the surface of Echo Lake;

when moonlight,
its bass note turned up loud,
hurts some building in Boston,
when the truly beautiful lie together.
I think of this, surely,
and would think of it far longer
if I were not . . . if I were not
at that old fire.

I could admit
that I am only a coward
crying *me me me*
and not mention the little gnats, the moths,
forced by circumstance
to suck on the electric bulb.
But surely you know that everyone has a death,
his own death,
waiting for him.
So I will go now
without old age or disease,
wildly but accurately,
knowing my best route,
carried by that toy donkey I rode all these years,
never asking, "Where are we going?"
We were riding (if I'd only known)
to this.

Dear friend,
please do not think
that I visualize guitars playing
or my father arching his bone.
I do not even expect my mother's mouth.
I know that I have died before—
once in November, once in June.
How strange to choose June again,
so concrete with its green breasts and bellies.
Of course guitars will not play!
The snakes will certainly not notice.
New York City will not mind.
At night the bats will beat on the trees,
knowing it all,
seeing what they sensed all day.

June 1965

EDWIN S. SHNEIDMAN

The Enemy

"Individuals who are actively suicidal suffer—among their other burdens—from a temporary loss of the view of death-as-enemy," according to Edwin Shneidman. Schneidman claims that in most life-destructive acts there is at least a degree of ambivalence. Noting that it is possible to make the choice to die in many different ways, he explains that it is important to consider the degree of conscious and unconscious intention in bringing about one's death. In his analysis of intentionality in death-related behaviors, Shneidman counters the notion that our age is one of denial with his claim that the prospect of "megadeath in the nuclear age" has instead produced a death-oriented society. Yet, he concludes, the consequences of such an orientation are more often romanticization than acceptance of death. Though the examples he uses come from the late 1960s, the consequences of romanticization are equally prevalent today.

This may be an age of youth but it is also an age of death. Death is in the air; none of us is more than minutes away from death by nuclear incineration. Life has become both more dear and more cheap. And if it can be taken by others it can also be thrown away by oneself. Senseless killing and the wanton destruction of one's own mind reflect the same debasement of man's basic coin: life itself. In the Western world we are probably more death-oriented today than we have been since the days of the black plague in the fourteenth century.

The young reveal an acute sensitivity to life-and-death issues. I believe that they can best be seen as children of The Bomb. At Harvard last year my course on death was scheduled in a room with 20 chairs. Having been for over 20 years one of the few researchers who concentrated on death phenomena—my original focus was on suicide prevention—I had come to assume that only a few would want to deal with the subject. To my surprise more than 200 undergraduates from Radcliffe and Harvard showed up for the first session. Much of my recent work grew out of the introspective reports and papers completed by the participants in that course. The students' painful awareness of death, long before the season regarded as appropriate, has helped me to grasp the difference between individual death as it has long been perceived and the prospect of megadeath in the nuclear age.

At first thought, "death" is one of those patently self-evident terms, the definition of which need not detain a thoughtful mind for even a moment. Every mature person knows instinctively what he means by it. A dictionary defines death as the act or event or occasion of dying; the end of life. As far as

Source: Reprinted from *Psychology Today* Magazine, August 1970. Copyright © 1970 by Edwin S. Shneidman.

the person himself is concerned death is his end—the cessation of his consciousness.

In spite of death's seemingly self-evident character, reflection tells us that it might take a lifetime fully to understand the word "death." As Percy Bridgman pointed out, where either consciousness or loss of consciousness (including death) is involved, we must distinguish between *your* private experiences and *my* private experiences. You (privately) can experience my (public) death; we can both (privately) experience someone else's (public) death; but neither of us can experience his own (inexperienceable) death. You can never see yourself unconscious, hear yourself snore or experience your own being dead, for if you were in a position to have these experiences you would not, in fact, be unconscious, asleep or dead.

If you can never experience your own death, it follows logically that you can never experience your own *dying*. "Now, wait a minute," you might say. "Granted that I cannot experience my being dead but obviously I am still alive while I am dying and, unless I am unconscious, I can experience that." The fact is that you can never be *certain* that you are dying. "Dying" takes its only legitimate meaning from the fact that it immediately precedes death. You may think that you are dying—and survive, in which case you were not dying at that time. You can of course at the present moment keenly experience your *belief* that you are dying, and the experience can be deathly real. You can also in the present anticipate what will happen after you are dead. But these anticipations are at the time they occur always present-moment live experiences.

All this is not to gainsay the fact that people are often correct in thinking that they are dying because they do then die. During an extended period of dying (or supposed dying), a person, unless he is massively drugged or in a coma, is very much alive. The interval of dying is a psychologically consistent, often exaggerated extension of the individual's personality and life-style. His idiosyncratic ways of coping, defending, adjusting and interacting remain with him, coloring his inner life and characterizing his behavior. A standard textbook on clinical medicine succinctly states: "Each man dies in a notably personal way."

Termination is the universal and ubiquitous ending of all living things, but only man, because he can talk about his introspective life, can conceptualize his own cessation. Death is the absence of life—and life, *human* life, is the life of the self, the life of mind. Your life is the full accounting of your personal diary, your memory bank, including your experience of the present moment. It is the life of your mind as you look out on the world and reflect upon yourself. Of course by "the life of the mind" I do not mean to limit the notion only to those aspects of mind amenable to immediate or conscious recall.

Death is the stopping of this life. Bridgman said that " . . . my own death is such a different thing that it well might have a different word." I propose that we use the word *cessation*. Cessation ends the potentiality of any (further) conscious experience. It is essentially synonymous with the conclusion of conscious life.

In order to have a full appreciation of the role of cessation, we must understand a few additional terms:

Termination is the stopping of vital physiological function, including such gross measure as the heartbeat or the exchanges of gases between the person and his environment and such refined measures as what we now call "brain death." Physiological termination is always followed shortly by psychological cessation. The converse however is not always true: it is possible for (private) cessation to occur hours or even days before (public) termination. For example when a person's skull is crushed in an accident, cessation occurs at the instant he loses consciousness for the last time, but he might be kept alive in a hospital as long as he breathes and brainwave patterns are traced on the EEG. But his life ended the instant his mind was destroyed. Loved ones and hospital personnel saw him "alive" in the hospital but that could be an experience only for them. Because the moment of "death" is socially defined by termination, we need that concept even in a psychological approach to death.

Interruption is the stopping of consciousness with the expectation of further conscious experience. It is to use two contradictory terms, a kind of temporary cessation. Sleep—dreamless sleep—is perhaps the best example of an interruption. Other interruptions include unconsciousness, stupor, coma, fainting, seizures and anesthetic states, and can last from seconds to weeks. By definition the last interruption of a man's life is cessation.

Continuation is the experiencing of the stream of temporally continguous events. Our lives are thus made up of one series of alternating states of continuation and interruption.

As one would imagine, *altered continuation* implies the continuation of consciousness in a way that is different from an individual's usual or modal style of functioning. Examples would be intoxication, drugged states, hypnotic states, malingering, role-playing, spying, feigning and even "unplugging." "Unplugging"—a term suggested to me by Professor Erving Goffman—is getting out of one's ordinary track of life by drifting, seceding or uncorking, such as burying yourself in a book, going on a *Wanderjahr,* watching a Western or, more actively, going on an escapade, a binge or an orgy—in short, escaping, as opposed to sweating it out.

A neglected aspect of death is the role of the individual in his own demise. The current traditional (and in my view, erroneous) conceptualization that views death as an experience—noble, religious, frightening, beneficent, malign—makes too much of the individual's role in his own death. We have already decided that for the chief protagonist, death is not an experience at all. But there is still another traditional view of death that, curiously enough, makes too little of man's role in his own demise. That view can be seen in the way we conceptualize death in our official records.

In the Western world "death" is given its operational meaning by the death certificate. The death certificate can be divided into three parts, reflecting the three basic kinds of information that it is intended to convey: (a) the top third of the certificate identifies the decedent; (b) the second third of the certificate relates the cause or causes of death. The international manual lists around 140 possible causes of death, including pneumonia, meningitis, myocardial infarction; (c) the last third of the certificate is perhaps the most important for our interests. It is intended to tell us *how* the person died. It normally indicates one of four conceptual crypts into which each of us is eventually placed. I call this world-wide taxonomic scheme the NASH classification of death, standing for the four *modes* of death: natural, accidental, suicidal and homicidal. The main terms can be combined or modified: e.g., "Accident-Suicide, Undetermined" or "Probable Suicide."

It is evident that the *cause* of death does not automatically tell us the *mode* of death. "Asphyxiation due to drowning" or "barbituate overdose" does not automatically tell us whether the death was accidental or suicidal or homicidal. This NASH scheme tends to obscure rather than to clarify the nature of human death.

Much of this anachronistic classification can be traced to the 1600s when the English crown was interested in assigning blame. Natural and accidental deaths were by definition acts of nature or of God. The survivors could only be pitied and the legitimate heirs would come into their rightful inheritances. On the other hand, the culprit must be identified and punished in homicidal and suicidal deaths. Suicide was *felo-de-se,* a felony against the self, and the crown took the dead man's goods. The coroner's judgment thus could affect the fortunes of a family. From the beginning, certification of the mode of death served quasi-legal functions with distinct monetary overtones.

This anachronistic omission of the part that a man plays in his own death ties us to seventeenth-century Cartesian thinking and keeps us from enjoying the insights of contemporary psychology and psychiatry. In order to put man back into his own dying—a time of life when he is very much alive—we shall need to call upon social and behavioral science.

It can be argued that most deaths, especially in the younger years, are unnatural. Perhaps the termination of life might properly be called natural only in cases of death in old age. Consider the following confusions: if an individual (who wishes to live) has his chest invaded by a lethal steering wheel, his death is called accidental; if he is invaded by a lethal virus, his death is called natural; if his skull is invaded by a bullet in civilian life, his death is called homicidal. A person who torments an animal into killing him is said to have died by accident, whereas one who torments a drunken companion into killing him is called a victim of homicide. An individual whose artery bursts in his brain is said to have died with a cerebral-vascular accident, whereas it might make more sense to call it a cerebral-vascular natural.

In light of these confusing circumstances, I have proposed that we supplement the NASH classification by focusing on the *intention* of each person *vis-à-vis* his own death, that all human deaths be divided among those that are (a) intentioned, (b) subintentioned or (c) unintentioned.

Intentioned

In an intentioned death, the individual plays a direct and conscious role in effecting his own demise. Persons who die intentioned deaths can be divided into a number of subcategories:

1. *Death-seeker*. He has consciously verbalized to himself his wish for an ending to all conscious experience and he acts to achieve this end. The criterion for a death-seeker does not lie in his method—razor, barbiturate, carbon monoxide. It lies in the fact that *in his mind* the method will bring about cessation, and in the fact that he acts in such a manner that rescue is unlikely or impossible. An individual's orientation toward death shifts and changes. A person who was a death-seeker yesterday might take tender care of his life today. Most of the individuals who are death-seekers ("suicidal") are so for relatively brief periods; given appropriate surcease and sanctuary they will soon wish to live.

2. *Death-initiator*. He believes that he will die in the fairly near future or he believes that he is failing and—not wishing to accommodate himself to a less-effective and less-virile image of himself—does not wish to let death happen to him. Rather *he* wants to play the dominant role; he will do it for himself, at his own time and on his own terms. In investigations among persons in the terminal stages of disease, it has been found that some, with remarkable and totally unexpected energy and strength, take out their tubes and needles, climb over the bedrails, lift heavy windows and jump. When we look at the occupational history of such individuals we see that they have never been fired—they have always quit.

3. *Death-ignorer*. Some people who kill themselves believe that one can effect termination without cessation. But in our contemporary society even those who espouse a religious belief in a hereafter still put the label of "suicide" on a person who has shot himself to death. This is so probably because, whatever *really* happens after termination, the survivors are still left to mourn in the physical absence of the deceased. Thus this subcategory of death-ignorer or, perhaps better, death-transcender, contains those persons who, from their point of view, terminate themselves and continue to exist in some other manner.

   The concept of death-ignoring is necessary; otherwise we put ourselves in the position of making comparable a man who shoots himself in the head in the belief that he will meet his dead wife in heaven and a man who travels to another city with the expectation of being reunited with his spouse. We must consider that cessation is final as far as the human personality that we can know is concerned.

4. *Death-darer*. He bets his continuation (i.e., his life) on a relatively low probability of survival. Regardless of the outcome a person who plays Russian roulette—in which the chances of survival are only five out of six—is a death-darer, as is the uncoordinated man who attempts to walk the ledge of a tall building. The rule of thumb is, it is not what one does

that matters but the background (of skill, prowess and evaluation of his own abilities) against which he does it.

Unintentioned

At the other extreme an unintentioned death is any cessation in which the decedent plays no significant role in effecting his own demise. Here death is due entirely to trauma from without, or to simple biological failure from within. At the time of his cessation the individual is going about his own business (even though he may be hospitalized) with no conscious intention of hastening cessation and with no conscious drive to do so. What happens is that something occurs—a cerebral-vascular accident, a myocardial infarction, a neoplastic growth, a malfunction, an invasion—whether by bullet or by virus—that for him has lethal consequences. *It* happens to *him*.

Most traditional natural, accidental and homicidal deaths would be unintentioned, but no presently labeled suicidal deaths would be. Persons who die unintentioned deaths can be subcategorized as follows:

1. *Death-welcomer*. Although he plays no discernible (conscious or unconscious) role in hastening or facilitating his own cessation, he could honestly report an introspective position of welcoming an end to his life. Very old persons, especially after long, painful, debilitating illness, report that they would welcome the end.

2. *Death-accepter*. He has accepted the imminence of his cessation and is resigned to his fate. He may be passive, philosophical, resigned, heroic or realistic, depending on the spirit in which this enormous acceptance is made.

3. *Death-postponer*. Most of the time most of us are death-postponers. Death-postponing is the habitual orientation of most human beings toward cessation. The death-postponer wishes that cessation would not occur in the foreseeable future; that it would not occur for as long as possible.

4. *Death-disdainer*. Some individuals, when they consciously contemplate cessation, are disdainful of death and feel that they are above involvement in this implied stopping of the vital processes. They are in a sense supercilious toward death. Most young children in our culture, aside from their fears about death, are probably death-disdainers—as well they might be.

5. *Death-fearer*. He fears death—and even topics *relating to death*—to the point of phobia. He fights the notion of cessation, seeing reified death as something to be feared and hated. His position may relate to his wishes for omnipotence and to his investment in his social and physical potency. Hypochondriacs are perhaps death-fearers. (A physically well death-fearer might, when he is physically ill, become a death-facilitator.)

Imagine five older men on the same ward of a hospital, all dying of cancer, none playing an active role in his own cessation. Yet it is possible to distinguish different orientations toward death among them: one wishes not to die and is exerting his will to live (death-postponer); another is resigned to his cessation (death-accepter); the third will not believe that death can take him (death-disdainer); still another, although he takes no steps to hasten his end, embraces it (death-welcomer); and the fifth is frightened and forbids anyone to speak of death in his presence (death-fearer).

6. *Death-feigner*. It is of course possible to shout "Fire!" where there is no conflagration. It is also possible to yell or to murmur "Suicide!" when clearly there is no lethal intention. Calls like "Fire!," "Suicide!" or "Stop thief!" mobilize others. They are grab-words; they force society to act in certain ways. An individual who uses the semantic blanket of "Suicide!" in the absence of lethal intent is a death-feigner. A death-feigner simulates a self-directed movement toward cessation. He might ingest water from an iodine bottle or use a razor blade without lethal possibility or intent. He may seek some of the secondary gains that go with cessation-oriented behavior. These gains usually have to do with activating other persons— usually the "significant other" person in the neurotic dyadic relationship with the death-feigner.

Subintentioned

The most important death category—the one that I believe may be characteristic of a majority of deaths—is the *subintentioned* death, in which the decedent plays some covert or unconscious role in hastening his own demise. The evidence lies in a variety of behavior patterns that include poor judgment, imprudence, excessive risk-taking, neglect of self, disregard of medical regimen, abuse of alcohol, misuse of drugs—ways in which an individual can advance the date of his death by fostering the risk of his own dying.

Subintention is a somewhat mysterious concept, resting as it does on the powerful idea of unconscious motivation. It is "the subterranean miner that works in us all." The question is, as Herman Melville asked, " . . . can one tell whither leads his shaft by the ever shifting, muffled sound of his pick?"

Many deaths certified as natural have a subintentional quality about them. Many of us know of cases in which persons with diabetes, peptic ulcers, colitis, cirrhosis, Buerger's disease or pneumonia have, through psychologically laden commission, omission, disregard or neglect, hastened their own demise. In addition "voodoo deaths," inexplicable deaths in hospitals (especially in surgery), and some sudden declines in health can be considered subintentioned. There is a notion that the speed at which some malignancies grow may be related to deep inner psychological variables.

And if some natural deaths are subintentioned (and thus not entirely natural), many deaths certified as accident are even more so—and not entirely accidental. A run of inimical events in one person's life can hardly be thought to be purely accidental. Sometimes we see someone drive a car as though he were afraid that he might be late for his own accident; he may be hurling himself toward a subintentioned death. Many automobile fatalities are not quite accidents and may not comfortably be called suicides; they can be more meaningfully understood as subintentioned deaths.

Some suicides show aspects of the subintentioned death category. (This is especially true for many cases certified as probable suicides.) Indeed the entire concept of subintentioned death—which asserts the role of the unconscious in death—is similar in many ways to Karl Menninger's concepts of chronic suicide, focal suicide and organic suicide, except that Menninger's ideas have to do primarily with self-defeating ways of continuing to live, whereas the notion of subintentioned death is a way to stop the process of living. Cases of subintentioned death may in general be said to have permitted suicide.

Many fatal incidents certified as homicides might be better considered subintentioned deaths. It is obvious that in some close dyadic pairs (married couples, lovers, friends), the victim—like the chief mate of the *Town-Ho* in *Moby-Dick*—"sought to run more than half way to meet his doom." To provoke another person to kill you is an indirect participation, at some level of personality functioning, in the manipulation of one's date of death.

The hypothesis that individuals may play unconscious roles in their own failures and act in ways that are inimical to their own welfare seems to be too well documented from both psychoanalytic and general clinical practice to be safely ignored. Often death is hastened by the individual's seeming carelessness, imprudence, foolhardiness, forgetfulness, amnesia, lack of judgment or another psychological mechanism. Included in the subintention category would be many patterns of mismanagement and brink-of-death living that result in death.

Subintentioned death involves the psychosomatics of death; that is, cases in which essentially psychological processes (fear, anxiety, derring-do, hate, etc.) seem to play some role in exacerbating the catabolic processes that bring on termination (and necessarily cessation). Several types make up the subintentioned death groups:

1. *Death-chancer*. If a death-darer has only five chances out of six of continuing, then a death-chancer's chances are significantly greater but still involve a realistic risk of dying. It should be pointed out that these categories are largely independent of method in that most methods (like razor blades or barbiturates) can legitimately be thought of as intentioned, subintentioned or unintentioned depending on the circumstances. Individuals who "leave it up to chance," who "gamble with death," who "half-intend to do it," are subintentioned death-chancers.

2. *Death-hastener*. He unconsciously exacerbates a physiological disequilibrium so that his cessation (which would ordinarily be called a natural death) is expedited. This can be done either in terms of his life-style (the abuse of his body, usually through alcohol, drugs, exposure or malnutrition), or through the mismanagement or disregard of prescribed remedial

procedures. Consider the diabetic who mismanages his diet or his insulin, the individual with cirrhosis who mismanages his alcoholic intake, the Buerger's-disease patient who mismanages his nicotine intake. Closely allied to the death-hastener is the death-facilitator who, while he is ill and his psychic energies are low, is somehow more than passively unresisting to cessation, and makes it easy for termination to occur. Some unexpected deaths in hospitals may be of this nature.

3. *Death-capitulator.* By virtue of some strong emotion, usually his great fear of death itself, he plays a psychological role in effecting his termination. In a sense, he scares himself to death. This type of death includes voodoo deaths, the deaths reported among southwestern Indians and Mexicans in railroad-sponsored hospitals who thought that people went to hospitals to die, and other cases reported in psychiatric and medical literature.

4. *Death-experimenter.* A death-experimenter often lives on the brink of death. He consciously wishes neither interruption nor cessation, but— usually by excessive use of alcohol and/or drugs—he pursues a chronically altered, often befogged continuation. Death-experimenters seem to wish for a benumbed or drugged consciousness. They will often experiment with their self-prescribed dosages (always increasing them), taking some chances of extending the benumbed conscious state into interruption (coma) and even (usually in a lackadaisical way) running some minimal but real risk of extending the interruption into cessation. This type of death is traditionally thought of as accidental.

It is important to distinguish between subintention and ambivalence. Ambivalence is perhaps the single most important psychodynamic concept for understanding death—or any of life's major psychological issues. Ambivalence represents at least two simultaneous movements within the mind of one person toward divergent, even opposite, goals. Examples of such contradictory activities would be loving and hating the same person, yearning for both autonomy and dependence, and, at rock bottom, moving toward both life and death. The concomitant movement toward each of these diverse goals is genuine in its own right. One can ingest pills, genuinely wishing to die, and at the same time entertain earnest fantasies of rescue. The paradigm of suicide is one of the deepest ambivalence; to cut one's throat and to cry for help—in the same breath.

On the other hand subintention does not emphasize the dual character of man's behavior so much as, in its own way, it emphasizes the unconscious aspects of man's being. Subintentioned acts, whether toward death or toward the expansion of life, are essentially movements toward outcomes that are not conscious goals. They are life's maneuvers that well up out of unconscious motivations and thus are more subtle in their appearance and more difficult to account. Is smoking suicidal? Drinking? Driving? Skiing? These questions cannot be answered yes or no. The answer is "It depends," and it may depend on a number of factors including the individual's orientations toward death and toward others in his life.

With some passionate emphasis Arnold Toynbee makes the point that death is essentially dyadic—a two-person event—and that as such the survivor's burden is the heavier. When he considers his own situation, he writes:

> I guess that if, one day, I am told by my doctor that I am going to die before my wife, I shall receive the news not only with equanimity but with relief. This relief, if I do feel it, will be involuntary. I shall be ashamed of myself for feeling it, and my relief will, no doubt, be tempered by concern and sorrow for my wife's future after I have been taken from her. All the same, I do guess that, if I am informed that I am going to die before her, a shameful sense of relief will be one element in my reaction. This is, as I see it, the capital fact about the relation between living and dying. There are two parties to the suffering that death inflicts; and, in the apportionment of this suffering, the survivor takes the brunt.

In focusing on the importance of the dyadic relationship in death, Toynbee renders a great service to all who are concerned with death, particularly with suicide. The typical suicide is an intensely dyadic event. The crucial role of the "significant other" in prevention of suicide is one aspect of the new look in suicidology.

Although it is difficult to take a stance counter to Toynbee, I believe that in emphasizing the dyadic aspect of death he seems to leap from a sentimental attitude of burden-sharing in a love relationship—the noble husband's wish to save his beloved wife from the anguish of bereavement—to an unnecessarily romantic view of death itself. In cases of absolutely sudden and precipitous deaths, the total sum of dyadic pain is borne by the survivor (inasmuch as the victim cannot experience any of it). But in protracted dying the present pain and anguish involved in the frightening anticipation of being dead may very well be sharper for the dying person than the pain suffered then and afterward by the survivor. The algebra of death's suffering is complicated.

For all his wisdom I believe that Toynbee indulges in the romanticization of death. In my view the larger need is to deromanticize death and suicide.

Certainly one of the most remarkable characteristics of man's psychological life is the undiluted and enduring love affair that each of us has with his own consciousness. Trapped as he is within his own mind, man nurtures his conscious awareness, accepts it as the criterion for mediating reality, and entertains a faithful life-long dialogue with it—even (or especially) when he takes leave of his senses. Often man communicates with his mind as though it were a separate "other," whereas he is really communicating with himself. Indeed, the other to whom he talks is in large part what he defines himself to be. Death peremptorily decrees an abrupt, unwelcome and final adjournment and dissolution of what Henry Murray has aptly called "the Congress of the mind." Death—i.e., being—is total cessation, personal nothingness, individual annihilation. Should one traffic with one's greatest mortal enemy, rationalize its supposed noble and saving qualities and then romanticize it as an indispensable part of dyadic life?

One difficulty with death is that within himself each man is noble—indestructible and all-surviving. Being conscious is all one has. That is what one's life is. Consciousness defines the duration and the scope of life, and the scope can be rich or the scope can be arid, a partial death that can come long before one's cessation.

Our current attitudes toward death are unconscionably sentimental. The several notions—of "heroic death," "generativity" and "wise death" in mature old age—are culture-laden rationalizations, as though the cerebrator could ever be truly equanimous about the threat of his own naughtment or his annihilation.

Although there are undoubtedly special circumstances in which some individuals either welcome their own cessation or are essentially indifferent to it, for almost everyone the heightened probability of his own cessation constitutes the most dire threat possible. By and large the most distressing contemplation one can have is of his own cessation. Much of religion is tied to this specter—and perhaps all of man's concern with immortality. We must face the fact that completed dying (i.e., death or cessation) is the one characteristic act in which man is forced to engage.

In this context, the word *forced* has a special meaning. It implies that a characteristic that death shares with torture, rape, capital punishment, kidnapping, lobotomy and degradation ceremonies is the quality of impressment. The threat of being reduced to nothingness can be viewed reasonably only as the strongest and the most perfidious of forced punishments.

In all this I do not believe that I am echoing Dylan Thomas's "Do not go gentle into that good night. Rage, rage against the dying of the light." Rather I am saying that one should know that cessation is the curse to end all curses, and *then* one can, as he chooses, rage, fight, temporize, bargain, compromise, comply, acquiesce, surrender, welcome or even embrace death. But one should be aware of the dictum: Know thine enemy.

Death is not a tender retirement, a bright autumnal end "as a shock of corn to his season" of man's cycle. That notion, it seems to me, is of the same order of rationalization as romanticizing kidnapping, murder, impressment or rape.

Nor does it mollify the terror of death to discuss it in the honorific and beguiling terms of maturity, postnarcissistic love, ego-integrity or generativity, even though one can only be grateful to Erik Erikson for the almost perfectly persuasive way in which he has made a generative death sound ennobling and nearly worthwhile.

I wonder if it would not be better to understand generativity as reflecting pride and gratitude in one's progenitors and perhaps even greater pride and faith in one's progeny, without the necessity of deriving any pleasure from one's own finiteness and the prospect of one's demise. There is (or ought to be) a reasonable difference between experiencing justifiable pride in what one has been and is and has created, on the one hand, and, on the other hand, feeling an unwarranted equanimity when one reflects that he will soon no longer be. Maturity and ego integrity relate to the former; the later is supported largely by the romantic, sentimental rationalization that one's cessation is a blessing. Such a rationalization is nothing less than psychological willing what is biologically obligatory. It may be more mature to bemoan this fact and regret it.

All this means that death is a topic for the tough and the bitter—people like Melville, in "The Lightning-Rod Man": "Think of being a heap of charred offal, like a haltered horse burned in his stall; and all in one flash!" Or Camus, especially in Meursault's burst of antitheistic and antideath rage just before the end of *The Stranger*.

A look at another culture might throw some light on this problem. When I was in Japan a few years ago, it seemed to me that one of the most pervasive religio-cultural features of the country was the romantically tinged animism that infused the religious thinking. It was not a more primitive feeling, but rather a more personal and spirited feeling, especially about nature. For example the Japanese feelings about a cherry tree in its ephemerally beautiful bloom seemed totally different from the feelings that an average American would muster on looking at a blossoming apple tree. The Japanese closeness to nature, akin to deification, seems to lead to a special Japanese feeling toward death—which I would have to call romanticization.

When I addressed a group of Japanese university students, one youth asked me if I could give him any reason why he should not kill himself if he sincerely believed that he would then become one with nature. The very quality of this question illustrates this animizing and romanticizing of death. Further I recall a young engineer who sat beside me on the new Tōkaidō train and wrote out: "Cherry blossoms is blooming quickly and scattering at once. Better to come to fruition and die like the blossom." He added: "We have had many great men among our forefathers whose deeds remind us of the noble characteristics of cherry blossoms."

In this country, the romanticization of certain types of homicides is an especially troublesome part of our national heritage. The honorifics go to the man with the gun. We have glamorized our rural bandits and our urban gangsters. The romanticized myth of the Western frontier, built around the image of the man with a gun, has set its homicidal stamp on our culture. The problem for television may not be the effects of violence but the effects of the romanticization of violence.

This romanticization of death goes to the beginnings of our national history. We depict our revolutionary heroes as Minutemen with rifles—as though it were primarily guns that had won the war. Perhaps more appropriate monuments at Lexington and Concord—we have even lost the meaning of the word "concord"—might have been statues of Paine and Jefferson seated, with pens. Unquestionably these representations would have implied quite different values and might have shaped our culture in a somewhat different direction. Our recent inability to amend our gun laws in the wake of a series of catastrophic assassinations has been a national disaster and a grisly international joke, highlighting our irrational tie to our own essentially anti-intellectual legends of romanticized homicide.

Romantic notions of death are obviously related to suicide. Individuals who are actively suicidal suffer—among their other burdens—from a temporary loss of the view of death-as-enemy. This is the paradox and the major logical fallacy of self-inflicted death. It capitulates to the decapitator.

Suicidal folk have lost sight of the foe: they sail with full lights in the hostile night. They are unvigilant and forgetful. They behave in strange, almost traitorous ways. They attempt to rationalize death's supposed lofty qualities and—what is most difficult to deal with—to romanticize death as the noblest part of dyadic love. Loyal-to-life people are inured against nefarious propaganda leading to defection. One should not traffic with the enemy. Suicidal individuals have been brainwashed—by their own thoughts.

How could the de-romanticization of death help suicidal persons? Would it be salutary or beneficial to embark on programs of de-romanticizing death in our schools—with courses in "death education"—or in our public media? In the treatment of the acutely suicidal person what would be the effects of directing his mind to a view of death as an enemy? Would such a psychological regimen hasten the suicide, have no effect at all, or would it make a death-postponer of him? In my own mind, the nagging question persists: would not this type of effort, like practically every other earnest exhortation in this alienated age, itself be doomed to an untimely figurative death?

But perhaps even more important is the question: how would the de-romanticization of death reduce the number of those especially *evil* deaths of murder, violence, massacre and genocide? Here, paradoxically, I am a trifle more optimistic. If only we can recognize that our three crushing national problems—the black citizen, the war in Vietnam, and the threat of nuclear death—all contain the common element of dehumanizing others (and, concomitantly, brutalizing and dehumanizing ourselves), then acting out of the urgent need to reverse our present national death-oriented course, we might bring new dimensions to life. But in order to avert the death of our own institutions we shall, in addition to being the home of the brave and the land of the free, have to become the country of the humane.

KENNETH P. COHEN

Hospice: A Caring Community

Within the general orientation of the hospice programs, several different approaches are possible. Here, Cohen outlines models of hospice care for home, independent facility, or hospital. Because cure of the patient is no longer the objective, the attention shifts to treatment of symptoms that cause discomfort and to psychological support for the patient and family.

To live without feeling or exciting sympathy, to be fortunate without adding to the felicity of others, or afflicted without tasting the balm of pity, is a state more gloomy than solitude: it is not retreat, but exclusion from mankind.

Samuel Johnson, *Rasselas*

Attend a workshop or meeting with hospice-interested people, and a sense of camaraderie pervades the setting. Not only are old friendships renewed, but the feeling of sharing, and an indescribable sensitivity brought about by dealing with death, ripple through the discussions both at the formal sessions and at the informal social gatherings. This sense of sharing is different and more intense than I have found at similar gatherings of hospital-interested people. There is also no comparable tone in meetings of those who do not provide personal services in their everyday lives. Barbara Hill, former executive director of Hospice of Marin, described this special hospice feeling beautifully at the Third National Hospice Symposium:

> My belief is that a specific environment needs to be created to develop a hospice—that of the love relationship. I believe that in a truly accepting, undemanding love environment the source exists for growth of the individual. It matters not whether that love is the love of husband and wife, therapist and client, mother and child, or hospice staff member and hospice family—when that mutual love and trust develop, miracles happen.[1]

Plant contends that "hospices are gaining favor in the U.S. because they are a curious amalgam of reactions and responses." She claims that one reaction is against the cure-at-any-cost syndrome that pervades the acute-care hospital. Another is the rebellion against hospital regulations that tend to keep

Source: Reprinted from *Hospice: Prescription for Terminal Care,* © 1979, Aspen Systems Corporation, Rockville, Md.

patients and families apart in times of crisis. A third reaction is against certain of society's attitudes about death that prevent the provision of the best care to the dying. The responses are all part of the slowly emerging movement toward death with dignity and the search for alternatives to institutionalization.[2]

All programs that care for the dying and their families are not necessarily hospice programs.[3] "A hospice is not a hospital and not a nursing home. The hospice is inspired by a different philosophy of care, relates to different goals, and provides different services to an entirely different population of cancer patients."[4] The hospice concept does not suggest a deficit in hospital care, but rather recognizes the fact that neither general, teaching, nor research hospitals are staffed for and oriented to providing care for terminally ill patients.[5]

Hospice Models

As noted earlier, a hosice is not necessarily an institution; a hospice is a program of care. It may be a home care program, a free-standing institution, a separate hospital department, or an interdisciplinary team that moves within a general hospital to wherever the patients may be located within the facility. It may offer outpatient services or day care; it may offer the home care in conjunction with the institutional settings, or it might combine variations of these models. A controversy is currently brewing over which of these models is the best for terminally ill patients. There is, however, no one "best" model.

Home Care and Institutional Hospice Services

Most people, given the choice, would prefer to die at home. Hence, home care hospice services seem to be most appropriate. Yet, a point may come in the home care regimen when the patient may have to be sent to an institutional hospice for a time to control new symptoms, provide the psychological boost of a fresh environment, or to provide relief and rest for the family members who must provide 24-hour-per-day aid to the patient.

The patient, then, will be transferred to the institutional hospice for a few days before being returned to the home and familiar surroundings so important to the terminally ill.

> The dying have the right to a great many things that hospitals and nursing homes simply cannot provide. They need life around them, spiritual and emotional comfort and support of every sort. They need "unsanitary" things, like a favorite dog lying at the foot of the bed. They need their own clothes, their own pictures, music, food, surroundings that are familiar to them, people they know and love, people they can trust to care about them. Hospices can provide this in their inpatient units; and yet, for many individuals and their families, it is much better for it to happen at home.[6]

Free-Standing Versus Hospital-Based Hospices

At this writing, the National Cancer Institute has provided funding for three separate free-standing hospices. At this writing, only one is operative:

Hillhaven Hospice in Tucson, Arizona. Under construction is Hospice, Inc., in New Haven, Connecticut, and to become operational by mid-to-late 1978 is Kaiser-Permanente Medical Care Program in Los Angeles. Although British hospices are almost exclusively free-standing, it appears unlikely that United States hospices will emerge as free-standing facilities.

Several additional free-standing facilities will probably be built in the future, but growth of the movement will depend on expansion of the home care and hospital-based models. Home care–based hospices will grow because of the inherent cost-saving features, and hospital-based hospices will proliferate because of the excess hospital beds available throughout the country. Because of the excess hospital beds, capital construction funds are and will be extremely difficult to obtain. Lawrence Burke of the National Cancer Institute feels that "it would more than compromise and complicate the [hospice] program to have it initiated within a general hospital."[7] On the other hand, Balfour Mount of the Royal Victoria Hospital questions the economic feasibility of free-standing hospices. "Analysis of the economics of maintaining such institutions . . . suggests that society cannot afford to support an adequate number to meet the need."[8]

A major objection to the hospital-based hospice unit is the almost diametrically opposed philosophies of *acute* care and *palliative* care. Opponents reason that the terminally ill patients are torn apart by observing hospital patients who will be leaving the hospital in the matter of a few days well on the road to recovery. To be in a hospital and know that patients in other parts of the hospital will be *cured* of their illnesses is a tremendous psychological barrier to the effective care of the hospice patients. Then, too, the acute-care training of personnel has run counter to that needed for hospice care. Hospital personnel will frequently refer to the hospice unit as the "dead end," or they may make other disparaging remarks that only serve to antagonize the hospice personnel and that may result in counter-productivity to the type of care to be provided to hospice patients.

The Mixed-Community Hospice

A 1950 study of cancer patients concluded that facilities for the care of terminal cancer patients should not be set up as specialized institutions operated solely for the care of *cancer* patients, as places where patients go to die from cancer. The report wisely proclaimed that, "specialization of this type is almost inhuman in the emotional trauma it produces for the patient and his family."[9] British hospices do not care only for the terminally ill, nor do they concentrate only on problems associated with advanced cancer. For example, St. Joseph's Hospice in Hackney, London has always had a well-mixed community of patients, and it has a home care program in its geographical area for anyone dying of anything. It also has a unit for long-term rehabilitation and home support. St. Christopher's Hospice in Sydenham, London has a wing for frail elderly and has a number of longer-stay patients with various diagnoses in its wards.[10]

Appropriate Treatment

The distinction between appropriate and inappropriate treatment of patients is a paramount concern of hospices. "This distinction means concentration on control of symptoms when definitive treatment for disease is no longer possible," writes Sylvia Lack. She adds that the best way to do this is with a centrally coordinated service of in-patient beds and a home care program under an autonomous hospice administration.[11] When a person's life is in its last few hours, that person needs a quiet place in which to die naturally. Most patients in a hospice die peacefully with no intravenous injections or gastric tubes, but if such treatment is appropriate, it is used.[12]

Patients come to hospices only when they have terminal illnesses that can no longer be treated or cured. The omission of further surgery or radiotherapy for these patients is the omission of extraordinary and optional means of prolonging the dying process. Thus, hospices do not practice dysthanasia; they practice JUCTO (justifiable use of conservative therapy only).[13]

> Formerly, when most people died at home, children grew up with a realistic understanding of death from which they are now shielded. Yet watching someone die in the loving and caring surrounding of a hospice surely does less emotional damage to a young child than watching even one evening of television violence.[14]

> Britain's 30-odd hospices are homelike places of care where terminally ill patients, with or without money, are given everything possible to allow them to die with dignity and to avoid unnecessary prolongation of life. The hospices are constantly developing new techniques to reduce pain, and doctors and nurses are devoting their entire careers to furthering this aim.[15]

Elements of a Hospice Program

The most common indication for admission to hospices—in some 40 percent of cases—is the need to give respite to relatives. On the other hand, 20 percent of admissions are social isolates with no one able or willing to care for them. At the same time, 60 percent of admissions need help with better control of their pain. Thus, hospice patients represent a mix of social and clinical need.[16]

A hospice program then, is not just a program that purports to care for the terminally ill. It is a program for meeting a wide range of physical, psychological, social and spiritual needs, a program of health care delivery consisting of ten clearly identifiable elements:

1. Service availability to home care patients and inpatients on a 24-hour-a-day, seven-day-a-week, on-call basis with emphasis on availability of medical and nursing skills
2. Home care service in collaboration with inpatient facilities
3. Knowledge and expertise in the control of symptoms (physical, psychological, social, and spiritual)

4. The provision of care by an interdisciplinary team
5. Physician-directed services
6. Central administration and coordination of services
7. Use of volunteers as an integral part of the health care team
8. Acceptance to the program based on health needs, not ability to pay
9. Treatment of the patient and family together as the unit of care
10. A bereavement follow-up service[17]

Not all existing hospice programs incorporate all ten of these elements. For example, some are entirely home care oriented, while others are exclusively institution based with no home care services; some have very limited bereavement follow-up service, while others have extensive bereavement service; many have services available on a 24-hour-a-day, seven-day-a-week basis; while some have more limited hours. Nevertheless, the ten elements represent the ideal to be achieved by any hospice program.

Home Care Plus Inpatient Services

The goal of hospice care is to help a patient continue life as usual—working, being with a family, doing what is especially significant before life comes to a close, and feeling a part of the ongoing life—not being different. Much of this type of care is fostered through the home care and outpatient programs. Hospices place primary emphasis on home care so that patients can maintain their life styles as long as possible, but they usually supplement the home care with their own inpatient unit, or they may have an arrangement with a local palliative-care hospital unit. The practical needs are to relieve families for a while, to provide 24-hour medical supervision when symptoms cannot be controlled at home, and to guarantee the professional care that is necessary during the final weeks of life. The overriding ideological and practical need, however, is continuity of care, for without a hospice-run inpatient unit, patients must enter hospitals or nursing homes and lose touch with the special symptom-control measures and medication regimens that typify hospice care.[18] The knowledge that a hospice bed is available in the inpatient facility often makes it possible for the patient to remain at home longer than either the family or the patient consider possible.

Emotional and Psychological Support

Emotional and psychological support is as essential an element of care as symptom control. Each patient is seen as part of a family unit, whose total well-being and lifestyle affect and are affected by care. Flexibility geared to the patient's mental and physical comfort characterizes the inpatient unit. Visiting hours are flexible (usually 24 hours per day), very young children and even pets are welcome at any time, meals are provided on demand, and wine and liquor are served in moderation. Patients also wear their own clothing and can bring favorite possessions, including furniture from home.[19]

In an article in the popular press, English hospice residents were described as being able to move about and enjoy days filled with a variety of activities, including art classes, pottery, crafts, bingo games, musical entertainment by volunteers, gardening, and automobile drives. All this while the patients were heavily dosed with pain-killing narcotics—yet most seemed alert.[20] For the patient with too much time to think, the systematic use of games of all kinds, under the supervision of the occupational therapist, is necessary.

In English hospices, even mealtime is a social event. Sherry or beer is always served before the meals. This stimulates the appetite and relaxes the patient as well as contributes to the nutritional state. Each course is then brought in separately and served to the patient in small portions. The nurse or volunteer takes the necessary care and time to make the patient feel wanted. This is unlike American hospitals, where large portions of food are placed on a tray in front of the patient, and personnel return in one-half to three-fourths of an hour to remove the usually uneaten meal.[21]

In an age of specialization and fragmentation, when a variety of medical specialists may be fascinated by the disease process and forget the patient, it falls to the nurse to reaffirm the personal identity and unique worth of the patient. However, care must be exercised that the staff address the patients as adults who understand. It is all too easy to talk down to patients, as though they were children or mentally deficient.[22] If this is done, the patient's emotional needs will not be met and all the good work of the hospice will be undone.

Little things are important, such things as washing a patient's hair, helping the patient to write a letter, moving the bed closer to the window to afford a better view of outdoor activities; these services can all be performed by either nursing personnel or volunteers. And of course physical touch is extremely important. Holding hands, caressing the face, stroking the hair—these are all forms of intimate communication, communication that does not depend on the spoken word. These continual personal reassurances to the dying patient speak of love, deep compassionate love between human beings.

The Interdisciplinary Team Approach

Fundamental to the hospice concept is the interdisciplinary team approach. No one person has all the answers to the problems of the dying patient and the family; such problems are multitudinous. The team is usually headed by a clinical physician. "The hospice program of care usually is directed by a physician for two reasons: first, symptom control, the focus of hospice care, is a medical concern, and second, a medical director is best able to generate understanding and support for the hospice concept among other physicians."[13]

It is the physician who gives general direction to members of the other disciplines—nurses, social workers, chaplains, physiotherapists, psychiatrists, dieticians, pharmacists, and volunteers. The composition of the interdisciplinary team will, of course, differ with each hospice.

Clearly the roles of doctor, priest and nurse are not going to be in neat compartments, for at times they will be completely interchangeable. To be instantly responsive to the patient's needs, one requires nurses who can alter the dosage of drugs, recognize when to give a wide range of "when necessary" prescriptions, and insert a urinary catheter. One needs doctors who can also be spiritual advisers and clergymen who can competently impart a grave prognosis. It is the widening of the scope of one's work, closer to the traditional role of the old-time family doctor, which is the principal attraction in care of the dying.[24]

Because the physician, the psychiatrist, and the nurse have acquired the image of being too busy, the person whom the patient and family frequently confide in about their deepest concerns is the volunteer, who is seen as the one person who has time and understanding.[25] Volunteers are utilized both in inpatient and home care programs. There are no standards for numbers of volunteers who might be used in various programs, but for home care programs a ratio of 12 lay volunteers to each professional is suggested.[26]

The legal counselor can be an important part of the interdisciplinary team. An attorney can help with legal, financial, or estate-planning needs, drafting the documents necessary to guarantee that patients' dependents will be sensibly provided for. Patients will then at least have peace of mind knowing that their wishes will be honored and that their loved ones will be protected.[27]

When unpleasant symptoms are under control and the patient is able to return home from the hospice facility for a time, then a social worker can be the liaison between the two and can help to deal with the economic consequences of a disease that has destroyed a person's earning capacity. All financial worries should be resolved before the death.[28]

Some of the team members may experience the "burn-out" phenomenon, especially the nursing personnel. Dealing with death, becoming intensely involved emotionally with patients and their families day after day, can affect a care giver psychologically and emotionally. The emotional drain caused by several deaths occurring in a relatively short period of time can take its toll in pent-up emotions screaming to be released; therefore, some hospice facilities are providing "scream rooms" to provide this release. Jerry Coash, director of the Encino Hospital palliative care unit, explained that he copes with this problem by having the nurses who spend the majority of their time in the hospice unit occasionally rotated to other nursing units within the hospital, even though continuity suffers.[29]

The Family as Patient

To the hospice team, the "patient" is undeniably the patient and the family. The family, in the broad sense, includes not only the natural family (immediate and other relatives), but also the extended family (natural family plus friends, and even pets) and the adopted family (the care givers).[30] Figure 1 shows the relationship of the elements of care to the unit of care: the terminally ill patient and the family.

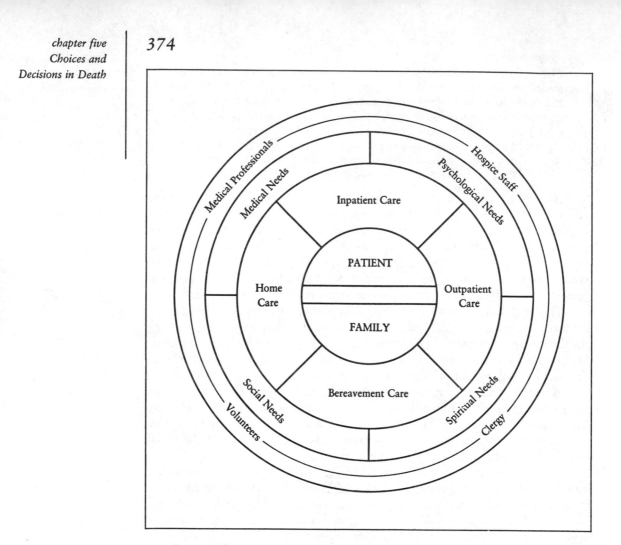

Source: "The Hospice Movement," Management Services Special Report, unpublished (Newport Beach, California: Advanced Health Systems, Inc., October 1977), p. 4. Reprinted by permission of Advanced Health Systems, Inc., 881 Dover Drive, Suite 20, Newport Beach, California 92663.

Naturally, some relatives will be part of the caring team, some will be patients along with the dying person, while others will alternate between the two roles. It may be that they will need to be put up in the facility overnight, if they are too distressed to return home alone, or if they want to be close at hand when death is imminent.[31]

Because they are also patients, relatives need to be cared for as well. For this reason, some hospices have a "relative's day off," when visiting of all but the most severely ill patients is discouraged. This releases the friend or relative who feels a duty to be visiting the loved one as much as possible and who consequently never gets out. Otherwise, visiting is unrestricted.[32]

The death of a person should leave the family with no feelings that they did not do enough. They should be directly involved in the patient's care. The team can teach the family various health care measures that will enable the patient to remain at home and, when inpatient care becomes necessary, should encourage the family to participate in that care too, by helping the nurses with feeding, turning, washing, and so on. Since this is their last offering, they want to be as close as possible to their loved one.[33]

Bereavement Services

Since grief begins at the moment when the patient's illness is diagnosed as terminal, relatives should not be told of this condition and then left to their own devices. They should be invited to come back and talk over their distress and to ask questions.[34] "To support a family through grieving before and after bereavement demands understanding and tolerance from the care givers. Understanding implies a familiarity with the patterns and processes of normal grief, while tolerance implies a capacity to accept the variable forms the process may assume."[35]

Bereavement follow-up is an essential part of hospice care. Follow-up can last for any length of time and take various forms, including home visits by team members who had treated the patient, phone calls, notes, or assisting a lonely spouse in finding a job. Such follow-up helps to support not only the family at a time when its members are particularly vulnerable to physical and psychological stress, but also the hospice team, which has also suffered a loss in the death of a patient.[36] William Lamers, in an interview describing the operation of Hospice of Marin, stated, "When our nurses and counselors have worked with a family and ultimately death occurs, each individual who worked with that family attends the funeral. Then we see that families are followed by our nurses and counselors for a period of a least a year after death has occurred."[37]

In a hospice there are often a number of bereaved people who are working through their grief by doing voluntary work for a few months following the death.[37] Thus, this activity is therapeutic for the survivors. Yet most hospices permit this only for a period of, say, six months to a year after the death.

Notes

1. Barbara Hill, "The 'How To' of Hospice Care," Proceedings of the Third National Hospice Symposium, Dominican College Campus, San Rafael, California, May 26–28, 1977, p. 18.

2. Janet Plant, "Finding a Home for Hospice Care in the U.S.," Hospitals, Journal of the American Hospital Association 51 (July 1, 1977): 53–62.

3. Sylvia Lack, "I Want to Die While I'm Still Alive," Death Education 1, no. 2 (Summer 1977): 165–76.

4. Letter from Lawrence D. Burke, Program Director for Rehabilitation Treatment, Re-

habilitation and Continuing Care Branch (DCCR), National Cancer Institute, HEW, December 15, 1977.

5. Ibid.

6. Sandol Stoddard citing William Lamers, *The Hospice Movement: A Better Way of Caring for the Dying* (Briarcliff Manor, N.Y.: Stein and Day, 1978), p. 51.

7. Burke letter.

8. Balfour M. Mount, "The Problem of Caring for the Dying in a General Hospital: The Palliative Care Unit as a Possible Solution," *Canadian Medical Association Journal* 115 (July 17, 1976): 119–21.

9. *Terminal Care for Cancer Patients* (Chicago: Central Service for the Chronically Ill of the Institute of Medicine of Chicago, 1950). p. 15.

10. St. Christopher's Hospice, "Annual Report, 1976–1977," p. 12.

11. Lack, "I Want to Die While I'm Still Alive."

12. Ibid.

13. D. G. McCarthy, "Should Catholic Hospitals Sponsor Hospices?" *Hospital Progress* 57 (December 1976): 61–5.

14. Ibid.

15. Richard Kolbe, "Inside the English Hospice," *Hospitals* 51 (July 1, 1977): 65–7.

16. E. Wilkes, "Terminal Care and the Special Nursing Unit," *Nursing Times* 71 (January 9, 1975): 57–9.

17. Sylvia Lack, "Philosophy and Organization of a Hospice Program," Unpublished paper, n.d.; "I Want to Die While I'm Still Alive."

18. Plant, "Finding a Home for Hospice Care in the U.S."

19. Ibid.

20. Michael Satchell, "How to Enjoy Life—Up to the Last Moment," *Parade*, October 16, 1977.

21. M. A. Rose and Walter J Pories, "Some Additional Notes on Hospices," *Ohio State Medical Journal* 73 (June 1977), 379–82.

22. *Palliative Care Service: October 1976 Report* (Montreal: Royal Victoria Hospital, McGill University, 1976), p. 75.

23. Plant, "Finding a Home for Hospice Care in the U.S."

24. Richard Lamerton, *Care of the Dying* (Westport, Conn.: Technomic Publishing Co., 1976), p. 22.

25. Lack, "I Want to Die While I'm Still Alive."

26. Burke letter.

27. Barton E. Bernstein, "Lawyer and Counselor as an Interdisciplinary Team: Interfacing for the Terminally Ill," *Death Education* 1 (Fall 1977): 277–91.

28. Lamerton, *Care of the Dying*, p. 21.

29. "Hospice Care—A New Concept for the Care of the Terminally Ill and Their Families," Workshop at UCLA Extension, Los Angeles, April 8–9, 1978.

30. Robert Woodson, "The Concept of Hospice Care in Terminal Disease," *Breast Cancer*, ed. J. M. Vaeth (Basel, Switzerland: Karger, 1976), pp. 161–79.

31. Lamerton, *Care of the Dying*, p. 20.

32. Ibid., p. 21.

33. Ibid., p. 40.

34. Ibid., p. 125.

35. *Palliative Care Service*, p. 84.

36. Plant, "Finding a Home for Hospice Care in the U.S."

37. "Hospice," Interview with William Lamers, Jr., Medical Director, Hospice of Marin, *Thanatos*, March 1977, pp. 6–11.

38. Lamerton, *Care of the Dying*, p. 129.

ROBERT KASTENBAUM

Exit and Existence: Alternative Scenarios

Hospice programs, once part of a visionary scenario, are now institutional realities. Robert Kastenbaum looks ahead in the following article sketching contrasting scenarios for the exit from existence. Noting that society has the power to develop scripts for the whole human life span, Kastenbaum explores the range of decisions available for expanding the quality of life during the latter part of the life span. Through a series of life-affirming decisions, society can make age a positive value.

How It Will Be from Now On: A Scenario

This projection is organized with reference to the way society has been answering the following question: what value is there in being an old, dying, or dead person?

It is useful to introduce one further concept: "the death system." This term refers to the functional network through which a society comes to terms with death, including people, places, objects, and symbols.[1] Some of these components are identified primarily, and permanently, by their role in the death system—for example, the funeral director, cemetery, death certificate; other components may be recruited into the system as the occasion demands. The death system performs several vital functions: predictions and warnings of the possibility of death and actions intended to prevent it; care of the dying or otherwise doomed person; physical disposition of the corpse; consolation and reintegration of survivors and the establishment of an orientation toward or relationship with the dead. Explanations and rationalizations of death are part of the system. Those actions which have the effect of bringing about death are as much a part of the system as the components of prediction and prevention. Certain aspects of the society's economic function and structure are, of course, part of the death system. How much money do you suppose changes hands in our society each year for death-related reasons? The answer to this question would include much if not all of the national defense budget; "life" insurance premiums, payments, and commissions; floral offerings; the pet-food industry; newspaper income from death notices; and so on.

These functions can be discerned in all societies; relative emphasis varies,

Source: Selection from Robert Kastenbaum, "Exit and Existence: Society's Unwritten Script for Old Age and Death," in David D. Van Tassel, ed., *Aging, Death and the Completion of Being,* © 1979, Case Western Reserve University. Published by University of Pennsylvania Press, Philadelphia, 1979.

however, from one society to another, or within the same society in different periods. The relative proportions of children, adults, and elderly adults at a given time will be a factor; but so will the prevailing system of religious beliefs and practices or a cycle of good or poor harvests.

The scenario for the future that suggests itself for our own society is based on the assumption that certain current trends will become dominant while other already entrenched attitudes and practices will continue. It is important to emphasize that this present-tense description represents one view of the way things *might* be. One approach to this scenario can be obtained by working backward from death itself.

1. There is no point in being dead. This view has now been made palpable by the systematic conversion of burial grounds to other, more utilitarian, purposes. Except for those relatively few cemeteries now designated as historical sites, the burial ground has virtually disappeared from the landscape. Again, with few exceptions, the recently deceased are not commemorated by conspicuous, space-wasting monuments. This practice has been losing much of its vitality for decades, anyway, as suggested by the increasing standardization of tombstone inscriptions. Other kinds of memorial practices have also been reduced to a minimum that a previous generation might not have thought possible. Traffic is no longer held up by the slow-moving cortege of limousines and mourners. Busy people no longer miss a day's work to stand in the wind or rain while a deceased colleague is lowered into the earth. Efficiency and common sense have at last prevailed. Our death system's gradually lessened interest in relating to or utilizing the dead, a phenomenon observed by a few in previous years, has moved from the mental–emotional sphere to the physical and official change of visible practices associated with disposal of the dead and with remembrance.[2] Naturally, services are available for those deviant and troubled individuals whose functioning is impaired by unresolved feelings about a dead person. According to the latest clinical and scientific reports, systematic desensitization to bereavement as a routine activity of the behavior modifiers has had reasonably consistent success.

2. There is little point in dying. In fact, as compared with the previous generation or two, there is relatively little "dying" per se. One reason for the diminished significance of dying, of course, has been the perfection of an integrated, computerized system for (a) determining a person's level of viability; (b) evaluating availability and cost of alternative treatment and maintenance procedures; and (c) resolving the problems of terminal care and body disposal. The United States Public Health Service operates the Super-Euthanasiac Computer, into which all relevant data are constantly programmed. When the computer detects and validates a critical configuration of disability, prognosis, and cost estimate, a quick and painless termination is accomplished—including selection of the appropriate body-disposal route. It is no wonder that the president of the American Medical Association has expressed unstinting approval of this technique. The need to make life-and-death decisions that began to weigh so heavily upon medical personnel in the

1960s and 1970s has now been almost entirely eliminated. Moreover, the unacceptable expense of maintaining incurable and unproductive citizens has been sharply reduced (although it must be admitted that the cost of the new computer system has been considerably higher than anticipated). Some observers were surprised, however, when the Pope herself expressed strong approval. Few could quarrel, however, with her assertion that the new system would promote favorable reallocation of scarce resources for safeguarding the lives of those who still had a chance. The development of the Church's own Vaticaniac Computer Program to guide determinations of viability of Catholic patients based on applicable tenets of their religion no doubt had something to do with the acceptability of the system as a whole.

Another reason for the reduced significance of dying and of being a dying person is more psychosocial than technological. Dying retained some importance as long as there was any point at all in being dead. Now that the status of the dead has become so attenuated, little significance need be attributed to the preparatory phase. The "exit" phase of existence has become relatively unimportant and vestigial. It is not a critical part of the transition from one social status to another; there is little significance that dying can borrow from its destination. "I am not going to be anything to anybody when I am dead; therefore, as I approach dead-status through the process of dying, my value progressively diminishes." Much of the individual's social value is depleted, then, before the moment of death arrives.

3. There is no point in being old. This is in part a function of the reverse sequence we have been describing. Society has no use for the dead, and therefore little use for the dying. For many years, being old has meant a general reduction in social value for reasons not directly associated with death. However, with the shift in mortality peaks from early to late in the lifespan, and with other socioeconomic and attitudinal changes, a more specific association has also been strengthened between *advanced age* and death. Now when a person is recognized as "old," this status initiates a trajectory of dysvalue that moves inevitably through dying- and dead-status. "I am an old person, which means that before long I will be a dying person; therefore, as I approach dying-status through the aging process, my value progressively diminishes." Old, dying, and dead are stations of life still differentiated by our society, but collectively they represent an essentially trivial postscript to authentic existence as a person in society.

This situation was anticipated by the low priority which society gave for many years to the care of the aged. Moreover, the growing trend for the aged to die in an institutional setting, coupled with the usual way in which institutions responded to the dying and the dead, provided a firm model for progressive dysvaluation.[3] Aged residents were likely to observe that the dying were isolated, and the dead removed quickly. Implicit were the messages that "Nobody has died," and "Dying and being dead are nothing." These messages registered with the impact that "Nobody has been alive," and I *will have been* nothing when I *become* nothing." So thoroughly were the aged dying and dead ejected from the scene that the fact that they had ever been alive (and perhaps valuable) seemed entirely inconsistent. With this sort of rehearsal for their own deaths, the institutionalized aged saw their present existence drained of value.

Today, the transitions from old to dying to dead are better managed. Much of the ambiguity has been eliminated, along with the accompanying tension and occasional guilt on the part of caregivers and family as well as the aged themselves. Only a few of the factors contributing to this change can be cited here.

One important development was the change in official recognition of the start of old age, from sixty-five to seventy.[4] Although gerontologists argued, with good evidence, that even seventy is "too young to be old" for many people today, a compromise at seventy prevailed. In retrospect, the identification of official old age with the biblical specification of "threescore and ten" seems to have proved fortuitous. People in their sixties now receive a full share of benefits and privileges. The slide of value-into-dysvalue throughout the seventh decade of life has been sharply reduced. Other factors in the change include the development of more flexible retirement plans, the cultivation of multiple careers, and the increased prominence of women in the work force.

Perhaps the single most important factor, however, has been the great success of the voluntary-termination plan. Once surrounded by prohibitions and negative emotions, suicide has become, under certain circumstances, an action with great positive value. This trend was anticipated some years ago. It was shown that the implicit preferences of most Americans regarding the "ideal" way to die included the following characteristics: (1) an identifiable and rational cause; (2) some element of control; (3) an acceptable physical setting; (4) occurrence at the right time; (5) little or no suffering or experiencing; (6) rapid onset; (7) consistency with the individual's distinctive or most valued style of life. It was predicted that all of these characteristics could most dependably be invoked by suicide.[5] The suicide would, of course, have to meet certain pragmatic and moral criteria, which were also discussed in some detail.

Apparently, two major factors in the success of the voluntary-termination plan were the decades-long subjection of the aged to low-priority status and the rapid diminution of the value of the dying and the dead in our death system. People simply incorporated these cultural orientations into their own attitude structures, and when they had themselves grown old, they began to act upon the implicit commands.

The well-achieved suicide (to use the old-fashioned expression) bestows upon the old person's exit a value that it can attain in no other way. Instead of fading into a prolonged phase of senescence and dysvalue, the man or woman on the brink of old age now can elect a self-termination mode that consolidates and validates his or her existence up to that point. A good citizen, having lived a good life, no longer faces the prospect of a retroactively spoiled identity because of unnecessary aging and dying.

381

Kastenbaum
Exit and
Existence:
Alternative
Scenarios

An Alternative Scenario

It is possible to accept the background facts and trends that generated the above scenario and yet arrive at a different one. This requires the recognition of several other trends and options that have not yet been mentioned.

"The Road Doesn't End Here Anymore"

The county historical society almost lost in its campaign to preserve the street in its old form as a designated reminder of how things used to be. Little could be said in favor of the structures themselves. The aesthetic appeal was virtually nil, and somehow the "bad vibrations" seemed to cling to the walls. Yet enough people appreciated the moral and educational value of preserving the row of "nursing homes" and "funeral homes" to allow the historical society to keep this relic of the not-so-distant past before contemporary eyes.

Surprisingly, the street has proved to be a popular if sobering attraction. "So this was the end of the road," a visitor may say, shaking his head as though to clear away disbelief. "You have to wonder how people felt when they turned down this street. It must have been like leaving life behind, entering a kind of slaughterhouse district, but with most of the bleeding *inside,* in the heart. How could people let the road end that way?"

The street of nursing homes and funeral homes—peculiar remnants of the past—certainly is out of place now. Old age and death once were considered the end of the road, almost functionally equivalent in many people's minds. This inaccurate assumption no longer burdens society. Advances in scientific knowledge have contributed to the change: increasingly, it has been recognized that many of the so-called inevitable changes "caused" by the aging process can in fact be attributed more accurately to a variety of specific factors. Each new rank of chronologically old men and women reaches a particular age checkpoint in better health and with greater functional capacity than the preceding one. There was no single "breakthrough"; instead, health maintenance throughout the lifespan has steadily improved. The physical impairment and vulnerability to chronic disease that were fostered by sedentary, careless, and unmonitored life styles have been sharply reduced. Sixty-five-year-olds are more physically active today than many forty-year-olds of a few generations back. Good nutritional habits carefully cultivated in the early years of life are now paying good dividends in the later decades. Specific changes, such as the enrichment of beer with vitamins, have helped to preserve the functioning of memory and the overall integrity of personality among people who in the past might have suffered deterioration not much past midlife.

The overall change, however, has occurred in the minds both of the elders themselves and of the allied health professionals. Suffering, impairment, and disease are no longer considered especially "natural" in old age. More can be done to prevent problems and to correct or compensate for them when they do occur.

Gerontologists from a variety of disciplines have helped to clarify the distinction between growing old and becoming ill. A core of processes remains that could be characterized as "normal aging," although even this core is still subject to continuing review and experimentation.

In similar fashion, a clearer distinction has been recognized between growing old and "getting stale." As developmental psychologists finally enlarged their horizons to encompass the whole lifespan and to establish appropriate ways of assessing behavior and experience from infancy through old age, it became evident that individual patterns are at least as significant as age-related changes. There was no escaping the conclusion that some men and women have "staled out" by their forties or fifties—or even their twenties or thirties—while others show few, if any, of the stereotypical age changes after they have passed their seventieth, eightieth, or ninetieth birthday. Circumstantial evidence has long suggested the importance of individual patterns; now, abundant research supports this view in detail.

In both biomedical and psychosocial terms, then, the assumption of a close link between old age and deterioration—and therefore between old age and death—has been shown to be faulty. While it is still true that some chronologically old people are physically ill and impaired, and some very limited in their ability to experience and adapt to their environments (not necessarily the same persons in both cases), such difficulties and illnesses no longer *define* old age. In addition to the greater national commitment to the maintenance of physical health throughout life, there is now more encouragement of continuing personal growth. Recreation, for example, has become more re-creational for many people; education is now a lifelong process for a greater number; and self-development groups have survived the fad stage to become an effective and respected part of the cultural milieu. While, of course, some people continue to reach the end of the road early in life, this is no longer the expected pattern. Chronological age simply does not have much to do with the quality of one's life. As old age (in the once-traditional chronological sense of the term) has been liberated from its association with the end of health and mental vigor, so the association with dying and death has been reduced to more realistic dimensions. People still die old if they do not die young, but they are not surrounded by clouds of gloom and dysvalue while they still walk the earth.

Many other changes have contributed to the revised image and reality of old age. Reaching a particular age (and remember when that was as young as sixty-five!) once meant a virtually complete exit from the social scene. The individual stepped (or was pushed) across a single threshold and from that point on was little more than an occasional offstage voice. Now, of course, fewer of the exits are controlled by chronology. Mandatory retirement did not tremble and fall with an overwhelming crash after a fierce struggle; it just gradually passed away.

More flexible ideas of what constitutes a working life have made the single-career pattern just one among several. The framework of young adult to

383

Kastenbaum
Exit and
Existence:
Alternative
Scenarios

elderly retiree has altered just as the nine-to-five workday has given way to more flexible arrangements. Now, people move into and out of occupations in a variety of patterns, taking a year out here for re-education, six months there for community service, and so on. The availability of a large number of vigorous, skilled elders who are interested in part-time or temporary employment has proved extremely helpful to many industries and government agencies. The "average" person now may have, in effect, "retired" several times before reaching age sixty-five and yet, in another sense, not have retired at all. The ever-changing flow of workers of various ages and degrees of development of their capacities has made age-based mandatory retirement anachronistic— and eliminated one of the main symbols of exit from social participation.

The great improvement in the status of women has also been very important. The woman of today must have an informed sense of history in order to recognize that once her life might have been considered over when the last child had left the "nest," or when she became a widow (as often happened to women in earlier generations before the longevity of males improved). Today's woman, fully competent in the management of her life outside as well as inside the home, brings many skills, achievements, and interests to the later years of her life. She is seldom faced with a confusing and unfamiliar world of financial management, for example, or frustrated by other problems that someone else would have looked after in the past. She is resourceful and successful throughout her life and has no reason to be otherwise as she reaches any particular chronological-age mark.

Both men and women, of course, have found the toppling of assumptions and prohibitions regarding sexual intimacy in later life to be a truly liberating development. In the past, physical death seemed almost an afterthought for some people when they had already exited (in society's view) from the life of labor and the life of love. Now, better general health has contributed to the general maintenance of sexual tone in elders; but the change in attitudes has also been very important. The overall maturation of public opinion in relation to many aspects of human development shows some of its most favorable results in relation to old age and intimacy. There was a period in which the existence of only two "kinds" of women was generally acknowledged: "good women," and those who enjoyed sex. Then, as women achieved sociopolitical equality with men, sexual liberation followed, sometimes accompanied by new problems for some men. It took some time for many men to adjust to women who were at least their equals in all spheres, and there *were* some "casualties" along the way. Now, however, adults share sexual intimacy at all points of the life span.

In general, men and women, now able to function well physically, maintain and develop personality strengths, participate fully in the work and productivity of society according to their individual interests, and remain sexually active, seldom regard any chronological age as the end of the kind of lives they have made for themselves. Those who choose, or are forced, to leave a particular domain in which they have functioned successfully can open other doors to a rewarding life. The humanization and individualization of technology has provided many more possibilities for maintaining control after such functions as muscular strength, mobility, reaction time, and sensory acuity have been impaired. In other words, a person is not necessarily rendered powerless and isolated just because a particular physical function has become less dependable. This ability to compensate for age-related deficits has, in turn, greatly reduced passive yearning for death, as well as active suicide, among older adults.

In essence, society has come to realize that within its power is the ability to develop alternative "scripts" for the whole human lifespan. The *programmed impetus* given to each person as a birthright may run its course around midlife, if not before: the "job specifications" written into the genes have completed their schedules.[6] For many centuries there was no concerted effort on the part of society to augment this partial script for a human life; few people survived long enough to require it. Now, however, a variety of alternative paths exists for the second half of life, and the variety is constantly increasing. Development through old age is almost as enthusiastically demanded and expected—and applauded and enjoyed—as development through the childhood years.

Society places greater value on the *completed person*.[7] Although a child of ten may be, in one sense, all that he or she can be, true fulfillment of human possibilities is now seen as requiring a long life in which knowledge increases and is enriched over the years. The young are fresh and daring; middle-aged people (the term now applies to a much longer space of life) would please Aristotle with their balancing of the novel and the familiar, the necessary and the possible; elders integrate all the qualities of previous years with a cultivated sense of perspective.

The Exit from Existence

Being old has shifted to a positive value. Yet dying and death have not been banished from the human condition, nor have they continued to operate secretly and to bizarre effect under the lugubrious apparatus of massive denial. Compared with the situation in the past, in fact, dying and death are much more out in the open today. This is due, in part, to the increased value placed upon *life* in old age. As a number of keen observers have remarked over the centuries, the person who has lived well and fully does appear more at ease with mortality.

But part of the new attitude is a result of a greater appreciation of dying, death, *and the dead* per se. When the old death system was functioning at its peak, the elderly progressed on a sort of assembly line from old age through dying to death and oblivion.[8] It is perhaps easier to understand this progression in reverse. For a time, honoring and memorializing the dead became a greatly attenuated process. Funeral processions, the use of cemetery space, and most forms of integrating the dead psychologically into the lives of individual survivors and the culture were under attack and erosion. In effect, the dead seemed to have no role in the symbolic life of society, with a few notable exceptions.

The nonutility of the dead was a phenomenon which then worked ahead in time. It made the dying person more of a threat, annoyance, or burden than a gathering place for social values and concern. There was no point in "being dead," hence little point in being a person who would soon be forgotten. This part of the process often was exemplified in congregate facilities for the care of the aged. The nonutility of the dying person worked forward in time to strip value from the old person. The elder would die, and the dead would blow away like the wind with its debris. Little wonder that many aging men and women, taking their cues from mandatory retirement, the death of a spouse, or some other major change in their lives, would disassociate from themselves just as society was pulling away from them.

Today, the aged have been liberated in both directions. In life, there is no longer an age-determined exitus from full participation and status. On the side of death, society has regained its sense of history and continuity. We no longer feel so lost, shift our feet, and avoid eye contact at leave-taking rituals. Death is not seen as a failure by the individual or the health professions. Thoughts and feelings toward the dead are accepted as a vital thread of continuity that symbolizes our existence as members of the human race rather than as solitary individuals. The neutral, objective-functional abandonment of the dead once in vogue has yielded to a more intuitive relationship, one that gives the present generation more in common with ancestors across the centuries than with those of just a few years ago. In caring about the dead and the dying, those who have barely started to approach their own elder years are already preparing the way for a personal sense of continued value throughout all the bright days and deep nights of life's seasons.

Notes

1. R. Kastenbaum and R. B. Aisenberg, *The Psychology of Death* (New York: Springer Publishing, 1972); R. Kastenbaum, *Death, Society, and Human Experience* (St. Louis: C. V. Mosby, 1977).

2. Kastenbaum and Aisenberg, *Psychology of Death*; R. Blauner, "Death and Social Structure," *Psychiatry* 29 (1966):378–94; R. Kastenbaum, "Two-way Traffic on the River Styx" (Paper presented at the annual meeting of American Psychological Association, 1969); R. Fulton, private communication.

3. E.g., R. Kastenbaum and S. E. Candy, "The 4% Fallacy: A Methodological and Empirical Critique of Use of Population Statistics in Gerontology," *Aging and Human Development* 4 (1973):15–22.

4. This was a futuristic proposition when presented at the conference; it is now becoming the law of the land.

5. R. Kastenbaum, "Suicide as the Preferred Way of Death," in *Progress in Suicidology*, ed. E. S. Schneidman (New York: Grune & Stratton, 1976), pp. 425–43.

6. R. Kastenbaum, "Theories of Human Aging—The Search for a Conceptual Framework," *Journal of Social Issues* 21 (1965):13–36.

7. R. Kastenbaum, "Time, Death, and Ritual in Old Age," in *The Study of Time*, ed. J. T. Fraser (New York, Heidelberg, Berlin: Springer-Verlag, 1975), 20–38.

8. R. Kastenbaum, *Death, Society, and Human Experience*.

structured exercises

Before beginning these exercises, please read "Note to the Instructor" on page xxi.

1. The bureaucracy of death throws a harsh light on death's aftermath. The objective details of death that are required for the official forms that accompany the disposition of the body offer a sharp contrast to what Shneidman has described as the "romanticization of death." In order to focus on the *facts* of death, conduct the following fantasy exercise: Assume that you have died in some chosen manner at some future time. Now, take fifteen minutes to visualize the circumstances of "your death" and complete the "Certificate of Death" found in Appendix C–4 at the end of this book.

   After each member of the class has finished, break up into groups of four to discuss the results of the exercise. Answer the following questions.

   a. How did you die? When? Where?
   b. What was the mode of death? The cause of death?
   c. Was there an autopsy? The cause of death?
   d. How might others assess the "intentionality" of your death? On what would they base their assessment?
   e. What effect has this exercise had on you? How has it affected your attitude toward the physical facts of death?

2. As the medical choices in extending life have increased, the general public has become more aware of the choices that must be made. Have the students review the "Guidelines for the Determination of Death" in Appendix A–2. The last several years have seen the growing interest in documents such as the "Living Will" reproduced in Appendix C–1 (although at the present time they have no legal status). A California statute provides for a legally binding "Directive to Physicians" (see Appendix C–3). Such proposals respond to the individual's fear of being forced to endure unnecessary prolongation of life, and his desire for a voice in medical decision making,

but the full implications of a particular proposal may go unnoticed until it is applied to specific situations.

Three illustrative cases are given below. Working as a class, discuss each case using the proposed criteria for the determination of death in Appendix A–2 to ground the discussion. Refer to the directive given in Appendix C–3 and answer the questions following each example. Compare and contrast the three cases, considering the relative suitability of the directive to each.

At the end of your discussion, list any changes you would propose to the directive or the safeguards you would write into a "Right to Die" law.

Case 1: As a result of a drug overdose, a 16-year-old boy has remained in a deep coma for six months. His physician judges the coma to be irreversible but cannot state that recovery at a distant time in the future is impossible. In the meantime, the boy is unable to breathe without mechanical aid from a respirator, although there is evidence of residual subcortical functioning. The boy's parents are reluctant to let their son go, but continued financial burdens threaten the stability of the home.

a. Does continued maintenance on a respirator meet the criterion for a "life-sustaining procedure" as given in the proposal (see Appendix C–3)?
b. If you were the parents, would you want the boy to be maintained on the respirator? For how long?
c. A teenager is unlikely to consider signing a document like a living will and is legally too young to sign a directive such as the one given in Appendix C–3. If the boy had indicated in previous discussions with his parents that he would not have wanted to be maintained indefinitely on a respirator, what action would you recommend?

Case 2: Mr. V., age 48, is suffering from a malignant brain tumor and is in a semi-comatose state. He has been referred by the family physician to the tumor ward of a Veteran's Administration hospital for terminal care. The VA oncologist suggests to Mrs. V. that a new drug might have some positive effects: an "extraordinary" treatment but one without painful side effects. Mrs. V. gives permission for treatment and subsequently Mr. V. recovers sufficiently to live comfortably for another twelve months.

a. From the description, do you consider that the drug represented a "life-sustaining procedure" as defined in the proposal?
b. If you were Mrs. V., what would you have decided, regardless of whether Mr. V. had signed such a directive?
c. If Mr. V. had signed the directive six months earlier, in his current semi-comatose condition would there be a way to allow his receiving the treatment?

Case 3: A 68-year-old grandmother with terminal bone cancer is being maintained on heavy doses of pain-relieving drugs. Since the cancer has not spread to vital organs, she faces an indeterminate period of intense pain before death occurs, most likely from a complication of the cancer such as pneumonia. In the course of her long illness she has reached the limit of her physiological tolerance to narcotics; increasing the dosage to alleviate her pain is likely to result in a fatal overdose. She has indicated unwillingness to sign the directive. Her husband is urging the physician to act to prevent further suffering, yet the doctor realizes the serious risk to the patient in administering higher doses of drugs.

a. As an observer what do you feel the doctor should do? Would your response differ if you were the husband? The patient?
b. How do you believe the final decision should be made?
c. Had the woman signed the directive, what options, if any, would the doctor have?

3. The study of death and dying forces a reexamination of personal goals and values. In Chapter One, the first exercise ("Coat of Arms") asked you to identify some of your values. The concluding exercise in this chapter is meant to help you assess your resources for realizing those values.

Take ten to fifteen minutes working quickly to list as many answers as you can for each of the following questions. Share your responses with other members of the class. As you discuss your responses, you may wish to add to your list.

a. When do I feel fully alive? What things, events, activities, etc., make me feel that life is really worth living, that it's great to be me and to be alive?
b. What do I do well? What have I to contribute to the life of others? Over what skills do I have mastery? What do I do well for my own growth and well-being?
c. Given my current situation and given my aspirations, what do I need to learn to do?
d. What wishes should I be turning into plans? Are there any dreams I've discarded as "unrealistic" that I should start dreaming again?
e. What underdeveloped or misused resources do I have? (Resources might be material things, talents, friends, etc.)
f. What should I start doing *now*?
g. What should I stop doing *now*?

questions

1. Define the following terms. Those marked with an asterisk are terms that the authors of the selections expect readers to know. If you are not familiar with the meanings of those terms, consult a dictionary.

Fletcher

  elective death
  *a right
  vitalistic error
  euthanasia (active, passive,
    direct, indirect,
    voluntary, involuntary)
  radical vitalism
  dysthanasia
  "mercy killing"
  *morals
  *ethics
  situation ethics
  *humanism
  *truism
  *pragmatic heresy
  heroics
  moral dying

Shneidman

  megadeath
  cessation
  termination
  interruption
  continuation
  altered continuation
  death-seeker
  death-initiator
  death-ignorer
  death-darer
  unintentioned death
  subintentioned death
  death-chancer
  death-hastener
  death-capitulator
  death-experimenter
  genocide

Bayles

  perfectionist standard
  utilitarian standard
  *anencephalic
  *Down's syndrome
  *duodenal atresia
  reasonable-person test

Cohen

  acute care
  palliative care
  dysthanasia

Kastenbaum

"death system"
"script"
programmed impetus
completed person

2. Opponents of euthanasia often argue that an acceptance of elective death would ultimately result in a "cheapening of life." But Joseph Fletcher claims that "prolonging life beyond any personal or human state" is as likely to end in a mockery of life. Write brief arguments for each side of the following debate resolution: That prolongation of life beyond natural limits undermines respect for life.

3. In another paper, "The Price of Life" (*Ethics* [1978] 89:20–34), Bayles argues that it is not only rational and morally permissible to place a price on one's own life but that there is also a morally accepted method of using pricing to determine some social policies. List as many examples as you can of ways in which society implicitly prices life. Begin with the building of a skyscraper, the purchase of life-saving equipment, and the budgeting of additional medical facilities. What competing values are apparent in your list?

4. Shneidman infers conscious or unconscious motivation from the patterns of behavior that he presents as illustrations of orientations toward death. Describe five cases of death in which you might infer "subintention." List the criteria you would use in determining the appropriateness of your inference. Consider how you might test the hypothesis that someone was "rushing to his own funeral."

5. a. In "Suicide Note," Anne Sexton writes:

> But surely you know that everyone has a death,
> his own death,
> waiting for him.
> So I will go now
> without old age or disease . . .

Do you share her view? Why, or why not?

   b. To what extent do you think that the writings prior to an author's death reveal his or her motivation?

6. Much of the discussion of death in the poetry of Anne Sexton centers on the "tools" of death. Using the views outlined in Shneidman's paper, "The Enemy," develop an explanation for why suicides may discuss method more than decision.

7. Extrapolating the consequences of Kastenbaum's statement in the scenario "Being old has shifted to a positive value," consider the practical consequences for advertising, education and social policy.

8. a. Shneidman condemns the romanticization of death for blurring the realization that death is "the enemy." What does he mean by the term *romanticization?* If death is viewed as "the enemy," can acceptance be possible? Explain.

   b. To what extent do you believe that our culture romanticizes death? Use examples from the media or literature.

9. a. The continuum of choices suggested by the range of papers in this chapter could extend to a consideration of altruism and martyrdom. List several examples of altruistic acts involving risk (e.g., the donation of an organ to a child, fighting a forest fire). How would you explain the difference between altruism and martyrdom? Are there contemporary martyrs? If so, give examples and state what benefits their martyrdom produced.

   b. What are the possible motivations for the acts you listed in 9a? Try to apply Shneidman's descriptive categories of orientations toward death to your examples. Would you describe the individuals in your examples as death-seeking? Why, or why not?

10. The selections in Chapter Five return the reader to a central question: What is an appropriate death? Or to put it another way, what is death with dignity? Identify both the implicit and the explicit conceptions of death that are expressed by the Van Dusens, Socrates, Fletcher, Sexton, and Shneidman. Compare and contrast their views. Describe the role of "choice" in each view.

11. a. List the factors that should be taken into account in choosing palliative care over acute care in the case of a terminal illness. Whose decision is it?

    b. In what ways should public policy recognize hospice concepts? What factors should be taken into account in determining the appropriate proportion of public funds for palliative care?

12. Argue the following proposition: Since refusing heroics is, in a sense, a shortening of one's life and is widely accepted as a valid option, shortening one's life by other means should also be an acceptable option.

13. Have your own ideas concerning the role of personal decision in death been influenced since the opening discussions in Chapter One? In what ways?

projects for further study

1. Research recent news coverage of cases such as that of the English sculptor described by Bayles. Analyze the actions taken or requested and the arguments advanced on each side. Classify the actions and the arguments according to the principles and tests put forth by Bayles. Was the outcome of each case consistent with the principles that Bayles advances? Are you satisfied with the decision regardless of the consistency of the argument? Why or why not?

2. In recent years many communities have developed "hot lines," and "suicide prevention centers," to meet the crisis of suicide or attempted suicide. The movement has greatly increased our understanding of the demographics and the dynamics of suicide, thereby improving our chances of preventing suicide.

   a. Research the dynamics of suicide, differentiating between the long-term personality and adjustment of the suicide victim and the precipitating events which most commonly precede a suicide attempt. The Los Angeles Suicide Prevention Center has developed a procedure for rating the "lethality" of a suicide threat as a means of evaluating the immediate, self-destructive potential of a suicide threat. From your own research construct a description of a high lethality suicide attempter, a low lethality attempter. Include in your profile personality factors, existing sources of psycho-social support, and the immediate motivation for the suicide attempt. Lethality scales and crisis intervention are covered extensively in the collection of papers contained in *The Cry for Help*, edited by Farberow and Shneidman.

   b. Community "hot lines" deal with many personal crises besides suicide and they are often staffed by student volunteers working under professional supervision. Suicide prevention centers, on the other hand, are specialized efforts to deal with self-destructive behaviors and, consequently, are staffed by a higher proportion of health care professionals to lay volunteers. Visit a suicide prevention center or "hot line" in your area to research the training that lay volunteers receive, the concrete steps they are trained to take, the point at which a referral to a professional is made, and the steps that the professional is likely to take.

3. Death has proven a most abundant theme in literature where the tensions between the rights of the individual and the rights of society can be sensitively searched. Identify categories for the study of literary presentations of death—e.g., death in the war novel, death and disease, death and self-definition and death in poetry—then select one work to study individually. Read the work carefully and then develop a critique of the presentation of death in that work. Include in your report responses to the following.

a. Why did you select this particular work?
b. How was death portrayed in the work? (Who died? Why? With what effect on the other characters?)
c. To what extent was the presentation of death realistic? Clinical?
d. What attitudes does the author convey about death?
e. What symbols of mortality are used in the work?
f. In what ways did individual choice or decision affect the death?
g. What are your reactions to the presentation of death in the work?

After all students have completed their individual reports, the class can divide into groups on the basis of the categories they previously decided to study. In the small groups, each student can report on the work he read, then the group members can work together to identify features in the presentation of death that are common to the specific category. The bibliographic references that follow may serve as a beginning.

Death in the War Novel
Catton, Bruce. *A Stillness at Appomattox*. New York: Doubleday, 1954.
Crane, Stephen. *The Red Badge of Courage*. New York: Grosset & Dunlap, 1952.
Deighton, Len. *Bomber*. New York: Signet, 1971.
Remarque, E. *All Quiet on the Western Front*. Boston: Little, Brown, 1958.

Death and Disease
Alsop, S. *Stay of Execution*. Philadelphia: Lippincott, 1973.
Craven, Margaret. *I Heard the Owl Call My Name*. New York: Doubleday Books, 1973.
Lund, D. *Eric*. Philadelphia: Lippincott, 1974.
Solzhenitsyn, A. *Cancer Ward*. New York: Farrar, Straus & Giroux, 1969.

Death and Self-Definition
de Beauvoir, Simone. *A Very Easy Death*. New York: Warner Books, 1973.
Fuentes, Carlos. *The Death of Artemio Cruz*. New York: Farrar, Straus & Giroux, 1964.

Plath, S. *The Bell Jar*. New York: Harper & Row, 1971.
Shaw, Bernard. *Saint Joan*. New York: Penguin, 1951.

Death in Poetry
Plath, Sylvia. *Ariel*. New York: Harper & Row, 1966.
Sexton, Anne. *The Death Notebooks*. Boston: Houghton Mifflin, 1974.
Tennyson, Alfred, Lord. *In Memoriam*. New York: W. W. Norton, 1974.

4. To explore society's attitude to aging, collect samples (pictures or tape recordings) of advertisements portraying people over sixty-five years of age. Observe your materials carefully for indicators of the subject's degree of engrossment in society, physical condition, and advertised need. You might want to make a comparison with similar materials portraying younger adults. Speculate on how each subject would allocate his time on a daily basis, and what other people he would see frequently.

for further reading

Alvarez, A. 1972. *The savage god: A study of suicide.* New York: Random House.

Bayles, M. D., ed. 1978. *Medical treatment of the dying: Moral issues.* Cambridge, Mass.: Schenkman.

Carse, J. P., and A. B. Dallery, 1977. *Death and society: A book of readings and sources.* New York: Harcourt Brace Jovanovich.

Crane, Diana. 1975. *The sanctity of social life: Physicians' treatment of critically ill patients.* New York: Russell Sage Foundation.

Farberow, N. L., and E. S. Shneidman, eds. 1961. *The cry for help.* New York: McGraw-Hill.

Gorovitz, S., A. L. Jameton, R. M. Macklin, J. M. O'Connor, E. V. Perrin, B. P. St. Clair, and S. Sherwin, eds. 1976. *Moral problems in medicine.* Englewood Cliffs, N. J.: Prentice-Hall.

Korein, J., ed. 1978. *Brain death: Interrelated medical and social issues.* New York: New York Academy of Sciences.

Maguire, D. C. 1974. *Death by choice.* New York: Doubleday.

McCarthy, D. G., and A. S. Moraczewski. 1981. *Moral responsibility in prolonging life decisions.* St. Louis: Pope John Center.

Menninger, K. 1966. *Man against himself.* New York: Harcourt Brace Jovanovich.

Perlin, S., ed. 1975. *A handbook for the study of suicide.* New York: Oxford University Press.

Veatch, Robert M. 1976. *Death, dying, and the biological revolution: Our last quest for responsibility.* New Haven, Conn.: Yale University Press.

———. 1979. *Life span: Values and life-extending technologies.* San Francisco: Harper & Row.

Williams, Preston N., ed. 1969. Ethical issues in biological medicine. *Proceedings for the Symposium on the Identity and Dignity of Man.* Boston: Boston University Press.

appendices

appendix a | *Additional Materials for Structured Exercises*

1. *Kidney Machine Psychological Reports Sheet**

Re: Patients for Kidney Machine
From: Hospital Psychological Staff

In routine preadmission interviews the following patients were examined and evaluated as per the following data:

Re: Alfred—He is presently distraught about his physical condition and reports that it interferes with his work. Seems very committed to his work and appears to be legitimately on the verge of an important cancer discovery. It was hard for the staff to get him to talk about his work in terms that they could understand.

Family relations seem strained and have been for some time because of his commitment to his work. The staff feels that he is a first-rate scientist and scholar who has contributed much and could contribute more to medical research. But they also believe him to be a mentally disturbed individual who, in time, will probably need psychiatric help.

Re: Bill—He is a well-oriented Negro, who does not appear to be swayed by the blandishments of black extremist groups. He is strongly devoted to his family and appears to be an excellent husband and father.

Bill's capacity for growth in his chosen occupation, however, seems limited. His high school record was poor, although he had no record of delinquency and was always regarded by his teachers as a student who tried hard. Therefore, he will probably not succeed with his business plans and will remain employed at a fixed rate permanently.

His wife is trained as a legal secretary. Her prognosis for employment is good, although Bill has discouraged her from seeking work because of mutual agreement to have her be a full-time mother. Bill seems unaware of the serious implications of his illness.

---

*Editors' Note: The Kidney Machine Psychological Reports Sheet is to be used in conjunction with Structured Exercise number two ("Kidney Machine Decision") in Chapter One.

*appendix A
Additional
Materials for
Structured
Exercises*

400

Re: Cora—One of the staff members evaluating Cora described her as a *professional Jew*. She is president of the local Hadassah organization and seems able to talk about nothing but her religion and her children. Although her recently found interest in interior decorating may be a sign of change, it was not clear to the staff whether this interest was real or only generated artificially when she heard of the interview requirement.

She seems resigned to her illness and likely death. Her husband works long hours, is in good health, and enjoys the respect and love of his children. Cora's mother, who also lives with the family, handles most of the child care.

Re: David—Typical of young student activists, David is a bright—almost straight "A"—student who enjoys the respect of most of his teachers and friends. But he appears confused about his future and demonstrates a penchant for jeopardizing it by involving himself in various student "causes." Indeed, his college's dean of student affairs regards him as an individual who will "demonstrate for anything."

He is bitter, almost paranoid, about his illness. His father has invested a good deal of money, time, and emotion in him and has always hoped that David would become a lawyer. His relations with his father are presently strained, however, and he seems only mildly concerned about his two sisters, although they still think highly of him. His future father-in-law, who is a highly successful businessman, expects him to enter the family enterprise upon college graduation.

Re: Edna—She is a self-contained, inner-directed woman and a model of the "career girl." It was clear to the staff that her natural aggressiveness and combative tendencies militated against any sort of marital attachment, and it is not impossible that she has lesbian tendencies.

Her employers regard her as indispensable. Her work record is superb, and her activities in church and charitable groups have been very effective. She is well regarded by all who know her, although she seems to have few, if any, close friends. She appears resigned to her death. In fact, she indicated that she would prefer to have someone other than herself go on the machine. Her offer did not seem in the least insincere.

2. Guidelines for the Determination of Death

Report of the Medical Consultants on the Diagnosis of Death to the President's Commission for the Study of Ethical Problems in Medicine and Biomedical and Behavioral Research*

The advent of effective artificial cardiopulmonary support for severely brain-injured persons has created some confusion during the past several decades

*Source: *Journal of the American Medical Association*. November 13, 1981. Vol. 246, pp. 2184–2186. Copyright 1981, American Medical Association.

about the determination of death. Previously, loss of heart and lung functions was an easily observable and sufficient basis for diagnosing death, whether the initial failure occurred in the brain, the heart and lungs, or elsewhere in the body. Irreversible failure of either the heart and lungs or the brain precluded the continued functioning of the other. Now, however, circulation and respiration can be maintained by means of a mechanical respirator and other medical interventions, despite a loss of all brain functions. In these circumstances, we recognize as dead an individual whose loss of brain functions is complete and irreversible.

To recognize reliably that death has occurred, accurate criteria must be available for physicians' use. These now fall into two groups, to be applied depending on the clinical situation. When respiration and circulation have irreversibly ceased, there is no need to assess brain functions directly. When cardiopulmonary functions are artificially maintained, neurological criteria must be used to assess whether brain functions have ceased irreversibly.

More than half of the states now recognize, through statutes or judicial decisions, that death may be determined on the basis of irreversible cessation of all functions of the brain. Law in the remaining states has not yet departed from the older, common-law view that death has not occurred until "all vital functions" (whether or not artificially maintained) have ceased. The language of the statutes has not been uniform from state to state, and the diversity of proposed and enacted laws has created substantial confusion. Consequently, the American Bar Association, the American Medical Association, the National Conference of Commissioners on Uniform State Laws, and the President's Commission for the Study of Ethical Problems in Medicine and Biomedical and Behavioral Research have proposed the following model statute, intended for adoption in every jurisdiction:

Uniform Determination of Death Act

An individual who has sustained either (1) irreversible cessation of circulatory and respiratory functions, or (2) irreversible cessation of all functions of the entire brain, including the brain stem, is dead. A determination of death must be made in accordance with accepted medical standards.

This wording has also been endorsed by the American Academy of Neurology and the American Electroencephalographic Society.

The statute relies on the existence of "accepted medical standards" for determining that death has occurred. The medical profession, based on carefully conducted research and extensive clinical experience, has found that death can be determined reliably by either cardiopulmonary or neurological criteria. The tests used for determining cessation of brain functions have changed and will continue to do so with the advent of new research and technologies. The "Harvard criteria" (*Journal of the American Medical Association* 1968;205:337–340) are widely accepted, but advances in recent years have led to the proposal of other criteria. As an aid to the implementation of

appendix A
Additional
Materials for
Structured
Exercises

402

the proposed uniform statute, we provide here one statement of currently accepted medical standards.

Introduction

The criteria that physicians use in determining that death has occurred should (1) eliminate errors in classifying a living individual as dead; (2) allow as few errors as possible in classifying a dead body as alive; (3) allow a determination to be made without unreasonable delay; (4) be adaptable to a variety of clinical situations; and (5) be explicit and accessible to verification.

Because it would be undesirable for any guidelines to be mandated by legislation or regulation or to be inflexibly established in case law, the proposed Uniform Determination of Death Act appropriately specifies only "accepted medical standards." Local, state, and national institutions and professional organizations are encouraged to examine and publish their practices.

The following guidelines represent a distillation of current practice in regard to the determination of death. Only the most commonly available and verified tests have been included. The time of death recorded on a death certificate is at present a matter of local practice and is not covered in this document.

These guidelines are advisory. Their successful use requires a competent and judicious physician, experienced in clinical examination and the relevant procedures. All periods of observation listed in these guidelines require the patient to be under the care of a physician. Considering the responsibility entailed in the determination of death, consultation is recommended when appropriate.

The outline of the criteria is set forth below in boldface letters. The lightface text that follows each heading explains its meaning. In addition, the two sets of criteria (cardiopulmonary and neurological) are followed by a presentation of the major complicating conditions: drug and metabolic intoxication, hypothermia, young age, and shock. It is of paramount importance that anyone referring to these guidelines be thoroughly familiar with the entire document, including explanatory notes and complicating conditions.

The Criteria for Determination of Death

An individual presenting the findings in *either* section A (cardiopulmonary) *or* section B (neurological) is dead. In either section, a diagnosis of death requires that *both cessation of functions*, as set forth in subsection 1, *and irreversibility*, as set forth in subsection 2, be demonstrated.

A. An individual with irreversible cessation of circulatory and respiratory functions is dead.

1. *Cessation* is recognized by an appropriate clinical examination.

Clinical examination will disclose at least the absence of responsiveness, heartbeat, and respiratory effort. Medical circumstances may require the use of confirmatory tests, such as an ECG.

2. *Irreversibility* is recognized by persistent cessation of functions during an appropriate period of observation and/or trial of therapy.

In clinical situations where death is expected, where the course has been gradual, and where irregular agonal respiration or heartbeat finally ceases, the period of observation following the cessation may be only the few minutes required to complete the examination. Similarly, if resuscitation is not undertaken and ventricular fibrillation and standstill develop in a monitored patient, the required period of observation thereafter may be as short as a few minutes. When a possible death is unobserved, unexpected, or sudden, the examination may need to be more detailed and repeated over a longer period, while appropriate resuscitative effort is maintained as a test of cardiovascular responsiveness. Diagnosis in individuals who are first observed with rigor mortis or putrefaction may require only the observation period necessary to establish that fact.

B. An individual with irreversible cessation of all functions of the entire brain, including the brain stem, is dead. The "functions of the entire brain" that are relevant to the diagnosis are those that are clinically ascertainable. Where indicated, the clinical diagnosis is subject to confirmation by laboratory tests, as described in the following portions of the text. Consultation with a physician experienced in this diagnosis is advisable.

1. *Cessation* is recognized when evaluation discloses findings of a *and* b:
a. Cerebral functions are absent, and . . .

There must be deep coma, that is, cerebral unreceptivity and unresponsivity. Medical circumstances may require the use of confirmatory studies such as an EEG or blood-flow study.

b. brain stem functions are absent.

Reliable testing of brain stem reflexes requires a perceptive and experienced physician using adequate stimuli. Pupillary light, corneal, oculocephalic, oculovestibular, oropharyngeal, and respiratory (apnea) reflexes should be tested. When these reflexes cannot be adequately assessed, confirmatory tests are recommended.

Adequate testing for apnea is very important. An accepted method is ventilation with pure oxygen or an oxygen and carbon dioxide mixture for ten minutes before withdrawal of the ventilator, followed by passive flow of oxygen. (This procedure allows $PaCO_2$ to rise without hazardous hypoxia.) Hypercarbia adequately stimulates respiratory effort within 30 seconds when $PaCO_2$ is greater than 60 mm Hg. A ten-minute period of apnea is usually sufficient to attain this level of hypercarbia. Testing of arterial blood gases can be used to confirm this level. Spontaneous breathing efforts indicate that part of the brain stem is functioning.

Peripheral nervous system activity and spinal cord reflexes may persist after death. True decerebrate or decorticate posturing or seizures are inconsistent with the diagnosis of death.

appendix A
Additional
Materials for
Structured
Exercises

404

2. **Irreversibility** is recognized when evaluation discloses findings of a and b and c:

a. **The cause of coma is established and is sufficient to account for the loss of brain functions, and . . .**

Most difficulties with the determination of death on the basis of neurological criteria have resulted from inadequate attention to this basic diagnostic prerequisite. In addition to a careful clinical examination and investigation of history, relevant knowledge of causation may be acquired by computed tomographic scan, measurement of core temperature, drug screening, EEG, angiography, or other procedures.

b. **the possibility of recovery of any brain functions is excluded, and . . .**

The most important reversible conditions are sedation, hypothermia, neuromuscular blockade, and shock. In the unusual circumstance where a sufficient cause cannot be established, irreversibility can be reliably inferred only after extensive evaluation for drug intoxication, extended observation, and other testing. A determination that blood flow to the brain is absent can be used to demonstrate a sufficient and irreversible condition.

c. **the cessation of all brain functions persists for an appropriate period of observation and/or trial of therapy.**

Even when coma is known to have started at an earlier time, the absence of all brain functions must be established by an experienced physician at the initiation of the observation period. The duration of observation periods is a matter of clinical judgment, and some physicians recommend shorter or longer periods than those given here.

Except for patients with drug intoxication, hypothermia, young age, or shock, medical centers with substantial experience in diagnosing death neurologically report no cases of brain functions returning following a six-hour cessation, documented by clinical examination and confirmatory EEG. In the absence of confirmatory tests, a period of observation of at least 12 hours is recommended when an irreversible condition is well established. For anoxic brain damage where the extent of damage is more difficult to ascertain, observation of 24 hours is generally desirable. In anoxic injury, the observation period may be reduced if a test shows cessation of cerebral blood flow or if an EEG shows electrocerebral silence in an adult patient without drug intoxication, hypothermia, or shock.

Confirmation of clinical findings by EEG is desirable when objective documentation is needed to substantiate the clinical findings. Electrocerebral silence verifies irreversible loss of cortical functions, except in patients with drug intoxication or hypothermia. (Important technical details are provided in "Minimal Technical Standards for EEG Recording in Suspected Cerebral Death" [*Guidelines in EEG 1980*. Atlanta, American Electroencephalographic Society, 1980, section 4, pp. 19–24].) When joined with the clinical findings of absent brain stem functions, electrocerebral silence confirms the diagnosis.

Complete cessation of circulation to the normothermic adult brain for more than ten minutes is incompatible with survival of brain tissue. Documentation of this circulatory failure is therefore evidence of death of the entire brain. Four-vessel intracranial angiography is definitive for diagnosing cessation of circulation to the entire brain (both cerebrum and posterior fossa) but entails substantial practical difficulties and risks. Tests are available that assess circulation only in the cerebral hemispheres, namely radioisotope bolus cerebral angiography and gamma camera imaging with radioisotope cerebral angiography. Without complicating conditions, absent cerebral blood flow as measured by these tests, in conjunction with the clinical determination of cessation of all brain functions for at least six hours, is diagnostic of death.

Complicating Conditions

A. Drug and Metabolic Intoxication

Drug intoxication is the most serious problem in the determination of death, especially when multiple drugs are used. Cessation of brain functions caused by the sedative and anesthetic drugs, such as barbiturates, benzodiazepines, meprobamate, methaqualone, and trichloroethylene, may be completely reversible even though they produce clinical cessation of brain functions and electrocerebral silence. In cases where there is any likelihood of sedative presence, toxicology screening for all likely drugs is required. If exogenous intoxication is found, death may not be declared until the intoxicant is metabolized or intracranial circulation is tested and found to have ceased.

Total paralysis may cause unresponsiveness, areflexia, and apnea that closely simulates death. Exposure to drugs such as neuromuscular blocking agents or aminoglycoside antibiotics, and diseases like myasthenia gravis are usually apparent by careful review of the history. Prolonged paralysis after use of succinylcholine chloride and related drugs requires evaluation for pseudocholinesterase deficiency. If there is any question, low-dose atropine stimulation, electromyogram, peripheral nerve stimulation, EEG, tests of intracranial circulation, or extended observation, as indicated, will make the diagnosis clear.

In drug-induced coma, EEG activity may return or persist while the patient remains unresponsive, and therefore the EEG may be an important evaluation along with extended observation. If the EEG shows electrocerebral silence, short latency auditory or somatosensory-evoked potentials may be used to test brain stem functions, since these potentials are unlikely to be affected by drugs.

Some severe illnesses (e.g. hepatic encephalopathy, hyperosmolar coma, and preterminal uremia) can cause deep coma. Before irreversible cessation of brain functions can be determined, metabolic abnormalities should be considered and, if possible, corrected. Confirmatory tests of circulation or EEG may be necessary.

*appendix A
Additional
Materials for
Structured
Exercises*

406

B. Hypothermia

Criteria for reliable recognition of death are not available in the presence of hypothermia (below 32.2°C core temperature). The variables of cerebral circulation in hypothermic patients are not sufficiently well studied to know whether tests of absent or diminished circulation are confirmatory. Hypothermia can mimic brain death by ordinary clinical criteria and can protect against neurological damage due to hypoxia. Further complications arise since hypothermia also usually precedes and follows death. If these complicating factors make it unclear whether an individual is alive, the only available measure to resolve the issue is to restore normothermia. Hypothermia is not a common cause of difficulty in the determination of death.

C. Children

The brains of infants and young children have increased resistance to damage and may recover substantial functions even after exhibiting unresponsiveness on neurological examination for longer periods compared with adults. Physicians should be particularly cautious in applying neurological criteria to determine death in children younger than 5 years.

D. Shock

Physicians should also be particularly cautious in applying neurological criteria to determine death in patients in shock because the reduction in cerebral circulation can render clinical examination and laboratory tests unreliable.

appendix b | *Social Facts of Death*

1. Average Length of Life in Years, by Race and Sex: United States, Specified Years, 1950 to 1982

Year	All races			White			All other Total			Black		
	Both sexes	Male	Female	Both sexes	Male	Female	Both sexes	Male	Female	Both sexes	Male	Female
1982 (est.)	74.5	70.8	78.2	75.1	71.4	78.7	70.9	66.5	75.2	69.3	64.8	73.8
1981 (est.)	74.1	70.3	77.9	74.7	71.0	78.5	70.3	66.1	74.5	—	—	—
1980	73.7	70.0	77.5	74.4	70.7	78.1	69.5	65.3	73.6	68.0	63.7	72.3
1979	73.9	70.0	77.8	74.6	70.8	78.4	69.8	65.4	74.1	68.5	64.0	72.9
1978	73.5	69.6	77.3	74.1	70.4	78.0	69.3	65.0	73.5	68.1	63.7	72.4
1977	73.3	69.5	77.2	74.0	70.2	77.9	68.9	64.7	73.2	67.7	63.4	72.0
1976	72.9	69.1	76.8	73.6	69.9	77.5	68.4	64.2	72.7	67.2	62.9	71.6
1975	72.6	68.8	76.6	73.4	69.5	77.3	68.0	63.7	72.4	66.8	62.4	71.3
1970	70.8	67.1	74.7	71.7	68.0	75.6	65.3	61.3	69.4	64.1	60.0	68.3
1960	69.7	66.6	73.1	70.6	67.4	74.1	63.6	61.1	66.3	—	—	—
1950	68.2	65.6	71.1	69.1	66.5	72.2	60.8	59.1	62.9	—	—	—

Note: For 1981 and 1982, based on a 10 percent sample of deaths; for all other years, based on final data.
Source: U. S. National Center for Health Statistics, *Monthly Vital Statistics Report,* Vo. 31, No. 13, October 1983.

2. Death Rates, 1960 to 1979, and Deaths, 1970 to 1979, from Selected Causes

Cause of Death	Crude Death Rate per 100,000 Population[1]					Age-Adjusted Death Rates per 100,000 Population[1]		
	1960	1970	1975	1978	1979	1970	1975	1979
All causes	954.7	945.3	888.5	883.4	869.5	714.3	638.3	588.8
Major cardiovascular diseases	515.1	496.0	455.8	442.7	435.4	340.1	291.4	259.3
Diseases of heart	369.0	362.0	336.2	334.3	333.1	253.6	220.5	203.5
Percent of total	38.8	38.3	37.8	37.8	38.3	35.5	34.5	34.6
Rheumatic fever and rheumatic heart disease	10.3	7.3	6.1	6.1	3.5	6.3	4.8	2.6
Hypertensive heart disease[2]	37.0	7.4	5.2	4.7	11.2	4.9	3.2	7.0
Ischemic heart disease	321.8	328.1	301.7	294.3	250.5	228.1	196.1	152.8
Other diseases of endocardium		3.3	2.1	1.9	2.9	2.3	1.4	1.9
All other forms of heart disease		15.9	21.2	27.2	64.9	12.0	15.0	39.1
Hypertension[2]	7.1	4.1	3.0	2.5	3.3	2.9	1.9	1.9
Cerebrovascular diseases	108.0	101.9	91.1	80.5	77.0	66.3	54.5	42.5
Atherosclerosis	20.0	15.6	13.6	13.3	13.1	8.4	6.6	5.7
Other	11.0	12.5	12.0	12.2	8.9	8.8	8.0	5.6
Malignancies[3]	149.2	162.8	171.7	181.9	183.3	129.9	130.9	133.2
Percent of total	15.6	17.2	19.3	20.6	21.1	18.2	20.5	22.6
Of digestive organs and peritoneum	50.8	46.6	46.8	48.3	49.6	35.2	33.6	33.8
Of respiratory and intrathoracic organs	22.2	34.2	40.7	45.8	46.9	28.4	32.5	35.8
Of breast	13.4	14.7	15.2	15.9	15.7	12.6	12.5	12.4
Of genital organs	21.6	20.3	20.2	20.7	20.6	15.6	14.6	13.9
Accidents and adverse effects	52.3	56.4	48.4	48.4	47.8	53.7	44.8	43.7
Motor vehicle	21.3	26.9	21.5	24.0	24.3	27.4	21.3	23.7
Falls	10.6	8.3	7.0	6.3	6.0	5.7	4.5	3.7
Drowning	2.9	3.1	3.1	2.7	2.6	3.1	3.1	2.6
All other	17.5	18.1	16.7	15.4	14.9	17.5	15.9	13.7
Chronic obstructive pulmonary diseases and allied conditions[4]	([5])	15.2	12.0	10.0	22.7	11.6	8.6	14.9
Bronchitis, chronic and unspecified	([5])	2.9	2.2	2.0	1.7	2.1	1.6	1.0
Emphysema	([5])	11.2	8.8	7.2	6.2	8.4	6.2	4.1
Asthma	3.0	1.1	.9	.9	1.2	1.0	.8	.9
Other	([5])	([5])	([5])	([5])	13.7	([5])	([5])	8.8
Pneumonia and influenza	[6]37.3	30.9	26.1	26.7	20.5	22.1	16.6	11.4
Pneumonia	[6]32.9	29.0	24.1	24.9	20.2	20.8	15.4	11.2
Influenza	4.4	1.8	2.0	1.9	.3	1.3	1.2	.1
Diabetes mellitus	16.7	18.9	16.5	15.5	15.1	14.1	11.6	10.0
Chronic liver disease and cirrhosis	11.3	15.5	14.8	13.8	13.5	14.7	13.8	12.2
Certain conditions originating in the perinatal period	37.4	21.3	12.5	10.1	10.7	(x)	(x)	(x)
Suicide	10.6	11.6	12.7	12.5	12.4	11.8	12.6	11.9
Homicide and legal intervention	4.7	8.3	10.0	9.4	10.2	9.1	10.5	10.4
Nephritis, nephrotic syndrome, and nephrosis	7.6	4.4	3.8	4.1	7.1	3.5	2.8	4.4
Congenital anomalies	12.2	8.3	6.2	5.9	6.1	7.6	6.4	6.2
Septicemia	1.1	1.7	2.6	3.6	3.6	1.4	2.0	2.4
Ulcer of stomach and duodenum	6.3	4.2	3.2	2.5	2.7	3.2	2.2	1.7
Benign neoplasms	2.7	2.4	2.3	2.3	2.7	2.0	1.9	2.0

Cause of Death	Crude Death Rate per 100,000 Population					Age-Adjusted Death Rates per 100,000 Population[1]		
	1960	1970	1975	1978	1979	1970	1975	1979
Hernia of abdominal cavity and intestinal obstruction[7]	5.1	3.6	2.9	2.6	2.4	2.6	1.9	1.4
Other infective and parasitic diseases	2.6	1.9	1.9	2.2	1.9	1.7	1.7	1.6
Anemias	1.9	1.7	1.5	1.5	1.4	1.3	1.1	1.0
Cholelithiasis and other disorders of gallbladder	2.6	2.0	1.4	1.3	1.4	1.3	.9	.8
Infections of kidney	4.3	4.0	2.1	1.4	1.3	2.8	1.3	.7
Nutritional deficiencies	(5)	1.2	1.2	1.3	1.0	.8	.7	.5
Tuberculosis	6.1	2.6	1.6	1.3	.9	2.2	1.2	.7
Meningitis	1.3	.8	.8	.7	.6	.8	.7	.6
Hyperplasia of prostate	2.5	1.1	.6	.4	.4	.6	.3	.2
Acute bronchitis and bronchiolitis	(5)	.6	.3	.3	.3	.5	.3	.2
Viral hepatitis	.5	.5	.3	.2	.3	.5	.3	.3
Symptoms, signs, and ill-defined conditions	11.4	12.7	14.9	14.4	12.5	10.4	12.3	9.9
All other causes	48.9	55.0	60.3	66.4	51.2	45.2	46.3	36.3

Note: Beginning 1970, excludes deaths of nonresidents of the United States. Age-adjusted death rates were prepared using the direct method in which age-specific death rates for a population of interest are applied to a standard population distributed by age. The standard population for this table is the total population of the United States enumerated in 1940. Age adjustment eliminates the differences in observed rates between points in time or among compared population groups that result from age differences in population composition. Deaths for 1979 classified according to ninth revision of *International Classification of Diseases*; for earlier years, classified according to revision in use at that time.

X = Not applicable.

[1]Based on resident population enumerated as of April 1 for 1960 and 1970 and estimated as of July 1 for other years.

[2]With or without renal disease.

[3]Includes other types of malignancies not shown separately.

[4]Prior to 1979, data are shown for bronchitis, emphysema, and asthma.

[5]Included in "all other causes." Comparable data not available separately.

[6]Excludes pneumonia of newborn.

[7]Without mention of hernia.

Source: U.S. Bureau of the Census, *Statistical Abstract of the United States, 1982–83.*

3. Suicide Rates, by Sex, Race, and Age Group, 1970 to 1979

| | Male | | | | | | | | Female | | | | | | | |
| | White | | | | Black | | | | White | | | | Black | | | |
	1970	1975	1978	1979	1970	1975	1978	1979	1970	1975	1978	1979	1970	1975	1978	1979
All ages[1]	18.0	20.1	20.2	20.0	8.0	10.0	10.8	11.6	7.1	7.4	6.9	6.6	2.6	2.7	2.8	2.8
5–14 years	.5	.8	.7	.6	.1	.1	.3	.2	.1	.2	.2	.3	.2	.1	.2	.1
15–24 years	13.9	19.6	20.8	21.0	10.5	12.9	13.4	14.4	4.2	4.9	5.0	5.1	3.8	3.3	2.7	3.4
25–34 years	19.9	24.4	25.8	26.2	19.2	24.3	24.4	26.3	9.0	8.9	8.5	8.0	5.7	5.6	5.6	5.7
35–44 years	23.3	24.5	22.5	22.5	12.6	16.0	16.9	16.9	13.0	12.6	10.9	10.1	3.7	3.9	4.6	4.1
45–54 years	29.5	29.7	24.7	23.9	13.8	12.1	13.8	13.0	13.5	13.8	12.1	11.7	3.7	4.0	4.2	2.9
55–64 years	35.0	32.1	29.3	26.6	10.6	10.8	10.2	12.9	12.3	11.7	10.3	10.2	2.0	3.5	3.2	4.0
65 and over	41.1	39.4	40.8	39.2	8.7	11.3	11.7	12.9	8.5	8.5	7.9	7.3	2.6	2.3	2.3	2.5

Note: Rates per 100,000 population in specified group.

[1]Includes other age groups not shown separately.

Source: U. S. National Center for Health Statistics, *Vital Statistics of the United States,* annual.

appendix c | The Bureaucracy of Death

1. A Living Will

To My Family, My Physician, My Lawyer and All Others Whom It May Concern

Death is as much a reality as birth, growth, maturity and old age—it is the one certainty of life. If the time comes when I can no longer take part in decisions for my own future, let this statement stand as an expression of my wishes and directions, while I am still of sound mind.

If at such a time the situation should arise in which there is no reasonable expectation of my recovery from extreme physical or mental disability, I direct that I be allowed to die and not be kept alive by medications, artificial means or "heroic measures". I do, however, ask that medication be mercifully administered to me to alleviate suffering even though this may shorten my remaining life.

This statement is made after careful consideration and is in accordance with my strong convictions and beliefs. I want the wishes and directions here expressed carried out to the extent permitted by law. Insofar as they are not legally enforceable, I hope that those to whom this Will is addressed will regard themselves as morally bound by these provisions.

(Optional specific provisions to be made in this space)

Optional proxy statement: I hereby designate _____
to make treatment decisions for me in the event I am comatose or otherwise unable to make such decisions for myself.

Optional Notarization:

"Sworn and subscribed to

before me this _____ day

of _____, 19_____."

_____
Notary Public
(seal)

Signed_____

Date _____

Witness_____

Witness_____

Copies of this request have been given to _____

_____   _____

(Optional)   My Living Will is registered with Concern for Dying (No. _____)

Source: Reprinted with permission of Concern for Dying, 250 West 57th Street, New York, NY 10107.

2. A Gift of Life: Uniform Donor Card

TO MY FAMILY AND PHYSICIAN

It is my wish that upon my death, my body, or any part of it, be used for the benefit of mankind.

I, therefore, execute the following Deed of Gift, under the Anatomical Gift Act, and I request that in the making of any decision relating to my death, my intentions as expressed herein shall govern.

I am of sound mind and 18 years or more of age. I hereby make this anatomical gift to take effect upon my death. The marks in the appropriate places and words filled into the blanks below indicate my desires.

I give: my body _____; any needed organs or parts _____; the following organs or parts _____

I give these to the following person or institution: the physician in attendance

at my death _____; the hospital in which I die _____; the following named

physician, hospital, storage bank or other medical institution _____

the following individual for treatment _____

for any purpose authorized by law _____; transplantation _____;

therapy _____; research _____; medical education _____.

Dated _____   _____
                                                signature of donor

Signed by Donor in presence of   _____
following who sign as witnesses   address of donor

_____   _____
          witness   witness

UNIFORM DONOR CARD

_____   _____
Name of Donor   Date of Birth

In the hope that I may help others, I hereby make this anatomical gift, if medically acceptable, to take effect upon my death. The words and marks below indicate my desires. I give:
(a) ____ any needed organs or parts (b) ____ only the following organs or

Specify: _____

_____   _____
Signature of Donor   Date & Place Signed

_____   _____
Witness   Witness

This is a legal document under the Uniform Anatomical Gift Act.

3. A Proposal for Right to Die Legislation: Directive to Physicians

The directive and list of definitions appear in the Natural Death Act passed in California in September 1976. The bill authorizes the withholding or withdrawal of life-sustaining procedures from adults who have a terminal condition and who have executed such a directive.

DIRECTIVE TO PHYSICIAN

Directive made this _____ day of _____ (month, year).
I _____, being of sound mind, willfully, and voluntarily make known my desire that my life shall not be artificially prolonged under the circumstances set forth below, do hereby declare:

1   If at any time I should have an incurable injury, disease, or illness certified to be a terminal condition by two physicians, and where the application of life-sustaining procedures would serve only to artificially prolong the moment of my death and where my physician determines that my death is imminent whether or not life-sustaining procedures are utilized, I direct that such procedures be withheld or withdrawn and that I be permitted to die naturally.

2   In the absence of my ability to give directions regarding the use of such life-sustaining procedures, it is my intention that this directive shall be honored by my family and physician(s) as the final expression of my legal right to refuse medical or surgical treatment and accept the consequences from such refusal.

3   If I have been diagnosed as pregnant and that diagnosis is known to my physician, this directive shall have no force or effect during the course of my pregnancy.

4   I have been diagnosed and notified at least 14 days ago as having a terminal condition by _____, M.D. whose address is _____, and whose telephone number is _____. I understand that if I have not filled in the physician's name and address, it shall be presumed that I did not have a terminal condition when I made out this directive.

5   This directive shall have no force or effect five years from the date filled in above.

6   I understand the full import of this directive and I am emotionally and mentally competent to make this directive.

Signed _____

City, County and State of Residence _____

The declarant has been personally known to me and I believe him or her to be of sound mind.

Witness _____

List of Definitions

a. "Attending physician" means the physician selected by, or assigned to, the patient who has primary responsibility for the treatment and care of the patient.

b. "Directive" means a written document voluntarily executed by the declarant in accordance with the requirements of Section 7188. The directive, or a copy of the directive, shall be made part of the patient's medical records.

c. "Life-sustaining procedure" means any medical procedure or intervention which utilizes mechanical or other artificial means to sustain, restore, or supplant a vital function, which, when applied to a qualified patient, would serve only to artificially prolong the moment of death and where, in the judgment of the attending physician, death is imminent whether or not such procedures are utilized. "Life-sustaining procedure" shall not include the administration of medication or the performance of any medical procedure deemed necessary to alleviate pain.

d. "Physician" means a physician and surgeon licensed by the Board of Medical Quality Assurance or the Board of Osteopathic Examiners.

e. "Qualified patient" means a patient diagnosed and certified in writing to be afflicted with a terminal condition by two physicians, one of whom shall be the attending physician, who have personally examined the patient.

f. "Terminal condition" means an incurable condition caused by injury, disease, or illness, which, regardless of the application of life-sustaining procedures, would, within reasonable medical judgment, produce death, and where the application of life-sustaining procedures serves only to postpone the moment of death of the patient.

4. Certificate of Death

It is easy to lose sight of the physical facts of death, particularly in the interim between the moment of clinical death and final rites. Yet a complex bureaucracy exists to deal with the many stark details of closing out a civil existence; the following forms chart the passage from dying person to physical remains. Although they are official records from one state, they can be considered representative documents for other regions; the information reported tends to be standardized to facilitate nationwide collection of health statistics.

CERTIFICATE OF DEATH
STATE OF CALIFORNIA

5. *Authority for Autopsy*

AUTHORITY FOR AUTOPSY

———— Date ———————— Hour ————.M

    The undersigned hereby authorize the above named hospital to permit its Pathologist, and/or such doctors and assistants as he may desire, to perform an autopsy and complete post-mortem examination upon the body

of ————————————————, deceased, including the taking of tissues for special study and microscopic examination, for the purpose of determining the exact cause of death.

Witnesses: Signed ————————————————

————————————————————   Relationship ——————————

————————————————————   Signed ————————————————

                          Relationship ——————————

---

6. *Permit for Disposition of Human Remains*

PERMIT FOR DISPOSITION OF HUMAN REMAINS

NAME OF DECEDENT		SEX	DATE OF BIRTH	DATE OF DEATH
PLACE OF DEATH—CITY OR TOWN	PLACE OF DEATH—COUNTY (OR STATE IF NOT IN CALIFORNIA)	NAME AND ADDRESS OF SPOUSE OR OTHER INFORMANT		
NAME OF FUNERAL DIRECTOR (OR PERSON ACTING AS SUCH)	CALIFORNIA LICENSE NUMBER			

TYPE OF PERMIT. CHECK <u>ONLY ONE</u> OF THE FOLLOWING TYPES OF DISPOSITION

☐ 1. BURIAL (INCLUDES ENTOMBMENT)

☐ 2. CREMATION AND BURIAL (INCLUDES INURNMENT)

☐ 3. CREMATION AND DISPOSITION OTHER THAN IN A CEMETERY

☐ 4. SCIENTIFIC USE

☐ 5. DISINTERMENT AND BURIAL (INCLUDES ENTOMBMENT)

☐ 6. DISINTERMENT. CREMATION. AND BURIAL (INCLUDES INURNMENT)

☐ 7. DISINTERMENT. CREMATION. AND DISPOSITION OTHER THAN IN A CEMETERY

☐ 8. DISINTERMENT AND REINTERMENT OF CREMATED REMAINS (INCLUDES INURNMENT)

☐ 9. DISINTERMENT OF CREMATED REMAINS AND DISPOSITION OTHER THAN IN A CEMETERY

FOR THE PURPOSE OF ISSUING THIS PERMIT. DISINTERMENT IS DEFINED AS THE REMOVAL OF HUMAN REMAINS FROM ONE SPECIFIED PLACE OF DISPOSITION TO ANOTHER SPECIFIED PLACE OF DISPOSITION. COMPLETE EACH ITEM REQUIRED FOR THE TYPE OF PERMIT SPECIFIED ABOVE AND INVALIDATE EACH LINE NOT REQUIRED FOR THE SPECIFIED DISPOSITION

BURIAL	NAME AND ADDRESS OF CEMETERY WHERE REMAINS ARE TO BE INTERRED	COUNTY
CREMATION	NAME AND ADDRESS OF CREMATORY WHERE REMAINS ARE TO BE CREMATED ⎮ DATE CREMATED	SIGNATURE OF PERSON IN CHARGE OF CREMATORY ▶
INTERMENT AFTER CREMATION	NAME AND ADDRESS OF CEMETERY WHERE REMAINS ARE TO BE INTERRED	COUNTY
BURIAL AT SEA OR DISPOSITION OTHER THAN IN A CEMETERY OF CREMATED REMAINS	ADDRESS. NEAREST POINT ON SHORELINE. OR OTHER DESCRIPTION SUFFICIENT TO IDENTIFY FINAL PLACE AND <u>COUNTY</u> OF DISPOSITION	
ACKNOWLEDGMENT OF APPLICANT	This is to certify that I am the person having the right to control the disposition of the remains of the above named decedent under provisions of the Health and Safety Code, and I hereby acknowledge that trespass and nuisance laws apply and understand that this permit gives no right of unrestricted access to property not owned by me.	SIGNATURE OF APPLICANT ▶ / DATE SIGNED
SCIENTIFIC USE	NAME AND ADDRESS OF FACILITY RECEIVING REMAINS	
LOCAL REGISTRAR	THIS PERMIT IS ISSUED IN ACCORDANCE WITH PROVISIONS OF THE CALIFORNIA HEALTH AND SAFETY CODE AND IS THE AUTHORITY FOR THE DISPOSITION SPECIFIED IN THIS PERMIT ⎮ AMOUNT OF FEE PAID ⎮ DATE PERMIT ISSUED	SIGNATURE OF LOCAL REGISTRAR ISSUING PERMIT ▶
CERTIFICATION OF PERSON IN CHARGE OF DISPOSITION	I CERTIFY THAT THE SPECIFIED DISPOSITION WAS MADE ON_____ (ENTER DATE)	SIGNATURE OF PERSON IN CHARGE OF DISPOSITION ▶

<u>COPY 1</u> OF THE PERMIT ACCOMPANIES THE REMAINS TO THE STATED PLACE OF DISPOSITION. THE PERSON IN CHARGE OF DISPOSITION IS RESPONSIBLE FOR COMPLETING THE PERMIT AND FORWARDING THE COMPLETED PERMIT WITHIN 10 DAYS TO THE LOCAL REGISTRAR OF THE DISTRICT IN WHICH DISPOSITION OCCURRED OR TO THE LOCAL REGISTRAR OF THE DISTRICT NEAREST THE POINT WHERE THE CREMATED REMAINS WERE BURIED AT SEA.

COPY 1   STATE OF CALIFORNIA—DEPARTMENT OF HEALTH SERVICES—OFFICE OF THE STATE REGISTRAR OF VITAL STATISTICS   (REV. 5-78) FORM VS-9

appendix d | Additional Teaching Resources

After approximately twenty-five years of formal study in thanatology, a considerable array of teaching materials is available. Appendix D consists of: (1) a topical list suited for designing classroom presentations for audiences with specialized interests or for assigning individual or class research tasks; and (2) an annotated list of media resources, keyed to each chapter of this text. Additional teaching material will be found in Daniel Leviton, "Death Education," in *New Meanings of Death*, ed. H. Feifel, New York: McGraw-Hill, 1977; and H. Waas, C. A. Corr, R. A. Rachelski, and C. M. Sanders, *Death Education: An Annotated Resource Guide*. Washington D.C.: Hemisphere Press, 1980.

1. *Topical Suggestions for Curricular Planning on Death and Dying*

abortion
accidental death
accident-proneness
actuarial science
aggression and violence
afterlife
alternative funeral rites
amniocentesis
assassination
autopsy

Biblical tradition
bullfighting
burial rites

causes of aging
cemeteries

chemical and biological warfare
children's literature
class and cultural differences in
    life expectancy
courage and death
cremation
cryonics

death and mysticism death customs
death fantasies
death in painting and music
death of a culture
death of God
death of a soldier
demographics of death

different cultural approaches
documentary treatments
donation of body parts
Down's syndrome
dynamics of prayer and supplication

elective death
embalming
epidemics
epitaphs and eulogies
ethics and medical experimentation
euphemisms for death
experimentation with life-saving techniques
exploitation

facing surgery
factors in life expectancy
fear of death
film treatments
funerals

genocide
geriatric wards

heart transplant
Holocaust experience
human sacrifice

images of death
immortality
infanticide
infant mortality
isolation and alienation

last words of the dying
legal rights of the dying and dead
life review

martyrdom
mass hysteria
media presentations
memorial art
millennial themes
mourning customs
myths of death and rebirth

natural disasters
nuclear threat

organ transplant
out-of-the-body experience

perception of time
personality factors in facing death
population and ecological control
post-mortem changes
poverty and death
pricing of life
psychopathologies of aging

racial segregation of the dying and the dead
reincarnation
resistance to torture by war prisoners
resurrection
ritual

samurai
science fiction/time machines
siblings' response to terminal illness
"sudden infant death" syndrome (SIDS)
survival in extreme environments
support groups
surrogate mothers
survivors of suicide
symbols for death

tomb
transformation

uncertainty of dying
use of sedatives

violence
voodooism, magical rites, occultism

war memorials

2. Multimedia References for Death and Dying

Chapter One: The Study of Death: Attitudes and Reflections

Chillysmith Farm—Film, color, 55 min. Filmakers Library, 133 E. 58th St., Suite 703A, New York, New York 10022. Documenting the responses of individual family members to the death of "Gramp," the film raises issues on values, family life, birth, death, and aging.

Confrontations of Death—Film, color, 35 min. Oregon Division of Continuing Education Film Library, P.O. Box 1491, Portland. Oregon 97201. Seminar participants discover their personal feelings about their own death through listening to music, viewing slides on death, and writing their own eulogies.

Day of the Dead—Film, color, 14 min. Pyramid Films, P.O. Box 1048, Santa Monica, California 90406. Mexico's Festival for the Day of the Dead in a film produced by Charles and Ray Eames.

Dead Man—Film, musical soundtrack, 3 min. Center for Thanatology Research, 391 Atlantic Ave., Brooklyn, New York 11217. Stark portrayal of the naked, dead body of an old man.

Chapter Two: The Experience of Dying

Death—Film, black and white, 43 min. Filmakers Library, 133 E. 58th St., Suite 703A, New York, New York 10022. Depicts the isolation of the dying in a hospital setting. Presents 52-year-old cancer patient portraying problems of meaningful communication with family, friends, and hospital staff.

Dying—Film, color, 91 min. King Features Entertainment, 235 East 45th St., New York, New York 10017. Cinema vérité portrayal of incidents in the dying of three cancer patients and the responses of their families. Contrasts different styles of dying in nonjudgmental fashion.

Joan Robinson: One Woman's Story—Videocassette, color, 165 min. Time-Life Video, Time & Life Building, New York, New York 10020. An intimate and powerful record of a woman, her husband, physician, and friends, as they face the anguish of her terminal illness. Explores issues of pain management and family relationships.

The Physiology of Dying—Videocassette. 56 min. Newmedia, 242 St. Joseph Avenue, Long Beach, California 90803. Presents the different physiological modes of dying—vital organ failure, brain tumor—and discusses the effects upon the patient.

Terminal Illness—Videotape, six programs. Instructional Media Services Booking, DG-10, University of Washington, Seattle, Washington 98195. Interviews with the patient, his family, and those who attended to his physical and spiritual needs. Interviews with the patient—25 min. The role of the physician—41 min. Pain management—37 min. Religion and the clergy—35 min. The grieving process, Part I—25 min., Part II—45 min.

To Die Today—Film, black and white, 50 min. Filmakers Library, 133 E. 58th St., Suite 703A, New York, New York 10022. Kübler-Ross describes five emotional stages she believes must be recognized in successfully relating to a dying person. Contains an interview with a patient and an evaluation session with a class of students.

Why Me?—Film, color, 10 min. Pyramid Films, Box 1048, Santa Monica, California 90406. Animated film humorously portraying the reactions of a man who learns that he only has five minutes left to live. With conciseness and levity, the film portrays the full range of responses described by Kübler-Ross.

Chapter Three: Grief, Mourning, and Social Functions

The Crisis of Loss—Film, color, 32 min. American Journal of Nursing Co., 555 W. 57th St., New York, New York 10019. Loss and mourning are examined within the framework of crisis theory. Examples support the importance of the perception of control and responsibility in coping with loss.

Death, Grief, and Bereavement—Audiocassettes. Series of 24 programs. Connie Goldman Productions, 3034 M Street N.W., Washington, D.C. 20007. Examines viewpoints by various authorities on death.

Grieving: Suddenly Alone—Film, color, 26 min. University of Southern California, Film & Video Distribution Center, School of Cinema–Television, University Park MC 0111, Los Angeles, California 90089. Chronicles the aspects of bereavement experienced by a middle-aged widow whose life-style is dramatically changed as the result of her husband's death.

Journey's End—Film, color, 28 min. University of Southern California, Film & Video Distribution Center, School of Cinema–Television, University Park MC 0111, Los Angeles, California 90089. Stresses the importance of making essential preparations for death. Encourages long-range planning for death by the preparation of wills, acquiring a knowledge of probate procedures and specifying funeral arrangements.

The Long Valley: A Study of Bereavement—Film, color, 51 min. Films Incorporated, Public Media Inc., 733 Green Bay Road, Wilmette, Illinois 60091. Dr. Colin Parkes talks to a group of doctors, clergy, social workers, and bereaved people about the process of grief. He emphasizes the essentiality of the grieving process.

Chapter Four: Death and the Child

All the Way Home—Film, black and white, 103 min. Films Inc., 5625 Hollywood Boulevard, Los Angeles, California 90068. The effects of a man's death on a six-year-old boy. The mother's initial withdrawal into grief and the family's inability to deal with the boy's need to understand. Based on James Agee's novel *A Death in the Family*.

Children's Conceptions of Death—Videocassette, color, 30 min. American Journal of Nursing Co., 555 W. 57th St., New York, New York 10019. Depicts children's attitudes toward and understandings of death at different stages of development.

The Dead Bird—Film, color, 13 min. Bureau of Audio-Visual Instruction, P.O. Box 2093, Madison, Wisconsin 53701. Four children discover a dead bird and prepare a funeral for it.

Last Rites: A Boy's Reaction to Death—Film, color, 30 min. Filmakers Library, 133 E. 58th St., Suite 703A, New York, New York 10022. A young boy attempts through fantasy to bring his dead mother back. A stranger's support helps him to accept the reality of her loss.

Winning Battles: Children With Cancer—Film, color, 8 min. Filmakers Library, 133 E. 58th St., Suite 703A, New York, New York 10022. Presentations of a pilot program at Stanford University Children's Hospital, where the family is actively involved in the child's treatment. Death is discussed openly while at the same time hope for the future is maintained.

Chapter Five: Choices and Decisions in Death

Born Dying—Film, color, 20 min. Research Press, Box 3177Y, Champaign, Illinois 61821. The film presents the agony of parents faced with legal/ethical dilemmas concerning the quality of life of severely handicapped newborns.

Everybody Rides the Carousel: The Later Years—Film, color, 9 min. Pyramid Films, Box 1048, Santa Monica, California 90406. Based on Erikson's view of the final stage of life, contrasting two couples who live their final years in vastly different ways.

Gravity Is My Enemy—Film, color, 30 min. Churchill Films, 662 N. Robertson Boulevard, Los Angeles, California 90069. Portrait of a young artist paralyzed from the neck down and the relationship of his work to his life.

The Last of Life: A Positive Look at Aging—Film, 28 min. Filmakers Library, 133 E. 58th St., Suite 703A, New York, New York 10022. Directed to health-care professionals, the film presents aging as a normal part of human development and urges that the individuality of elderly patients be valued.

Suicide: But Jack Was a Good Driver—Film, color, 15 min. CRM/McGraw-Hill Films, P.O. Box 641, Del Mar, California 92014. As the friends of a teenager killed in an automobile crash leave his funeral, they come to the realization that his death was probably a suicide.

Will to Die—Film, color, 18 min. American Journal of Nursing Co., 555 W. 57th St., New York, New York 10019. Views death from the point of view of theology, law, and medicine, and presents both positive and negative views on euthanasia.